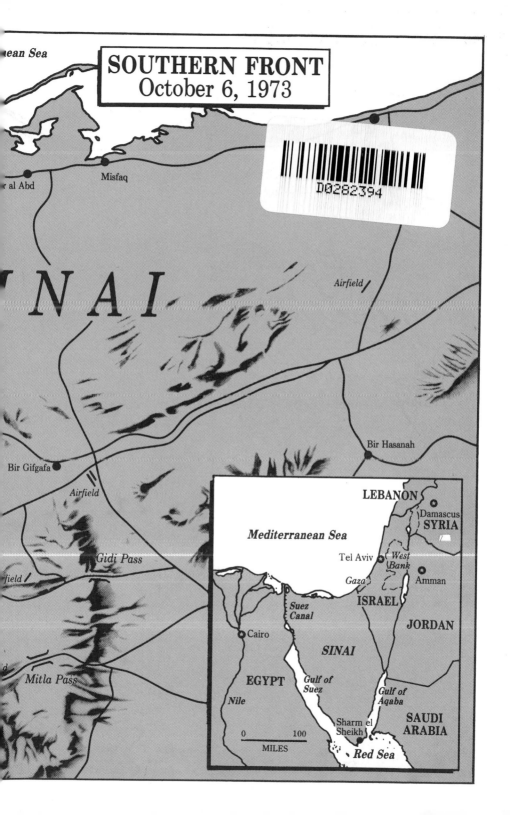

ean Sea

SOUTHERN FRONT
October 6, 1973

D0282394

al Abd   Misfaq

I N A I

Airfield

Bir Hasanah

Bir Gifgafa

Airfield

Gidi Pass

field

Mitla Pass

LEBANON

Damascus
SYRIA

Mediterranean Sea

Tel Aviv   *West Bank*

Gaza   Amman

ISRAEL

Suez Canal

JORDAN

Cairo

SINAI

EGYPT   *Gulf of Suez*

Nile

Gulf of Aqaba

SAUDI ARABIA

Sharm el Sheikh

0   100

MILES

Red Sea

WARRIORS
AGAINST
ISRAEL

Also by the author:

Warriors at Suez
Warriors for Jerusalem

WARRIORS
AGAINST
ISRAEL

by

DONALD NEFF

PUBLISHED BY AMANA BOOKS,
58 ELLIOT STREET
BRATTLEBORO, VERMONT 05301
MANUFACTURED IN THE UNITED STATES OF AMERICA

1 3 5 7 9 10 8 6 4 2

LIBRARY OF CONGRESS CATALOGING IN PUBLICATION DATA

NEFF, DONALD, 1930—
    WARRIORS AGAINST ISRAEL: HOW ISRAEL WON THE BATTLE TO BECOME AMERICA'S
ALLY 1973

    BIBLIOGRAPHY: P.
    INCLUDES INDEX.
    1. ISRAEL-ARAB   WAR   1973—DIPLOMATIC   HISTORY. 2. ISRAEL-ARAB   CON-
FLICTS. 3. JEWISH-ARAB RELATIONS—1967-1973 I. TITLE.
DS128.12.N44   1988   956'.048   88-6246

For George Ramonas
who did the impossible

CONTENTS

MAPS

CAST OF CHARACTERS

AMERICA

Donald Bergus, head, special interests section, Egypt
Henry A. Kissinger, secretary of state/national security adviser
Richard M. Nixon, President
William P. Rogers, secretary of state
Joseph Sisco, assistant secretary of state
James Schlesinger, secretary of defense
Michael Sterner, diplomat

EGYPT

Ahmed Ismail Ali, war minister
Mohammed Fawzi, general
Adbul Ghani Gamasy, general
Mohamed Heikal, journalist
Hafez Ismail, national security adviser
Gamal Abdel Nasser, president
Mahmoud Riad, foreign minister
Anwar Sadat, president
Ali Sabri, politician
Mohammed Sadiq, minister of war
Saad Shazly, army chief of staff

ISRAEL

Avraham Adan, general
Haim Bar-Lev, former southern commander
Moshe Dayan, defense minister
Simcha Dinitz, ambassador to the United States
David Elazar, chief of staff
Shmuel Gonen, southern commander
Golda Meir, prime minister
Yitzhak Rabin, ambassador to the United States
Ariel Sharon, general

JORDAN

Hussein ibn Talal, king
Wasfi Tal, prime minister

LIBYA

Muammar Qadhafi, ruler

PALESTINE

Yasser Arafat, chairman Palestine Liberation Organization
Abu Iyad, Fatah official

SAUDI ARABIA

Faisal ibn Abdul Aziz, king
Ahmad Zaki Yamani, oil minister

SOVIET UNION

Leonid Brezhnev, chairman
Anatoly Dobrynin, ambassador to the United States
Andrei Gromyko, premier
Andrei A. Grechko, marshal
Nikolai Podgorny, president
Vladimir Vinogradov, ambassador to Egypt

SYRIA

Hafez Assad, president

UNITED NATIONS

Gunnar Jarring, special negotiator
Keith Howard, military observer

PROLOGUE

Almighty and eternal God, creator of the world and the Father of all creatures, bless this new highway which you have permitted man to open in the midst of your creation. Make of this river not only a passage to universal prosperity, but make it also a royal road of peace and of justice; of the light, and of the eternal truth. O God, may this highway bring men together, but above all may it bring them to Thyself; and may it be to everyone propitious, for time and for eternity.

—Prayer delivered by Monseigneur Bauer,
at the opening of the Suez Canal, November 16, 1869

There was at the time no particular reason not to share the soaring sentiments of the good Apostolic Delegate to France and Confessor to Empress Eugenie. The Suez Canal was indeed the great engineering marvel of the mid-nineteenth century, and its conclusion after ten arduous years was an occasion of great wonderment, pride and festivity. The Empress Eugenie herself was in Egypt for the gala ceremonies inaugurating the canal as were six thousand invited guests, the royalty of Europe and Arabia, their expenses paid by the profligate and proud Khedive Ismail, the ruler of Egypt. Thousands of others of the curious, the adventurous and the resentful uninvited paid their own way to marvel at the world's newest wonder in the cradle of wonders. As Monseigneur Bauer noted, excavation of the 101-mile canal was the accomplishment of an ancient dream that finally linked East and West, a watery umbilical cord through desert wastes that was certain to increase enormously trade and travel, cutting the route from Europe to Asia by as much as half, conquering, as he exulted, "one of the most formidable enemies of mankind, which is distance."

"Henceforth, the Indian Ocean and the Mediterranean Sea are a single flood. The history of the world has reached one of its most glorious stages."

But enemies more formidable than distance would confront mankind at the Suez Canal. Rather than a royal road of peace and justice, the canal

5

almost immediately became a battle line both symbolic and actual, an excuse for war and a magnet for warriors.

• •

First of the warriors to arrive were the British who coveted the canal as a royal highway to the jewel of the crown, India. Britain invaded Egypt thirteen years after the canal's opening, thus assuring the uninterrupted operation of the waterway, and remained in Egypt for seventy-two years. During that time British troops fought Turco-German forces along the canal in World War I, endured guerrilla attacks by Egyptians after World War II, and then were humiliated in the Suez crisis of 1956, which finally marked in public perfidy the end of the empire. Through it all the Suez Canal had remained under Anglo-French ownership, its smooth operation assured by foreign pilots, foreign administrators and a foreign company, the Compagnie Universelle du Canal Maritime de Suez, that had become a country-within-a-country.

When British troops finally withdrew for the last time in 1956 at the end of the Suez War, the canal lay blocked by sunken Egyptian ships, the\ detritus and destruction of war lining its northern banks and its ownership, for the first time, firmly in Egyptian hands. It was a proud and momentous moment for the Egyptians, whose ability to operate the waterway was widely and arrogantly doubted. Soon after the war's end, however, Egypt reopened the canal amid much fanfare and proved to the world it was capable of operating the waterway smoothly and competently.

Eleven years later, Israeli troops struck in a blitzkrieg across the Sinai Peninsula and occupied the east bank of the canal. Once again the waterway was closed, this time for years. By 1973, the waterway, still closed, was merely a stagnant demarcation between two opposing armies. Rather than being a conduit for peace and justice, as Monseigneur Bauer had prayed, the canal had now ignobly become, as Israeli Defense Minister Moshe Dayan said, "one of the best anti-tank ditches available."

On the east bank Israel had erected with sand and stone and steel what was considered one of the most formidable defense barriers in the world, the Bar-Lev Line. It consisted of a chain of mutually supporting fortresses with deep underground bunkers and stores of oil that when released would turn the waters of the canal into an inferno for attackers. The Bar-Lev Line itself was a seventy-foot high sand rampart that had been piled up along almost the entire distance of the canal from the Mediterranean to the Gulf of Suez and beyond it in the Indian Ocean. Behind this line bristling with weapons, Israel felt secure. "Egypt has no military option at all," Israeli

6

Deputy Prime Minister Yigael Allon noted contentedly in the summer of 1973.

So, indeed, it seemed. In front of the Bar-Lev Line stretched the canal's waters, 155 yards wide, fifty-five feet deep, a stark killing field. On the west bank of the canal stood Egypt's army, thwarted by the nearly two football field's width of the open waterway and the guns of the Bar-Lev Line. On its side of the canal, Egypt had established the most sophisticated and densest antiaircraft system in the world. The complex was a gift of the Soviet Union and consisted of a maze of missiles, rapid-fire and long range guns, and extensive radar systems that could track and destroy planes from near ground level up to 70,000 feet. The Soviet Union had also been generous in providing Egypt with a large tank force, jet warplanes and other modern weapons—a cornucopia of the instruments of war to match the massive armaments given to Israel by the United States.

The backing by the two superpowers of the opposite sides in the Arab-Israeli conflict made the confrontation between Egypt and Israel a reflection in miniature of the American and Soviet conflict. When war came, as it did in the fall of 1973, it would be fought with the superpowers' most advanced armaments short of nuclear weapons. The waters of the canal would run red. And once again the superpowers would be brought to the brink of war.

• •

In 1973—the year 5734 in the Hebrew calendar and 1393 in the Arabic— October 6 occurred during the Islamic holy month of Ramadan, a time of fasting and prayer, and on the holiest of all Jewish days, Yom Kippur, the day of atonement. It was on this religious day, just four months after Deputy Prime Minister Allon had boasted that Egypt had no military option, one hundred and four years after Monseigneur Bauer prayed that the Suez Canal would bring men together in peace and justice, that four thousand Egyptian guns opened up along the whole length of the Bar-Lev Line, raining 10,500 shells on the Israeli defenders in the first minute. Twenty minutes later, one thousand assault rafts began transporting the first waves of five infantry divisions—80,000 men—across the roiled waters of the canal. In another ten minutes the first Egyptian flag was flying from the Bar-Lev Line. It took just one hour for the first of the supposedly impregnable Bar-Lev fortresses to fall. Others followed like dominoes. Soon portable bridges spanned the channel and Egyptian tanks began rumbling into the Sinai under the cover of roaring warplanes. Simultaneously, similar advances were made by Syrian forces in the north on the barren Golan Heights overlooking

7

the lush fields of the Upper Galilee, Israel's northernmost territory. Now, from the west and from the north, Israel, to everyone's surprise, was under fierce attack on two fronts, and its unprepared forces were reeling.

At 6:15 that evening, Prime Minister Golda Meir announced over national radio: "Citizens of Israel, at around 1400 today the armies of Egypt and Syria launched an offensive against Israel....We have no doubt about our victory but we consider the resumption of the Egyptian-Syrian aggression as tantamount to an act of madness."

By that time, despite Meir's bold words, Israel's forces in both the Sinai and on the Golan Heights were staggering under the deadly blows of the Arabs. Thousands of men and tanks were engaged in vicious combat. The war that no one thought could happen, the fourth Arab-Israeli war, had begun. And the Arabs were winning.

When the fighting stopped nineteen days later, the Egyptians were firmly entrenched on both sides of the Suez Canal, determined never to give it up again. It was an extraordinary accomplishment and a historic return to Egypt of control of the canal. Egypt celebrated its victory by cleaning out the bombs, mines and other souvenirs of war from the fabled waterway. Then, amid festive celebrations, this time with Anwar Sadat leading a convoy of ships in the waterway, Egypt reopened the canal on June 5, 1975—exactly eight years after the start of the war that had closed it.

There could be no honor in a sure success,
but much might be wrested from a sure defeat.

T.E. Lawrence, Seven Pillars of Wisdom

PART ONE: NO WAR, NO PEACE

1967 to 1973

CHAPTER I

The Death of Nasser

IT WAS 6 PM when Anwar Sadat was awakened from his usual afternoon nap and told to go to the President's Cairo residence for a "very important reason." He quickly dressed and traveled to the Manshiat al-Bakri section of the ancient and overcrowded city. It was a drive he had made many times, through dusty streets choked by cars and carts, fume-belching buses and trucks, and occasional donkeys, the drivers shouting and the vehicles blaring their horns, the sidewalks so crowded with war refugees and fellahin clad in gallabiehs, the peasants' traditional long robes, that the mass of humanity spilled over into the roadway, snarling even more the traffic. Cairo, a city with sewers and electricity and roads for around two million, was in 1970 the home of nearly six million people.

The modest residence in the Manshiat al-Bakri suburb was a familiar sight to Sadat, the same villa President Gamal Abdel Nasser had been living in since he was a lieutenant colonel nearly two decades earlier. But this time Sadat, a figurehead vice president and loyal follower of Nasser for much of his adulthood, found a numbing scene. Nasser, aged fifty-two, lay in his bed in pajamas, surrounded by doctors and senior government officials, all of them obviously agitated and in high emotion.

Nasser, *el rais*, the boss, as he was affectionately known, was dead.

For eighteen years Nasser had ruled Egypt as his personal fiefdom, a revered if flawed figure who had given Egyptians and the Arab world a new sense of pride. Now his passing left his aides in stunned confusion, ravaged by emotions ranging from their personal grief to anxiety for their careers and the future of their country. Nasser had died without anointing a successor. He had left no political will, no instructions for carrying on, no guide to the future. There had never been a transfer of power, that most delicate and perilous process in a country's national life, since Nasser and

13

the Free Officers had overthrown Egypt's crumbling monarchy in 1952. There was no tradition for informing the nation that it had no leader or for forming a new government or for choosing a new leader. The void created by Nasser's death was complete, the confusion suffered by the inner circle of the government total.

Sadat exclaimed to the doctors: "It's not true...what you're saying is wrong....It can't be right." General Mahmoud Fawzi, the Egyptian minister of war, groaned: "Everything is over." The physicians, reportedly in tears, explained they had worked on the stricken President for two hours, using an electronic cardiac pulser, but in vain. The heart attack had been massive, ending a career that had made Nasser the greatest Egyptian in modern history, the leader of the Arab world, the embodiment of a resurgent Islam and the most fearsome of Israel's enemies.

Now, September 28, 1970, Egypt was suddenly without him.

Formally, as vice president, Anwar Sadat stood next in line. But he was so little regarded by his colleagues and such a butt of malicious humor that no one thought of him as anything but a transitional figure. He was considered something of a clown by foreign diplomats and Egyptians alike because of his sycophancy toward Nasser, his exaggerated rhetoric, his obsession with sartorial splendor and fascination with play acting. Although he was a member of the original Free Officers that overthrew King Farouk, he had nearly missed the revolution by going to a movie on the night of the coup.

The general judgment in the West of Sadat was expressed by Milton Viorst in a column in The Washington Star: He "is considered an incredible incompetent whom Nasser kept around out of regard for loyalty."

Nasser himself had relished poking fun at Sadat, who although an old colleague was never a friend or close adviser. One of Nasser's jibes made a French pun out of Sadat's first name, Anwar—ane noir, black donkey, referring to Sadat's dark skin. At other times, Nasser called him Bikbashi Sah, "Major Yes, Yes," explaining: "If he would occasionally vary his way of expressing agreement instead of forever saying sah [quite right], that would be easier on my nerves." According to a popular joke, when Sadat appeared anonymously before God and was asked what his outstanding characteristic was, he replied: "There is nothing outstanding about me." "Ah, yes," replied God, "you must be Anwar Sadat."

Sadat had been made vice president the previous December 20 by Nasser, but even that had seemed off-handed, more a whim of the president than a confrontation with his own mortality. According to journalist Mohamed Heikal, who later became a bitter enemy of Sadat's, when he asked Nasser why he had chosen the comparatively obscure Sadat for the honor, the President had laughed and said: "All the others have been vice president at one time or the other; it's Anwar's turn."

As the gravity of their predicament weighed on the officials standing around Nasser's corpse, they retired to the ground floor sitting room to try, somehow, to avert a power struggle that could lead to chaos and worse, perhaps even civil war and their own demise. So far the nation remained unaware that the great leader had died. The officials were not sure how the public should be informed or who should do it or how the populace would react.

Sadat was as confused as the rest, perhaps more so since even at this early hour it was obvious that the poor boy from the Nile Delta was, quite unexpectedly, in a position where by adroit maneuvering he might become the next president of Egypt. Turning to Hcikal, the vice president asked the journalist what he thought should be done.

"We should...follow the rules laid down in the constitution," said Heikal. Then he added pointedly: "This states that on the death of a president the vice president should take over for a period of sixty days until a plebiscite to choose a successor can be held."

Sixty days. Implicit in mentioning that duration was the promise that it would provide time enough to sort things out in a more orderly manner, time to determine the true new leader. As Heikal put it with his characteristic acid in his biography of Sadat, written with bile after Sadat's assassination. "Certainly, all of us taking part in this meeting were conscious of his limitations, but I felt strongly that the need for continuity overrode all other considerations."

Conspicuous among the others taking part in the anxious discussions at the Nasser home was Ali Sabri, a former prime minister (1964-5), who after Nasser was considered by many the strongest man in Egypt. Sabri's power rested on two bases, his close ties with the country's superpower patron, the Soviet Union, and his leadership role in the Arab Socialist Union, the one political party tolerated by Nasser. The ASU served as both the confessional of the people's complaints and the ideological sounding board for the Nasser revolution. It was one of the few diffuse power centers allowed by Nasser, along with the military, the intelligence services and the secret police. Otherwise Nasser had kept all power in his own hands and operated through his personal secretariat.

Sabri was widely disliked. A long stint in air force intelligence had left him obsessed by secrecy and fascinated with covert operations. He was opportunistic, leftist, pro-Soviet and, much to his own peril, openly scornful

15

of Sadat, an attitude reciprocated by Sadat with fervor. Westerners who dealt with Sabri variously described him as an "artful bureaucratic intriguer" and "an unattractive and unscrupulous personality who hardly ever had a kind word to say about anybody...." Years later Sadat in his autobiography accused Sabri of having a "natural inclination to spy on people, hatch intrigues, and play underhand games." In addition, Sadat wrote, Sabri "would not make a decision on anything" and was "by nature afraid of responsibility." This was one of the men Sadat now had to cultivate and lull into support if he wanted to be president of Egypt.

On his side, Sabri obviously thought that of all his competitors, Sadat was the narrowest, the weakest and the most easily influenced. As Heikal noted later: "The group which afterwards became known as the 'centers of power' [i.e., the opponents of Sadat] were content with Sadat as president because they thought he was a weak man whom they could manage." Ali Sabri eventually found out how woefully mistaken that assessment was, but for the moment it seemed an obvious and realistic judgment.

At the end of their meeting, it was decided that Sadat, as acting president, would inform the people of their leader's death. But first a red alert was flashed to the army to guard against a possible attack from Israel or an internal insurrection. Then a tearful Sadat went on television and said: "The U.A.R., the Arab nation and humanity have lost the most precious man, the most courageous and most sincere man."

The reaction throughout the Arab world was a profound sense of loss. Wrote an American magazine: "From Algiers to Aden, Marrakech to Muscat, Nasser's death united Arabs in grief. Everywhere the plaintive cry went up: 'Why do you leave us, Gamal?' From loudspeakers atop minarets in a thousand towns and cities wafted the reedy, lugubrious voices of muezzins chanting verses from the Koran."

Spontaneous demonstrations of grief erupted throughout the Middle East. Weeping men in towns far removed from Egypt bore empty coffins in mock funerals. Some 75,000 Palestinians paraded through the Old City of Jerusalem, now in its fourth year of Israeli occupation. In Cairo, no less than five million people poured into the streets for the state funeral, which was also attended by twenty-seven heads of state, eleven prime ministers and twenty-two other foreign delegations, including Aleksei N. Kosygin, the premier of the Soviet Union. The United States, which had no formal diplomatic relations with Egypt, was represented by only a mid-level cabinet member, Health, Education and Welfare Secretary Elliot Richardson.

Such an outpouring of affection and depth of mourning only confirmed to the government what the inner circle already knew: despite his many

16

failures, the towering stature of Gamal Abdel Nasser would be the Egyptian people's measuring rod of his successor. It would not be easy to measure up.

Meanwhile, the constitutional process went forward. Sadat, duly supported by the heirs of Nasser, was put forward as the late president's legitimate successor. On October 15, Sadat was confirmed as President in a plebiscite with a vote of 90.04% and officially sworn in two days later. Among his first appointments was Ali Sabri, whom he named as one of his two vice presidents. For the moment Sadat had assured his exalted office by assuaging Sabri's ambitions.

CHAPTER II

Diplomacy vs Force

SADAT'S ASCENDANCY TO THE PRESIDENCY of Egypt was only one of four major changes in leadership in the Middle East in 1969 and 1970, changes that would have profound reverberations throughout the region. New leaders had also emerged in Libya and Syria on the Arab side and in Israel.

Golda Meir had succeeded Israel's moderate Prime Minister Levi Eshkol after his death February 26, 1969. Golda, as she was universally known, was seventy years old when she finally reached the top after long service as Israel's first ambassador to Moscow, minister of labor, minister of foreign affairs and, most recently, secretary general of the socialist Mapai Party. Born Goldie Mabovitch in Kiev, Ukraine, her family had emigrated to Milwaukee when she was eight. In the United States, she became a school teacher and a fervent Zionist and socialist. In 1919, at the age of twenty-one, she emigrated to Palestine to join the early pioneers of the Jewish state.

She had endured all the ideological and physical struggles leading toward Israel's statehood, and in the process Golda Meir had evolved into a complex mixture of the archetypical Jewish mother and iron-willed Zionist zealot. As Time magazine described her in 1969: "The essence of the woman is conviction, without compromise, and expressed with all the subtlety of a Centurion tank. She seldom loses an argument...." In the jaundiced opinion of former Austrian Chancellor Bruno Kreisky, himself a Jew who dealt with her many times, Golda Meir was "a tough, obstinate, unintelligent woman, without discernment, wisdom or poise." Despite such stern opinions, which were shared by many who knew her well, Golda Meir was immensely popular, particularly in the United States where she was regularly selected in various polls as the world's most admired woman.

18

No one doubted that Golda planned to retain as much as she could of Israel's conquests from the 1967 war.

The speed and sweep of Israel's stunning six-day military victory had won widespread admiration, especially in the United States, releasing a surge of pride and unprecedented confidence in Israel. The upwelling of optimism in turn fed ambitions for territorial expansion, for what was perceived as a new, better and more secure life. Although there were about a million Palestinians living in the occupied lands, there was tremendous pressure among some Israelis, particularly among extreme nationalists like Menachem Begin and his far right Gahal coalition, to retain much of the land, especially revered Jerusalem, the storied West Bank of the Jordan River, the Samaria and Judea of ancient Israel, and the strategic Golan Heights. Begin's Gahal opposition party was a major part of Israel's national unity government that Golda now headed and, as a result, its highly aggressive views exerted considerable restraining influence on any Israeli policy tending toward withdrawal or compromise on the occupied territories. It was this confident mood in Israel and the hardlining Golda Meir that Sadat would now have to confront and to match wits with in his first tenuous days of rule.

The other new leaders coming on the turbulent scene were Hafez Assad and Muammar Qadhafi. A month after Sadat's election, on November 13, 1970, Assad, the proud, calculating, and cool minister of defense and former air force commander, staged a bloodless coup against the radical civilians of the Baathist government and became Syria's new leader at the age of forty-four. A career military man and member of the Alawite cult of Shia Islam, a sect that represented about 11% of the largely Sunni Moslem population, Assad was the strongest and shrewdest leader Syria had had since winning its independence from France at the end of World War II. He was to bring unprecedented stability to modern Syria, which had suffered almost as many coups as it was years old. In the process, he would show himself every bit as determined to regain Syria's land occupied by Israel as Golda was in retaining it. He would also become a strong competitor of Sadat for the leadership of the Arab world.

A year before Assad's rise, on September 1, 1969, Qadhafi led a coup against King Mohammed Idris, the pro-western ruler of Libya since its independence in 1951. Qadhafi was a twenty-seven-year-old Moslem totally unknown outside of Libya. He would soon create endless headaches for the West. His first action in coming to power was to announce that America's lease on Wheelus Field would not be renewed when it came up the following year; America's major base in Africa was thus lost. In his

19

first speech, the young signals officer called for Arab unity, saying it was the "answer to the challenges from imperialism and Zionism."

Qadhafi's rantings would have received scant attention except for the fact that his desert country had the one resource that Europe was totally depended upon: high grade light oil. In 1969, Libya was supplying a quarter of all of Western Europe's oil, and oil income had soared from $3 million in 1961 to $1.2 billion at the time of Qadhafi's takeover. He quickly recognized the West's dependence on Libya's precious resource and saw that it could be used as an ideological weapon of great potency. From now until the 1973 war, Qadhafi and Libya would be in the forefront in threatening the oil weapon. His message was clear: if the West did not modify its support of Israel it would pay dearly.

Adding muscle to Qadhafi's threats was a little noted trend developing in 1970 that would have ominous implications for the United States and Western Europe. First, in July, Algeria demanded a 50% rise in its taxes on oil produced by French companies, increasing the cost of a barrel 77 cents to $2.85. It made the price rise retroactive to January 1969. A short time later, on September 4, Libya forced the independent Occidental Petroleum Company to increase its taxes to 58% from 50% and to raise by 30 cents the price of a barrel of oil, to $2.53. Other oil firms operating in Libya were soon brought to heel and made similar concessionary agreements, thus bringing about the largest price increase ever and the first major hike in thirteen years. The writing was already clearly on the wall. The oil countries were determined to profit from their own oil and use it to influence the Arab-Israeli conflict.

Now, with the coming to power in a short period of time of Sadat, Assad and Qadhafi, the Middle East by the fall of 1970 had three new Arab leaders who were all relatively young, all nationalists, all recently released from Western colonialism, all distrustful of Israel and all oriented by necessity—if not inclination—toward Moscow.

Within the broader Arab world, then, there now existed a new group of Soviet-dependent states, anti-Zionist and secular or at least antimonarchist in form, that served as an alternative to the conservative royal governments ruling Jordan, Saudi Arabia and the Persian Gulf emirates. Intriguingly, those countries with oil—which included the world's largest proven fields—were suddenly finding themselves for the first time in a powerful position to influence western countries dependent on their oil. These countries also happened to be the monarchies of Saudi Arabia and the Gulf emirates. But now they shared a common goal with the new states—anti-Zionism.

• •

The task facing Sadat as Egypt's new leader was monumental. He had no constituency, no natural sector of public support, no real experience in governing. At fifty-one years of age, he had spent four of those years in prison as a revolutionary and the rest of his adult life as an army officer, an editor of a daily newspaper, chairman of the Afro-Asian Solidarity Council and as speaker of the impotent National Assembly, Egypt's rubberstamp parliament. In short, he had been a loyal party functionary, an obedient follower and willing factotum for Gamal Abdel Nasser. But he had not in any sense been a leader or mover in the mainstream of forming or carrying out Egypt's policies at home or abroad.

In part, Sadat's isolation now proved to be an asset since he could hardly be accused of causing Egypt's predicament, which in the autumn of 1970 was grave. The lot of the fellahin, the long-suffering Egyptian peasant farmers, was as miserable as it had been during the monarchy that Nasser had overthrown in 1952. A water buffalo still cost more to hire, 69 cents a day, than a man, 58 cents. The average per person income had increased during Nasser's reign from $120 a year to only $170, most of that eroded by inflation and increased taxes. Foreign exchange was so scarce that even imports ranging from scotch for tourist hotels to cosmetics were almost nonexistent; rationing limited meats and shop shelves were often empty. The country's liquid assets were so meager that the government had trouble finding money to pay its large corps of bureaucrats. Disenchantment was so great that during the previous year 150 Egyptians a day sought visas to work in the United States.

Aggravating this daily struggle for survival was the country's soaring birth rate. The population had jumped from 21 million at the start of Nasser's rule to 33.3 million at his death; it was now nearly double its 1948 level when Israel was born. At least half were illiterate and 90% lived subsistence lives. This mass of humanity was crowded into less than 5% of the country's land, mainly in the fertile Delta and Nile Valley that sliced for nearly a thousand miles through the barren desert. The Aswan High Dam, Nasser's greatest achievement, added 1.2 million additional acres of cultivatable land but even this bountiful contribution of technology was incapable of keeping up with the burgeoning population. By the time the acreage was available the population increase was so large that the ratio of people to arable land was the same as before the dam.

The press of humanity and the plethora of poverty were a volatile mix that continually threatened the government's stability. Along with Sadat's rivalry with Ali Sabri, his inter-Arab competition with Assad and his confrontation with Golda Meir, Egypt's social ills were a pressing factor threatening Sadat's survival.

• •

In the dangerous early days of his presidency, Anwar Sadat moved slowly, cautiously, to consolidate his power and avoid abrupt policy changes. He promised the people of Egypt to continue the policies of Abdel Gamal Nasser, thereby lending a sense of continuity and legitimacy to his own rule, and he began wooing his own constituency among the bourgeoisie by loosening controls on private property and among the poor by lowering the prices on such staples as tea, sugar and cooking oil. He spoke on radio and television in a soft, vernacular Arabic, radiating rustic charm and extolling not socialism but belief in God. He cultivated the press, the judiciary, the universities and, especially, the army. He bearded his enemies in their power center, the ASU, the Arab Socialist Union, Egypt's only political party, and made it name him chairman.

Still, discontent and restlessness were widespread, in large part because of Egypt's enervating, unending, unwanted and costly war with Israel. Particularly inflammatory was the continued presence of Israeli troops across the Suez Canal left over from the 1967 war. They were still there three years after Israel had captured Egypt's Sinai Peninsula, Syria's Golan Heights and Jordan's West Bank, including Jerusalem, a loss that rivaled the humiliation suffered by Islam when the Crusaders captured Jerusalem nearly nine hundred years earlier in 1099. The disgrace, the shock and depression, the raw humiliation, had been overwhelming. Nasser had called it in public "the setback." But in fact it had been a catastrophe, a stunning blow not only to Nasser but all Arabs and Islam itself. Nasser never really recovered from the trauma of having his air force destroyed in several hours, his army decimated in six days and the whole of the Sinai lost.

Sadat, in one of the seemingly sincere expressions in his revisionist "autobiography," expressed the anguish felt by most Arabs: "I myself was completely overwhelmed by our defeat. It sank into the very fabric of my consciousness so that I relived it day and night. As its real dimensions were daily revealed to me, my agony intensified—and my sense of helplessness....That Egypt should survive became my dominant passion....The basic task was to wipe out the disgrace and humiliation that followed from the 1967 defeat."

Thus, despite Egypt's overwhelming domestic problems, it was the conflict with Israel that, by necessity, absorbed Sadat's anguished and obsessive

22

attention. As a result, the 1967 war never really was allowed to end. Rather, a ceasefire stopped the fighting briefly, then fighting escalated violently into a year-and-half-long battle along the Suez Canal that became known as the War of Attrition.

Another ceasefire was finally achieved August 7, 1970, shortly before Nasser's death. But it was for only ninety days, and it was due to expire in less than a month after Sadat's official assumption of the presidency. This timetable caused him his most pressing business in his first days in office. Emotions ran high about the continued Israeli occupation of Egyptian land. Students regularly demonstrated for the return of the territory, by war if necessary. Indeed, the war was still present. Along the canal zone, windows and automobile headlights remained painted in dark blue in order to hide from Israeli gunners, and in Cairo buildings were still piled high with sandbags and tape covered windows.

These reminders of no war-no peace added to the frustrated, depressing atmosphere gripping Egypt, and to Sadat's problems. While a new ceasefire was desirable, peace without the return of land was not possible politically. Yet the fighting along the canal during the war of Attrition had been so costly that Sadat was not anxious to resume it. In addition, the Soviet Union, which Egypt depended so heavily on for aid, advisors and diplomatic support, had early made it known to Sadat that it preferred a peaceful solution to the conflict with Israel. This message had been passed directly by Soviet Prime Minister Aleksei Kosygin when he visited Cairo for Nasser's funeral. Kosygin had a series of meetings at the time to look over the new leadership and explain Moscow's policies.

"Kosygin's message was one of caution," reported journalist Mohamed Heikal, who was considered with suspicion by the Russians. "He had made it plain that the Russians wanted the ceasefire to be extended." The trouble with this advice was that the continuation of no war-no peace meant stagnation, which meant Israel's continued occupation of Egypt's land. It was not an acceptable situation for a weak and new leader.

After Kosygin's departure, Sadat delegated a group of top officials, including Heikal and the commander-in-chief of the armed forces, General Mohammed Fawzi, to study the question of Egypt's preparedness. Heikal believed that with the ceasefire due to expire November 7, there was too little time for the new President to be expected to take the momentous decision of going to war. To buttress his argument, Heikal asked for a professional opinion from Fawzi—and received an answer that showed how tenuous Sadat's position remained.

"Tell me, from a purely military point of view, are you ready for a

23

resumption of hostilities,?'' he asked the general.

"I am a soldier," said Fawzi, adding pointedly: "If I am given an order in writing, I will do whatever is required of me by the political leadership."

The condition that Fawzi required written orders stunned Heikal, who later noted that "never, while Nasser was alive, had [Fawzi] asked for any written orders."

To Heikal and others, it was clear the old general had come under the influence of the Ali Sabri group.

In the end, Fawzi admitted that Upper Egypt was still unprotected by SAM missiles and that the armed forces were not ready for war. The group recommended to Sadat that the ceasefire be extended for a further three months. Shrewdly, the new president did not risk public wrath by personally making the decision public. Instead, he acquiesced in a U.N. General Assembly resolution on November 4, which called for Israel's withdrawal and a continuation of the ceasefire for ninety days. There was considerable subtlety in this maneuver, a level of shrewdness equal to Nasser that would eventually become recognized as Sadat's style. Rather than taking a public stand, Sadat simply let the ceasefire continue, thereby appearing to bow to the wishes of the world community while at the same time defusing resentment from his hawks at home.

He manipulated this deliberate ambiguity to keep Israel off balance and to take a tough posture before the armed forces. "We are not committed to anything," he said in a speech November 13. "Nothing restricts our movement after this period." Renewed fighting was "very possible," he warned. At the end of the month, he vowed a new ceasefire extension would be granted "only if there is a definite timetable for Israeli withdrawal."

Sadat thus early displayed an unexpected subtlety and diplomatic agility in his handling of the sensitive ceasefire issue. It earned him no great praise but it allowed the new leader to surmount his first hurdle. But underground his enemies, especially Ali Sabri, were gathering their forces, keen, as Sadat noted, "to have a showdown with me."

CHAPTER III

The Nixon White House

ALTHOUGH HE WAS IMPATIENT WITH DETAILS, disliked the nitty gritty of negotiating and valued his leisure over regular office hours, in short, he was lazy but imaginative, Anwar Sadat understood all too well the convoluted strategic problem facing him. Without some movement toward the return of Egypt's land, his country would remain obsessed with the conflict with Israel, Egypt and its teeming masses would have no chance of winning the more basic war against poverty and he, of course, would not long last as Egypt's ruler. Yet Sadat's choices were severely limited. War was out of the question. There was a war plan, known as Granite I, but there was also a deathtrap known as the Bar-Lev Line. The world's military experts, Egyptians included, agreed the towering Israeli sand barrier of fortresses and gun emplacements on the east side of the Suez Canal was so formidable that it could be overwhelmed, if at all, only at enormous cost in blood. The Bar-Lev Line ran the hundred-mile length of the Suez Canal, sealing off the Sinai Peninsula from Egypt as securely as a closed iron gate. The road to war was shut, or so it appeared.

The only other avenue lay in diplomacy. But Israel had repeatedly demonstrated that it was so strong, and growing stronger with generous infusions of American aid, that it would return Egypt's land, if at all, only on its own terms. Repeated efforts had already shown Sadat that these were terms his countrymen would not accept.

Sadat's solution to this conundrum was worthy of Metternich—on the surface; underneath his strategy was basically flawed because he failed to appreciate the depth of Israel's influence in America. He shrewdly concluded that the shortest distance to peace lay not through nearby Tel Aviv but six thousand miles to the west, through Washington. Instead of confronting

Israel head-on, he would ignore the Jewish state. He would open a backchannel to Washington and through it manipulate Israel into a solution. His reasoning appeared subtle and profound. It went something like this: Since Washington's strategic interests lay in friendly relations with the oil-rich Arab world, it was to America's advantage to have good relations with the Arab countries. Since America's global efforts were aimed at stemming communism, then in the Middle East this could be accomplished only by carrying out an evenhanded policy. And, finally, since Israel needed Washington more than Washington needed Israel, America could pressure Israel. Without America, Israel could not long maintain its military superiority or survive its isolation in the world community.

What could be simpler—and ultimately more wrong?

On its surface, however, it was an insightful analysis of the strategic situation and it seemed to be an especially shrewd reading of the character of President Richard Milhous Nixon, now entering the third year of his presidency.

• •

Nixon had come to power in 1969 less encumbered by Middle East preconceptions or political dependence than any President since Dwight D. Eisenhower. He had lived through the traumatic Suez crisis of 1956 as vice president and had visited the Middle East as a private citizen before returning to the White House as President. His attitude toward both Israelis and Arabs was cool-eyed. He had sent former Governor William Scranton on a pre-inaugural swing through the Middle East in late 1968 to study the area, which, following the 1967 war, had become increasingly intrusive in U.S. foreign affairs because of America's succession to France as Israel's major supporter. Scranton, on his return, reported that in his assessment U.S. policy should be "evenhanded" in order to protect American national interests. The remark brought protests from Israel, which considered such an attitude close to anti-Israel. But Nixon did not disavow Scranton's remarks beyond having his press secretary point out that "Scranton remarks [are] not Nixon remarks." Privately, Nixon was heard to say: "We cannot let the American Jews dictate policy."

Nixon considered himself less beholden to Jewish votes than any of his predecessors and therefore impervious to the formidable pressures of the Israeli Lobby. However, Nixon, a consummate politician, was sensitive to these pressures, as his memoirs revealed: "One of the main problems I faced...was the unyielding and shortsighted pro-Israeli attitude in large and influential segments of the American Jewish community, Congress, the media and in intellectual and cultural circles. In the quarter-century since

26

the end of World War II this attitude had become so deeply ingrained that many saw the corollary of not being pro-Israel as being anti-Israeli, or even anti-Semitic. I tried unsuccessfully to convince them that this was not the case."

At the beginning of his administration, before the Watergate scandal overwhelmed him, Nixon's attitude toward Israel and the Arabs was fairly benign and oriented toward a just resolution of the long conflict. He agreed with the principles of U.N. Resolution 242, passed in 1967 and calling for a return of land in exchange for peace.

More than most politicians, Nixon displayed an understanding of the subtleties of the local rivalries that raged in the region. But his mindset and his responsibilities as the leader of the Western world were such that he viewed conflicts in global, superpower terms. This attitude was reinforced by the debacle in Vietnam where vast quantities of American blood were being shed in an essentially local conflict, although that was not how various administrations, including his own, publicly described it. But the inescapable fact of Vietnam was that Americans were dying to prop up a local government incapable of sustaining itself.

This question of whether the Vietnam conflict, and by extension, the Arab-Israeli conflict, was essentially a superpower conflict or a local rivalry was an exceedingly complex and subtle one, since it was indeed part of both. The confusion lay in discerning the ratio between its local and global aspects. The dispute was the basis of a running agrument between bureaucrats and Nixon Administration officials during all of Nixon's tenure and beyond.

In general, the supporters of Israel, and Israel itself—as did the supporters of the Vietnam War—emphasized the view that Israel's troubles all flowed from the opposition of the Soviet Union. That being the case, they argued, the United States should support the Jewish state as an ally in its global contest with communism. Opposing this stance were the Arabists of the state department and the Central Intelligence Agency. These men and women for the most part had served in the region, knew many of its leading personalities and had seen up close the prickly local issues that underlay the conflict. Almost unanimously, they regarded the conflict as local in origin and only incidentally global in context.

"I constantly wrote cables trying to explain that it was a local conflict and that the Soviets were only there because we were so totally pro-Israel," recalled the CIA's station chief in Cairo during the early 1970s, Eugene Trone. Others wrote similar reports. But these messages were largely ignored in the White House where combating global communism was more

27

attractive, and politically more profitable, than trying to mediate the Middle East's serpentine local issues.

• •

In his subtle and wily way, Anwar Sadat tried to involve the United States in Egypt much as Nasser had the Soviets, and essentially for the same reasons. What he had not counted on was the depth and strength of Israel's supporters in America, among them Nixon's national security adviser, Henry Alfred Kissinger. Officially, Kissinger was effectively removed from the administration's concerns with the Middle East. This came about at the start of the administration when Nixon was overwhelmed with the war in Vietnam and massive antiwar protests, and as he developed his larger plans to make an opening with China and achieve detente with the Soviet Union. It was a full agenda and Nixon deliberately assigned the Middle East to his old friend, Secretary of State William Pierce Rogers, about the only substantive area given Rogers because Nixon and Kissinger were determined to supervise the rest of the nation's foreign affairs.

"I did this partly because I felt that Kissinger's Jewish background would put him at a disadvantage during the delicate initial negotiations for the reopening of diplomatic relations with the Arab states," Nixon recalled in his memoirs. In explaining his decision to Kissinger, Nixon added: "You and I will have more than enough on our plate with Vietnam, SALT, the Soviets, Japan and Europe." As indeed they did.

Nonetheless, Kissinger, strongly pro-Israel, ambitious and jealous of Secretary of State Rogers' stature, if not his effectiveness, bridled at not having more influence on Middle East policy. Kissinger's ruthless infighting against Rogers and his publicly scornful attitude toward him were an open scandal, and did nothing to help the administration formulate a coherent Middle Eastern policy.

As Kissinger himself later admitted: "Neither Rogers nor I mustered the grace to transcend an impasse that we should have recognized was not in the national interest. If we had been prepared to overcome our not inconsiderable egos, we could have complemented each other's efforts." But they never did. As a result, "In the end, [Nixon] probably spent as much time mediating between Rogers and me as between the Arabs and Israelis."

Rogers was a highly successful corporation attorney who had served with Nixon in Eisenhower's Administration as attorney general. An upright, proud man, perceptive and socially ambitious, he took seriously his writ to find a fair and equitable settlement in the Middle East. Part of his problem, however, was that Rogers did not believe in working long days and

28

he did not bring the energy or the personal commitment to the Middle East problem that Kissinger did.

• •

Henry Kissinger came to his post as national security adviser with strong biases but little knowledge about the region. He had never visited an Arab country and had been to Israel only three brief times during the previous decade. Despite this, his attitudes fairly closely paralleled those of Israel's staunchest supporters, of which he openly included himself as one.

Kissinger knew firsthand about the brutality of rampant anti-Semitism. He had grown up in the Bavarian village of Furth, a town with a population of about eighty thousand with three thousand Jews in the days before World War II. With the rise of Nazism in the 1930s, life increasingly became a nightmare for Furth's Jews. Kissinger's father, Louis, a teacher, soon lost his job. Kissinger and other Jews were expelled from the Gymnasium and forced to attend an all-Jewish school. Jewish boys were no longer welcome to play in soccer games or attend social events. Hitler Youth roamed the streets, picking fights, roughing up Jews. By the time Kissinger was fifteen, in 1938, the family, like many European Jews, had had enough and emigrated to New York. The move probably saved their lives. At the end of World War II, only seventy Jews showed up in Furth at the first postwar service; among the six million Jews killed by the Nazis were thirteen of Kissinger's relatives.

In Manhattan, Kissinger prospered beyond the bounds of even the usual expectations of the America dream. He survived the impoverishment of the new emigre by working odd jobs to get through high school as a straight A student, served as a sergeant in the army and then, in 1947, won a scholarship to Harvard. It was the start of a brilliant career as historian and nuclear strategist at that cloistered school. But, despite his great success, always in Kissinger's background there was the out-of-control Germany of the 1930s and the haven represented by the new state of Israel.

Thus when he later became national security adviser and then secretary of state, Kissinger brought with him to the corridors of power an abiding concern for the welfare of Israel. As he explained: "Look, anyone who has been through what I've been through has some very special feeling for the survival of the state of Israel." He remembered that he lost "many of his relatives in the concentration camps" and he viewed Israel as "a place of refuge for those who survived." Observed one of Kissinger's closest aides: "He's objective about Israel but not detached. How could he be? He has a strong sense of 'these are my people.' He's immensely

29

proud to be a Jew. When he pleads for changes in Israeli policy, it's precisely because he wants Israel and Jewry to prosper. It tears his guts out to be accused of treachery to his own.'' When Jewish leaders at one point accused him of acting against Israel, Kissinger replied: "How could I, as a Jew, do anything to betray my people?''

Kissinger shared Nixon's global outlook and primary interest in superpower relations, particularly the threat of nuclear war, and regarded regional conflicts as a reflection of superpower competition. As a result, he tended, when he looked at the Middle East beyond the frontiers of Israel, to see the region as a subsidiary pawn in the larger superpower chess game, a minor player whose interests could be sacrificed or ignored in pursuit of winning the global contest. For Kissinger, this meant that the prime goal of the United States should be to eject the Soviets from the Middle East, an aim that he concluded could be best accomplished by doing nothing and letting the Arabs stew in their own frustrations. By contrast, experts in the state department, sensitive to local issues, urged an active American role in seeking peace, restraint in arms aid to Israel and, like William Scranton, a more evenhanded policy.

Kissinger was on the opposite side of all these issues. He supported Israel's hardline policies, urged generous arms aid for the Jewish state and believed that stalemate was preferable to withdrawal without full peace. From his powerful office in the White House, Kissinger actively opposed State Department efforts to break the logjam.

"I thought delay was on the whole in our interests because it enabled us to demonstrate even to radical Arabs that we were indispensable to any progress and that it could not be extorted from us by Soviet pressure," Kissinger later observed. "The state department wanted to fuel the process of negotiations by accepting at least some of the Soviet ideas, to facilitate compromise. I wanted to frustrate the radicals—who were in any event hostile to us—by demonstrating that in the Middle East friendship with the United States was the precondition to diplomatic progress."

The problem with this analysis was that it ignored the basic injustice inflicted on the Palestinians. This myopia would distort Kissinger's view of the Middle East throughout his tenure in Washington.

Kissinger also disagreed with the general attitude in the state department that the impasse in the Middle East was due to Israeli intransigence, which of course was the essential reality. He blamed Arab radicals abetted by Soviet meddling. In this, Kissinger was occasionally in conflict with Nixon, who ''...leaned toward the departmental views that Israel's policies were the basic cause of the difficulties...." Nixon also disagreed with Kissinger's belief that continued Soviet failure to find a settlement was playing into Washington's hands because the Arabs would become disillusioned with Moscow. As Nixon shrewdly observed in a note to Kissinger: "We have been gloating over Soviet 'defeats' in the Mideast since '67—& State et al said the June war was a 'defeat' for Soviet. It was not. They became the Arabs' friend and the U.S. their enemy. Long range this is what serves their interest."

Beyond these disagreements, Kissinger and the state department were at loggerheads over the fundamental question of whether Israel was an asset or a deficit to U.S. interests in the Middle East. Kissinger saw Israel as an ally, strong and democratic, that could act in concert to promote and protect America's position. This argument was less than persuasive to experts on the area who had watched Soviet influence grow from nil in the mid-1950s to the pervasive strength it had achieved less than fifteen years later, mainly because of the diplomatic openings Arab grievances against Israel provided the Soviets. In addition, Palestinian guerrilla groups had grown explosively during the same period and were directly striking at Americans. In the view of the Arabists, the area was being radicalized in direct response to Israeli intransigence on the basic democratic principles of withdrawal from captured lands and its refusal to grant self-determination to the Palestinians.

Over these core issues Kissinger, the intellectual from Harvard, and Rogers, the successful Manhattan lawyer, would struggle viciously until one of them prevailed. If Anwar Sadat had been aware of the depth and deadliness of this bitter personal feud he might have chosen a different strategy.

• •

Kissinger and Rogers were given a chance to test against the unforgiving mirror of reality their conflicting views early in the Administration. It came in 1970 during the most dramatic terrorist operation of its kind. On September 6, guerrillas belonging to the Popular Front for the Liberation of Palestine, the PFLP, a radical offshoot of Yasser Arafat's Fatah, in quick succession hijacked a Swissair DC-8 with 155 passengers, a TWA Boeing 707 with 151 passengers and a PanAm 747 with 152 passengers. Attempts to take over a fourth airliner, an El Al jet, resulted in a shootout inside the plane. One of the hijackers was killed and the second, the notorious Leila Khaled, was wounded by security guards. Khaled, a young and attractive Palestinian, had gained renown throughout the Arab world when she took part in one of the first successful hijackings of a commercial airliner by Palestinians the previous year. The Swissair and TWA planes were flown with their passengers to a deserted airfield about twenty-five miles northeast of Jordan's capital of Amman. It was a barren area of lifeless salt flats near rude camps controlled by the PFLP, whose guerrillas soon surrounded the two planes. The third hijacked jet, a PanAm 747, was flown to Cairo where the passengers were released and it was blown up.

The jubilant Palestinians of the PFLP immediately named the old Dawson airfield in Jordan where the planes were being held "revolution airport" and demanded the release of commandos being held in Britain, Israel, Switzerland and West Germany. While the world marvelled at the spectacle of more than three hundred passengers, nearly all of them from America and Europe, and two modern jet aircraft being held hostage at the dirt airstrip in the desert wastes, the guerrillas delivered yet another shock. They hijacked a British jet on September 9. The BOAC VC-10 with 115 persons aboard was also forced to land at "revolution airport," which by now had become one of the best known airfields in the world. The PFLP said the jets and its passengers would be exchanged for the release of Leila Khaled, who had been flown to London and was being held there. Now there were three planes and a total of 421 hostages in the PFLP's hands.

Keeping the tension at a melodramatic level, the PFLP repeatedly set deadlines, threatening to kill all the hostages and blow up the planes. All three jets were wired with bombs.

A spokesman for the PFLP summed up the situation, as perceived by the desperate Palestinians: "The government can do nothing to stop us. If they move the army closer to the planes, they will be responsible for the consequences. We are calling the shots in Jordan, not the government. As for world opinion, where was world opinion when a million of our people were hijacked out of Palestine by the Israelis? The world didn't care about us, so why should we care about anybody? Now let world opinion—and King Hussein—understand the drastic measures we are prepared to take to dramatize our cause and win back our land."

Then the terrorists made a threat that directly involved Washington. They offered to release all the hostages except Israelis and Americans holding dual U.S.-Israeli passports, in return for the Europeans releasing their Palestinian prisoners. Israelis and American-Israelis would be released only when Israel freed the guerrillas it held. A seventy-two hour deadline was set for Israel to act.

In Washington, the skyjackings immediately exposed the animosity between Kissinger and Rogers. At their first meeting on the crisis, it quickly became obvious that Rogers and Kissinger had completely different concepts of how to respond. Rogers, a cautious man, pedestrian in imagination but upright and prudent, thought that in the end there was little that could be done by the United States. Military intervention would be extremely risky and, with several hundred thousand U.S. soldiers still fighting in Vietnam, would involve all of the country's strategic reserve, which amounted to a meager four brigades. As a result, Rogers wanted to reassure the Palestinians that America meant them no harm; he somehow thought that this could help calm the situation and open a dialogue. By contrast, Kissinger, like many academics newly exposed to raw power, was quick to threaten force; his reaction in this case was no different. He wanted to send stiff warnings to Arab governments, although at this point they were as impotent as was Washington.

The fact was that the situation already was far out of hand and it represented a major embarrassment to the United States. A few poorly armed terrorists were holding Americans and others in a desert and the United States was helpless to save them. That is what became clear at this first meeting. Nothing was accomplished, except to expose once again to insiders that the Secretary of State and the National Security Adviser could not stand each other.

Then occurred a bizarre scene.

Divided and devoid of solutions, the officials were summoned to another, this one in President Richard M. Nixon's Oval Office. The discussion swashed around aimlessly with no clear ideas emerging. Instead, Secretary of Defense Laird talked about using electronic devices to prevent future hijackings. Apparently appreciative of this diversion, Nixon chimed in, favoring both armed guards and electronic devices. He instructed Laird to take the "lead responsibility" and told Kissinger to "coordinate" the effort. As for the nominal purpose of the meeting—how to respond to the crisis in Jordan—Nixon ordered Rogers to press diplomatic initiatives.

That was it. The meeting ended with nothing being decided, no course of action agreed upon beyond "diplomatic initiatives," which would have been taken under any circumstances no matter how futile they were. The crisis was now in its third day but the Nixon-Kissinger Administration was as baffled as how to respond as was the rest of the world.

In his memoirs, Kissinger expressed the bewilderment that presumably gripped all of the participants in the presidential meeting: "My confusion as to what all this meant was not cleared up when the President wandered into my office ten minutes after the meeting and said he recognized he had

33

a 'terrible bureaucratic problem;' the Cabinet officers all wanted to 'do something;' he had given them each something to do; I should sort it out. He did not say how, or even exactly what he intended.''

It was this vacuum that allowed the energetic Kissinger to become the prime mover in the crisis over the next seventeen tension-filled days. From the beginning of the crisis, Kissinger took charge. No one else seemed to want to, or indeed to know what to do. His first action was to activate the National Security Council's crisis machinery, WSAG, the Washington Special Actions Group, on September 9. Membership of WSAG included the state department's area specialists and policy analysts plus representatives of the CIA, the Pentagon and other experts who could contribute to the solution of problems. At WSAG's initial meetings it became clear that America's options were not many. A rescue operation, as Rogers had early realized, was considered by all of WSAG's officials as far too risky.

The reality was that despite nuclear weapons, supersonic jets and super-sophisticated electronics, America was essentially powerless to rescue the hostages alive. Rescue, it was realized almost immediately, would be attempted only if the terrorists began attacking the hostages. Instead, the group concentrated on how, in Kissinger's self-promoting words, ''to begin conveying determination and start exerting pressure....American resolution was alike crucial for the fate of the hostages and for the survival of the King. Indeed, in a curious way the future of the King and of the hostages had begun to merge.''

The first effort to project a powerful image came the next day, September 10, when Nixon authorized placing the 82nd Airborne Division on ''semi-alert'' at Fort Bragg, North Carolina, and six C-130 cargo planes were flown to Incirlik air base in Turkey for possible evacuation of the American hostages. The next day the aircraft carrier *Independence* was ordered to sail off the coast of Lebanon with its task force of four destroyers; two more destroyers were ordered to join the group on September 12 and four more C-130s were ordered to Turkey with an escort of twenty-five F-4 Phantoms warplanes.

These aggressive moves reflected Kissinger's usual pugnacity in a crisis and his rather simplistic—or cynical—belief that the Soviet Union was the motivating power. ''In my view,'' wrote Kissinger, ''the Kremlin was playing the Jordan crisis....It made formally correct noises but did nothing constructive to reverse the drift toward crisis.'' In fact, as later studies reveal, Moscow was cautious throughout the crisis. Despite this, Nixon, by now deeply involved in the November congressional elections, supported Kissinger's confrontational view. Both men chose to regard the developing crisis mainly in East-West superpower terms. The reaction of the guerrillas to the U.S. military gambits was predictably violent. On September 12, the sixth day of the crisis, the PFLP retaliated by blowing up all three commercial jetliners. Then, all but fifty-four of the hostages, thirty-four of them Americans, were released unharmed. The remaining hostages were divided into small groups and hidden in various neighborhoods. The PFLP said it considered the American hostages as though they were Israelis. It continued to threaten dire consequences if Israel and other countries did not soon release Palestinian prisoners.

The wanton destruction of the airliners was a catalyst in the heavy, moody atmosphere in Jordan. Like a stroke of lightning, it ignited a storm of fighting and hastened the complete collapse of order. Battles flared, sputtered to an uneasy halt and then flared again in Amman and in the northern regions of the country where the guerrillas were strongest. But still King Hussein, torn by conflicting advice, hesitated to give the fateful order to crush the guerrillas. Yet the time for hesitation was clearly ending.

Speculation was rife that King Hussein would not last long.

• •

Hussein ibn Talal ibn Abdullah ibn Hussein Al Hashimi was a product of Bedouin legends and of Harrow and Sandhurst, a short, muscular ruler with a daredevil's instincts in automobiles but a statesman's caution in diplomacy. His desert country had been carved out of the Turkish Empire in 1921 by Winston Churchill in "one Sunday afternoon," as the former British leader liked to recall. Hussein's grandfather, Abdullah, had ruled Transjordan, as it was originally known, until his assassination by a Palestinian in Jerusalem in 1951. Hussein, then fifteen, had been by Abdullah's side and was hit by a bullet but not seriously injured. After a brief reign by his father, King Talal, who suffered from schizophrenia, Hussein officially took the constitutional oath as king of the Hashemite Kingdom of Jordan in May 2, 1953, five months short of his eighteenth birthday.

By 1970, King Hussein had ruled longer than any other Arab leader except Egypt's Gamal Abdel Nasser—but his reign now was in graver danger than ever before. Since the 1967 Arab-Israel war, the ranks of the Palestinian guerrilla organizations had grown dramatically and dangerously. According to U.N. studies, the war had produced 323,000 new refugees on top of the 726,000 who were made homeless by the 1948 war, another human flood of the homeless dispersed into their own diaspora. The new refugees flocked to the dismal refugee camps in Lebanon and Jordan and other countries, powerfully contributing to the destabilization of Hussein's rule.

35

A moderate and pro-Western, Hussein's attitude toward the Palestinian commando groups was cautious, as it had to be. At least half of his country's two million population was, by 1970, made up of Palestinians, mostly refugees, who provided a natural base of support for the guerrillas. There was no easy solution to Hussein's dilemma. On the one side, the fedayeen's existence was founded on its ability to launch raids into Israel. Yet the raids brought such punishing retaliatory attacks by Israel against Jordan that the King was losing his credibility as a ruler capable of protecting his population or even his own prestige. In addition, the guerrillas in the camps, and increasingly in the cities too, were a quasi-government unto themselves. They carried arms, collected taxes, often by force, and had their own foreign relations. Friction between the crown and the commandos, particularly the PFLP and even more radical groups like the Popular Democratic Front, which was openly challenging the monarchy, grew sharply. The confrontation between the increasingly bold guerrillas and the royal army was now at an explosive level. Hussein had to act or lose his crown.

Intelligence that war was imminent reached Kissinger on the evening of September 15 while he and many of his associates were at a black tie dinner in Virginia. Quickly gathering up the other members of WSAG, Kissinger flew by helicopter back to the White House and convened an emergency meeting at 10:30 PM. The consensus was to build up even more U.S. forces in the region, provide psychological and material support for King Hussein and, in Kissinger's words in his memoirs, to "match and overwhelm a Soviet response (including if necessary military intervention.)"

On September 16, as predicted by intelligence sources, Hussein finally took decisive action. The King dismissed his civilian government, replaced it with military officers and demanded that the guerrillas honor a previous truce to withdraw from Amman and collect the weapons of their supporters. When they instead declared a general strike and ordered all commandos to remain in place with their "fingers on the triggers," Hussein declared martial law throughout the kingdom.

Civil war was now unavoidable.

At dawn on September 17, Jordanian armor and troops entered Amman and fierce fighting broke out in the capital and the northern strongholds of the guerrillas. The tough Jordanian troops gave no quarter. Buildings were blasted pointblank by cannon fire, nests of guerrillas were routed by air and ground attacks and the leaders of the commando groups were hunted down. A total curfew was declared and citizens warned that anyone on the streets would be shot on sight.

The same day as the outbreak of heavy fighting, Nixon took the only

36

moves that seemed available. He dispatched two more aircraft carriers, the *Saratoga* and the *John F. Kennedy*, with a cruiser and twelve accompanying destroyers, to the eastern Mediterranean. An amphibious force with 1,200 marines was ordered to stay within thirty-six hours of Lebanon and an additional cruiser and the task force led by the helicopter carrier *Guam* were ordered to speed their way to the Mediterranean.

On September 19, reports of Syrian tank movements began reaching Washington, a possibility that for some reason no one in the administration seemed to have taken seriously. The report came from a British official in Cairo and was not directly routed to Washington, so Kissinger and WSAG discounted it. The next day, however, both Hussein and his close adviser, Zaid Rifai, Jordan's prime minister, urgently radioed Ambassador L. Dean Brown in Amman, reported major armored incursions by Syria and officially requested U.S. assistance. Shortly after noon on September 20, Rifai specifically asked for U.S. reconnaissance flights to see if more Syrian forces were heading toward Jordan. In all, there were now about one hundred Syrian tanks inside the country. If Syria staged an all out invasion, there was no way Jordan's tiny force of three hundred tanks and thirty-eight aircraft could stand up to Syria's 880 tanks and two hundred airplanes.

Although the Soviet Union was urging restraint, Nixon and Kissinger continued to view the crisis within the context of superpower relations. "...one thing was clear," Nixon wrote in his memoirs. "We could not allow Hussein to be overthrown by a Soviet-inspired insurrection. If it succeeded, the entire Middle East might erupt in war: the Israelis would almost certainly take preemptive measures against a Syrian-dominated radical government in Jordan; the Egyptians were tied to Syria by military alliances; and Soviet prestige was on the line with both the Syrians and the Egyptians. Since the United States could not stand idly by and watch Israel being driven into the sea, the possibility of a direct U.S.-Soviet confrontation was uncomfortably high. It was like a ghostly game of dominoes, with a nuclear war waiting at the end."

This was a highly colored misreading of the reality. It exaggerated Moscow's involvement and Israel's peril. The Soviet Union, as former National Security Council analyst William Quandt pointed out, was continuing to limit its statements to warnings that no nation should intervene. When the Sixth Fleet built up its forces in the eastern Mediterranean, the Soviets docilely got out of the way to avoid a confrontation. Additionally, the Israelis were in no way in any danger of being "driven into the sea." Their forces were far too strong for Syria to confront. Actually, it was Hussein who feared the Israelis might take advantage of the crisis and launch a ground attack to capture more of his country, a suspicion shared by some officials in Washington.

Nonetheless, with Nixon's approval, Kissinger sent stiff warnings to the Soviet Union and Syria. Also, an airborne brigade in West Germany was put on full alert and the Sixth Fleet in the Mediterranean was ordered to sail closer to Lebanon.

The question now was whether the United States or Israel would intervene if the King's position became graver. There had been early unanimity about one thing: There would be no joint U.S.-Israeli military operations since that would finally and completely destroy American interests in the Arab world by openly associating Washington with Tel Aviv. While Nixon kept his options open, Kissinger and WSAG believed that "our forces were best employed in holding the ring against Soviet interference with Israeli operations." In other words, as explained by Kissinger in his memoirs, "If Israel acted, everyone [in WSAG] agreed that the United States should stand aside but block Soviet retaliation against Israel."

Pressures on Nixon mounted. The need for action became urgent with the relay of an emergency message from King Hussein at about 8:20 PM on September 20. His extraordinary request, repeated twice that day to British diplomats in Amman for relay to the United States, was for immediate air strikes—preferably by the Sixth Fleet but even by Israel, if necessary—against the invading Syrian tanks. WSAG, which was propelled into practically nonstop meetings by these distraught messages, recommended yet more military preparations. The 82nd Airborne Division at Fort Bragg was brought to a full alert.

Within an hour of receiving the Hussein message, Kissinger and WSAG member Joseph Sisco decided Jordan's message should be passed onto Israel. However, the President was not in the White House. They eventually found him bowling alone at an out of the way bowling alley in the recesses of the basement of the Old Executive Building across from the White House. As the President stood listening, bowling ball in hand, Kissinger explained WSAG's plans. Nixon made his decision at once. He approved.

Now Kissinger had to find out if the Israelis were preparing to act. At about 10 PM, he found Israeli Ambassador Yitzhak Rabin in New York with Golda Meir who was addressing a United Jewish Appeal dinner. Kissinger's voice sounded urgent over the telephone as he said: "King Hussein has approached us, describing the situation of his forces, and asked us to transmit his request that your air force attack the Syrians in northern Jordan. I need an immediate reply."

The cautious ambassador, careful not to commit his country to such an extraordinary request, replied: "I'm surprised to hear the United States passing on messages of this kind like some sort of mailman. I will not even submit the request to Mrs. Meir before I know what your government thinks. Are you recommending that we respond to the Jordanian request?"

"You place me in a difficult position," said Kissinger. "I can't answer you on the spot."

Before he could get an answer, Kissinger was handed another urgent message from Hussein. He promised to call Rabin back and turned his attention to the latest bad news: At least two brigades of Syrian tanks, about two hundred and fifty in all, had poured into Jordan. The Syrian vehicles were all freshly painted with the red and olive-green emblems of the Palestine Liberation Army to make it appear as a Palestinian force, a ruse that fooled no one. The heavy Syrian force quickly dispersed Jordanian tanks trying to stop it and occupied Irbid in the north of Jordan. The Syrians were now in a position to roll right on to the capital, Amman. If the Syrian air force also joined the fight, Hussein's days would be numbered. Morale of the royal troops was collapsing.

Kissinger and Sisco now came to another important decision, the most major and the last significant recommendation they and WSAG had to make in the crisis. They concluded that, with U.S. military options limited and its troop strength in the region modest, the United States would do more than merely pass on Hussein's request for help. They would actively urge Israel to launch air strikes against the Syrian tanks. Together they telephoned Secretary of State Rogers at his home, where he foolishly spent most of this dramatic Sunday, thereby contributing to his reputation of indolence, and put forward their recommendation. For once, Rogers and Kissinger were in agreement. By 10:12 PM, Kissinger and Sisco retraced their steps to the bowling alley. They found Nixon still there. He approved an Israeli thrust and authorized Kissinger to approach Rabin with the proposal.

At 10:35 PM, Kissinger again telephoned Rabin in New York and said: "The request is approved and supported by the United States government."

"Do *you* advise Israel to do it?" asked Rabin.

"Yes, subject to your own considerations," replied Kissinger. He promised that the United States would replace all material losses and would counter Soviet interference.

At 11:30 PM, Rabin called back with Golda Meir's answer: Israel would fly a reconnaissance flight at first light. But it wanted a number of assurances, most importantly a commitment that the United States would protect Israel from any Soviet or Egyptian reaction. As the Kalb brothers reported in their biography of Kissinger: "...Nixon gave his approval. Their understanding was historic: Israel would move against Syrian forces in Jordan; and if Egyptian or Soviet forces then moved against Israel, the United States would intervene against *both*."

Israel soon began openly mobilizing and moving tanks and other forces to its frontier with Syria, signalling Damascus that Israel would not tolerate Syrian hegemony over Jordan. The Israeli increase in tank strength was dramatic, soon reaching 400.

But though there was general agreement between Tel Aviv and Washington, the Israelis insisted that if they moved they would have to use ground troops as well as air power. The issue caused delay because some U.S. officials were suspicious about Israel's intentions in using ground troops. As Talcott W. Seelye, a career foreign service officer who headed the state department's special task force during the crisis, recalled: "To us it was clear that what the Israelis wanted to do was to capitalize on this opportunity to extend their territory. We turned them down." In the end, Israel took no direct action beyond its showy mobilization.

• •

As suddenly as the crisis exploded on the world, it evaporated. Emboldened by America's support and Israel's professed willingness to participate, Hussein's armored force did better than expected against the Syrian tanks, estimated now at three hundred. More significantly, Syria's air force still had not intervened under the orders of Defense Minister Hafez Assad, who had differences with the Syrian leadership over the wisdom of the invasion. (Assad staged a coup the next year and has remained in power since.) With the skies free of opposition, Hussein's tiny but deadly air force had complete command of the skies. It began blasting at will the Syrian tank positions on September 22. By the end of the day there were indications that the Syrians were moving back home. The next day, the withdrawal was confirmed and the crisis ended without Israel taking any direct action in it.

The refusal of Assad to commit Syria's air force was more evidence of how deeply rooted in internal Syrian politics the invasion was, rather than in the global context of the superpowers posited by Nixon and Kissinger. But this political aspect was completely ignored in Washington. As NSC analyst Quandt observed: "In short, American policy in the crisis may well have had very little effect on the Syrian decision to withdraw its armor."

Diplomat Talcott Seelye, who had served most of his career in the Middle East and at the time was director of North Arabian Affairs, completely disagreed, as did others, with the Nixon-Kissinger assertion that the United

States had somehow backed down the Soviet Union. "Moscow's involvement in fomenting the crisis did not exist to the best of our knowledge," he said. "In fact, we had reliable intelligence reports indicating that the Soviets sought to restrain Syria—which conceivably might have contributed to Assad's decision to withhold his air force from helping the invading tanks." Seelye added: "The White House contention that we stood the Soviets down is pure nonsense."

Between September 25 and 29, all the hostages who had been held since the plane hijacking at the beginning of the month were released in return for the freeing of seven Palestinians held in Britain, Switzerland and West Germany, including hijacker Leila Khaled. Part of the original aim of the PFLP terrorists had been achieved even though the slaughter of Palestinians greatly harmed the guerrilla forces. To the end, Israel refused to bargain and the PFLP failed to get any Palestinians in Israel released.

Though the crisis with Syria was over, the civil war continued in Jordan. Thousands of Palestinians were killed during the heavy fighting between the guerrillas and royal Jordanian troops, and despite a ceasefire on September 24, firefights sputtered on. Women and children were dying of thirst in the capital. "God is my witness," proclaimed PLO Chairman Yasser Arafat. "Hunger and thirst are killing our remaining children, women and old men." The Arab world was up in arms at the spectacle of this continuing fratricide. Repeated meetings were held among Arab leaders, delegations were dispatched to Amman to seek a stop to the fighting and entreaties were made for Hussein and the Palestinian leaders to hold a peace meeting.

President Nasser called a meeting of the Arab heads of state and finally prevailed on King Hussein to travel to Cairo to talk peace. Arafat also attended. He had been hiding in Amman to escape assassins and had to escape disguised in Bedouin robes aboard an airplane being used by Arab peacemakers. On September 27, Hussein and Arafat joined with the Arab leaders in signing a fourteen-point peace plan tirelessly worked out by Nasser. It called for full support of the commandos but, significantly, it ordered the withdrawal of all fedayeen from Amman. Hussein, and Kissinger, had won.

The ceasefire generally held until the following summer. Then Jordanian troops finally finished their grisly business. The Palestinian survivors who had taken refuge in the northern hills of Jordan the previous September were then wiped out or chased from the country. After this, guerrilla influence was kept firmly under control in Jordan. But although they were defeated in Jordan they were by no means wiped out. The survivors, and new recruits to the cause, found new camps in Lebanon, adding to that wretched country's miseries. After this, unstable Lebanon became the major killing ground of Palestinians for Israel and the scene of an incredibly bloody civil war that continues to plague it.

• •

With the September ceasefire the Jordanian crisis was over as far as the United States was concerned. Nixon and Kissinger gleefully proclaimed the administration's first triumph in foreign policy, a timely boost for the Republican Party in the approaching November elections and in Nixon's own reelection two years hence. They bragged that Syria had been thwarted, the Soviet Union neutralized and Hussein saved. It was a sweet moment, made considerably sweeter by the opportunities it gave the President and his national security adviser to strut as the macho saviors of the moment. Neither Nixon nor Kissinger was bashful about his own self-proclaimed role in bringing about the end of the crisis. (When King Hussein was asked later by Ambassador Brown about Kissinger's memoir version of his own actions during the crisis, the King dryly replied: "I thought I had something to do with the war.")

In this euphoric atmosphere, deep appreciation of Israel's actions was expressed. Although the fighting ended before any Israeli forces had to be committed, Kissinger called Ambassador Rabin and effusively thanked him. "The President will never forget Israel's role in preventing the deterioration in Jordan and in blocking the attempt to overturn the regime there. He said that the United States is fortunate in having an ally like Israel in the Middle East. These events will be taken into account in all future developments."

Israeli leaders left no doubt that their country would have mobilized its forces in the face of Syrian tanks moving into Jordan anyway, but Golda Meir's coordination with Washington, though limited and conditional, was greeted as evidence of the value of Israel as a strategic ally. There was little attempt made to differentiate between the often conflicting national interests of the United States and Israel, or to recognize the regional nature of the conflict. Instead, Nixon and Kissinger emphasized the contest with Moscow and the benefits of cooperation with Israel, a popular stand for an administration under fierce criticism for its Vietnam policies.

On this flawed misreading of reality, the historic argument of whether Israel was a strategic ally was substantially won by Kissinger. But in far-off Cairo, Anwar Sadat was not aware of this fundamental shift in America's perception of the Middle East.

42

CHAPTER IV

Sadat Offers Peace

WHILE ANWAR SADAT had decided to base his strategy on Washington's support, the reality at the beginning of 1971 was that Israel's relations with the United States had never been stronger or Egypt's worse. There had been no U.S.-Egyptian diplomatic ties since the 1967 war, when Egypt broke relations, and in his last years Nasser had grown so disillusioned that he was content to have Moscow conduct what few official contacts there were with the United States. This peculiar arrangement symbolized how completely dependent Egypt had become on the Soviet Union. It was by now as reliant on Russia as Israel was on America.

Yet Sadat was no admirer of the Soviet Union. He sensed that the communist leaders were suspicious of his stability, refusing to provide him with the weapons he constantly sought and ready to sell Egypt short in favor of achieving detente with the United States. "This is how the Soviet Union always dealt with me," he groused in his memoirs in one of his numerous complaints about Moscow's refusal to provide him the weapons he sought. "It liked to see our hands tied, so that we were unable to take a decision." This aversion toward Russia was no doubt reinforced by Sadat's conflict with the Ali Sabri group, which enjoyed Moscow's trust and support. Repeatedly Sadat referred to the group as "Soviet agents" and the "Soviet power bloc."

Sadat's first approaches to Washington came in the form of conciliatory messages relayed by King Hussein of Jordan and King Faisal of Saudi Arabia toward the end of 1970 and in a direct approach to President Richard Nixon. On November 23, five weeks after his election, Sadat sent a personal letter to Nixon urging a resumption of U.N.-sponsored peace talks. He followed this up with another message on December 24 with a simple message: "I want peace; move fast."

Neither message produced a reaction in the White House. The problem was that Sadat was so little-known in Washington that the administration, in particular National Security Adviser Kissinger, was reluctant to take him seriously. Expressing the general judgment in the higher levels of Washington officialdom, Kissinger assumed that Sadat would last in power no "more than a few weeks."

The state department, however, was impressed and urged Nixon to convince Israel to return to U.N. talks that had been dragging on inconclusively since after the 1967 war. This the President did by a series of actions, including several letters to Israeli Prime Minister Golda Meir during December, promising that Israel would never be allowed to suffer military disadvantages. The administration also encouraged Israel's return to the U.N. talks by openly siding with the Jewish state diplomatically. On December 8, a U.N. General Assembly resolution endorsed the "inalienable rights" of the Palestinians to self-determination. Even though self-determination was one of the fundamental Wilsonian beliefs of the United States, Washington voted against the resolution to display its support for Israel.

On December 28, 1970, Israel, with such backing, agreed to return to the talks—but not to the borders of June 4, 1967. On this intractable issue, the talks were doomed to fail.

• •

Sadat, meanwhile, was faced with another deadline on the ceasefire. It was due to expire February 5, 1971, and the Ali Sabri group favored ignoring it and resuming limited war with Israel. Sadat, blaming Soviet procrastination in delivering missiles to protect Upper Egypt, contended Egypt could not resume fighting until the southern half of his country was defensible.

The issue was an emotional one for Egyptians, as was demonstrated at a rally Sadat held in January in the Delta town of Tanta. He pledged that "there will be no compromise and that unless a timetable is drawn up for Israeli withdrawal we shall not renew the ceasefire." Then he cried to the crowd: "Are you *really* fed up? Are you *really* tired of fighting?" The riled crowd shouted back: "We shall fight, we shall fight, Sadat. Lead us to liberation."

Privately, however, Sadat was listening not to the voice of the mob but to the advice of the state department. It was urging another extension of the ceasefire. Secretary of State William Rogers had called 1971 the "year of decision," and in a letter sent to Sadat on January 27, the secretary of

44

state personally promised that if Sadat extended the ceasefire again the United States would make an "all out effort to help the parties reach a settlement this year." Rogers also assured Sadat that Israel did not have a veto over U.S. policy, an oddly optimistic assurance in the face of the evidence to the contrary.

Sadat decided on a thirty-day extension, but with his usual flare for the dramatic, he kept his plans secret. As a result tension mounted as the day of the ceasefire expiry approached. Egyptian Foreign Minister Mahmoud Riad, a prickly, suspicious diplomat, added to the crisis atmosphere by warning that unless diplomatic progress was made then the resumption of hostilities would be inevitable.

Sadat cleverly used the escalating suspense to capture world attention for what he considered an extraordinary offer. On February 4, the day before the ceasefire's expiry, he went before the National Assembly and delivered a long speech about the Arab-Israeli conflict. It was apparent that in this forum he would reveal his decision on the ceasefire. The attention of the world press and of millions of Egyptians was focused on his words. Sadat capitalized on the suspense by delivering a detailed review of events since the 1967 war, in the process blasting America's "total support of Israel," before he addressed the issue that everyone wanted to hear about.

"We cannot, we have no right to, allow the ceasefire to be applied indefinitely while [diplomatic] efforts make no progress," Sadat said. "Otherwise the ceasefire lines will become a fait accompli, political lines similar to the 1949 armistice lines....This we cannot allow under any circumstances." But, he added, he had decided to bow to the pleas of the world community and a personal appeal by the secretary-general of the United Nations. "We shall refrain from opening fire for a period we cannot prolong beyond thirty days and which will expire on 7 March."

Then, while he had the world's attention, Sadat made a peace gesture. He offered to open the Suez Canal if Israel would withdraw its troops a limited distance as the first step toward full implementation of U.N. Resolution 242.

It was an historic offer which he immediately enumerated in a Newsweek interview. According to Sadat, Israel should withdraw about halfway across the Sinai to a line from Al Arish to Ras Mohammed. He also pointedly echoed Israel's demand for secure borders, adding: "The party that needs secure borders is us, not Israel....The Israelis have bombed our heartland, used napalm, with as many as 180 planes in 17 hours of raids in a single day....dropping between half to one million dollars worth of bombs."

Sadat put his offer of a peace treaty on the record officially on February

45

15. He thus became the first Arab leader publicly to agree to sign a peace agreement with Israel. But it was a gesture that received little response in the Nixon White House and only suspicion in Israel.

• •

By February 1971, Gunnar Jarring, the U.N.'s special envoy seeking a peace formula since the end of the 1967 war, was dispirited. None of his long and arduous exertions had produced the slightest result. In order to salvage something from his mission, the much maligned Swedish diplomat dropped his role as messenger between Egypt and Israel on February 8, and offered what he considered his own fair formula for peace. In fact, it was an extremely equitable formula with something for both sides but, as usual in the Middle East, fairness counted for little.

From Israel he asked an agreement in principle to withdraw to the pre-1967 war lines, subject to practical security arrangements. From Egypt he asked for a peace agreement with Israel, respect for Israel's independence, the right for Israel to live within secure and recognized borders, and freedom of navigation in the Suez Canal and the Straits of Tiran. It was, overall, a solution that implicitly gave Israel all that it had publicly been seeking: peace, secure borders, which implied minor rectifications of the 1967 lines, use of the Suez Canal and unhindered passage through the Tiran straits. But it did not allow what Israel wanted most: retention of east Jerusalem, the Golan Heights, Sharm el Sheikh at the tip of the Sinai Peninsula and the West Bank.

Sadat's response was positive; he agreed to sign a peace treaty with certain conditions. Israel's reply was bluntly negative. It declared: "Israel will not withdraw to the pre-June 5, 1967, lines." That said, Israel made what it termed an offer to negotiate without prior conditions. The prior condition of not returning to the prewar frontier, of course, was unacceptable to Sadat and the Jarring mission was again suspended. It was fitfully reviewed at the end of the year before Jarring's efforts finally ended in total failure.

• •

While he kept his Washington strategy secret, a close observer would have been able to detect by early 1971 that Sadat was embarked on a far different course from his predecessor Nasser. Starting on February 19, a series of important articles by Mohammed Heikal in the semi-official daily Al Ahram began openly examining the advantages of finding some accommodation with the United States. The Heikal series brought into public discussion the question of whether any settlement was possible without the active support of Washington. The articles obviously reflected the thinking of Sadat and were aimed at gaining public acceptance for his approach to the United States.

Heikal's series was typically bold and daring. He asserted the unspeakable by implicitly admitting that Israel was here to stay and observing that the United Nations was impotent because of the competing interests in the Middle East of the superpowers. As a result, he argued, the key to a settlement was to "neutralize the United States somehow." His prescription: "What we must do is to embarrass the United States by every possible means to push her away from the fighting front....The Egyptian people can defeat Israel if the United States of America is not with her on the front."

Despite such signals from Cairo, however ambiguous, President Nixon and his national security adviser displayed no interest. On the contrary, in his annual State of the World message to Congress on February 25, 1971, which Kissinger helped draft, Nixon demonstrated that he continued to regard the Middle East mainly in superpower terms. He vowed that the United States would not impose a peace settlement, thereby pleasing Israel and its supporters, and he made no mention of Sadat's February 4 offer to reopen the Suez Canal. Instead, he warned that the region was more dangerous than Indochina because of the possibility of a superpower confrontation. "Any effort by any major power to secure a dominant position could exacerbate local disputes, affect Europe's security and increase the danger to world peace," he said. "We seek no such position; we cannot allow others to establish one."

It was hardly a message to encourage Sadat, but the Egyptian leader, with no serious alternative available, pressed on. He was determined to attract Washington's attention. But, to his dismay, he managed only to arouse the curiosity of the Soviet Union.

CHAPTER V

Russia Becomes Suspicious

IF PRESIDENT NIXON and his national security adviser could not discern that Egypt was up to something significant, the leaders of the Soviet Union certainly did. They were becoming increasingly concerned about the plans of Egypt's new leader. They worried why Anwar Sadat was flirting with Washington and they were still unsure of the direction of Sadat's policies. "...they were still puzzled to know what to make of the new president," observed Heikal. "All the doubts and hesitations about Egypt which had been building up in their minds while Nasser was still alive were accentuated now that he was dead."

In addition, the shaky ceasefire along the Suez Canal could collapse at any time, causing renewed fighting and even perhaps all-out war. Russia was at the point of holding the Communist Party's 24th Congress in which the leadership planned to set out formally a policy of promoting detente with the United States, so an outbreak of combat in 1971 was especially worrisome to Moscow because, beyond the military dangers, it would complicate Moscow's evolving relations with Washington.

Soviet Ambassador Vladimir Vinogradov tried to communicate these concerns in late February to Foreign Minister Riad. But he was met by a harsh dressing down. Describing himself as "surprised and dismayed" by the ambassador's lecture "about the necessity of pursuing our political efforts for a peaceful settlement," Riad exploded: "You come to me now to speak about a peaceful solution? What have we been doing for the last three years?...What more do you expect us to do? I don't want to indulge in an argument with you but to communicate to your government that there is dissatisfaction in the army that the military equipment we have already contracted for has not yet been delivered, and we urge you to deliver it as soon as possible."

As the tense Riad-Vinogradov meeting indicated, relations between the two countries were deteriorating in the winter of 1971. Sadat sought to improve them by traveling to Moscow on a secret trip March 1-2. According to Sadat, it was not a pleasant visit.

Chairman Leonid Brezhnev and Primier Aleksei Kosygin personally met the Egyptian leader in the Kremlin. They wanted to know what his plans were if he really did refuse to extend the thirty-day ceasefire, due to expire March 7. "Have you studied the problem? Have you got a plan?" they asked. Brezhnev added: "You say you'll refuse an extension of the ceasefire. But what is going to happen on March 8th, or on the 9th or the 10th? Do you know what Israel's reaction will be? Are they going to attack you in depth? Are they going to attack your missile sites? If they do, what will you do? Will you take the initiative by military operations, and if so what operations? Are you going to cross the canal?"

Sadat did not deliver a direct answer. Instead, he said with what was regarded as typical hyperbole: "Our people are ready to fight for ten years, and to lose one million, two million, three million people killed, just as you lost 20 million in the war. We are prepared to see our institutions destroyed, but on one condition: that if the enemy hits us in depth, we hit him back in depth."

Sadat complained bitterly about delays in the delivery of weapons promised by the Soviets, particularly bridging devices to cross the canal and advanced aircraft to counter Israel's U.S.-made Phantom jets. He also objected violently to a Soviet demand that if it provided Egypt with advanced warplanes equipped with missiles that Moscow retain operational control. "I was livid with rage at this...," Sadat recalled. "Nobody is allowed to take a decision on Egyptian affairs except the people of Egypt itself—represented by me, the President of Egypt!

"I don't want the aircraft," he shouted at the Russians. According to Sadat, Brezhnev called him aside and promised him a large number of advanced planes. "In that case," Sadat said, "I'd take back what I said about our difference, provided, of course, that the pilots received their orders from me." Russia never did provide the planes.

Apparently the only light moment in the tense Moscow meeting came when Sadat mentioned in flattering terms Russia's swift 1968 invasion of Czechoslovakia. "Marshal Grechko should be proud of what happened," said Sadat.

"It's a nice idea," replied Brezhnev. "The West lost face because Czechoslovakia was occupied in only six hours. But it wasn't strictly speaking a military operation."

49

"No, no," insisted Sadat, "the way the West talks about it makes it a splendid achievement. In that very short time the operation was successfully completed."

"Has it given you ideas about occupying Tel Aviv in the course of a single night?" asked the usually dour Kosygin.

At that, there was general laughter before the meeting returned to reality.

• •

On his return to Cairo in early March, Sadat was once again faced with the dilemma of how to manipulate the ceasefire issue to Egypt's advantage. It was obvious that Egypt still remained too weak to challenge Israel militarily. Yet the granting of another extension of the ceasefire would be dangerous politically because it would be an implicit admission of Egypt's weakness, giving the Ali Sabri group yet more ammunition to use against him. Sadat, demonstrating what later was to become the hallmark of his diplomatic style, shrewdly gambled with his military weakness to encourage political movement. He definitely would refuse to extend formally the ceasefire. But at the same time he would not order the resumption of combat, thereby creating extreme suspense about what would happen. Simultaneously, he would push for a political settlement. It was a two-track policy, the public part to keep up war scares, the private part to find a diplomatic solution.

Sadat publicly hinted at his strategy when he announced on March 7 that the ceasefire had come to an end. He could not, he would not renew it. But at the same time, he pointedly added: "This does not mean that diplomatic activity will halt or that guns alone will speak." It was an open plea for a political settlement, a message he emphasized by publicly calling on the United States to "perform its duty" to pressure Israel to return all of the captured territories.

Sadat then launched an elaborate display of actions aimed at scaring the world into believing that war was imminent. Egyptian forces were put on alert, causing Israel in turn to increase the war readiness of its own forces. Egyptian civilians who had dribbled back to the blasted cities along the canal waterway during the ceasefires were once again dramatically evacuated. Sadat made a show of conferring with army commanders and investing provincial governors with special war powers. He presided over a meeting of a group named the Committee for Preparing the Country for War. Journalists were briefed on the "role of the press in the battle" and on ways for "mobilizing the masses for sacrifice." Every day Cairo's most influential newspaper, Al Ahram, ran several pages devoted to various aspects

50

of the efforts to prepare for war. One dispatch from the canal zone was headlined: "Waiting for the Order."

The foreboding sense that war could erupt at any moment became more acute daily. A news report from the United Nations said that the world's diplomats feared the military quiet could not last longer than a couple more weeks. By March 16, Secretary of State Rogers was warning that if a settlement was not achieved "...in the foreseeable future...there is a very dangerous situation that will develop and possibly lead to World War III." Sadat's efforts at creating a war scare were working—but not his efforts to find peace.

• •

Behind the scenes Sadat nonetheless kept working for a political solution. On March 5, in response to a letter from President Nixon the previous day that had urged renewal of the ceasefire, the Egyptian leader had sent a long letter to the White House explaining why he was not going to formally extend the ceasefire. He also pleaded with Nixon to launch an effort to get Israel to agree to an interim settlement along the lines of his February 4 offer to open the Suez Canal.

Nixon was encouraged enough to order the state department to pursue the issue with Israel, which was less than enthusiastic. That became even clearer on March 13 when Golda Meir publicly repeated the list of Israel's territorial ambitions. They included, as before, retention of all of Jerusalem, Gaza, Sharm el-Sheikh and the Golan Heights; enlargement of the border around Eilath and an access road to Sharm el-Sheikh through the eastern Sinai, demilitarization of all of the Sinai Peninsula and changes in the frontier of the West Bank. Menachem Begin's ultranationalistic opposition Gahal bloc roundly criticized Meir for being too conciliatory in making these demands, a complaint that was moot since no Arab state would make such sweeping concessions.

Begin represented the vanguard of a new harder-lining kind of Zionism that emerged in force in Israel after the stunning victory of the 1967 war. He and his growing number of followers were less interested in peace than land, less dedicated to democracy than a Jewishness theocracy, less concerned with the civil rights of the Arabs than with Jewish rights. It was Begin and his followers who articulated and reinforced the spreading desire in Israel to retain all the occupied lands, narrowing even further Golda Meir's diplomatic flexibility.

As Abba Eban, Israel's most distinguished elder statesman, noted later how Zionism changed, and with it Israelis, after the 1967 war: "We inter-

51

preted the war as not just a victory, but as a kind of providential messsianic event that changed history permanently and gave Israel the power to dictate the future.'' The liberal traditions of Zionism were spurned and a new Zionism emerged: ''It says that we will not give any territory back; if the Arabs don't like it here they can get the hell out, and if they stay we will not give them all of their human rights, and being Jewish is more important than being democratic.''

Despite this changing reality, which remained unperceived in Washington, Secretary of State Rogers tried to nudge Israel toward conciliation. During a press conference on March 16, he urged Israel to be more flexible and to rely on international guarantees for its security rather than territory that belonged to other countries. ''Although geographical considerations are important, it is not necessary to acquire territory to make adequate provisions for security,'' he said. He also repeated publicly that the United States believed Israel should withdraw totally from the Sinai Peninsula.

The reiteration of statements such as these, which in fact did faithfully reflect official U.S. policy, if not that advocated by Kissinger, had long made Rogers one of the most unpopular Americans in Israel. Golda Meir gave vent to these passions March 17 by roundly criticizing the secretary of state. ''At stake is not the fate of the United States but of Israel and the Jewish people, and in this we cannot rely on Rogers' planning....there must be a deterrent border so that no Sadat can in five or ten years try again.''

In order to stop the bickering, Washington urged Israel to put its position in writing. As an inducement, it announced on April 19 that twelve F-4 Phantoms would be sent to Israel. Israel's answer came the same day and it was again less than encouraging. It offered to withdraw a short distance from the east bank of the Suez Canal. But it then added a number of conditions: No Egyptian troops should cross to the east bank, Egyptian troops on the west bank should be thinned out, the ceasefire should be extended indefinitely and there would be no linkage between the withdrawal and U.N. Resolution 242—in other words, the minor withdrawal would be an isolated event unconnected to a larger process leading to total withdrawal. The Israeli position paper also asked for Washington's full support and a reaffirmation of its promise to protect Israel's security. Nixon responded affirmatively two days later, although he refused to provide America's full support for the Israeli negotiating position.

The Israeli conditions were too much for Sadat to accept, even as the basis for the initiation of negotiations. He rejected them on April 23 and, in the judgment of the National Security Council, the diplomatic effort appeared at an end.

• •

But Bill Rogers was not ready to give up yet, despite the opposition of Kissinger and Israel, and the pessimism of the NSC. He had good reason. Privately, Sadat had met with an old acquaintance, Michael Sterner, one of the few U.S. diplomats who knew the new President, and delivered a hopeful signal. Sterner had been a young political officer in the Cairo embassy in the early 1960s while Sadat was head of the National Assembly and they had come to know each other then. When Sadat officially visited the United States in 1966 as the head of the National Assembly, Sterner was chosen as his official escort and the two men had spent ten memorable days together in Washington and in touring the country.

Now, on April 22, 1971, Sterner was the director of Egyptian affairs in the state department on a tour of the Middle East, a middle level diplomat who normally would not be expected to meet with the President of Egypt. But because of his past association, Sterner was invited to see Sadat. With Bergus, Sterner traveled to the presidential house at the Barrage on the Nile where Sadat met them under the legendary fig tree, supposedly planted in the time of Mohammed Ali a century and a half earlier.

With a large map of the Sinai set up before them, Sadat enthusiastically talked about his plans for an interim agreement and the depth of Israel's withdrawal. Sterner and Bergus became so interested by the obvious desire of Sadat to conclude a limited agreement, albeit seen by Sadat as only the first step to total withdrawal, that the two American diplomats began nudging each other under the table. Bergus had heard some of these views in his many meetings with Sadat but this was the first time Sadat, as president, had been so specific in discussing the actual details of a withdrawal. The Egyptian's desire for peace was obvious to the American diplomats, his willingness to be flexible encouraging. And it was clear that he was putting forth proposals that he expected the United States to pass onto to Israel.

At the end of the interview, Sterner and Bergus returned to Cairo and sent a cable to the state department reporting that Sadat appeared to be both serious and desirous about finding a settlement to the Arab-Israel conflict, implying that chances for a breakthrough might be better than generally thought in Washington. This was the same conclusion the CIA had come to.

At this point William Rogers decided to gamble. He was more encouraged than Henry Kissinger, who continued to doubt the state department and CIA appraisals of Sadat's flexibility, and perhaps he was also more realistically fearful about the consequences of the continued stalemate that Kissinger advocated. Against Kissinger's wishes, Rogers decided to travel to the Middle East in May, the first secretary of state to visit the region since John Foster Dulles in 1953.

• •

Rogers' imminent arrival postponed Sadat's effort to make April the "decisive" month. Now May was that month, the time of "defining stands, the stage in which all parties reach the end of the road." Three days before Rogers' arrival, Sadat warned in his May Day speech that he was expecting more from Washington than it had so far produced. Said Sadat: "The country which gives Israel everything from a loaf of bread to Phantom bombers claims that it cannot pressure Israel. Isn't it ridiculous? In spite of everything we prefer to believe [what America says] and give it another, and perhaps the last, chance to make an effort for peace."

Rogers found Sadat charming, polite and expressing all the right formulations that indicated flexibility. But the one thing Sadat wanted most Rogers was not willing to give. That was to have the United States apply pressure on Israel to accept the peace-for-land formula of U.N. Resolution 242.

The Rogers-Sadat May 6 meeting was considerably friendlier than Rogers' two sessions immediately afterwards with Golda Meir in Jerusalem. The Israelis remained suspicious of Rogers, believing he might be pro-Arab, and Israel's and Egypt's positions continued to be far apart. In the end, Israel softened its stand somewhat by agreeing that it might allow Egypt to station civilians and technicians across the canal in Egypt's Sinai Peninsula, but no troops. However, it now insisted that the question of a pullback of Israeli forces should not be addressed until after the canal was opened. It was not much of a concession but Rogers jumped at it. Assistant Secretary of State for Near East and South Asia Affairs Joseph Sisco, who had accompanied Rogers, was delegated to go back to Cairo to pursue the talks while Rogers returned home.

On his way, Rogers stopped in Rome where he told reporters on May 8 that there was "some narrowing of the gap" toward a partial settlement. The next day, however, after a disappointing meeting with Sisco, the Egyptian foreign ministry publicly contradicted Rogers by announcing that "...the difference between the Israeli and Egyptian points of view is large and continuing. There has been no change at all in the situation." When Rogers insisted later in Washington that there was room for optimism, the Egyptian foreign ministry replied: "There is nothing that can be called agreement on any subject." And feisty Foreign Minister Riad directly attacked Rogers, charging the U.S. official had tried to "give the impression of a change in direction when in reality there was no such thing."

Neither side was ready to let Rogers off the hook, much to the detriment of the secretary of state. For Israel, Rogers' inability to achieve any diplomatic gains reinforced its contention that he was naive and out of his depth in the murky waters of the Middle East, a contention that justified the continuation of diplomatic stalemate and, consequently, the retention of occupied territory. As for the Egyptians, particularly Foreign Minister Riad who distrusted the sincerity of the United States and who had suspicions about the wisdom of Sadat's flexibility, they focused on the disparity of strength between America and Israel and found it impossible to believe that the United States was incapable of pressuring tiny Israel.

The Rogers' visit left Sadat with no accomplishment and great frustration. For Rogers, the result was devastating. His failure led to a steady erosion of his credibility as a Middle Eastern negotiator and the growth of Henry Kissinger's influence.

• •

In the midst of this international bazaar bargaining and Byzantine turf fighting in Washington, Anwar Sadat finally decided to act against his enemies at home.

CHAPTER VI

The Soviet-Egyptian
Friendship Treaty

IN THE SPRING OF 1971, Anwar Sadat was at last ready to consolidate his power by moving against his enemies. He was more secure after seven months in office and goading him on were reports of heightened activities by the Ali Sabri group. There were daily meetings and spates of anti-Sadat rumors emanating from the Sabri group. There was also a constant stream of complaints about Sadat's actions and his inability to make war—or peace.

Sadat suspected that his enemies were about to strike, but as yet he had no clear evidence. The spark that apparently fired Sadat's actions was a request by the Soviet Union to make Sharawi Gomaa, the interior minister and a close ally of Ali Sabri, prime minister of Egypt. Sadat saw this as an effort by Moscow to strengthen Sabri's position and he reacted immediately.

According to Sadat, the request was made around April 1971 by the Soviet ambassador, Vladimir Vinogradov. For his efforts, Vinogradov received a lecture in return. First Sadat bluntly refused the Soviet request, then he dropped a bombshell by saying, "Although I am eager to maintain my good relations with you, I'd like to inform the Soviet leadership that I have decided to remove Ali Sabri from the Egyptian political leadership. I have informed you of this, even though it is one of our internal affairs in which I can allow no one to interfere, because, I'm afraid, the Western press will say, when this happens, that I have removed Moscow's number one man in Egypt and so upset you. You should know that Moscow has no man in Egypt—you are dealing with a government, not with individuals. I'm

56

removing Ali Sabri because, although I accept differences of opinion, I cannot tolerate a power struggle.''

Ali Sabri's firing followed soon afterward. On May 2 a simple announcement said: "President Sadat has decided to relieve Ali Sabri from his post as vice president, with effect from today." Ali Sabri's friends implored Sadat to remove the word "relieve" in an effort to make it look like the vice president had resigned. But Sadat, determined to demonstrate his power in public, refused, adding to Ali Sabri's resentment and humiliation.

Now Sadat sat and waited to see how his enemies would react. It was not at all clear how powerful they were or how determinedly they would act—or even whether Sadat could survive a concerted attack.

The break came quite suddenly and unexpectedly. At 2 in the morning on May 10, a police officer, Major Taha Zaki of the ministry of interior, arrived at Sadat's Nile-side residence and demanded to see the President. His insistence finally convinced the guards to awaken a secretary, who in turn tried to explain the impossibility of awakening the President in the middle of the night. But the policeman persisted.

Major Zaki informed the secretary that he was attached to the interior department's office in charge of guarding recordings of tapped telephone conversations. The Ali Sabri group had been secretly conducting widespread tapping of telephones, including those connected to a private presidential circuit used only by about twenty-five top officials, including Sadat, the prime minister, the director of intelligence and the military chiefs. Zaki had brought along for Sadat's ears tapes of two revealing conversations. With this background, the secretary was finally convinced and awakened the President. A tape player was found and Sadat, clad in pajamas, sat down to listen. What he heard finally caused him to act.

The tapes revealed that Sadat had already escaped without knowing it a planned assassination attempt and that his enemies were plotting his overthrow. He stayed up all night listening to the tapes and pondering their fateful import. Fearful now of using his own telephone, Sadat waited until dawn and then had one of his daughters go to the house of his confidant, Mohamed Heikal. "It astonished me that he had not called me on the telephone or sent one of his secretaries," Heikal recalled in his memoirs. "I went at once, and found him sitting in an armchair, dressed in pajamas and a dressing-gown, and with a tape recorder in front of him."

It was immediately clear to both men that the army was the key to Sadat's survival. While Defense Minister Fawzi was a supporter of the plotters, the chief of staff, General Mohammed Sadiq, was a Sadat loyalist as was the commander of the presidential guard, General El-Leithy Nassif. Both enjoyed more support in the military establishment than Fawzi.

Sadat played his cards shrewdly. He kept his peace until May 12 when he finally managed to get Sadiq to give the assurance he needed. While on the way to deliver a speech to troops at a camp near Suez, Sadiq privately said to Sadat: "We understand your position." It was all Sadat had to hear.

The next day, Sadat moved forcefully. He fired Interior Minister Sharawi Gomaa, whom he identified publicly as the leader of the conspirators, and had all the recordings from tapped telephones seized. A short time later on the evening of May 13, the plotters took a concerted action that they thought would cower Sadat. They resigned en masse—the war minister, the information minister, the director of intelligence, the speaker of the National Assembly and some of the top officials of the Arab Socialist Union. They had apparently calculated that the country could not operate without them. It was, as Heikal correctly perceived, a "virtual coup d'etat."

Instead of being cowed, however, Sadat boldly welcomed the challenge. He accepted their resignations, put the officials under house arrest and ordered the news of their fate broadcast on radio and television. Heikal, who was with Sadat at the time, said the president was in "good spirits; his nerves were holding out well."

Sadat's swift moves completely destroyed his opposition. The populace failed to throw its support to the Ali Sabri conspirators and, with the army's firm backing, Sadat at last became the unopposed President of Egypt. He quickly solidified his position by dissolving the ASU, ordering it reorganized from the ground up, and demanding the drafting of a new national constitution. He vowed that at the end of his six-year term he would not stand for re-election. Sadat assured the people that he would give them freedom and democracy. He symbolized his commitment by changing the name of the National Assembly to the People's Assembly.

The Sadat era had at last begun. It had taken him exactly eight months from the time of being officially elected to his high post to the consolidation of his power. During that pregnant period, he had managed to maintain the ceasefire, launch his own peace initiative, initiate an opening to Washington while retaining his relations with Moscow, win the support of the Egyptian army and totally vanquish his domestic enemies. It was a significant achievement, but still it brought no recognition from Washington that in Cairo there was a leader worthy of attention.

• •

Sadat's first major official act produced yet another surprise—the signing of a Treaty of Friendship and Cooperation with the Soviet Union. On the heels of the deposing of the Ali Sabri group in mid-May, a high level delegation of Russians arrived in Cairo May 25, 1971. Two days later Sadat and Soviet President Nikolai Podgorny signed a treaty that pledged friendship between the two countries and, significantly, formally committed the Soviet Union explicitly to the defense of Egypt. It was the first time Moscow had ever made such a commitment to a noncommunist country of the Third World. During talks with Sadat, Podgorny again emphasized that the Soviet Union believed Egypt's diplomatic efforts in the Arab-Israeli conflict had not been exhausted. The Russians still did not want war.

But the Soviets did want influence, and the treaty was yet one more token marking their growing power in the region. They had paid dearly for it. During the War of Attrition between 1969 and 1970, Soviet pilots and missiles had assumed complete responsibility for protecting Egypt's skies against Israeli raiders, the first time Moscow had ever committed Soviet troops in large numbers outside of the communist bloc.

The calculated risk had not been an exercise in altruism. Russia since the time of the tsars had cast covetous eyes toward the warm waters and strategic lands of the Middle East but had been rebuffed by the Turkish Empire and later by the West. It was only in 1955 that the Soviets finally managed to get a foothold in the region when they broke the Western arms embargo and sold weapons to Egypt through their Czechoslovakian surrogate.

Since then, Soviet aid to Egypt and other Arab states had been bountiful, representing a counterweight to U.S. aid to Israel and a signal to the Third World that Moscow could be relied upon to provide what the West denied. For Egypt the association had been profitable. Aside from being the major armorer of its armed forces, which it trained and gave some of its most sophisticated weapons, Moscow was the paramount benefactor of Egypt's economy. It financed and helped build the Aswan High Dam, one of the greatest engineering marvels of its time, and such other prestigious projects as the Helwan steel plant and the 2,000 kilohertz nuclear research reactor at Alexandria. Soviet aid to Egypt was so generous, in fact, that there was criticism in the Eastern Bloc that communist nations were being short-changed in order that Moscow could help a noncommunist nation that gave no shrift to domestic communists. There were even rumors that this overly generous policy toward Egypt may have contributed to Nikita Khrushchev's fall in 1964.

If so, Khrushchev's successors gave no indication of changing the policy that had developed under Khrushchev or of limiting aid. Quite the contrary. The Soviets moved with surprising alacrity at the end of the 1967 war to take advantage of the hatred and humiliation Arabs felt at America's support of Israel. As Professor George Lenczowski observed:

Alienation from the West—with the United States a special target due to its arming and support of Israel—was expressed [in the Arab world] in many ways: rupture of diplomatic relations with Washington by six Arab countries, reduction in economic interchange, expulsions of Western residents in the area, closing and sequestering of American schools, universities and libraries, temporary oil embargoes, suspension of overflight rights, boycotts of Western shipping, trade and banking, total or partial nationalization of certain enterprises, and threats of drastic action against the oil companies. It was this alienation that the Soviet Union exploited to its own advantage by trying to substitute itself for the diminishing Western presence in the area.

The Soviets exploited with talent the Arabs' resentments after 1967. Foremost was the Soviets' replacement of Egypt's massive losses in the war. The Soviet rearmament supply operation was unprecedented. It surpassed in both quantity and quality the aid given to North Vietnam and the pace of the resupply exceeded that provided to any other allied or friendly country. In addition, from a prewar level of about five hundred advisers, the Soviet presence in Egypt after the 1967 war grew to several thousand. Postwar, Soviet advisers extended their functions from being primarily technical consultants on the operation of weapons into all phases of training, planning and air defense of the Egyptian military establishment.

In return for its exceptional generosity, the Soviet Union received more than just a symbolic presence in Egypt and the Middle East. The first postwar rewards came in January 1968 when Nasser formally granted the Soviet navy support facilities for maintenance, repair and provisioning of its ships at Mersa Matruh, Port Said and Alexandria on the Mediterranean. Three months later Soviet Tu-16 reconnaissance aircraft were given permission to use Egyptian airport facilities at Cairo West so they could fly surveillance flights over the U.S. Sixth Fleet and Israel. After acceding to Nasser's requests in January 1970 to protect Egypt's skies from Israeli warplanes, the Soviets gained even more access. They were granted exclusive jurisdiction over parts of six airfields and freedom to deploy missile and air defense personnel and pilots at their own discretion throughout Egypt.

Thus Moscow finally regained, and increased, the infrastructure in the eastern Mediterranean it had been seeking since Albania denied it a naval base at Vlone in 1961. With the Egyptian bases, Russia's naval strength in the region grew significantly. From 750 ship-days in 1963 the Soviet navy logged 1,624 in just the first half of 1970. The number of Soviet ships patrolling the Mediterranean now ranged between forty to seventy, hitting a high of seventy-one in September 1969, including 34 surface ships and 19 submarines. By late 1969, a Soviet N-Class nuclear-powered submarine visited Alexandria, the first time such a vessel anchored in a foreign port.

The Soviet Union at last was in a position to neutralize the Sixth Fleet, strengthen its antisubmarine warfare capabilities against U.S. Polaris submarines patrolling the Mediterranean and reconnoiter the Red Sea area of the Horn of Africa from Upper Egyptian airfields. It had never been so strong in the Mediterranean, nor had the United States ever been so directly challenged by Soviet strength in the region. As a CIA study concluded in the summer of 1970: "The Soviet Mediterranean Squadron is now sufficiently powerful in conventional as well as nuclear armament to threaten the Sixth Fleet and other NATO naval units. Submarines and surface ships armed with antiship cruise missiles are a significant threat to our surface ships—including aircraft carriers, and the torpedo attack submarines continue to pose a threat to allied naval forces. In fact, the Sixth Fleet is faced with the highest density of deployed Soviet submarines anywhere in the world."

Beyond that, the growth in Soviet strength in the Mediterranean helped to protect its important warm-water ports in the Black Sea. From these harbors forty to fifty percent of all of Russia's maritime activity originated and terminated. In addition, of course, such burgeoning strength not only influenced the Arab-Israel conflict but affected the strength of NATO as well. A Pentagon study noted in early 1970: "...the Soviets can hope to undermine the southern flank of NATO, erode American influence in the region, and create serious economic problems for West Europe—and for U.S. interests—by turning radical and possibly other Arab states against the West, the U.S. and its investments in Middle East oil."

It was all of these things that the Soviet Union was obviously now trying to do, with considerable success.

• •

Typically, William Rogers and Henry Kissinger disagreed over the implications of Egypt's new friendship treaty with the Soviet Union. Rogers told Nixon that the treaty "strengthens [Sadat's] hand vis-a-vis his own military by its emphasis on long-range military support. It could help maintain [his] flexibility on a Suez Canal settlement." This conclusion was later confirmed by the Egyptian leader's actions. The treaty did not inhibit his peace moves, which under any circumstances the Russians favored. Rogers was strongly supported by the CIA, whose station chief in Cairo, Eugene Trone, had concluded—and reported to Washington—that the treaty marked no radical change in Egypt's policies.

But Kissinger saw it differently on the geopolitical scoreboard. He warned the President: "Rather than strengthening Sadat's flexibility with respect to negotiating the canal settlement, the treaty could give the Soviet Union a veto over the future negotiations. Thus, whatever the outcome of the negotiations...recent events may have enhanced Soviet long-term influence."

Kissinger's response, however unintentional, was to play to the long-term interests of the Soviets by seeking the short-term gains that the support of Israel gave Washington in domestic politics. He sought to maintain the stalemate between Israel and Egypt until Cairo made even more concessions and Moscow could be shown impotent. Explained Kissinger: "Our strategy had to be to frustrate any Egyptian policy based on military threats and collusion with the Soviet Union. Therefore Sadat's Friendship Treaty with the Soviets, whatever its motives, did not galvanize us to help him as he might have hoped. On the contrary, it reinforced my determination to slow down the process even further to demonstrate that Soviet threats and treaties could not be decisive."

Rogers' sense of justness and urgency was more reflective of the reality, but Kissinger's biases, his sense of superpower global competition and his compulsive ambitions carried the day.

By all indications of his later behavior, Sadat still remained flexible and desirous of a comprehensive settlement with Israel after signing the treaty with Moscow. But in America, and in Israel, he continued to be considered a buffoon, unworthy of serious attention.

CHAPTER VII

Kissinger Prevails

IN MID-1971, there occurred a diplomatic flap that allowed Henry Kissinger to further denigrate the state department's abilities and advance his own ambitions to take over Middle East policy. It started when the Egyptian foreign ministry met with Donald Bergus, the head of the U.S. Interests Section in Cairo, in effect the U.S. ambassador in lieu of formal diplomatic relations. On May 20, Bergus was given a preview of the government's counterproposals as a follow up to Secretary of State Rogers' trip earlier in the month. Bergus found the communique so negative in tone that he believed it would create only anger in Washington. On his own he redrafted the message, changing the style but not the substance, which contained an expressed willingness to agree to an interim accord if it led to a comprehensive settlement. Bergus returned the message to the ministry on May 23, careful to label his suggestions as unofficial and reflecting his own belief as to how Egypt could present its case in the most favorable light to Washington. Nonetheless, when Sadat sent Egypt's response to the state department on June 4 it very closely followed the Bergus' wording, indicating that the Egyptians believed Bergus' suggestions reflected official policy.

Bergus' action, although not strictly within a diplomat's bailiwick, was not at all unusual among American diplomats who had friendly relations with the governments they were assigned to, particularly in the Third World. Nonetheless, Kissinger exploded when he heard of what Bergus had done. He once again accused the state department of amateurism and bungling.

Kissinger's ire was in part explained by the fact that relations between him and Rogers were by now so bad that the state department was cutting Kissinger out of its activities. The result was that Kissinger was not even aware of what became known as the "Phantom Memo" until three weeks after its delivery to the state department. Its existence was finally leaked to columnist Joseph Kraft, who wrote a story about it that appeared June 27 in The Washington Post and other newspapers. Kissinger hit the ceiling. "I was annoyed—to put it mildly—that none of these moves had been disclosed to the President of the United States," Kissinger protested.

Israel's foreign ministry was better informed than Kissinger, for the ministry's director-general, Gideon Rafael, was well aware of the Sadat-Bergus texts, apparently even before Kraft's story. "One fine morning in June I found copies of the Sadat-Bergus exchange in my in-tray," Rafael wrote in his memoirs. "They had reached my desk not exactly by the courtesy of the authors." Who provided the texts, Rafael coyly declined to identify, but it was entirely likely by one of Israel's many supporters working in the Nixon Administration, according to speculation by U.S. diplomats and intelligence experts. By this time the government was so filled with Israel's supporters that it was assumed by top intelligence officials like Central Intelligence Director Richard Helms that any secret concerning Israel was known by the Israelis as a result of illegal leaks by its supporters.

Regardless of how the Bergus memorandum got to Jerusalem, Kissinger was angered more about its contents. He felt, quite rightly, that it "revealed the state department's bias toward an interim accord that was a stage toward an agreed (and unattainable) comprehensive settlement." A comprehensive agreement, of course, was Sadat's basic demand but it also reflected official U.S. policy, first enunciated at the end of the 1967 war and since then repeated to Nasser and then Sadat. Nonetheless, Kissinger did not believe in it and continued to oppose it.

After Kraft's story appeared, the state department publicly disavowed the memorandum, saying it did not represent Washington's position. The Egyptians were stung and disillusioned, feeling that the United States was being deceitful. The Israelis, though obviously not surprised, expressed fury too, charging that the state department was egging Egypt on as a way of applying pressure on the Jewish state and failing in its commitment to keep Israel informed. The state department and the National Security Council were in deep confusion. The affair ended with the dolorous result that once again there was general disarray and bitterness between all the players in the Middle Eastern diplomatic game.

That may have been exactly the conclusion desired by Egyptian Foreign Minister Mahmoud Riad. Like Kissinger, he opposed the state department's initiative, but for different reasons. Riad continued to suspect strongly that Sadat was not firm enough toward Israel and he was suspicious of

Washington's sincerity because of its close ties with Israel. Despite these suspicions, Riad remained under pressure from Sadat to achieve some diplomatic movement, and was being criticized by the president for being too negative. He was in an irritable and impatient mood at this time. Perhaps to prove that his pessimism was justified, Riad leaked to Joseph Kraft a distorted version of the background of the Bergus memorandum, charging that he did not know the origin of the memorandum and assumed it reflected Israel's policy, thereby implying that Washington was now so yoked to the Jewish state that it was merely passing on its dictates. He complained that Washington was falsely generating optimism about a settlement as a way to sway Egypt and make it more conciliatory.

Actually, there could be no doubt about the personal nature of Bergus' role because Riad's assistant, Mohammad Riad, had noted in Arabic on the memorandum that it contained points unofficially put forward by Bergus. But by raising in public the question of the memorandum's origin and distorting its background Riad forced the state department into the awkward position of either having to deny complicity or publicly siding with Egypt against Israel. When the state department denied complicity, the denial confirmed to Riad his suspicions about the lack of American sincerity and effectively derailed the idea of an interim agreement that he so strongly opposed.

Bergus, who dealt closely with Riad, concluded: "Riad wanted to kill the whole thing. He was of the school that felt the Arabs had to show no flexibility because justice was on their side. All they had to do was explain the justice of their cause and everything would be all right. A lot of Egyptians felt like Riad and so among his other problems Sadat also had to fight many of his own advisers."

• •

Michael Sterner, the state department's Egyptian desk officer in Washington, was back in Cairo in July to meet once again with Sadat. By this time, the Egyptian President was understandably impatient. Sterner and Bergus tried to allay Sadat's growing disillusionment, assuring him that the state department remained committed to a comprehensive settlement.

On their side, the American diplomats were particularly interested in the meaning of the Friendship Treaty with the Soviet Union. They were fishing for reassurances for use in the bureaucratic turf battle with Kissinger, who was using the signing of the treaty as evidence of Egypt's unreliability. Sadat gave it to them. He assured Sterner and Bergus that the treaty did not limit his freedom of action, that he had in no way modified his offers for peace. "He was absolutely serious about wanting a settlement," Sterner said later.

Then Sadat asked: what is going to happen next? To that, Sterner and Bergus had no answer. The most they could do was assure Sadat that his views would be studied and Washington would get back to him about the next step. But, in fact, the U.S. initiative by now was essentially a dead issue. President Nixon had his eye on bigger things as election year approached. Kissinger at this time was on his way for his secret trip to China on July 7 to 9, secret talks were being held with North Vietnam to try to end the continuing war and secret negotiations were going on with the Soviet Union for a Nixon-Brezhnev summit. Beside these global events, the Middle East was not only an annoyance and no-win situation but an issue so prickly that it repeatedly caused the President political problems from the influential American supporters of Israel.

The press was reporting anger among Jewish Americans about Rogers' continuing efforts to pressure Israel, anger that manifested itself by vicious personal attacks on the secretary of state and snide reports in the press. Senator Stuart Symington of Missouri publicly called Rogers a "laughing stock" because of his inability to control Kissinger. As early as January of the previous year, Columnist Jack Anderson reported that "American Jewish leaders are up in arms over a statement attributed to...Rogers behind closed doors, that his Middle East concessions have their approval and that...Meir's sharp objections were intended strictly for home consumption....Jewish feelings are running so high that several depositors withdrew their money from the Chase Manhattan Bank after press reports ascribed a backstage role to David Rockefeller, the bank president, in guiding Middle East policy."

Grumblings from the Jewish Lobby remained a steady background noise to each of Rogers' forays into Middle East policy. By the middle of 1971, the volume was getting louder as the presidential campaign began to take shape. Columnists Rowland Evans and Robert Novak, for instance, wrote on June 4 that "leaders of the American-Jewish community are already incensed about what they regard as the tough, heavy-handed treatment accorded...Golda Meir by...Rogers in their first meeting in Jerusalem May 27....Rogers' total frankness in his conversations with Israeli leaders angered not only the Israelis but some of their friends in Congress." A short time later, Evans and Novak reported that Jewish Americans were becoming so restive that there was concern among Nixon's political advisers that "the American Jewish community will not be very forthcoming in 1972 campaign cash for Mr. Nixon...."

With such political perils and constant criticism accompanying every Middle East initiative, Nixon's enthusiasm for Rogers' efforts steadily cooled as the election neared. This was an evolution happily encouraged by Kissinger, who by now was seeing his chance to take over the last substantive area of policy left to Rogers.

• •

Frustrated at his humiliating inability to get any peace process underway, Sadat reverted to threats. On July 23, Sadat picked up Rogers' theme that 1971 was a "year of decision." At a meeting of the completely reconstituted Arab Socialist Union, Sadat said that "we must escape from this stagnation of no war, no peace. I shall not allow 1971 to pass without this battle being decided....1971 will be a decisive year." He added a conciliatory note: "We must move, but politically as well as militarily." The 1,700 delegates of the ASU gave Sadat "full powers" to take whatever actions were necessary to recover all Arab land from Israel.

Throughout the rest of the year Sadat repeated the "year of decision" threat with increasing urgency, but with no discernible impact on Israel or the Nixon Administration. In fact, as the weeks and months went by without any movement, either military or diplomatic, the repeated threat became a source of growing embarrassment for Sadat. It was a public reminder of how helpless Egypt was, yet another humiliation for him and by extension for all Egyptians and Arabs. Sadat became desperate. He still felt he did not have the weapons he needed to challenge Israel directly and Moscow was showing no urgency in providing them, although it was continuing a steady supply—but too slow, in Sadat's opinion.

In addition, his relations with Moscow had cooled again as a result of his support in mid-July for President Jaafar Nimeiry against an attempted coup d'etat by communists in the Sudan. The Soviets had requested Sadat's assistance for the arrested communists but he refused. The most he would do was seek to assure the safety of one of the plotters, Shafie Ahmed Sheikh, a winner of the Lenin Prize for Peace. Sadat telephoned Nimeiry, but when the Egyptian asked for clemency for Shafie, he was told: "It's too late; he's just been hanged."

To repair his relations and to urge speedier delivery of weapons to bear out his "year of decision" threat, Sadat asked the Russians for a top level meeting. But now there was an ominous silence from Moscow.

67

It was while Kissinger was secretly on his way to China in early July to make the historic opening with that ancient country that he heard Rogers was seeking presidential approval for yet another trip to the Middle East. Kissinger objected to this latest effort by the state department. "From Saigon I cabled that such a trip would now only accelerate tensions in the Middle East and should be deferred." Nixon agreed. No action was taken until Kissinger returned and a formal meeting of the National Security Council was held July 16. At the meeting, it was agreed that Assistant Secretary of State Joseph Sisco could make a low-keyed effort to see if there was any flexibility in Israel's position. But, Nixon added, he would not promise to put pressure on Israel.

Between July 30 and August 5, Sisco stayed in Israel to try to find agreement for a two-stage Israeli drawback followed by the positioning of only a token Egyptian force on the west bank. Golda Meir demanded some show of U.S. good intentions, specifically the sale of more Phantom jets. But requests for the airplanes by Sisco were turned down by the President and as a result he was left with no bargaining leverage. His talks were so fruitless that Sisco returned directly to Washington, not even bothering to stop in Cairo, a slight that infuriated the increasingly impatient Sadat.

This latest failure by the state department and the approaching election gave Kissinger his chance to take over Middle Eastern policy. As he later recounted: "[Nixon] was afraid that the state department's bent for abstract theories might lead it to propose plans that would arouse opposition from all sides. My principal assignment was to make sure that no explosion occurred to complicate the 1972 election—which meant in effect that I was to stall." That Henry Kissinger was more than happy to do.

But first, Bill Rogers made one desperate effort to retain his turf. On October 4, 1971, he delivered an address to the United Nations urging Israel to accept an interim agreement for withdrawal from the Suez Canal. He stuck by his maximum plan by adding that such an accord would be "merely a step" toward a comprehensive agreement, exactly what Kissinger opposed. Rogers also urged the two sides to begin proximity talks with Sisco acting as mediator.

Egypt agreed, but Israel refused. Israel once again used the talks issue as a way to insist that it first needed U.S. assurances on arms aid. Nixon had stalled for the past six months in signing a new arms accord with Israel in the hope of being able to influence Israeli policy and because of a conviction that Israel's military might remained superior. Such stalling was now becoming politically dangerous. The day after Rogers' speech, seventy-eight senators signed a resolution urging the administration to supply more F-4 Phantoms to Israel.

Under such pressures, and in a attempt to get Israel to negotiate, the Nixon Administration agreed to put into effect the exchange of technology envisioned in the Master Defense Development Data Exchange Agreement signed the previous year. A Memorandum of Understanding, initialed in November, began a massive and lucrative transfer of technology to Israel, assuring the country the capability to produce many of its own weapons. In addition, the understanding also granted the sale of jet engines to Israel for construction of its own warplane, the Kfir. This aircraft was being constructed on the basis of blueprints for France's Mirage III fighter, which had been stolen from a Swiss firm and transported to Israel, all nearly 200,000 of them, during a year-long Israeli intelligence operation in 1968-9.

But still, Israel refused to join the proximity talks.

• •

After two months of waiting, Sadat, by now raging at Moscow's cold shouldering of him, finally received a message that the Soviet leadership would meet with him October 11. "Although I had had enough...I didn't show that I was upset in the least and did leave for Moscow," Sadat recalled in his memoirs. "At the talks I repeated the words I had said to them in March: 'I don't mind, my friends, if you keep me one step behind Israel [in armaments] but I find it a bit too much to be twenty steps behind her!'"

The supply of weapons dominated the talks. When Sadat emphasized Egypt's shortages, Brezhnev responded: "We have heard we have not supplied you militarily with all your demands. This may be true, since the military never cease making demands....The question, however, as was posed today, is whether or not the Egyptian army is capable of undertaking major operations to liberate Sinai. I will asked Marshal Grechko to give his views on this."

Andrei Grechko began by stating that there were three factors that defined the capability of an army: the number of men and the quantity of their arms, the quality of the arms and morale. The veteran general pointed out that between Egypt and Syria they had a two-to-one edge in men and arms, including tanks, artillery and air-defense missiles against Israel. They had the same advantage in airplanes and an overwhelming superiority in naval arms. The Soviet Union had provided engineering equipment to cross the canal, it had recently given equipment to clear minefields and jam electronic equipment. Then Grechko made a cutting remark that did not endear him to the Egyptian leader: "The first two you have but as for the third you will have to consult your own consciences.''

Brezhnev observed that the figures showed Egypt was on a par with Israel—reinforcing the strong implication that what the country was lacking was morale, not Soviet arms. At any rate, he said, "you should pursue your political efforts and continue the contacts with Nixon.'' He then pledged a major increase in weapons aid, including a squadron of MiG-23s, missile-equipped Tu-16 bombers and 240mm mortars. Though the arms package was generous, it was as nothing compared to the breadth of weapons, money and technology the United States was providing Israel, a point not lost on Sadat.

With impressive insight, Sadat told the Russians that he believed the "imperialist powers'' were trying to "drive a wedge between us and the Soviet Union. This can only serve America and Zionism. As I've said, my conviction is that America has three targets, and that in this they are eye to eye with Israel. First, they want to remove the Soviet presence from the area and create misunderstandings between the Arabs and the Soviets. Secondly, they want to achieve the isolation of Egypt, because Egypt has shown how it is possible to build up a modern country, while they want it to remain a backward African country, no more important than Gabon. Thirdly, they want to liquidate all progressive regimes in the Arab world, which would be easy for them once Egypt had been isolated.''

Sadat told the Soviets that Egypt had "made every effort possible to attain a peaceful settlement'' and that now "force and only force is the method'' to deal with Israel. But the Soviets prevailed and Sadat signed a joint communique calling for a peaceful settlement based on U.N. Resolution 242. Like American interests at this point, Soviet attention was focused elsewhere than the Middle East.

At the end of the talks, Foreign Minister Riad, who had attended, observed that the Soviets had "refrained from sharing in the responsibility of a decision for war which demanded, in their view, that Egypt have the will to fight. I felt, after listening to Grechko's report, that our decision in favor of war should not be delayed any further, and I said as much to Sadat on our way back to Egypt.''

In the balance between war and peace, the tilt from now on would increasingly go toward war.

• •

The Soviets wanted Western credits and technology, and toward that end the Twenty-fourth Congress of the Communist Party in March 1971 had formally approved a policy of detente with the United States. The two countries hoped to solidify detente the next year when Nixon was going to visit Moscow to achieve substantive agreements on arms control. The Soviet leaders' attention was also focused on Asia. They had just been outflanked by Nixon's opening with China and in addition there were severe tensions building in the subcontinent between India and Pakistan, two other countries that were aligned on opposite sides of the superpowers and were about to go to war. Moscow wanted a war in the Middle East no more than did Washington.

As a result, when Sadat returned to Cairo in full expectation of a massive infusion of Soviet arms to make good his "year of decision," he was in for another serious disappointment. Sadat claimed "there was no sign of anything throughout October and November," although U.S. news reports were saying that Tu-16s bombers were being flown to Egypt along with loads of war materiel. It is likely both Sadat and the press were right in the sense that the bombers were arriving but not all the materiel Sadat wanted. At any rate, Sadat recalled bitterly in his memoirs: "I summoned the Soviet ambassador, sent messages to the Kremlin, and so on, but received no reply whatsoever....It was the end of December when the Soviet ambassador called to tell me that the Soviet leaders were very busy at the moment but that they'd willingly see me in Moscow on February 1 and 2, 1972."

Meantime, in his supreme frustration—and with his "year of decision" embarrassingly running out—Sadat's trust in the United States finally turned to complete disillusionment. Despite repeated expressions of optimism by Rogers, the United States obviously was not putting any pressure on Israel and the Jewish state was still refusing even to attend proximity talks.

Sadat resorted to increasingly bold threats, but without effect. On November 11, Sadat declared that "1971 must be a decisive year because we cannot remain forever suspended in this state of no peace and no war." Nine days later, he warned: "There is no longer any hope whatsoever of peaceful or other solutions...war is at hand." The next day he revealed in an address to troops along the canal that he had "cut off all contacts with the United States for a peaceful solution." He told the troops they must "fight ferociously to prove to the world that we are a fighting people. I have come to tell you the battle is at hand."

Washington responded the next day by saying that it was dropping its mediation efforts. Any effort by the United States to find peace in the Middle East was now dead and so too was any hope Sadat had of making

71

• •

1971 a year of decision.

With the state department admitting failure, all that was left to formalize Kissinger's role as head of Middle East policy was for President Nixon to assign the region to him officially. This he effectively did in a White House meeting with Golda Meir on December 2, 1971. The President accepted an Israeli request that Kissinger establish a secret backchannel that would bypass the state department. Under the pressures of the coming election, Nixon also promised not to pursue the quest for a comprehensive settlement, thereby assuring Israel's continued occupation of Arab lands, and he pledged a major increase in U.S. arms for Israel.

A short time later, the United States signed another Memorandum of Understanding with Israel promising the sale of an astonishing forty-two F-4s and ninety A-4s warplanes. It also pledged it would not initiate any talks with the Arabs without first discussing the initiative fully with Israel. As historian William Quandt observed: "If the memorandum were taken literally, the United States had tied itself almost completely to the Israeli position."

After the signing of this latest Memorandum of Understanding, Israel finally agreed to join proximity talks. But by this time Sadat was so disillusioned that he refused.

"By the end of 1971, the divisions within our government...had produced the stalemate for which I had striven by design," recalled Kissinger with satisfaction. The result was a deliberately imposed period of neglect over the next two years. It was a sterile period of U.S. diplomacy, based in large part on the mistaken belief that the Arabs were simply too backward and weak to challenge Israel militarily.

CHAPTER VIII

Emergence of Black September

As ANWAR SADAT'S public humiliation grew over his inability to make 1971 the "year of decision," the first evidence of a new, more vicious and merciless fedayeen terror organization came with dramatic suddenness on November 28, 1971 in Cairo. Wasfi Tal, prime minister and defense minister of Jordan, the man widely blamed throughout the Arab world for the slaughter of the fedayeen during the 1970 Black September civil war in Amman, was gunned down on the entrance steps of the Sheraton Hotel as he was returning to his room. Two young gunmen, backed up by two others, assaulted Tal, firing at least ten shots. As Tal lay dying, a Jordanian officer reverently knelt down and kissed his forehead. One of the assassins also knelt. He gleefully licked the blood flowing from Tal's body.

Black September thus made its entrance on the world stage. It was not a month but a movement, an expression of rage and hatred and numbing despair named after the violent events of September 1970 in Jordan. Its aim was brutally simple: Terror.

Black September was the latest of a sequence of fateful reverberations stemming from the rout of the Arab armies in 1967. That victory had produced a dramatic growth of Palestinian commando groups. It was the Palestinians who bore the brunt of the defeat. They lost their homes and more of their land, and the totality of the defeat made it obvious that the Palestinians could not depend on other Arabs to secure their fate.

Up to the 1967 war, the Palestine Liberation Organization, the first official Palestinian resistance group, founded in 1964, had been the major Palestinian organization. But it was essentially a front for Egypt. It had been devoted mainly to controlling the more radical elements of the Palestinians rather than working for the benefit of the Palestinians themselves. It was suspect from the beginning. Underground factions like Fatah, which had taken a vague shape in the late 1950s under the leadership of Yasser Arafat, known by the nom de guerre of Abu Ammar, a short, soft-spoken engineer, continued to thrive even after the PLO's founding.

Fatah began attacks against Israel at the beginning of 1965, and by the end of the 1967 war it was the best known, most respected and largest Palestinian guerrilla movement. It was essentially non-ideological, careful not to be dominated by any Arab nation and it concentrated on the liberation of Palestine through attacks by fedayeen, Arabic for self-sacrificers. As such, it was supported by the more conservative Arab states like Saudi Arabia and Kuwait and attracted mainly Moslem activists unencumbered by political slogans of the right or left.

But by the end of the 1967 war disillusionment had become so great that more radical groups of fedayeen sprang up. The most important was the PFLP, the Popular Front for the Liberation of Palestine, a coalition of three small groups which was founded by a Palestine-born Christian physician, Dr. George Habash. Unlike Fatah, the PFLP was deeply ideological, committed to Marxism-Leninism with a heavy lacing of Maoism and opposed not only to Israel but also to Arab monarchies like Jordan and Saudi Arabia. Most significantly for Washington, it was violently anti-imperialist, by which it meant in particular the United States. It reversed the priorities of Fatah by stressing that the long term aim was not the establishment of merely a Palestinian state but transformation of the whole Arab world. "Unlike...some other groups, we saw the liberation of Palestine as something not to be isolated from events in the rest of the Arab world as a whole," Habash said in explaining his philosophy. "We saw the need for a scientific and technical renaissance in the Arab world. The main reason for our defeat had been the scientific society of Israel as against our own backwardness in the Arab world. This called for the total rebuilding of Arab society into a twentieth-century society."

Although Habash had been comparatively moderate before the war, he had completely changed his attitudes by the time he formed the PFLP in 1967. "The only language which the enemy understands is that of revolutionary violence," he declared in his inaugural statement on December 11, 1967. He added that the historic task of the moment was to start a struggle so fierce that it would turn "the occupied territories into an inferno whose fires consume the usurpers." Later he explained the PFLP's objections to peace: "We do not want peace. Peace would be the end of all our hopes. We shall sabotage any peace negotiations...." Terrorism was necessary for the PFLP, he claimed, for its "shock value....We had to shock both an indifferent world and a demoralized Palestine nation....The world has

74

forgotten Palestine. Now it must pay attention to our struggle.....What we are after is liberation of Palestine. If we must blow up a dozen El Al planes, then we will.''

• •

On December 15, 1971, slightly more than two weeks after Tal's assassination, Black September's anger exploded again. Two Jordanian ambassadors were the targets of attacks. Zaid Rifai, one of Hussein's closest friends and a hardliner against the fedayeen, was shot in his automobile in London, where he was serving as ambassador. At least thirty to forty bullets were fired by two men, but Rifai suffered only a minor hand wound. The other attack was aimed at Ambassador Ibrahim Zreikat in Geneva. A suspicious package addressed to him was delivered to the Jordanian mission. It exploded when it was opened by Swiss police, seriously wounding two of them. The terrorists were back in operation—with a vengeance. Soon their targets would extend beyond Jordan and its representatives.

• •

King Hussein's subjugation of the fedayeen was highly unpopular in the Arab world, which felt that he was doing, as Palestinians had complained, "Israel's dirty work," whether willingly or not. His drive against the Palestinian commandos deprived them of their most valuable location for launching attacks against Israel; meanwhile, the region had remained suspended in the limbo of no war—no peace. The year of 1971, Sadat's year of decision, had ended as it had begun, with Israel remaining on Arab territory and increasingly strengthening its hold. In addition to the restlessness and expectations that had been provoked by Sadat's repeated threats to go to war, the dramatic rise of Black September further inflamed the Arab bloodlust for revenge.

In this charged atmosphere, Sadat, much to his humiliation, had to explain in public that Egypt had been too weak to go to war in 1971. On January 13, 1972, he admitted that the Pakistan-India war at the end of the previous year had caused the Soviet Union to divert weapons from Egypt, leaving his troops underequipped. Indeed, the Soviets apparently had taken Sadat's war threat more seriously than his own people, because they had removed air-defense equipment around Aswan as much for India's aid, purportedly, as to warn Sadat not to go to war.

To add to his discomfort, Sadat foolishly tried to imply that a fog bank in the Sinai, a highly unlikely phenomenon under the noon day desert sun, had prevented an attack by ready Egyptian troops in December. This led to a series of pointed jibes among the joke-loving Egyptians: "Why didn't you fight in the war, daddy?" "Because, son, I was lost in the fog." The Israelis were also merciless in mocking Sadat's "year of decision." They called the end of the year "December 32nd," indicating that the year would never end for Sadat because he was too cowardly to make war.

Worse for Sadat, the United States, on the same day as his admission of weakness, made public the signing of the Memorandum of Understanding the previous November 1 giving Israel the technology to produce its own U.S.-designed weapons. It was all too much for Cairo's angry, impatient students. On January 16, 1972, the students' repressed emotions exploded.

In nine days of demonstrations, sit-ins and rioting, thousands of students took to the streets, demanding that Sadat keep his promise and go to war. If not, they warned, he should be replaced with a "real government of mobilization." In his turn, Sadat blamed the riots on outside agitators. Nonetheless, he promised that his pledge to go to war was "not mere talk but a reality....There is no other path than the battle."

In an effort to pacify the students, Sadat shuffled his cabinet, taking the opportunity to sack Foreign Minister Mahmoud Riad and thus tighten his grip on foreign policy. But the riots continued. Finally, Sadat launched a tough crackdown that resulted in fifteen hundred students being arrested. Although he managed to subdue the students, the message to Sadat was abundantly clear. He urgently needed a victory. He had to make the Israelis withdraw, by diplomacy if possible, by war if necessary, if he was to survive.

CHAPTER IX

Israel Gets a New Chief of Staff

THE PALESTINIAN GUERRILLAS forced out of Jordan in 1970 and 1971 had only one place to go, southern Lebanon. It was the sole area left where they could launch attacks against Israel. Syria would not allow them to operate openly from its territory, although it sanctioned several training camps, nor would Egypt. Only Lebanon, with its weak government and feuding sects, could be cowered into accepting the guerrillas. Their appearance was unwelcome by the largely Moslem Shiite villagers in southern Lebanon, since the presence of the guerrillas brought with it heavy attacks by Israel, raids that frequently hit civilian and PLO structures indiscriminately. But there was little the villagers could do to oust the heavily armed fighters and the result was that they became caught in the middle of the unrelenting war, doomed to untold suffering.

Shelling from Lebanon in early January 1972 caused no damage inside Israel but brought an immediate response. Israeli jets bombed and then its troops entered southern Lebanon and blew up several buildings in retaliation, the first time Israel had gone into the area in eleven months. That same month, Israeli planes bombed guerrilla camps in southwestern Syria for the first time since June 1970.

These manifestations of new Israeli toughness came just days after a new chief of staff was appointed for the Israeli Defense Forces at the beginning of the year. He was David ("Dado") Elazar, forty-six at the time, a compact, darkly handsome Yugoslavian who had emigrated to Israel in 1940 and joined the Palmach, the elite strike force of the Jewish underground army before independence. He stayed in the army and quickly gained recognition as a calm and tireless and hard leader. By the time he was thirty-six, he was a major general and head of the armored corps, a proud wearer of the corps' black beret. He later became commander of Northern Command, the region of Upper Galilee along the frontier with Lebanon, Syria and Jordan. During the 1967 war, while he headed Northern Command, Israel broke a ceasefire and attacked Syria, capturing the Golan Heights. In the mini-war of attrition that developed after 1967 on the northern front, Elazar operated with a simple, if harsh, philosophy: "To make life bearable for us and unbearable for them."

Elazar served for five years as head of Northern Command, the top field command after Southern Command, which included Sinai and the strategic frontier with Egypt. He was a cool, calculating fighter, a natural leader of men, so successful in Northern Command that he was promoted in 1970 to Chief of General Staff (G Branch), the traditional stepping stone to the army's top job. Two years later, on January 1, 1972, Elazar succeeded Haim Bar-Lev to become Israel's ninth chief of staff.

It would be this tough, fun-loving and totally dedicated soldier who would direct Israel's campaign in the approaching war.

Elazar's assumption of command marked a period in which Israel carried out some of its harshest and bloodiest attacks on its neighbors. Shortly after the first of the guerrillas' raids of 1972 from southern Lebanon, Elazar warned that such attacks would bring "disaster" to the Lebanese villages. He was as good as his word. When three Israelis were killed by infiltrators in late February 1972, Elazar's response was to send a force into southern Lebanon for four days that killed sixty persons and wounded a hundred others. Under Elazar, such incursions became routine, despite repeated condemnations by the U.N. Security Council.

• •

While Elazar was instrumental in forging Israel's new hard line against the guerrillas, the far more significant strategic decision that faced Israel in the post-1967 war period had already been taken. It was Israel's conscious choice to stay on the east bank of the Suez Canal. In the final analysis, all that occurred up to the 1973 war pivoted on that basic decision.

A major consequence of the decision was the conversion of the entire 101-mile length of the Suez Canal into one great battle line of fortified positions by the time of Elazar's appointment. Troops and guns lined both sides, Egyptian facing Israeli, both ready for the next exchange of fire. Less than two hundred yards—an easy rifle shot—separated the combatants along most of the canal. Between was the placid water of de Lesseps' creation, now undisturbed by maritime traffic. It had remained closed since the 1967 war, its passage blocked by sunken ships and mines, leaving fifteen merchant

78

ships from eight nations stranded by the outbreak of fighting. Two of the ships were American: the Observer, lying motionless with broken down engines in the northern reaches of the canal, and the African Glen, which was clustered with the other thirteen vessels in the southern part in a body of water appropriately named Great Bitter Lake. Skeleton crews manned the rusting hulks, about 150 men in all, Americans and British, French and Swedish, now united in what they facetiously called the Great Bitter Lake Association. But there was nothing facetious about their predicament. They were stranded between two bitter armies.

The conversion of the canal into a battle zone came about with the construction the Bar-Lev Line. It was a towering sand embankment erected by Israel on the east side of the canal as its frontline defense against an Egyptian attempt to regain the Sinai Peninsula. It was a massive barrier, studded with heavily fortified forts, artillery emplacements, barbed wire and gun positions. It had come about as Israel's answer to murderous artillery attacks launched by Egypt to vent its frustration against the no war-no peace period following 1967.

Heavy artillery barrages caused Israel to face a seemingly simple but ultimately momentous question: How best to preserve Israel's hold of the east bank of the Suez Canal? In the face of a determined enemy such as Egypt, this was not an easy military problem. The range of choices lay between systems of static and mobile defense, and in the end the answer had to take into consideration political aspects as well. It was a puzzle without an elegant solution.

Major General Avraham (Bren) Adan was put in charge of the problem. Adan was a short, husky disciplinarian, blond and rugged, a veteran armored forces commander who had fought in all of Israel's wars. He was also going to play a significant role in the coming war. Adan was naturally sympathetic to mobility, which was Israel's forte, but not blinded by its glamor. The country's stunning triumph in 1967, when its tanks had thrust across the 100-mile width of the Sinai Peninsula to reach the east bank of the Suez Canal in three days, had made the armored corps the most dashing and storied of the ground services. After the war, it attracted the brightest and most ambitious of Israel's officers. It was now the premier ground service and figured prominently—too prominently, critics would later argue— in Israel's determination to hold onto the east bank.

The consideration that ultimately swayed Adan's decision was not military but political. It was the fear that Egyptian forces might manage to cross the canal and to hold some land, even a sliver, long enough for the superpowers to impose a ceasefire. Such a feat would be hailed as a major victory

79

by the Arab world. "We faced a dilemma," observed Adan in his memoirs. "On the one hand, we had ideal conditions for a mobile defense and, on the other, the sensitive political-strategic considerations of a small nation for which 'trading' territory was anathema." Israel was determined, for psychological reasons as much as any other, to deny Egypt the small symbolic victory of being able to recapture even a bit of its land.

Adan attempted to solve this problem by combining both static and mobile defense tactics into a coordinated plan. In the process, he set the battleground for the coming war.

Adan's first conclusion was that Israel's most immediate requirement was the capability to detect an attack immediately. From that basic conclusion grew like topsy what later would be one of the most fortified war zones in the world.

To assure early detection, Adan decided that electronic sensors were needed to cover the length of the canal. As Adan pointed out in defense of his plan, the canal was particularly suited for projecting electronic beams because it ran level and straight for most of its course. One sensor at ten kilometer intervals would be adequate. But here was the conundrum. Such sensors meant that there had to be an Israeli presence at the canal's bank to operate, maintain and monitor the devices. Thus emerged the fateful sequence: To protect the sensors and their operators, fortresses must be constructed along the canal; to assure the security of the fortresses, troops must be stationed; and to protect the troops, artillery and tanks were needed. The world's latest Maginot Line thus came into existence.

Eventually thirty forts were constructed out of gabions of stone, sand bags and steel rails torn out of the railroad General Edmund Allenby's British forces had constructed in their attack across the Sinai during World War I. The fortresses were highly elaborate affairs and included such amenities as commercial telephones so soldiers could call home. Each fort was built to survive direct artillery hits and had firing positions interconnected by trenches, deep underground bunkers and storehouses for ammunition, food, water and medical supplies to last for several days. Mine fields and barbed wire surrounded the forts. Between thirty and ninety men were normally stationed at each fort, not a number large enough to hold back a major invasion but judged to be sufficient for defensive purposes. To add to their protection, a system of fuel tanks was installed with outlets into the canal so its waters could be set afire during an enemy crossing.

The general staff approved Adan's plan around the end of 1968. A massive construction program began immediately, involving thousands of civilians and soldiers, adding significantly to the $500,000,000 Israel spent on defenses in the Sinai before the 1973 war. By the time of Elazar's appointment as chief of staff, the Bar-Lev line was already the centerpiece for Israel's defense of the occupied Sinai.

CHAPTER X

Sadat Ousts the Soviets

ANWAR SADAT, faced with the aggressive tactics of Israel's new chief of staff and the seeming impregnability of the towering Bar-Lev Line, besieged by domestic discontent, frustrated in his futile Washington strategy and still in search of weapons, once again turned to the Kremlin for help in the winter of 1972. He flew to Moscow February 2 and held a series of uncomfortable talks over the next two days with the Soviet leadership, pleading as usual for more weapons.

"In October you promised me equipment that hasn't arrived; more was promised by Podgorny in May, and it hasn't arrived; more was promised by Ponomarev in July, and that has not arrived either. Why the delay?" he asked of the Soviet leadership.

Leonid Brezhnev replied that he personally was to blame. The delays were due to paperwork and red tape, he said. Sadat writes that he was "beside myself with rage. I reiterated what I had told them on my previous visits, particularly that we didn't want Soviet soldiers to fight our battle for us and that we sought no confrontation between them and the United States. The meeting ended with them reading out a list of weapons which they promised would be shipped 'forthwith.'

"They were not the essential weapons I wanted but they were better than nothing."

To add to Sadat's unhappiness, on February 5, the day after he left Moscow, Washington made public its generous new arms package for Israel, which included an astonishing 42 F-4 Phantom jets and 90 A-4 Skyhawks. Moshe Dayan contentedly commented: "We got the main items we feel we should have got."

Concluded Sadat: "Back in Egypt, I realized my patience had run out."

82

Unrecognized by much of the world, Sadat was about to profit from a historic convergence of supply and demand. The small cloud of looming oil shortages suddenly became a stormhead in early 1972. The Arab oil states of the Persian Gulf, including Saudi Arabia, raised their oil prices in January by 8.49% to $2.42 a barrel. By April, it finally became clear to some parts of the administration that an energy crunch was approaching. Interior Secretary Rogers C.B. Morton warned that "we are facing a fuel and power crisis." America's oil consumption was increasing dramatically, and domestic production was failing to keep pace. A nation with 6% of the world's population was consuming one-third of the globe's energy output. It was predicted that if the trend continued, the United States would have to import half of its oil by 1980. Twice during the rest of the year quotas on oil imports were raised; at the end of the year they were lifted completely on fuel oil to avoid anticipated shortages during the winter.

The Office of Emergency Preparedness warned that "we are becoming more and more dependent on Middle East sources of crude oil."

But, beyond words, little serious attention was given to the approaching crisis. The administration's attention was focused instead on the scheduled summit meeting in Moscow in May 1972 between Richard Nixon and Leonid Brezhnev, their first face to face meeting. It was causing considerable concern in Cairo and other Arab lands.

President Sadat was suspicious that the Russians, in pursuit of detente with the United States, would sacrifice the Arab cause. He was keenly aware that the national interests of the two superpowers overrode regional problems, a situation that encouraged both superpowers to support the continuation of the region's stalemate. The major business of the summit was the signing of the first SALT agreement, the Strategic Arms Limitation Agreement, and the formalization of detente, "Basic Principles of US-Soviet Relations."

Against these grandiose issues, the Middle East was a sideshow. On April 12, Sadat expressed his worries to Brezhnev in a letter. "Any new American policy will certainly be against our interests," he warned.

He also brought up the sensitive issue of the emigration of Russia's Jews, the largest reservoir of Jews outside of the United States, estimated at about three million—equal to Israel's population. In response to its efforts to cultivate detente, the Soviet Union had begun allowing unprecedented numbers of Soviet Jews to emigrate to Israel. In 1970, only about 1,000 Jews were allowed to leave the Soviet Union. Suddenly, in 1971, as Moscow and Washington opted for detente and the Russians recognized the sensitivity in America of the Jewish question, the floodgates opened. The figure skyrocketed to 13,000 in 1971 and went beyond an unprecedented 30,000 in 1972. Noting the increased immigration, Sadat wrote: "Some of them are young men, intellectuals and scientists, who are going to be of great material assistance to Israel."

Sadat's unhappiness with Russia's willingness to allow Jews to emigrate to Israel was only one of numerous contentious issues continuing to disturb harmonious relations between the two countries. The main one, of course, was the constant bickering over the supply of weapons, which caused deep resentments on both sides. Beyond that, however, was the Soviet Union's opposition to the idea of Egypt launching a war. In part, this was likely due to its doubts about the military capabilities of the Arabs, who in three wars had not shown themselves able to defeat Israel. But it had most to do with the Kremlin's global ambitions and especially its detente with the United States. War would certainly pit the two superpowers on opposite sides, with the ever-threatening possibility of a direct nuclear conflict between them. This the Soviet Union had consistently shown it wanted to avoid.

Underlying many of the irritants in the Cairo-Moscow relationship were the cultural differences between the two countries. Egyptians considered Soviet advisers insensitive and heavy handed, and they resented Russian efforts to isolate part of Cairo West Airport from Egyptian control for their exclusive use. There was also resentment at the Soviets' refusal to mix in Egyptian society, living instead in closed compounds open only to Russians. "Never did they mix with Egyptians, to share a meal or even a cold drink, but kept only to themselves....They were not even lighthearted," observed Sadat's wife Jehan.

The Soviets had their own grievances. They were worried about Egyptian emotionalism that might propel the region into a major war and they wondered what Sadat's true intentions were. The Egyptian leader was still something of an unknown quantity. In addition, the Soviets were aware that he had assured a Saudi Arabian official early on that he would evict the Soviets if it would get his land back. The Saudis had relayed the message to Washington where Senator Henry Jackson, one of Israel's staunchest supporters, promptly leaked it, presumably as a way to embarrass Sadat and damage relations between Egypt and Russia. The leak did its damage, since it left the Soviets suspicious and uncertain about Sadat's intentions.

• •

For the third time in eight months, Sadat traveled to the Soviet Union on April 27, 1972, to try to harmonize relations and seek reassurance about the May summit meeting. The visit only added to the Egyptian's growing resentment. He suffered the humiliation of being publicly snubbed by the failure of Brezhnev to welcome him at his arrival or bid farewell at his departure. Then his visit was abruptly cut short by twenty-four hours with the lame excuse that "common understanding and unity" had "enabled us to reach the desired end in the shortest possible time."

These were public slights that the proud Egyptian leader was not likely to forgive or forget. Nonetheless, Sadat managed to extract from the Russians a promise that they would finally fulfill all of their arms commitments by the coming November. "The idea was that we should be adequately prepared by November, when a new American President would have been elected, to resort to military action if all avenues to peace continued to be blocked. They agreed to this...." In addition, Sadat also extracted a pledge from the Russians that they would send him a report on any discussions with Nixon involving the Middle East.

Back in Cairo, Sadat was again subjected to scorn because of the Soviet slights and charges by his right wing critics that Egypt had become a Russian vassal. In his May Day speech, the Egyptian leader sought to downplay the snubs in Moscow by reporting that Brezhnev, despite a 104-degree temperature, had met with him for nine hours. "Our enemies were very pleased," said Sadat. "They said Brezhnev did not receive Anwar Sadat at the airport. This means that the visit was a failure...."

In fact, as Sadat was able to point out, the visit had produced an important and tangible achievement for Egyptian foreign policy. In the joint communique issued at the end of Sadat's visit on April 29, the Soviet Union for the first time sanctioned the Arabs' right to resort to the use of arms to retrieve their territory. Charging that Israel and the United States remained hostile to a political solution, the communique said that "the Arab states...have every reason to use other means to regain the Arab lands captured by Israel." The Soviet Union had never previously made such an acknowledgement, a fact that the Cairo press went out of its way to comment on—but which received little attention in the White House.

• •

The long-anticipated summit took place in Moscow as scheduled toward the end of May. But June came and went without the Soviets supplying Sadat with the promised report on the talks. The public documents released at the end of the summit on May 29 certainly gave the Egyptian leader reason for extreme anxiety. They were, he recalled, a "violent shock."

Only two paragraphs were devoted to the region in the communique, calling for a "military relaxation" and reaffirming both sides' commitment to "a peaceful settlement in the Middle East in accordance with Security Council Resolution 242." A set of "general working principles" was no less disappointing from Sadat's view. It listed seven agreed points, all of them rehashes of previous positions taken by the two sides, including the call for an end of belligerency.

These boilerplate formulations, and particularly the joint call for a peaceful resolution and a military relaxation, were all that Sadat had feared and exactly what Henry Kissinger had sought. Kissinger later admitted, "...I sought the blandest possible Middle East formulation in the communique....The upshot was a meaningless paragraph....it was practically an implicit acceptance of the status quo and was bound to be taken ill not only in Cairo but elsewhere in the Arab world." As for the general working principles, observed Kissinger, they "did not go beyond the existing United Nations resolutions or were so vague as to leave wide scope for negotiation in implementation. Their practical consequence was to confirm the deadlock."

Kissinger added: "As far as we were concerned, our objectives were served if the status quo was maintained until either the Soviets modified their stand or moderate Arab states turned to us for a solution based on progress through attainable stages."

Sadat had other ideas. In a letter to Brezhnev June 7, Sadat again voiced some of his fears about the continuing stalemate. "In my opinion, there will be no settlement unless positive pressure is exerted on America and Israel. Unless Israel feels that the military balance is tilting against it, and that we can apply military as well as political pressure, there will be no settlement. I fear that the postponement of any movement by us, either military or political, for month after month, only helps to consolidate Israel's position in the occupied territories." He again urged that weapons deliveries be speeded up. But there was only silence from Moscow, much to Sadat's growing fury.

By this time, the uneasy relations between Soviet and Egyptian officers were raw. Both sides held each other in open scorn, the Russians considering the Egyptian soldiers lazy and inept, the Egyptians feeling the Russians were arrogant and disparaging. The Egyptians grumbled about obsolete Soviet equipment, inferior to American weapons, and about being kept deliberately low on ammunition and spare parts.

Beyond these bad relations in the military, which were eating away at

Sadat's strongest pillar of support, Egypt was suffering in other ways. The economy was desperate; tomatoes, onions and sugar, the staples of the peasants' diets, were scare. There were shortages of many consumer items, unemployment was high, productivity low and waste and corruption were appalling. Students remained restless and impatient, facing an uncertain future and a frustrating present. It was they who were raising in public the question of why Russia would allow Jews to emigrate to Israel, thus strengthening Egypt's enemy. All this added up to a serious threat to Sadat's rule.

A well-informed report in The Washington Post spoke openly of a mood in Cairo of "uncertainty and frustration," and speculated that "many believe a [coup] could happen within a year." It added:

> Sadat's continuing vacillation on a no peace—no war policy appears to be slowly eroding his authority, both among the civilian population and among his own government officials. More ominously, there are reports of growing dissatisfaction within the army circulating....One of the President's problems seems to be a credibility gap. The truth, as a number of diplomatic observers here see it, is that despite all the belligerent talk Sadat is not prepared to go to war with Israel because he knows that Egypt would lose once again. Sadat' continuing postponement of 'zero hour' since the so-called year of decision ended in December has not been overlooked....Many here see his latest deadline as one more postponement of the inevitable moment when Sadat must acknowledge that Egypt cannot successfully take on the Israelis again without Soviet help—which Moscow has declined to provide.

In all, Sadat's continuing close relationship with the Kremlin was beginning to carry more liabilities than assets. This was especially true of his relations with Saudi Arabia. The Saudi ruling family was rabidly anti-communist and suspicious of the Soviets' presence in Egypt. Sadat early on had worked hard to improve relations with the Saudis, which under Nasser's socialism had been badly strained, and he continued to court them.

It then occurred to Sadat, who so relished the dramatic gesture, that there was a way to capture Washington's attention and at the same time significantly improve his ties with Saudi Arabia. These goals, he realized, could be achieved by taking an unexpected action: expelling the Russians.

The idea no doubt was reinforced during the summer when Saudi's minister of defense, Prince Sultan, stopped in Cairo on his way back from Washington where he had met with Nixon and Kissinger. His message was that the Americans would not put any pressure on Israel as long as the Russian advisers remained in Egypt. The expulsion of the Russians would also be very popular with the Saudis, who along with Kuwait and Libya, were the main source of Arab aid to Egypt—120 million pounds sterling a year, about $250 million, since the 1967 war closed the Suez Canal, denying Egypt of its revenues.

●   ●

It was not until July 8 that Brezhnev sent Sadat an analysis of the summit talks (although a preliminary report had been sent earlier). The letter was more than two and a half pages long and said, in sum, that no progress had been made on the Middle East question because "it was the U.S. election year." It made no mention of why weapons were still not arriving on schedule or of Egypt's war option, except in the last five lines. And these were insulting. The Soviets, reported Sadat, "said simply that we were unable to start a battle, that they had experience in this respect, and that they had made an unusual effort to persuade Nixon that Security Council Resolution 242 should be implemented."

Brezhnev urged Sadat to raise the morale of the army, "to fill them with courage, determination and vigilance, and to educate them in the struggle against imperialism and Zionism." It was not the kind of message Sadat expected or wanted to hear. He turned to Soviet Ambassador Vinogradov, who had personally delivered the letter, and asked: "Is this *the* message?"

"Yes," he said.

"You were, weren't you, with us in Moscow last April and you did hear us agree that the weapons should be sent to us before the U.S. elections took place"   .

Vinogradov said he had.

"Well, this message doesn't mention that," Sadat said.

"This is the message I have received," replied Vinogradov.

"Well, I cannot accept it, and indeed reject the Soviet leaders' method in dealing with us."

Then Sadat dropped his bombshell.

"I have decided to dispense with the services of all Soviet military experts [about 15,000] and that they must go back to the Soviet Union within one week from today."

The only other person in the room was Sadat's national security adviser,

88

Hafez Ismail, who had not been let in on the momentous decision. His jaw dropped. Vinogradov was incredulous. He "didn't believe it. He thought it was an attempt at blackmail," observed Sadat.

But it was true. The first thing the next morning, Sadat called the war minister and ordered him to carry out the decision. By the time Sadat publicly announced the expulsion on July 18, nearly 15,000 Soviet military advisers were already starting to go home.

• •

The ouster caught everyone by surprise, including the United States. "It was a total, total surprise," said Eugene Trone, the CIA station chief in Cairo at the time. "There was never even a hint."

It was vintage Sadat, a monumental decision arrived at privately, kept closely held and executed with dramatic swiftness. Henry Kissinger, while admitting that he was as surprised as everyone, thought that Sadat could have gotten more profit from the action: "I had expected that at some point down the road, Sadat would be prepared to offer to trade Soviet withdrawal for progress with us. But, still handicapped by my underestimation of the Egyptian president, I never guessed that he would settle the issue with one grand gesture, and unilaterally."

Simultaneously, Sadat had made another fundamental assessment. He concluded that William Rogers and the state department were essentially impotent. He thus decided to deal directly with the White House through a backchannel bypassing Foggy Bottom, causing at times some considerable confusion. For while the Egyptian foreign ministry and the state department were holding an on-going dialogue, Sadat and his foreign affairs adviser, Hafez Ismail, were at times taking entirely different positions in the CIA backchannel with Nixon and his national security adviser. CIA station chief Trone, undercover as the political officer, the number two man in the Special Interests Section behind Bergus, was in charge of the backchannel and thus at times better informed than his nominal boss. So too, of course, was Kissinger, putting him in an ideal position to further undercut the authority of the secretary of state.

Henry Kissinger hailed the expulsion of the Soviets as a great triumph for his policies, which in part it was, since American inflexibility had indeed forced Sadat to do something drastic. But the action had dramatic implications unimagined by Kissinger. Instead of profiting the United States at the expense of the Soviet Union, the expulsion of the Russians meant that Sadat was now denied the Soviets' moderating advice. As Sadat's wife observed: "The only barrier to Anwar's pledge to avenge our honor was the Russians." Now the Russians were not around any more. Yet at this juncture such restraint was especially needed, since Sadat felt he had only one way to go: War.

• •

On June 17, 1972, a little noted break-in occurred in the Democratic headquarters in Washington's Watergate complex. It would have far reaching repercussions not only for Nixon's presidency but also for the Middle East. But like Sadat's dramatic expulsion of the Soviets, the Watergate event was little appreciated by Kissinger and the White House.

CHAPTER XI

Massacre in Munich

WASHINGTON'S ATTENTION WAS FOCUSED on matters other than the Middle East in the summer of 1972. The presidential election was in high gear and the Republicans were making special efforts to woo the Jewish vote. Richard Nixon was using Henry Kissinger on occasion to brief influential Jewish voters. Israeli Ambassador Yitzhak Rabin, appreciative of the enormous support Nixon and Kissinger had given his country, was openly urging the President's reelection among Jewish groups. Polls were showing that the Republicans were going to win New York, with its heavy Jewish vote, for the first time since Calvin Coolidge.

Democratic candidate George McGovern, at first moderately critical of some Israeli policies, soon began trying to out-do Nixon in his pro-Israel statements. He proposed that the U.S. Embassy be moved from Tel Aviv to Jerusalem, which almost no country recognized as Israel's capital except Israel itself. The open pandering to the Jewish vote became so blatant that columnist Nicholas Von Hoffman was moved to write a scathing article condemning the "dangerous quiet of bipartisan agreement [which] stifles questioning and discussion" of Middle East policy. Von Hoffman went on to criticize "our present policy [which] makes neither moral nor political nor economic sense." Then he riled sensitivities further by labelling Israel the "Prussia of the Middle East, a baby Junker state" that was "making the Sinai safe for lebensraum." The uproar was horrendous, with an outpouring of outraged letters inundating the newspapers that carried the column, a vivid demonstration, if any was needed at this point, of how sensitive the Middle East had become in American politics.

Equally diverting Nixon's attention from the Middle East was the continuing Vietnam war. Secret peace talks in Paris with North Vietnam were entering their final phase. The end of the war was to have been Nixon's top

91

achievement. But now, nearly four years after coming to office, all Nixon could show was that during his term the country had squandered $50 billion more on the war, lost 20,492 more American lives as well as hundreds of thousands more Vietnamese.

Nor was Kissinger concerned with the Midddle East at this time. He had been delighted with the expulsion of the Soviets, but puzzled by Sadat's handling of the matter. In Kissinger's estimate, Sadat deserved no American gratitude since he had not been shrewd enough to bargain with Washington about the expulsion.

The U.S. media was not much impressed either with Sadat's dramatic gesture. The Washington Post concluded that the expulsion of the Soviets "graphically demonstrates Egypt's realization that it has no military option for solving the Middle East crisis." When Sadat vowed in a speech that Egypt still planned to wrest its territory back from Israel, The New York Times poked fun at him, echoing Israeli gibes about his repeated empty boasts by saying his threats rang "more futile and foolish than ever."

Now Sadat was left with a resentful Soviet patron, an indifferent administration in Washington and a world community that generally considered him a silly bag of wind.

•   •

Despite the expulsion, Sadat had not given up hopes that he could still persuade the Soviets to give him the war weapons he wanted. But first he would have to mollify the Kremlin's hurt feelings. Although both sides conducted themselves with dignity during the expulsion crisis, in private the Soviet leadership expressed bitterness. A post-expulsion letter from Brezhnev had dropped the usual salutation of "Dear Friend" or "Dear Comrade" and simply addressed Sadat as "Dear Mr. President." In response, Sadat sent a long and thoughtful letter at the end of August to "Dear Friend" Brezhnev explaining in detail why he had ordered the Soviet advisers out.

> I would like, my friend, to reveal briefly my impressions...because it is your right as a friend to know the reasons which, I believe, justify my decisions. The [conflict with Israel] is 'frozen,' and no means of breaking the present deadlock are available. The American claim that the United States, and the United States alone, is capable of finding a solution has been increasingly vindicated, even after the Moscow [summit]

meeting. Israel's unbridled actions in our Arab region continue unchecked. The statement issued by the Moscow meeting calls for 'military relaxation' in the region after the solution of the problem.

Your message of July 8 completely ignores the measures we had agreed upon and which we believe to be absolutely necessary insofar as they would enable us to resort to military action, if need be, after the U.S. elections. The United States continues to give unlimited amounts of weapons to Israel, and is moderniz-ing the Israeli air force, apart from other types of armaments. Your attitude...reveals that the partial embargo you have im-posed on us for the last five years, in regard to 'retaliation weapons,' has been extended at this critical period to cover basic necessities which I had specified in my message to you but which you completely ignored.

In view of all these considerations, my decision to terminate the mission of the advisers has been designed to give us a pause—to mark the inevitable end of a certain era and the begin-ning of another based on fresh concepts, recalculations and redefinition of our stands....

To be completely honest, however, I have to state that your very first priority in establishing the cooperation you wish to have with us should be to enable us to liberate our land. We wish to consolidate our cooperation with you to the greatest possible extent—though such an extent will be commensurate with the extent of assistance we shall receive from our friends in the Soviet Union, toward solving our basic and paramount problem, that of liberating our land....The problem of liberating our land is everything to us—our very life, conduct, relations, and actions

In concluding, Sadat offered to send his prime minister to Moscow "to help our relations to proceed in the future from a firm basis of trust, and cooperation based on mutual frankness to serve our common interests." The Russians agreed but the visit of Aziz Sidqi was a flop. The Kremlin leadership was still angry. "Dr. Sidqi came back with nothing but a bunch of promises that were never kept," noted Sadat bitterly.

His cause, his burning mission, the issue on which his presidency dan-gerously pivoted—the return of Egypt's land—appeared hopeless. His im-

93

potence was emphasized by an announcement by Israel that since the 1967 war it had established forty-four settlements on occupied Arab territory in the Sinai, the Golan Heights and the West Bank. Jews were relentlessly moving onto Arab land and there was nothing Anwar Sadat could do about it.

• •

The terrorists of Black September thought they had an answer to Israel's continuing settlement of the occupied territories. They undertook an operation that riveted world attention and caused a greater impact than even the massive hijackings of airliners in September 1970. It began when eight Black September members slipped over the wire mesh fence of the athletes' village at the Munich Olympic Games early September 5, 1972. They were armed with Kalashnikov rifles and hand grenades and headed straight to Block No. 31, the Israeli pavilion. They entered through an unlocked door and ran into a weightlifter and a wrestling trainer. Both Israelis were killed. In the confusion, several Israeli athletes fled the pavilion; nine others were captured by the terrorists. The twenty-hour drama that became the horror of the Munich Olympics was about to begin on worldwide television.

The Olympic operation had been planned by Fatah's Abu Iyad, a close associate of PLO Chairman and head of Fatah Yasser Arafat, as a spectacle that would bring world attention to the Palestinian cause and upstage the radical PFLP, whose increasingly bloody terrorist actions were making Fatah and the PLO appear timid and uncommitted. Publicity was guaranteed. There were six thousand journalists covering the Olympics with some of the most advanced television equipment ever assembled. On the morning of the eleventh day of the Olympics, the powerful camera atop the television tower turned from the stadium and zeroed in on Block No. 31, where it would remain glued through the day as the tragedy unfolded, the TV images bouncing from satellites to receivers around the world.

The terrorists demanded the release of two hundred Palestinians held in Israeli prisons. The Germans wanted to negotiate. But Israel flatly refused. "We do not bargain, but we must defend ourselves," Israel's ambassador to West Germany told the German government. "That means, in this case, that there must be an immediate counterattack. My government will accept nothing else." Israeli security men were immediately sent to Munich to advise the Germans. Their orders were that there must be no negotiations, no bargaining. The terrorists had to be subdued or killed.

Deadlines were repeatedly set and then extended by the terrorists. At last, at 10:06 PM, seventeen hours after the crisis erupted, the terrorists were talked into a trap. They were told a jetliner was waiting to take them and their hostages to Cairo where they could complete an exchange with Israel. The eight terrorists and nine Israeli hostages were flown in two helicopters to Furstenfeldbruck military airport twenty minutes from Munich where a brightly lit Boeing 707 sat waiting.

Unseen by the terrorists were five German sharpshooters, six hundred Frontier Guardsmen and a number of police armed with automatic weapons.

When the helicopters landed, the two pilots jumped out followed by two terrorists, covering them at pointblank range. Two other terrorists walked over to the jetliner, little more than a football field away.

Then they froze. There was no crew aboard the waiting plane. At that point the sharpshooters fired. The two men guarding the pilots were immediately killed. One of the two Palestinians returning from the jetliner was also cut down. The other terrorists, all of them still in the helicopters, shot back, killing one of the sharpshooters. Then a sudden, dramatic stillness descended on the grim scene made stark by the harsh illumination of floodlights.

In Arabic, German and English, authorities pleaded with the men through loudspeakers to surrender. There was no answer from the helicopters. At 1:05 AM, September 6, the second anniversary of the mass jetliner hijackings two years earlier, the Germans opened fire again. One terrorist jumped from a helicopter, turned and lobbed a hand grenade inside. At the other helicopter, another terrorist fired his automatic weapon inside. The Germans in armored cars moved in and witnessed the ghastly result. They found all the Israeli athletes dead. So too were all but three of the Palestinians.

The operation was a disaster for Fatah. It had indeed received attention throughout the world, but not the kind anticipated. There was universal condemnation at the violation of the joyous spirit of the Olympics, at the wanton deaths of young athletes, at the savagery of the Middle East moved into a European setting. A letter in Time Magazine summed up the revulsion felt by many: "...the Black September mob are truly the scum of the earth." Longer term, it did make some non-Middle Easterners begin to wonder what was going on in the region that possibly could motivate such extremism. But, in the end, Munich was one of the most disastrous operations Fatah had ever undertaken.

There was an immediate backlash in Germany and other countries against all Arabs. Popular sentiment in West Germany turned violently anti-Arab. Several hundred Arab residents were expelled, two Arab social groups were outlawed and Arabs trying to enter the country were closely interrogated; 1,900 were refused entry. In some cafes signs were put up reading "Arabs

95

not wanted.''

In response, Libya refused entry to West Germans and Cairo demanded that all West Germans obtain visas before entering Egypt. In the United States, President Nixon publicly denounced the killings, the U.S. Senate and House passed resolutions urging all nations to boycott countries harboring terrorists. The FBI, the state department and the immigration service joined in a program to interrogate and keep an eye on all suspicious Arabs.

Israel's reaction was instant and violent. Two days after the Munich killings, as many as eighty Israeli jets launched the heaviest air raids since the 1967 war, blasting targets deep in Syria and Lebanon. Between two hundred to five hundred Lebanese, Syrians and Palestinians, mostly civilians, were killed. The next day, September 9, Syrian and Israeli jets fought in the skies over the Golan Heights. Three Syrian planes were downed. Syrian artillery responded and the country declared a war alert. Israel followed suit the following day and also went on war alert.

The U.N. Security Council considered a resolution condemning Israel for its indiscriminate attacks against Lebanon and Syria but the United States vetoed it September 10, only the second time Washington had employed a veto. The vote was 13 to one with one abstention. The American delegation explained the draft resolution had been unfair because it did not equally condemn terrorist attacks against Israel.

On September 15 two Israeli soldiers were killed in an ambush on the Golan Heights. The next day, instead of hitting Syria, an Israeli force of three thousand troops protected by tanks and air cover invaded fifteen miles into Lebanon and marauded for a day and a half. Israel said ''at least sixty'' guerrillas were killed; the Palestinians reported thirty-five guerrillas, eighteen Lebanese soldiers and twenty-three civilians killed.

On the same day, September 16, a letterbomb killed the agriculture attache in the Israeli Embassy in London. A month later to the day, Abdel Wael Zuaiter, Fatah's representative in Italy, was gunned down by unknown assailants. The PLO claimed Israeli agents were responsible; Israel denied it. The covert war of secret agents and assassinations was about to spill yet more blood.

• •

An aggressive new anti-guerrilla policy was invoked on October 15 by Israel. It was, in effect, a declaration of war fully supported by Chief of Staff David Elazar. As explained by an Israeli spokesman, the Jewish state would no longer wait to be attacked before retaliating. Now it would attack whatever guerrilla targets it could find. ''We are no longer waiting for them to hit us first," said the spokesman. "This is the operative phase of our pledge to hit the terrorists wherever they are, and they are in Lebanon and Syria." Former head of Israel's military intelligence, Chaim Herzog, explained: "We are not engaged in reprisal, but a war against terror. The very presence of terrorists...is a provocation."

That same day, about twenty Israeli jets dropped bombs and launched rockets against what were described as terror targets in Syria and Lebanon. Only Lebanon reported casualties, two civilians killed and sixteen wounded.

Despite Israel's new policy, the terrorists continued to score successes. At the end of the October, on the 29th, two Black September terrorists hijacked a Lufthansa Boeing 727 over Turkey and forced West Germany to release the three terrorists captured during the Munich massacre. The three were flown to Libya and freedom. Israel's response was sharp. It hotly criticized West German capitulation, as did the United States, and the next day launched heavy air raids deep inside Syria. Damascus reported more than sixty civilians killed and seventy wounded. The guerrillas placed their losses at fifteen dead.

For the next several months, Syria and Israel exchanged stiff blows almost daily, raising fears of a all-out war between the two countries.

• •

By the end of 1972, the Middle East was locked in a spiral of rising tensions and increasingly brutal actions. Egyptian Prime Minister Aziz Sidqi reiterated once again in December to the People's Assembly that he saw no alternative to war. "We have tried every method to restore our rights through a just settlement of our cause, but Israel—backed by the United States—is challenging the whole world and continues to occupy our land," he said.

At about the same time, the U.N. General Assembly passed three resolutions condemning Israel for its razing of 15,855 Palestinian houses in Gaza, urging it to accept back Palestinians driven from the homes in the 1967 war and declaring that Palestinians had the right of self-determination.

But these actions and statements elicited no response in Israel or the United States.

• •

Sadat finally took the only step left to him to get the requisite weapons of war. Once again he did it by surprise. Without bargaining or attempting to extort concessions, he unilaterally granted in December the Kremlin what it wanted most from Egypt: Renewal of its five-year agreement, due to expire the following March, on strategic naval facilities in Egypt. He also found a treasure chest to pay for the weapons he needed. The donor was Saudi Arabia. With a new naval bases agreement and hard cash in hand, the Soviets reacted with alacrity. Moscow at last was ready to sell Egypt the weapons it needed to go to war.

CHAPTER XII

Nixon Searches for Peace

RICHARD NIXON BEGAN THE SECOND TERM of his presidency determined to be active in finding a solution to the festering Middle East conflict. The January 27, 1973 ceasefire in Vietnam had finally brought America's involvement to a formal end, and attention and interest turned toward the Middle East as the next explosive area that desperately needed pacifying. In Nixon's eyes, that meant getting Israel to become more flexible. To that effect he sent a strong note to Henry Kissinger in February.

K—you know my position of standing firmly with Israel has been based on broader issues than just Israel's survival—Those issues now strongly argue for movement toward a settlement. We are now Israel's only major friend in the world. I have yet to see one iota of give on their part—conceding that Jordan and Egypt have not given enough on their side. This is the time to get moving—and they must be told that firmly.
The time has come to quit pandering to Israel's intransigent position. Our actions over the past have led them to think we will stand with them regardless of how unreasonable they are.

Kissinger, after working closely with the President for four years, believed that Nixon "deep down wanted to...impose a comprehensive settlement sometime during his term in office....Nixon was convinced that he owed nothing to Jewish votes and that he could not increase his Jewish support regardless of what he did....He believed that Jews formed a powerful cohesive group in American society; that they were predominantly liberal; that they put the interests of Israel above everything else; that on the whole they were more sympathetic to the Soviet Union than any other

99

ethnic groups; that their control of the media made them dangerous adversaries; above all, that Israel had to be forced into a peace settlement and could not be permitted to jeopardize our Arab relations.''

Yet, Kissinger noted, despite all this, ''in every crisis Nixon stood by Israel more firmly than almost any other President save Harry Truman. He admired Israeli guts. He respected Israeli leaders' tenacious defense of their national interest. He considered their military prowess an asset for the democracies.''

If Nixon's emotions about Israel were confused and conflicted, Kissinger's were not. ''Though not practicing my religion,'' he wrote, ''I could never forget that thirteen members of my family had died in Nazi concentration camps. I had no stomach for encouraging another holocaust by well-intentioned policies that might get out of control. Most Israeli leaders were personal friends. And yet, like Nixon, I had to subordinate my emotional preferences to my perception of the national interest. Indeed, given the historical suspicions toward my religion, I had a special obligation to do so. It was not always easy; occasionally it proved painful. But Israel's security could be preserved in the long run only by anchoring it to a strategic interest of the United States....''

In the end, as events would show, Kissinger was far less successful in protecting American interests than he hoped or later pretended.

• •

While Nixon searched for peace, Anwar Sadat was planning for war. He had begun seriously considering war after expelling the Soviets in the summer of 1972. His numerous military threats up to this period had been largely show, saber-rattling to force a political settlement and protect his own position. Now the reality had become inescapable. War was the only alternative. The original deadline he had set for completion of preparations for combat was November 15, 1972. The timing was significant, as Sadat later observed: ''The U.S. presidential elections would be over in the early days of November and I wanted to give the President-elect a chance to try to find a peaceful solution to the problem. So, if nothing was achieved in this direction by then, we would be ready to take military action.''

As the deadline neared, Sadat summoned a meeting of the supreme council of the armed forces on October 24 for a report on the state of readiness. To his chagrin, he discovered that little had been done. Beyond that, even his war minister continued to oppose his strategy for a limited engagement. General Mohammed Sadiq and Sadat had been having an increasing number of disagreements over recent months, particularly over the question of strategy. Sadat believed that a canal crossing that resulted in recapturing even a small spit of Egyptian land would pay major political dividends. Sadiq favored a more ambitious undertaking, but at the same time constantly complained that the armed forces did not have the necessary weapons to undertake any aggressive action.

Sadat was stunned when his generals told him that they were not only unready to go to war but that their defenses against an attack were inadequate.

"We're completely exposed, sir," said Major General Abdel Munim Wasil, commander of the Third Army. "Any attempted concentration of forces this side of the canal would be spotted by the Israelis, so that we'd be attacked before any crossing is made." The commander of the Second Army, Major General Saad Mamun, gave a similar assessment.

The reason, it turned out, was that General Sadiq had discontinued the practice of matching every Israeli increase of the height of its sand rampart on the east bank. The result was that Israel's rampart now soared to about fifty feet, and growing, while Egypt's was only around ten feet high.

'I'm sorry, but you must know I am very upset," said Sadat. "When I came to see you I expected you to be ready to carry out any plan we might choose to lay down and now I find that you haven't even a defensive plan ready. How could we hope to launch an offensive when we're not even prepared for defense?"

Within two days, Sadat staged a purge of his top officers, firing Sadiq and his deputy, the commander of the navy and others. The man chosen to replace Sadiq was Achmed Ismail, fifty-five years of age. Ismail was a highly regarded professional soldier, "the classic officer, the soldier par excellence," as Mohamed Heikal described him, "an infantryman, professional, honest, wholly above politics." Best, from Sadat's viewpoint, was Ismail's understanding of the subtle relationship between war and politics. While not brilliant, he was a husky six-footer who by shear doggedness and hard work had succeeded. He was stolid, a stickler for discipline, gruff and dedicated. He had his early training under the British and later at Russia's Frunze Academy. At the time of his appointment as minister of war, he was the chief of the national intelligence service.

It was Ismail who would formulate the final plan for war and oversee its operations in less than a year.

Helping him were two brilliant generals: Saad Shazly, the chief of staff since early 1971, and Abdul Ghani Gamasy, Shazly's director of operations since the previous February. Shazly, fifty, was a flamboyant paratrooper, husky and handsome, a derring-do field officer much beloved by his troops.

Even as a general he had continued to jump. Diplomatic tours in London and the United Nations gave him a worldliness usually lacking in Egyptian officers. His reputation as a fighter preceded him in the 1967 war. In that humiliating rout, Shazly escaped through the Mitla Pass, much to the disappointment of Bren Adan, the Israeli general who designed the Bar-Lev Line. "...I really wanted to capture Shazly," recalled Adan in his memoirs, "but he ruined his reputation by being one of the first to flee. The legend was shattered, to be replaced by contempt." The two men would compete on the field of battle soon again. This time the contempt would be replaced by admiration.

The other member of Achmed Ismail's team was Mohammed Gamasy, fifty-one, a former tank commander, the intellectual among the top three Egyptian generals. He was an avid reader, quiet and thoughtful, and non-political.

Sadat had at last formed a topnotch command to direct his war. But there was a basic problem. Ismail and Shazly detested each other. In fact, when Shazly heard of Ismail's promotion, his resentment was such that he considered retiring. But, he concluded, "We were preparing a battle of destiny....It would have been too much to leave the armed forces and the fruits of my labor to others....But the most persuasive reason was that, if I resigned now, it would be seen as support for general Sadiq. It would be assumed I shared Sadiq's view that we could not start a war now or in the near future."

The troubles between Ismail and Shazly, polar opposites in personality and outlook, stretched back to 1960 when they were both posted in the Congo and had such bitter words over how to command an Egyptian U.N. mission that Shazly took a swing at Ismail. When Ismail was named chief of staff in March 1969, Shazly had immediately resigned. It required a promise from President Nasser personally that Ismail would not interfere with Shazly to persuade him to return to the armed forces. Sadat now made a similar pledge.

The first task for the new Egyptian team was to heighten the vulnerable sand rampart along the canal. By the end of 1972, they had overseen the construction of thirty massive sand ramps reaching seventy feet into the air and each containing 230,000 cubic yards of sand. Now Egyptian and Israeli soldier could look eyeball to eyeball across the narrow waters of the Suez Canal on an equal footing.

Their next task was more complex. It was how to refine plans to cross the open canal, that veritable killing field, and penetrate Israel's dense rampart in the face of Israel's undoubted might.

As with any military operation, it had to have a name. They designated the crossing Badr, after the first victory by Mohammed during Ramadan in 624; the battle itself was labelled Sharara, Arabic for spark, a spark meant to set alight the diplomatic world.

• •

The continuous round of terrorism and harsh Israeli attacks against both Lebanon and Syria were keeping emotions high throughout the Middle East. Egyptian students were again restless. At the end of 1972, hundreds of disgruntled students occupied the main building of Cairo University to protest school policies and the government's lack of progress in getting Arab lands back. They were particularly critical of Sadat. Fifty students were arrested; in retaliation thousands of students rioted on New Year's day 1973. The riots quickly spread to Alexandria and other cities. Thousands of police and students fought a pitched battle on January 3 in Cairo's streets, the police using tear gas and clubs. The government managed to quiet the the students only by ordering the closing of Cairo University and dozens of other colleges and educational institutions in the country for four weeks.

Still, passions continued to seethe and they were further stoked January 8 by extensive air and ground battles between Israeli and Syrian forces. At least a dozen planes from each side tangled in the skies above the Golan Heights, ending with the loss of three to six Syrian planes. Six Syrian tanks and four radar stations were also knocked out in the fierce combat. During the day's fighting, Damascus radio repeatedly urged other Arab countries to "go into battle immediately with Israel and not let Syria stand alone and take the enemy blows." Such appeals inflamed radicals throughout the Arab world and prompted them to put pressure on their governments to act against Israel, thus heightening the tense atmosphere.

Syria charged that during the battle Israeli jets had entirely destroyed the village of Dail, near the Jordan border, in air attacks that Damascus claimed killed five hundred civilians. Israel called the report "a lie." A U.N. investigating team later reported eyewitnesses confirming at least 125 civilian deaths.

Three days after the fighting, Israel announced its losses in combat and terror incidents during all of 1972. It reported nineteen soldiers had been killed during the year in fighting and thirty-four civilians in terror incidents, including twenty-eight, mostly Puerto Rican civilians, who eventually died as a result of the attack by Japanese terrorists at Lod Airport in May. No similar Arab figures were released but they numbered in the hundreds.

The next month brought other Israeli actions that caused more outrage in the Arab world. On February 21, Libyan Arab Airlines civilian flight 114 strayed over the Sinai, forbidden to commercial traffic, and headed eastward toward the highly sensitive installation in the Negev Desert at Dimona where Israel conducted its nuclear experiments. Two U.S.-made Israeli Phantoms rose to meet the Boeing 272 and attempted to force it to land. The plane began to descend and lower its landing gear, then it suddenly veered westward, back toward Cairo, its intended landing place. With Chief of Staff Dado Elazar's personal approval, the Israeli jets shot down the airliner despite its flight westward away from the Sinai, killing 106 persons.

Earlier that same day, Elazar had presided over one of Israel's boldest raids to date. A force of paratroopers had gone by ship and helicopters to Tripoli in northern Lebanon, 125 miles north of the Israeli frontier, and attacked two Palestinian guerrilla bases. Thirty-one persons were killed, including thirteen civilians.

While praised in Israel for the Tripoli operation, Elazar came under considerable criticism for the downing of the Libyan airliner. Prime Minister Golda Meir, who had appointed him, assured Elazar that his job was not in jeopardy. "...I want to tell you that I don't just appreciate you, I admire you," she said. "And I don't just believe in you, I have full confidence in you."

Arab response to the Israeli actions was vehement. In Libya's capital of Tripoli, demonstrators smashed the windows of the U.S. Embassy and burned the American flag. Syria called the airliner downing "overt piracy" and Egypt warned Israel that it "shall pay dearly at the hands of the Arabs."

• •

In search of a new initiative in the Middle East amid such carnage, Nixon arranged meetings with representatives of Jordan, Egypt and Israel in February and early March 1973. In preparing for the White House sessions, Kissinger sent the President a memorandum listing three strategic options: First, to "stand back and let the two sides reflect further on their position," in other words, continued stalemate; second, to seek an interim agreement and, finally, to work privately toward a comprehensive agreement.

Nixon bridled at the idea of continued stalemate. On the margin of Kissinger's memorandum, he wrote: "K—Absolutely not. [Ambassador Yitzhak] Rabin must be told this categorically before I see [Golda Meir]. I have delayed through two elections and this year I am determined to move off dead center—I totally disagree. This thing is getting ready to blow." He made no comment on the second course. He liked the third—secret talks, as "the preferred track for action. At the same time keep the public track going for external appearances—but keep it from interfering with the private track." This instruction gave Kissinger the authority to conduct substantive negotiations while leaving the state department with only sterile public actions.

King Hussein of Jordan was Nixon's first Middle East visitor in 1973. In two sessions February 6 and 27, he was less sanguine about the meaning of Sadat's expulsion of the Soviet advisers, correctly perceiving that one of Sadat's motives was to free himself from Moscow's opposition to war. He also accurately predicted that Russia would increase its arms supplies to Egypt as a way to retain it position with Cairo and would continue to pour weapons into Syria to prevent it from following Egypt's example. Hussein, as usual, expressed considerable flexibility in seeking peace. He said Jordan was ready to talk directly with Israel—in fact, he had personally met in secret with Israeli leaders a number of times since the war, but to no avail.

What was needed, Hussein said, was not another Jordanian proposal but an American one. Then he made the only miscalculation of his visit, and it was a dangerous one. He suggested that the United States had about two to three years to find a settlement before the region exploded. This helped lull Nixon and Kissinger into thinking they had more time than they did.

Next to arrive at the White House was Hafez Ismail, Sadat's national security adviser who called on February 23. He carried with him a note from Sadat warning that "the situation in our region has deteriorated almost to the point of explosion." Like Hussein, Ismail also expressed flexibility. Cairo was ready to give security guarantees and an end of belligerency to Israel in return for a complete withdrawal. But final peace could only come with a solution to the Palestinian problem. Nixon, to Kissinger's surprise, now voiced support of such an interim settlement, saying a comprehensive agreement was too difficult to achieve all at once. He urged Ismail to conduct secret talks with Kissinger to see if they could find a peace formula.

The two security advisers met for two days of secret talks February 25-6 in the suburban New York home of an old Nixon friend, Donald M. Kendall, board chairman of Pepsico. The state department was not informed of the meetings, more evidence of how totally strained relations now were between Rogers and Kissinger. The Kissinger-Ismail sessions served more as a get-to-know-you opportunity than a negotiation. Kissinger warned Ismail that he thought little could be accomplished until after Israel's elections, set for the end of October. Privately, Kissinger felt the talks left little room for optimism but the two men, believing time was on their side, promised to meet each other again in several months.

Last to arrive at the White House was Golda Meir. For good reason, she was in high spirits. Israel had never been stronger, thanks to Nixon's generosity, and in her estimation there was no urgency to find a final settlement because the Arabs had no military option. When she saw the President and Kissinger on March 1, she said, "We never had it so good." She sang Nixon's praises, allowed that she would be willing to enter peace talks but could not commit herself to their outcome and left the strong impression that she was in no hurry to see a new diplomatic initiative. Then she pressed the President for what she wanted most: more arms. Nixon, always pliant in Meir's hands, consented to give Israel another large number of warplanes and other concessions. It would get twenty-four more Phantoms and an equal number of A-4 Skyhawks, an enormous addition to its already overwhelming strength.

Because of Arab sensitivities, Nixon and Meir agreed to keep the aid package secret. Predictably, it leaked within days and caused a major uproar in the Arab world, which was probably the result sought by the unidentified leaker. Disclosure of the arms deal immediately wiped out the good will established by Hafez Ismail's visit. The incident was compounded by the fact that a newspaper story had earlier reported, incorrectly, that an arms deal had been made while Ismail was on his way back to Cairo. The timing of the story made it seem aimed at embarrassing the Egyptians and Kissinger hastened to assure Ismail that the report was untrue. When Nixon then did approve such a deal, the reaction in Cairo was understandably "great disappointment."

Sadat was explicit in his disappointment. In an interview with Newsweek a short time later, he complained: "Everything was discouraging. Complete failure and despair sum it up....Every door I've opened has been slammed in my face by Israel—with American blessings....The time has come for a shock....Everything in the country is now being mobilized for the resumption of the battle—which is now inevitable." During this same period, Sadat made repeated warnings that the area was headed to war—in fact, too many warnings in the opinion of even some of his own countrymen. A group of the country's most celebrated writers and intellectuals had become so fed up that at the beginning of the year they issued a public statement urging Sadat not to use the word "battle" any more. The word, they complained, had "lost its power, effectiveness, as well as credibility."

Nonetheless, Sadat kept up his warnings. On March 29, he declared himself the military governor of Egypt with powers to declare martial law; the next month he announced plans to form a people's militia to help in the "total confrontation" with Israel. The difference now was that the Egyptian leader was serious. But the leaders of the West and Israel and even his own subjects were so used to such antics by now that they paid little attention.

At the same time, peace efforts were not encouraged by statements coming out of Israel. When Golda Meir returned home, she said there was "no basis or reason for changing our policy." Moshe Dayan urged Israelis to settle in the occupied territories since there was no chance of Arab-Israeli negotiations for "ten to fifteen years." At about the same time, a poll showed that a vast majority of Israelis opposed returning most of the occupied territories.

* *

On the same day that Nixon was meeting Golda Meir in Washington, another terrorist outrage occurred. Eight terrorists in a Fatah vehicle crashed through the gate of the Saudi Arabian Embassy in Khartoum and invaded a party being thrown for U.S. deputy chief of mission, George C. Moore. Guests fled in all directions as the eight men came in with automatic weapons firing. All but six of the guests escaped or were released. Held by the terrorists were Moore, U.S. Ambassador Cleo A. Noel Jr., and Belgian chargé d'affaires Guy Ein, as well as the Saudi and Jordanian ambassadors and the Japanese chargé. Both Moore and Noel were immediately tied up and unmercifully punched and kicked. Noel had just arrived in the Sudan and Moore was on his way home.

The terrorists wanted the release of Abu Daoud, a Fatah leader, and sixteen comrades who were being held under death sentence in Jordan for attempting to overthrow King Hussein. When after a day of threats Jordan refused to give in, the terrorists received a radio message from Beirut ordering them to kill three of the hostages. Moore, Noel and Ein were taken to the cellar and cold bloodedly machine gunned to death. The terrorists surrendered to Sudanese authorities the next day. They were later freed.

The murders may have seemed justified to those who suffered Israeli attacks, but their effect in the United States was to turn Americans even more against the Palestinians.

Israel struck back at the terrorists in a dramatic way the next month. Under repeated urgings from Chief of Staff Dado Elazar, Defense Minister Moshe Dayan finally consented to a daring commando attack in the middle of Beirut. Its purpose: the assassination of three Palestinian guerrilla leaders. Early in the morning darkness of April 10, an Israeli force stormed an apartment building on rue Vertun and killed Kamal Nasir, a Fatah spokesman; Kamal Adwan, a Fatah operations officer, and Yossef Najjar, also known as Abu Yussef, a suspected leader of Black September. Najjar's wife was also killed as was a seventy-year-old Italian woman who made the mistake of opening her apartment door to see what was happening. Unknown to the Israelis was the fact that bigger fish were just buildings away. Yasser Arafat and his top lieutenant Abu Iyad were both in Beirut that night.

All told, twelve persons were killed in the Israeli operation: four Palestinians, two Lebanese civilians, two Lebanese policemen, three Syrians and the Italian woman. Twenty-nine others were wounded. Elazar told a news conference that same day that the raid was carried out in retaliation for "the intensification of terrorist acts in Europe and other places in the last months." He added that "there is no possibility of honoring the sovereignty of Lebanon and its capital as long as it is serving as a complete haven for terrorists."

Elazar's mention of an intensification of terrorists acts was all too true. Since the beginning of the year, the secret war between Israeli and Palestinian agents had been escalating. On January 25, Hussain Bathir, a PLO official, had been killed by a bomb blast in his Cyprus hotel room. The next day, Israeli agent Baruch Cohen was shot to death in Madrid. On March 12, another Israeli, Simha Gilzer, was shot and killed in Cyprus; three weeks later, on April 6, Basil Kubaisi, a PFLP member, was shot to death in Paris. Even after Israel's Beirut raid, the killings went on. On April 27, Vittorio Olivares, described as an Israeli agent working for El Al Airlines, was shot dead in Rome; Mohammed Boudia, a Black September member, was killed by a bomb in Paris on June 28. Three days later the Israeli air and naval attache in Washington, Yosef Alon, was shot dead in suburban Chevy Chase. Later in July, on the 21st, Israeli agents gunned down Achmed Bouchiqi in Norway, only to discover that he was merely a waiter with no guerrilla ties.

More dramatic operations followed. On August 5, two Black September terrorists attacked the Athens airport terminal with automatic weapons and hand grenades, killing three and wounding fifty-five; two of those killed were Americans, the other an Austrian. Israeli warplanes on August 10 forced an Iraqi Airways passenger jet with seventy-four passengers, en route from Beirut to Baghdad, to land in Israel in the expectation that PFLP leader George Habash was aboard; he was not and the plane was allowed to fly on. The incident brought another unanimous condemnation of Israel from the U.N. Security Council and a question by Foreign Minister Abba Eban whether "our government was still in full contact with international reality.''

And so it went, the secret war waged among agents in the dark streets and alleys of Europe and Cyprus while the more publicized raids, hijackings and terror actions took place in full public view around the world, all adding in their way to the tensions and hatreds of the Middle East.

• •

Unknown in Washington and Tel Aviv, the month after President Nixon's meeting in March with Prime Minister Golda Meir, a secret meeting took place in Egypt between Anwar Sadat and Syria's Hafez Assad. Chief of Staff General Gamasy submitted to the two leaders a top secret, hand written list. It contained the names of three months: May, September and October. They were the recommended dates that, from a military view, would be the most favorable for starting war.

A choice was made—October 1973.

CHAPTER XIII

The Politics of Oil

KING FAISAL IBN ABDUL AZIZ WAS AN AUSTERE, ascetic, severe ruler. In 1973, he was sixty-nine years old and had been King of Saudi Arabia for nine years, a reign enlightened by his devotion to national planning and hard work. With his lean and lined face, his hooked nose and brooding eyes, Faisal was a son of the desert; but he also was a man of the world. He was the spiritual head of Islam, the custodian of Islam's holy places, including Jerusalem, and the country he ruled held the largest reserves of oil in the free world. This pious and powerful man had finally decided to use, if necessary, his oceans of oil as a political weapon in the Arab-Israeli conflict, a potent threat in this period when oil prices were climbing and storages forecast.

Faisal believed the world's two major evils were Zionism and Communism, a subject he lectured on endlessly despite the obvious contradiction between the two beliefs. Nonetheless, he held to his views passionately, convinced, as he told one interviewer, that "Zionism is the mother of Communism." To the observation that the two creeds were pitted against each other in the Middle East, he replied: "It's all part of a grand plot, a grand conspiracy. Communism...is a Zionist creation designed to fulfill the aims of Zionism. They are only pretending to work against each other."

Faisal had never gotten on well with Egypt's Nasser but he and Anwar Sadat were old acquaintances and enjoyed each other's company. When Sadat came to power, Faisal was quick to establish a private channel with the Egyptian. Sadat, recognizing the value of Faisal's friendship and of his enormous treasury, did all he could to cultivate the relationship. It was in part under Faisal's encouragement that Sadat expelled the Soviets, an act that made the old King think even higher of Sadat as a statesman and devout Moslem.

THE POLITICS OF OIL

It was in 1972, after Washington's failure to respond to Sadat's expulsion of the Soviets and Nixon's election-inspired major increase of arms to Israel, that Sadat confided to the King that he had finally concluded only war could get back Arab lands. For Faisal, as for all other Arabs, the continued occupation of Jerusalem, the third most holy city in Islam, was unacceptable. He responded to Sadat's confidence by promising to finance the war and, more significantly, to employ the oil weapon if the United States did not modify its pro-Israeli policy.

Faisal contacted other Persian Gulf leaders and soon collected a kitty of $300 million to $500 million for Egyptian arms purchases. He also assured a fund of $400 million to $500 million to cover Egypt's balance of payments needs as well as the continuation of an annual $250 million subsidy for Egypt's loss of Suez Canal revenues. Faisal's advice to Sadat was simple: "Only make sure when you fight that you keep on fighting."

Suddenly, with hard cash available, the good communists in Moscow were much more interested in supplying Egypt's military needs. In February 1973, both Sadat's security adviser, Hafez Ismail, and his new war minister, Achmed Ismail, traveled separately to Moscow for highly successful talks on new arms agreements. Within a month, the arms were flowing to Egypt and Sadat pronounced himself well satisfied. "Now they are supplying us with everything they can," he said in an interview. "I am completely satisfied." Asked if it was Soviet opposition that kept Egypt from going to war, Sadat brushed aside the idea. "The decision is not theirs," he declared.

•   •

Despite his pledge to finance Anwar Sadat's war, King Faisal apparently still retained some lingering hope in the spring of 1973 that a clash of arms could be avoided. From his vantage, Saudi Arabia and other Arab oil nations were by now doing the West a favor by continuing to pump large amounts of oil to keep pace with the West's gargantuan appetite. Saudi Arabia alone was producing 7.2 million barrels a day, earning more money than it knew what to do with. Yet it was being urged to expand production by 1980 to twenty million barrels daily. This was a depletion of its only natural resource that Saudi Arabia did not need to meet its economic obligations or even the extravagances of some of its profligate princes. Its high production was seen by the King mainly as a way to pacify the insatiable oil thirst of the West—even if it did happen to result in increasing his personal wealth immensely. Thus Faisal felt the West owed him a favor.

What the spiritual head of Islam wanted was the United States to alter its policies toward Israel so that holy Jerusalem would again come under Moslem control. If not, he concluded, then Saudi Arabia would not increase its production.

Faisal instructed his oil minister, Ahmad Zaki Yamani, to carry this tough message to Washington in April 1973. Yamani met separately with William Rogers, Kissinger, and Treasury Secretary George P. Shultz. Kissinger, who does not mention this meeting in his memoirs, responded by urging Yamani to keep the threat secret. "This should not go further," Kissinger said. "I hope you have not mentioned this to anybody else." He was disturbed to find that Yamani had already spoken with Rogers and Shultz.

"Afterwards the oil minister wondered why Dr. Kissinger should be so concerned to keep the threat of the Arab oil weapon a secret," observed Robert Lacey in his history of the Saudi royal family. "The security adviser had talked in terms of Arab image and of the importance of the Arabs not appearing threatening or extreme in American eyes.

"But Yamani, who like many Arabians, feels that Dr. Henry Kissinger's Jewishness hampers his impartiality in Middle Eastern matters, did not accept the security adviser's counsel at face value. Dr. Kissinger, in the oil minister's opinion, could not care less about the Arabs' posture for the Arabs' sake; the security adviser was concerned to prevent the American public from reflecting too deeply on the price they might have to pay for supporting Israeli military conquests...."

Yamani's response was to give an interview to the The Washington Post on April 18 in which he warned that the United States must become more evenhanded in its Mideast policies. "We'll go out of our way to help you," he said. "We expect you to reciprocate."

Although The Post noted "this was the first time that Saudi Arabia...has publicly linked the flow of its oil to the United States with Washington's Middle East policy," the newspaper was not impressed. The day after the interview ran, the Post published an editorial criticizing Yamani's threats and told its readers that "it is to yield to hysteria to take such threats as Saudi Arabia's seriously."

• •

The Nixon Administration was not impressed either. In an extraordinary display of self-delusion, and with the active encouragement of Israeli officials, it preferred to think that Yamani was acting without the authority of King Faisal. This was a wholly self-serving avoidance of the problem, since there was no way a Saudi minister would act independently of his King. Saudi Arabia, as was well-known but somehow in this case ignored, was an absolute monarchy and Faisal's powers were absolute. Saudi subjects were not distinguished by their tendency to exceed their orders.

The administration's indifference to Yamani's message annoyed King Faisal. To emphasize that Yamani had carried his personal message, he granted for the first time in his life an interview to American TV, the first filmed interview he had given anyone since 1967.

"America's complete support of Zionism against the Arabs makes it extremely difficult for us to continue to supply U.S. petroleum needs and even to maintain friendly relations with America," he said.

"He means what he says," Faisal's son warned journalists.

But the general consensus shared the Israeli assessment that the King was bluffing. Israel's Foreign Minister, Abba Eban, declared that "there isn't the slightest possibility" of an oil boycott. "The Arab states have no alternative but to sell their oil because they have no other resources at all."

Inside the state department, Joe Sisco and his Middle East experts concluded that Faisal was being pressured by Sadat to give his support for the Arab cause against Israel and as a result was merely making his threats to placate the Egyptian leader. But the old King was entirely serious, as he repeatedly tried to make clear up to the outbreak of war.

In May, Faisal summoned to his Riyadh palace Frank Jungers, board chairman of the Arabian American Oil Company, and warned him about the possibility of an oil boycott. Jungers passed the word to both the White House and state department. "It was ignored," he said later, even though the oilman knew Faisal "never acts on a whim. He never breaks his word. When he speaks, he never tells you anything unless he means it."

That same month Faisal told four other leading oilmen that Arab passions were rising and American interests in the Middle East could be threatened. "You may lose everything," Faisal warned. "Time is running out."

The oilmen tried to warn the Nixon Administration about the seriousness of Faisal's warning but no one in the White House, the state department or the Pentagon took them seriously. They attempted to see Kissinger; he refused even to grant them an appointment.

The board chairman of Standard Oil Co. of California, Otto N. Miller, became so concerned that he urged in a company letter to the firm's nearly 300,000 shareholders and employees to foster "the aspirations of the Arab people [and] their efforts toward peace in the Middle East. There is now a feeling in much of the Arab world that the United States has turned its back on the Arab people...." Although he made no direct mention of Israel, there was such an explosion of protest by Jewish groups, some of which urged a boycott of Standard Oil products, that Miller was forced to back

113

down. He later issued a statement saying that peace, of course, had to be based on "the legitimate interests of Israel and its people as well as the interests of all other states in the area."

Another oilman, Maurice F. Granville, chairman of Texaco, also tried to warn that Faisal meant business. He publicly appealed to Americans "to review the actions of their government in regard to the Arab-Israeli dispute and to compare these actions with its stated position of support for peaceful settlement responsive to the concerns of all the countries involved." He was no more successful than Miller.

• •

Throughout the summer, King Faisal, other Arab leaders and oilmen all repeatedly warned that an explosion was coming and the oil weapon would be used. In September, the King told Newsweek that "logic requires that our oil production does not exceed the limits that can be absorbed by our economy." Washington, he added, should disavow "Zionist expansionist ambitions."

It was yet another clear warning but Washington remained unimpressed. Treasury Secretary George Shultz spoke condescendingly of Arab "swaggering" and Nixon archly observed that "oil without a market...does not do a country much good." When asked if he would change policy toward Israel as a result of Arab threats, Nixon replied he would not. "We are not pro-Arab," he said. "And we are not pro-Israel....We are pro-peace."

In view of such attitudes, Faisal's resolve hardened. The oil weapon was now in lock-step with Egypt's and Syria's preparations for war.

CHAPTER XIV

Confronting the Bar-Lev Line

THE PROBLEMS FACING THE EGYPTIAN ARMY were as complex and as challenging as any ever faced by warriors. Before the Egyptians could think about engaging Israeli forces in combat, they first had to get across the Suez Canal, a feat few thought possible. Indeed, the obstacles seemed unconquerable, even in terms of the usual willingness of political leaders to squander blood.

There were four major obstacles that had to be overcome before the real fighting could begin.

First, and most daunting, there was the canal itself. It had been dug through sand, about 150 yards wide on average but not suitable over its entire 101-mile length for a military crossing. Only about a half of the canal lent itself to an amphibious assault, and this in only three areas: between Qantara and Ismailiya in the north, Ismailiya and the Great and Little Bitter Lakes in the center and the lakes and Suez City in the south. The lakes themselves and the intractable salt marshes in the north between Qantara and Port Said were essentially unusable for large military forces. To hold up the canal's sandy banks, they had been cemented from the canal bed fifty-five feet underwater to beyond the waterline. At high tide, the concrete wall extended a yard above water; at low, two yards and in some stretches three yards. Tanks and amphibious vehicles could not climb this steep, cemented bank without ramps.

Next there was the sand rampart that Israel had piled up on top of the residue dumped on the east bank during a century of canal dredging. It soared as high as seventy feet with steep slopes of 45 to 65-degree gradients. Its face merged with the canal bank, leaving no room for landing craft or men to gain a foothold or maneuver. The rampart served not only as a for-midable physical obstacle but as a screen behind which Israeli armor and artillery operated hidden from prying eyes.

Then came the thirty forts of the Bar-Lev Line, deeply dug in the sand rampart, impervious to anything less than 1,000-pound bombs, and protected by mine fields, barbed wire and firing positions. From their high posts, Israeli soldiers had a clear field of fire over the expanse of the canal's waters.

The final barrier was the hellish fire devices Israel had installed to set aflame the waters of the canal. Vats filled with inflammable liquids were buried in the banks with outlets underwater. When released, the fluid would float to the surface and be set afire, turning the canal into a curtain of flames.

All these obstacles had to be overcome before the Egyptians could begin fighting what many observers considered one of the best armies in the world. Israeli Chief of Staff Dado Elazar had declared that the obstacles were such that, if Egypt attacked, the Bar-Lev Line would become "the Egyptian army's graveyard." Most military observers agreed with him.

The biggest question of all facing the Egyptian military planners was: What kind of war could Egypt realistically hope to wage against Israel's might? For most of the world's strategists, the answer was simple—none. Unanimously, the military experts in Israel and the United States, and most other countries, agreed that Egypt had no serious military option against Israel.

But a cool assessment of the strengths and weaknesses of the two sides told an entirely different story, one that the hubris of Israel and its victories blinded nearly all the world from seeing. The Egyptian general staff thought it saw several intriguing openings.

First, the Egyptian generals conceded, Israel's air force was unchallengeable. There was no doubt that it was as good as any in the world in both its American-made equipment and its experienced pilots. Israeli flyers trained more and had more actual combat experience than any in the world, although against no serious opposition from competing air forces. The country had 513 combat aircraft, including 160 A-4 Skyhawks, 120 F-4 Phantoms and 35 French-built Mirages IIIs. Egypt's air force had been completely destroyed in the 1956 war and then again in the 1967 war, along with many of its pilots. Although the Soviet Union had since then rebuilt it, there had not been enough time for Egyptian flyers to get the training and combat experience for Egypt to risk taking head-on Israel's air force. Furthermore, the MiG-21, Egypt's main combat plane with 210 available, was no match for the Phantom. Thus, as a starter, Egypt's strategists had to accept that they would go to war lacking air superiority, an almost unacceptable disadvantage in any conventional war.

116

CONFRONTING THE BAR-LEV LINE

Counterbalancing this, however, was a major strength. It was Egypt's nearly impregnable air defense system. By 1973 it was the densest in the world. It had been steadily reinforced since the start of the War of Attrition ceasefire in the summer of 1970 and it bristled with sophisticated weapons. These included SA-2 and SA-3 missile networks entrenched every two miles along the canal and concentrated in a "box" between the canal and Cairo. In all, there were a total of 840 ready missiles.

The SA-2 was a two-stage weapon with a 288-pound warhead designed to combat planes flying at medium to high altitudes, with a slant range of twenty-eight miles and a ceiling of around 70,000 feet. But it was impotent against fast planes flying under a thousand feet because of its slow acceleration. In addition, the SA-2 had been widely employed by North Vietnam against American warplanes and the United States had developed effective ECM, electronic countermeasures, which both warned the pilot of the missile's approach and jammed the missile's terminal homing frequency, causing it to veer off course. The United States was providing Israel with the sophisticated ECM devices. To overcome this, the Soviets had given Egypt the SA-3, a two-stage missile effective in a range between 500 and 40,000 feet with advanced radar and electronic systems that were less vulnerable to electronic countermeasures.

The most potent Egyptian missile, however, was the Soviet-made SA-6, a single-stage guided missile effective from less than 100 feet to 100,000 feet with a 25-mile range. It packed a warhead of nearly 90 pounds. It was mobile, operated with both optical and radar guidance and was transportable on one armored carrier that fired three missiles. There were an estimated 120 mobile SA-6 carriers, adding another 360 mobile missiles to Egypt's air defense.

Equally important was a thick forest of antiaircraft guns provided by Moscow. It ranged from the shoulder-fired SA-7 to the 37mm towed gun and stationary 85mm and 100mm guns reaching as high as 45,000 feet. Altogether, Egypt had about 1,000 antiaircraft guns, including the deadly ZSU-23/4, a four-barrelled, radar-controlled, rapid fire weapon capable of spewing out 4,000 rounds of 23mm slugs a minute. Egypt's estimated 800 ZSU-23/4s could put up a nearly impenetrable curtain of fire.

As long as Egyptian troops could remain under the protection of this formidable air defense umbrella they would be comparatively immune from Israel's air force. On the other hand, this imposed a limit on how far Egyptian troops could venture beyond the east bank. If they pushed forward too far—in this case, beyond approximately ten miles—they would be chewed up by Israel's air forces.

117

The major asset of the air defense sysem, and its limitation, heavily influenced all of Egypt's strategic choices.

Israel enjoyed two other major advantages the Egyptian analysts had to consider. These were the technological and tactical superiority of its troops as exemplified by its excellence in mobile ground operations by armored forces—although never against a properly trained opponent—and its certainty of receiving abundant supplies from the United States.

Off-setting these assets were a number of little recognized vulnerabilities. Foremost, concluded an Egyptian study, was the "wanton Israeli conceit." Major General Hassan Badri, the leading historian of the Egyptian armed forces, believed that "Israel's over-self confidence and contempt for the Arabs [are] two attributes that went far beyond the reasonable and led her into mazes of foolish conceit."

Two comparatively easy wars had lulled Israel into believing its own admirers about the ability of its armed forces. In fact, as the Egyptians noted, the 1956 war had been no contest at all. Israel had colluded with Britain and France and, supported by those two powers, its forces had run over Egyptian Sinai defenses with little opposition. In 1967, Israel had launched a surprise attack that had essentially won the war in the first few hours when its air force destroyed on the ground the combined air forces of Egypt, Jordan and Syria.

Since then, Israel's soldiers had been widely hailed for their brilliance and bravery, accolades which Egyptian generals thought the Israeli warriors came not only to believe but to expect as their due. Frequent boasts by Israeli generals and politicians convinced the Egyptian planners that Israel overestimated the abilities of its armed forces and greatly underestimated the capabilities of the Arabs. Pride, concluded the Egyptians, goes before the fall.

Other areas identified by the Egyptians as Israeli weaknesses were its sensitivity to combat losses, its economic inability to withstand a prolonged war, its fear of a two-front war, its long lines of communication to the canal and the relatively small size of its standing army. Israel depended on advanced warning to call up the reserves of its citizen army. Its standing forces along the canal and on the Golan Heights facing Syria were relatively small, based on the assumption that it would always have advanced warning to get reinforcements to the fronts when needed.

The Egyptian analysts judged their country's strength to be, foremost, the justness of its cause. This provided the underlying meaning for its actions, buttressed the morale of the troops and attracted support within the international community. Beyond that, there was the ability of the Egyptian

CONFRONTING THE BAR-LEV LINE

infantryman in defense and Egypt's significant advantage in manpower, a population base of ten-to-one. If, added to this, Syria joined the war, with its six million people, Israeli resources would be stretched thin. Syria too had been given a strong air defense system by the Soviet Union. Additionally, Syria faced no barrier like the Suez Canal. Its forces directly confronted Israel's troops on the Golan Heights. Engagement, and perhaps breakthrough on those barren heights, could commence as soon as the order was given.

There was one other major factor that affected both Arabs and Israel equally. The Egyptian general staff concluded, as had its counterpart in Israel, that there was no way that a decisive war could be waged, even if the Arabs had the means. The superpowers would not allow a complete victory by either side. This consideration probably gave a false sense of security—and an unrealistic element of recklessness—to both sides.

Taking these various factors into account, the Egyptians concluded that the only viable option was a limited war, a campaign that would emphasize Egypt's and Syria's strengths in defense and exploit Israel's vulnerabilities.

The plan was straightforward, at least in terms of the irrationality accepted as normalcy in military matters. Its aim was to force Israel into a prolonged engagement where its powerful tank formations would be denied maneuverability, its air force neutralized by SAM defenses and its ground forces made to attack defensive positions on two fronts at great cost in blood. With the emergence of this grand strategic concept, General Achmed Ismail gave his order. He instructed the general staff to prepare to "undertake a limited offensive, to establish a bridgehead across the Suez Canal."

The underlying unknown in this order was the basic question of whether the Egyptian forces could establish a bridgehead. They first had to get across the canal. The overpowering of the Bar-Lev Line remained the essential prerequisite. But the puzzle had long been the focus of the Egyptian strategists, and they had come up with answers. Their solutions were ingenious and would make military history.

• •

Throughout the spring and summer of 1973, Richard Nixon had a more threatening crisis than any he had ever faced. It was Watergate. The Watergate break-in the previous year had by now burgeoned into a fullscale assault on Nixon's presidency. His two top assistants, H. R. Haldeman and John Ehrlichman, and his attorney general, Richard Kleindienst, all submitted their resignations at the end of April because of their implication in the burglary and the resulting attempt at covering up White House complicity. Another White House aide, John Dean, who was providing incriminating evidence against the administration, was being fired. Nixon was distraught. The administration was in disarray.

"The disintegration of a government that only a few weeks earlier had appeared invulnerable was shocking to observe," wrote Kissinger. "The President lived in the stunned lethargy of a man whose nightmares had come true." As the crisis grew, life in the White House was "like living on a volcano."

No one could be sure what Nixon would do or who could be trusted. The President was "isolated, secretive, paranoid," Kissinger had repeatedly told Alexander Haig, Kissinger's former deputy and now Nixon's new chief of staff. Haig confided that he was "never sure whether Kissinger was describing himself or Nixon."

In this atmosphere of uncertainty, suspicion and fear, which dragged on month after excruciating month as more and more revelations emerged, any hope that Nixon had of finding a Middle East settlement evaporated. At his second summit with Leonid Brezhnev, this one in Washington and San Clemente in June 1973, Nixon was satisfied with a communique that included only eighty-nine bland words about the Middle East. When Brezhnev, strongly warning that war might break out in the region, as he had reason to know, suggested that the USSR and the United States secretly agree to impose a comprehensive settlement, Nixon demurred. For Kissinger, as for Israel, the idea was anathema. "For Nixon to force the issue at the height of Watergate hearings would have added the allegation of engaging in a diversionary maneuver to the charge of betraying an ally," Kissinger observed.

The result was still more drift in the Middle East, welcomed by Israel and regarded by the Arabs as yet more proof that war was the only alternative.

CHAPTER XV

Countdown To War

DECEPTION WAS A MAJOR PART of Anwar Sadat's war strategy. He achieved it with prestidigitatorial mastery.

Stories began leaking out of Egypt in the spring and summer of 1973 about the poor state of Egyptian equipment and the sloppiness of its maintenance. A *Washington Post* story reported that Egypt's air defense system had been destroyed during the War of Attrition and not repaired since, that civil defense was in a shambles and that the weakness of the Egyptian war machine was such that renewal of war would be "suicide."

Aviation Week, the respected technical journal, reported: "Missile sites have all been closed as a direct result of the removal of Soviet military advisers, while the Egyptians don't have the technical know-how to maintain the system."

These false assessments, almost certainly planted by Egyptian intelligence, added to Israel's sense of well being.

Moshe Dayan expressed the euphoria of the times in a speech in early April atop Masada, the emotional symbol of Jewish resistance where nearly a thousand Jews reportedly committed suicide rather than submit to the Romans two thousand years earlier. "...now I believe that we are on the threshold of the crowning era of the return to Zion," Dayan said. Israel was blessed with a constellation of circumstances, "the likes of which our people has probably never witnessed in the past, and certainly not since the modern return to Zion."

The first of these factors was "the superiority of our forces over our enemies, which holds promise of peace for us and our neighbors." Others included Israel's occupation of Arab lands and the expulsion of the Soviets from Egypt. Privately, Dayan predicted Israeli troops would man the Bar-Lev Line, or slightly modified lines in case of an interim agreement, for

121

at least the next three years. He, as well as Israeli intelligence, assumed Egypt would not be strong enough to attack any earlier than 1976, if then. While Dayan was waxing lyrical about Israel's strength and blessings, other reports began appearing about Egypt's war plans. There is little doubt—but still no proof—that these leaks were all part of Sadat's orchestrated campaign of deception.

At the same time as stories were reporting Egypt's weaknesses, intelligence reports and newspaper stories began reporting detailed Egyptian military moves. A story in London's *Sunday Times* on April 8 predicted an Egyptian thrust into Sinai in May. Undercover sources reported that May 15 was the date and that the attack would involve five Egyptian divisions, which in fact was the overall Egyptian force used in October.

These reports, together with information about the resumption of Soviet arms shipments, the recent arrival of Libyan and Iraqi warplanes in Egypt, and Sadat's repeated warnings of war, caused Chief of Staff General Elazar to put Israel's forces on a heightened alert in mid-April. Elazar ordered the general staff to "act as if war were a certainty," although the chief of military intelligence, the top intelligence officer in Israel, Major General Eli Zeira, thought that the probability of war was low, "perhaps even very low." Nonetheless, with increasing Egyptian military activity clearly visible, Elazar ordered a partial mobilization in May.

With such divided assessments, Israel celebrated its twenty-fifth anniversary May 7 by strutting its military strength with a large parade in Jerusalem as a warning to its enemies. Thousands of Israeli soldiers, hundreds of tanks and other equipment paraded through the ancient city, mainly in Arab sections, while scores of Phantom, Skyhawk and Mirage warplanes roared overhead. The Jewish state never looked, and never had been, stronger in its quarter-century existence. Chaim Herzog, the general who had been head of army intelligence (1959-61) and was later to become President of Israel, wrote in the Independence Day issue of Israel's leading newspaper, Haaretz: "Israel is today a major military power in the Middle East that both the Middle Eastern states and the superpowers must take into consideration in any appraisal of events."

While the government kept a calm front, insisting that war was not near, the IDF, Israeli Defense Forces, remained on alert. The government's concern was that if there was a public war scare, it could be manipulated, cited as a danger too great for the superpowers to tolerate. The Soviet Union could pressure the United States and Israel to break the no war-no peace impasse by demanding a return to negotiations. There was also concern about the approaching elections at the end of October. The government did not want to give its political opponents the opportunity to attack it for provoking a war or for making concessions in peace talks. Thus a quiet facade was maintained.

• •

Behind the scenes, week after week during the summer of 1973, the Israeli general staff held intensive planning sessions about Egypt's possible war options and Israel's optimal riposte. But as one anticipated deadline after another passed with no attack, Eli Zeira's intelligence prediction that the chances of war were low began to prevail. The belief took hold that it had all been a false alarm. Sadat had been bluffing again, as he had since his ludicrous 1971 "year of decision." More public scorn was heaped on him and by mid-August—seven weeks before the attack—Elazar called off the alert. Complacency again set in among Israel's generals.

Adding to Israel's sense of well being was a declaration by Dayan that the ceasefire lines were frozen and no major war would erupt for the next ten years. Less than two months before war, he told the general staff: "The balance of forces is so much in our favor that it neutralizes the Arab considerations and motives for the immediate renewal of hostilities." He added, reflecting the general contempt Israelis felt toward the Arabs' fighting abilities: "Our military superiority is the double result of Arab weakness and our own strength. Their weakness derives from factors which, I believe, will not quickly change."

Arik Sharon, the impetuous commander of the southern command, declared that "there is no target between Baghdad and Khartoum, including Libya, that our army is unable to capture." He assured Israelis that "with our present boundaries we have no security problem." And Deputy Prime Minister Yigael Allon said flatly: "Egypt has no military option at all."

So confident were the Israeli generals and politicians that it was decided to cut Israel's compulsory military service of three years by three months, starting the next year.

An atmosphere of complacency and security prevailed in Israel. There was unanimity that the Arabs were too weak and the Israelis too strong for a major war to erupt. The partial mobilization of May had cost $11 million, and in hindsight it now seemed like a waste of precious money. Elazar would be extremely careful before he called another costly mobilization.

No outcome could have been more welcomed by Anwar Sadat and his generals.

123

After much trial and error, disappointments and dissections, the Egyptian general staff finally found the answers to the difficult problems facing its crossing of the Suez Canal. Egyptian analysts had early concluded that the paramount problem facing the army was the sand rampart, that barrier of sand as high as seventy-foot encrusted with the mighty forts of the Bar-Lev Line. If that could not be breached, then no crossing could take place, no engagement of the Israelis could occur. The problem was that stark. There was no way to envelop the barrier, no way to leap it, no way to burrow under it—and no way to ignore it. It stretched for nearly the whole of the 101 miles of the Suez Canal and it had to be assaulted head-on. In some way passages had to be driven through it so that tanks and artillery could move into the Sinai Peninsula. Without them, the infantrymen could not stand up to Israeli counterattacks.

But if the rampart could be penetrated, then the strategic equation would be dramatically altered. Then all other problems would become minor by contrast—except, of course, the actual combat itself.

The Egyptians had at first tackled the problem by experimenting with the logical device, explosives. From the size of their tanks and other vehicles, the Eygptians calculated they had to blast passages involving the clearing of 1,500 cubic meters of sand. They thought at first that the deeper they dug into the rampart and the more explosives they used, the more sand each detonation would remove. But they soon discovered they could not dig very deeply into the sand because it acted like a fluid, quickly erasing the digger's work.

Over several years of efforts, 300 various experiments had been tried. Artillery shells, aerial bombs, mines and rockets blasted the sand without the desired results. The shifting sand simply refilled the holes. Nonetheless, the Egyptians persevered, eventually evolving a method to clear a passage large enough for tanks. But it was extremely cumbersome and unsatisfactory.

Chief of Staff Shazly discovered it would take sixty men, five hundred pounds of explosives, a bulldozer and five to six hours of hard work to force one breach. This was in peaceful circumstances and involved only one passage. The Egyptians calculated they needed at least seventy passages to get the necessary amount of equipment into the Sinai. In war, "such knots of men would be irresistible targets for enemy artillery fire," Shazly observed dryly. He concluded: "It was an unrealistic scheme."

Then a young engineer, perhaps remembering how water pumps were used to scour sand away in the building of the Aswan High Dam, suggested the method be tried against the rampart. As the young engineer pointed out, the water was available in the canal. All that was needed were high pressure pumps.

The Egyptians experimented and discovered to their delight found that it worked. One cubic meter of sand could be removed with only one cubic meter of water. By using five high pressure British and West German pumps, the Egyptians could scour away 1,500 cubic meters of sand in as little as two hours. (In their own studies, the Israelis had concluded it would take at least twelve hours to breach the rampart.)

The Egyptian engineer corps established a rigorous training program in which teams practiced blasting 1,500 cubic meter passages twice a day and twice a night. The training was so extensive that it was estimated that it resulted in the movement of 1.5 million cubic meters of sand before the war. Eventually eighty teams became extremely efficient in gouging out passages through sand dunes. They used pumps that were gasoline-fueled and portable, and could be taken across the canal in boats.

The Egyptians at last had their Open Sesame—a method for breaching Israel's rampart, a method no one apparently had ever considered.

With the breaching problem solved, the Egyptian army could be assured that it would have the opportunity to get its armor into the Sinai and face the Israeli army on an equal footing. But there were still several fundamental obstacles to overcome, most pressingly how to destroy or neutralize Israel's system for setting afire the waters of the canal.

The Egyptians had seen Israel test one of the devices and found that it caused flames a meter high that burned for thirty to forty minutes at 700 degrees Centigrade. At first, the Egyptians experimented with men clad in fire-proof suits using palm fronds to beat out the flames. This obviously would not work under combat conditions. Another experiment was to use chemical fire extinguishers. General Shazly impatiently rejected both schemes. After much study, he concluded the only way to deal with the problem was to deny the Israelis use of the inflammable liquid so that there would be no fire in the first place.

The Israeli fire system consisted of three components: a reservoir holding about two hundred tons of imflammable liquid buried in the sand; an underground pipe leading to the canal; and an underwater outlet. At low tide, the outlet could be seen under about two feet of water. The Egyptians counted around twenty of them. Shazly's solution was to blast the reservoirs with artillery and satchel charges and to have rangers block the outlets by stuffing wet cement in their openings. In addition, he decreed that crossing points near the outlets should be upstream, so that the islands of flame would float harmlessly down stream.

Other factors facing the Egyptian general staff quickly fell into place. It was decided that the first assault wave would cross the canal in 720 boats carrying eight soldiers each, protected by a tremendous artillery barrage from four thousand guns. They would attack along the entire length of the canal. This was so they would present only a dispersed target and to confuse the Israelis about the thrust of their attack. Once ashore, they would face the strenuous task of scaling the high, steep rampart up rope ladders with full battle gear. It was estimated 32,000 troops would have to get across the canal in the first three hours in order to establish bridgeheads and begin the task of scouring passages through the rampart.

But here another problem cropped up. Since they would be fighting before armor came across, the assault troops needed to carry all the weapons, ammunition and water they could. But the average soldier can carry only about sixty-five pounds without suffering a marked drop in performance. The solution: Little golf-type carts were given to the soldiers so they could tote extra materiel. Experiments showed two men could drag as much as 375 pounds in the carts. During the war, 2,240 carts were used to transport 336 tons of equipment, an amount that it would have taken 22,400 porters to carry.

To sustain the bridgeheads, a thousand tanks and 13,500 support vehicles would have to cross within six hours after the ramparts had been breached. This meant bridges had to be constructed and ferries employed. To accommodate the heavy tanks, weighing thirty-six tons and up, ten heavy duty bridges would have to be placed across the canal. Five light bridges would also be put up to serve as decoys to attract enemy fire away from the heavy bridges. In addition, ten pontoon bridges would be constructed for infantry use.

The final major decision was to select the exact timing of the attack. After much study, the sixth day of October was chosen. Many factors were involved in the decision, including considerations about the height of the canal's tide, the time of moonset and the significant fact, as Egypt's generals thought at the time, that October 6 was Yom Kippur, the Jewish Day of Atonement, the most holy day in the Judaic calendar. On that day radio stations go off the air in Israel and nearly all Israelis are either at home fasting or in synagogues praying. It was also the tenth day of the Moslem holy month of Ramadan, Islam's month of fasting and prayer. The Egyptian generals calculated that Israel would least expect an attack during Ramadan.

The timing of the attack was set at 2 PM. This would mean the rays of the setting sun would shine in the eyes of the Israeli defenders along the canal. Another advantage of that time was that the canal would be in high tide both in its daily fluctuation and its monthly extremes. At its minimum, the tide changes two feet every six hours; at its maximum, as on October 6, it varies six feet between flood and ebbtide levels.

There was one other advantage in choosing October 6. On that day, the moon set at midnight, meaning the Egyptians would have partial moonlight while they were erecting the bridges in the evening and then total darkness for getting their vital armor across the canal. The final consideration was the fact that Israel was involved in the closing days of a hotly disputed election campaign, its attention diverted by the country's spirited domestic politics. The election was to take place October 28.

• •

Now, only one major aspect of Egypt's strategy was left—surprise.

The Israeli general staff assumed that it would have five to six days advance notice of an Arab attack—and at the worse no less than forty-eight hours—to mobilize its reserves and blunt any Arab attack. This seemed a safe assumption. It did not appear possible that any significant element of surprise could be achieved by the Arabs. The massing of modern armies, with their armor and motorized support vehicles and artillery and tens of thousands of men, appeared certain of detection in this day of air surveillance and electronic detection devices.

Nonetheless, Egypt correctly calculated that even in this area it could succeed. One of its most effective deceptions involved the repeated mobilization of its army. From the beginning of the year to the end of September, Egypt mobilized its reserves twenty-two times, holding them on duty for various periods from a few days to several weeks. The repeated mobilizations eventually served their purpose by making them routine and thus lulling Israel into taking them for granted. The deception continued to the outbreak of war. When the final mobilization began September 27, public announcements were made that the men would be released October 7.

All this activity took place within the framework of annual maneuvers. Since the 1967 war, Egypt and Syria had held fall maneuvers, indicating the depth of both countries' determination. One more maneuver, announced to start October 1, seemed much the same as earlier ones and raised no inordinate suspicions in Israel. Furthermore, Egypt and Syria had continuously maintained most of their armies on the frontline with Israel so that the administrative organizations already existed and were familiar to Israel. All that was needed to achieve deception was to flesh out the formations. This was done in Egypt by holding large maneuvers along the canal

127

by day, but when the units withdrew at night fewer left the canal than had arrived. Huge hidden storehouses were thus slowly stocked at the front line to provide the hundreds of tons of war material needed for Egypt's assault.

Syria did not need to be so cautious because of an incident that, while painful, turned out to be one of the biggest contributors to maintaining the secrecy of the war preparations. On September 13, a dogfight between Israeli and Syrian planes quickly escalated and resulted in the downing of twelve Syrian planes and one Israeli.

The aerial combat created a sensation, making headlines about the Syrians' defeat and sending a new sense of alertness through the armies in Syria as well as Egypt and Israel. As a result, from now until almost the hour of war, Israeli intelligence interpreted military preparations in both Syria and Egypt as stemming in large part from the September 13 air clash. The Israeli analysis was that Syria and Egypt apparently believed the incident was the precursor of an Israeli offensive and so their armies were taking defensive measures. In addition, of course, the incident was widely cited by Israelis and others as proof that the Arabs remained weak and had learned nothing since their 1967 defeat.

The Israeli general staff feared that Syria would retaliate, not by war but by an attack on one or more of Israel's settlements on the Golan Heights. Syria might make a land grab, Defense Minister Moshe Dayan suggested after the aerial combat. Chief of Staff Elazar doubted it but the three-day Rosh Hashanah holiday was approaching and so perhaps precautions should be taken "so we can rest easy on Rosh Hashanah," he said. He ordered reinforcements of twenty-five tanks onto the heights on September 26, the day before Rosh Hashanah. "We'll have one hundred tanks against their eight hundred," Elazar wisecracked. "That ought to be enough." Dayan told a reporter that day: "I hope the Syrians realize that any blow they land will hurt them more than it will us."

As the deadline to war approached, intelligence reports noted that Syria was going on a war footing. Its entire army was on alert and it had taken the unprecedented action of moving Sukhoi-7 warplanes to a forward air base. One report said Syria was going to attack with three divisions in an attempt to wrest back the heights. But such was Israeli overconfidence that, despite these accurate reports, the assessment of the Israeli general staff on September 30 remained that Syria was merely reacting to its own fears of an Israeli attack.

Disturbing reports about Egyptian preparations were also beginning to increase, but again the Israelis remained sanguine. Particularly reassuring to them had been a speech Sadat made on September 28, the third anniversary of Gamal Abdel Nasser's death. He had voiced no war threats. Indeed, he had spoken openly of Israel's power because of its support by the United States. True, he had said: "Perhaps you have noticed that there is one subject which I have not mentioned, the subject of the battle. I did this on purpose. We have had enough of words."

Anyone correctly assessing Sadat would have interpreted this as the warning it was. But in the eyes of Israeli intelligence chief Eli Zeira, Sadat was merely saying that he would not make the mistake again of declaring another "year of decision." Zeira advised the army and the government that war remained a "low probability."

Except for the unusual military activity, which could be explained by the annual maneuvers and the jitters caused by the September 13 air battle, most other indicators continued to point toward calm—as they were meant to. Egypt had insisted during the summer on a long debate in the U.N. Security Council that dragged through June and most of July. Only an American veto, the fifth ever cast by the United States, saved Israel from a strongly worded resolution condemning its continued occupation of Arab lands. Then Sadat deliberately leaked to a diplomat that he himself planned to go the United Nations in October, a story he expected would soon reach Israeli ears. Cleverly, Sadat was implicitly raising the question of why Egypt and he personally would be spending so much attention to the United Nations if the Arabs planned to go to war. In addition, the long debate in the United Nations had the advantage of reviewing all of the Arabs' grievances against Israel, reminding the world community that the Arab nation had legitimate complaints.

Beyond these false indicators of calm, the Arab world appeared hopelessly disunited, as usual. This was emphasized by a highly publicized and seemingly silly march in late July by 30,000 Libyans to Egypt. They were sent toward Egypt's border to dramatize Muammar Qadhafi's demand that union between his country and Egypt be achieved. The Egyptians stopped the Libyan horde at the border to prevent them from marching on to Cairo, as they vowed to do. It all appeared extremely embarrassing and caused more arch comments in Israel and America about impetuous and foolish Arabs.

Then came a dramatic development that galvanized Israeli and world attention. Probably as part of Egypt's deception plot (but never proved), two Palestinian guerrillas boarded a train carrying Soviet Jewish emigrants to a transit facility outside of Vienna on September 28 and took three hostages. They demanded the transit facility at Schonau Castle, operated by the Jewish Agency of Israel to help Soviet Jewish emigrants, be shut down. Chancellor

Bruno Kreisky complied, much to the consternation of Israel. Prime Minister Golda Meir was so outraged that she flew to Vienna to vent her rage. But the chancellor, a Jew but not a Zionist, refused to rescind his decision. The incident consumed Israel's irritation in the early days of October as the Arabs prepared for war.

By then, the Central Intelligence Agency had received enough disturbing reports that it asked Israel for its assessment of what was going on. One CIA report had said, with uncanny accuracy, that war was scheduled to start on the following Saturday, October 6. Israeli intelligence denied it. It replied that war was not near and its probability remained low. The activity in Syria and Egypt continued to be explained by Israel as the result of annual maneuvers and defensive actions.

Interestingly, the CIA had correctly predicted in a May 31 study that the "resumption of hostilities by autumn will become a better than even bet" if stalemate continued. But by the end of September that wisdom was ignored and all U.S. intelligence agencies agreed by consensus that war was not near. A subsequent House committee study of the failure of U.S. intelligence concluded that American analysts, like their Israeli counterparts, had suffered from an underestimation of the Arabs, believing that the Arab soldier "'lacks the necessary physical and cultural qualities for performing effective military services.' The Arabs were thought to be so clearly inferior that another attack would be irrational and, thus, out of the question," the report concluded. In short, racial prejudice helped prevent U.S. and Israeli intelligence analysts from interpreting correctly the data pointing to war.

While reports grew about Arab war preparations, Egypt's shrewd deception program continued to play on such prejudice and to confuse the picture. On October 2, Al Ahram published a brief story announcing that places were available for military officers who wished to visit the holy shrines at Mecca. On October 4, some 20,000 Egyptian reservists were reported to be demobilized. Diplomatic activity continued routinely. Preparations were underway for a visit to Egypt by Princess Margaret of England and the Rumanian defense minister was slated to see General Ismail on October 8.

• •

Hidden from view, ammunition and other stores were moved to the canal under darkness and camouflaged. Bridging equipment, difficult to hide, was not brought forward until the day before the attack. Units were now at full strength. All was in readiness on both the Egyptian and Syrian fronts.

130

COUNTDOWN TO WAR

Secretly, Sadat had already signed a "war order" on October 1 directing the Egyptian armed forces to attack Israel and to inflict the heaviest casualties so as to convince the enemy "that continued occupation of Arab land exacts a price that is too high for him to pay...." But still the world was lulled into believing nothing serious was occurring.

Israel even missed the significance on October 3 of another major clue that war was near. It came after Sadat and Assad informed the Russians that they had resolved to go to war. The impetuous Soviet reaction was to airlift its personnel out of the two countries, an action that Israel and the United States immediately detected but somehow missed its significance. On the same day, aerial photographs revealed to the Israeli general staff that the number of guns along the canal had grown from eight hundred to over 1,100 and that the five Egyptian divisions were up to full combat strength.

With all this mounting evidence, Israel finally became concerned enough to take action. On October 5, the eve of Yom Kippur, a "C Alert" was issued, the highest possible next to a general mobilization for war; it was the first declared "C Alert" since the 1967 war. Leaves were cancelled, the air force was put on a war footing and reinforcements were ordered for the both the Sinai and the Golan Heights.

But Defense Minister Dayan remained hesitant to call up reserves. Such an act might cause an Arab reaction and contribute to the spiraling military moves. More importantly, the general election was only weeks away. The Labor candidates' assurances of Israel's dominance were the principal domestic topic throughout Israel. For weeks the ruling Labor Party leadership had been reassuring the country that war was not imminent. If a mobilization were called now and then found to be unnecessary, it would reflect on the government and harm its leaders, particularly Dayan, at the ballot box.

As the streets of Israel's cities became deserted with the setting of the sun and the start of Yom Kippur on October 5, the day's newspapers gave no hint of a crisis. The elections were the big news. The Schonau Castle incident was still getting featured play. At a campaign rally, Golda Meir violently denounced Chancellor Kreisky, ending her speech with the declaration that "for as long as peace does not come we will remain in place where we are today—in the north, in the south and in the east." Only the day before, Chief of Staff Elazar had bragged: "The enemy must know that Zahal [Israel's army] has a long arm, and when this arm reaches the depth of his territory it turns into a fist!"

The other big news of the day was a story that Zaire had announced it

131

was breaking diplomatic ties with Israel because of its occupation of Arab land, the seventh African nation to do so in the past year. Counterbalancing that, Foreign Minister Abba Eban had just had a meeting with Henry Kissinger, who had become the fifty-sixth secretary of state on September 22. He found Kissinger "jocular and relaxed."

Eban told Kissinger that Israel did not believe war was near. "It seemed that American intelligence experts confirmed the Israeli view, and Kissinger was tranquil," recalled Eban in his memoirs. Then Kissinger said: "Well, you have your elections soon. In any case, nothing dramatic is going to happen in October." The meeting had taken place October 4.

The next day, Sadat formally signed his strategic directive to General Ismail. It ordered the armed forces to break the current ceasefire on October 6, to "inflict the greatest possible losses on the enemy" and to "work for the liberation of the occupied land."

Israel still was unaware war was near. Chief of military intelligence Zeira was by now concerned, but also as usual confused. He continued to insist that the possibility of a coordinated Arab attack was "lower than low" and a mass crossing of the canal "the lowest probability of all." Not even a telltale cancellation of all commercial air flights in Egypt and the dispersal of civilian planes the day before had convinced the Israelis about war. The cancellation mistake was quickly corrected but Shazly worried: "...surely the enemy would have learned of this and drawn the correct conclusions?" But it did not.

That same night, October 5, Egyptian rangers and frogmen slipped across the silent waters of the Suez Canal and neutralized the devices meant to set the canal's waters afire. They stuffed wet cement in the outlets and cut the fuel pipes while Israel's soldiers sat securely in their forts.

The war was less than twenty-four hours away. The five-to-six days that Israel had counted on for advanced notice had been missed. Not even the minimum time of forty-eight hours' warning was now possible. For all practical purposes, the Arabs had already achieved complete surprise.

• •

On the eve of battle, Egyptian Chief of Staff Saad Shazly climbed a forward observation tower at the edge of the canal to take a final look at the looming Bar-Lev Line. Less than three hundred yards away was the soaring rampart of sand. It looked, as many observers had attested, impregnable with its forts, artillery platforms, tank emplacements, pillboxes, barbed, razor and concertina wire, mines and booby traps—a daunting bastion stretching as far as the eye could see northward to the Mediterranean and

Europe and southward to the Red Sea and Asia. It was a stark and dramatic sight by the placid waters of the canal that had once been hailed as a highway to peace, making a mockery of monseigneur Bauer's inaugural address that the canal was the the victor over "one of the most formidable enemies of mankind, which is distance."

Directly in front of Shazly, across the narrow water of the canal, was Fort Purkan. The Egyptians called it Ismailia East because it was opposite that once-teeming canal city, long since emptied of its hundreds of thousands of civilians by Israeli bombardments. The fort dominated the Ismailia-Cairo road and was the strongest point in the central sector of the Bar-Lev Line. Anxiously, Shazly peered through a telescope at the Israeli stronghold. The thirty-three men inside were unaware of his attentions or of the approaching earthquake. There was no unusual activity. All was as quiet and undistrubed as the calm waters of the Suez Canal. The Yom Kippur prayers were soon to start. Shazly relaxed.

"The next time I saw that fort, I was convinced, it would be rubble in our hands," he thought.

•   •

That same night Shazly's Israeli counterpart drove home through the ghostly, deserted streets of Tel Aviv worrying whether he had not over-reacted by ordering a C Alert "on a day like this." Everything seemed so peaceful to General Elazar with the start of Yom Kippur.

133

PART TWO: WAR AND PEACE

October 6-25, 1973

CHAPTER XVI

October 6: War

SATURDAY

TEL AVIV

AT 4:30 IN THE MORNING the red telephone by the bed of Dado Elazar rang, waking the Israeli chief of staff after only a few hours sleep. It was his aide de camp, Lieutenant Colonel Avner Shalev, with "incontestable" intelligence information. Egypt and Syria were planning a coordinated attack at 1800 hours today. Elazar had "never imagined in his worst dreams" such peril facing Israel, such numerous enemies, such short warning time. He immediately ordered that his top commanders be informed. They were instructed to meet with him at general headquarters in Tel Aviv's Zahala district no later than 5:15 AM.

To his stirring wife on that fateful Saturday, Elazar said simply: "This is it. It's war."

From the start, Israel was plagued with bad luck. The attack was actually scheduled to begin at 1400 hours, four hours earlier than the Israeli command assumed. Somewhere along the chain of command, the initial report of an "afternoon" attack had become sunset and then became fixed at 6 PM. When Minister of Trade Haim Bar-Lev, the former chief of staff whose name adorned the Bar-Lev Line, questioned the odd timing, pointing out that it would be too late for Arab air attacks, he was told in a meeting with Elazar and Zeira later: "No, it will definitely be at 6 o''clock."

The error would add to the confusion and psychological shock throughout the day. Instead of an anticipated nearly fourteen hours, Israel in reality had only nine and a half hours left to prepare.

The short period of warning made Elazar almost wholly dependent on

137

the air force to blunt the initial Arab attack. Before leaving his house, he telephoned Major General Benyamin Peled, commander of the air force, and asked him how soon his planes could be ready. They would have to prepare to launch a preemptive attack and at the same time be ready to protect Israel's skies. Perhaps, Elazar suggested, a strong air strike could make the Arabs change their minds. He asked Peled the latest time he could order a preemptive attack. "Now, I must start preparing immediately," said Peled. Even with this much notice, it would take the air force until 11 AM to outfit warplanes and organize the attack. Elazar gave him the go-ahead to make preparations for an attack and then sped to the general headquarters.

Chief of Intelligence Zeira arrived at headquarters a short time after Elazar, still not convinced the Arabs would attack despite the "incontestable" information. "Let's act as if there will be a war," declared Elazar curtly. He ordered immediate mobilization of several thousand reservists and preliminary steps for a general mobilization. The final order would have to come from the political leadership, Prime Minister Meir and her cabinet.

By 6 AM, Elazar, Zeira and several others were in Defense Minister Dayan's Zahala office. Zeira continued to doubt there would be war, and he told Dayan that foreign sources were reporting all was quiet. Dayan tended to agree with the intelligence chief. After all, on that day many top Egyptian ministers were traveling around the world on "routine" business; the economic minister was in London, the commerce minister in Spain, the information minister in Libya and the foreign minister in Austria.

Sadat's finely honed deception plan was still in operation, still deceiving the Israelis.

Dayan refused Elazar's request for an air attack against the air forces of Egypt and Syria, thereby causing the air force to lose precious hours reconfiguring the weapons loads of its planes from the pre-emptive attack ordered by Elazar. Nor would he authorize mobilization of the 200,000 to 250,000 reservists Elazar wanted. With the elections only a short time away, and after the weeks of reassurances that there would be no war, Dayan was sensitive that if a general mobilization were called on the holy day of Yom Kippur and turned out to be a false alarm, he and the Labor Party would pay at the polls. Additionally, "I feared such moves would burden our prospects of securing the full support of the United States."

Elazar stood his ground. He demanded that four combat divisions, augmented by maintenance and artillery units, be called at once, but Dayan refused. To settle the question, the two men went to Prime Minister Golda

Meir's Tel Aviv office at 8 AM.

The meeting with Prime Minister Meir lasted until 9:20 AM. In the end, she too turned down a preemptive strike, mainly on grounds that she did not want to incur the anger of Washington, and compromised on the mobilization issue. Instead of the 50,000 men that Dayan favored and the quarter million that Elazar was demanding, she approved the mobilization of 100,000 to 120,000.

Meir next saw the U.S. ambassador, Kenneth B. Keating, who had arrived only that summer. She assured Keating that Israel would not launch a preemptive attack and would take no action to initiate hostilities. She requested that he ask Washington to contact Egypt, Syria and the Soviet Union and inform them that Israel was conducting a limited mobilization but had no desire for war.

As soon as he received Keating's report, Secretary of State Henry Kissinger personally telephoned diplomats from the three countries to convey the urgent message, but he was still "more than half convinced that Egyptian and Syrian [war preparations] grew out of a misunderstanding of Israeli intentions."

Dayan too remained unconvinced that war was near. Among other things, he obviously was still worried about the political impact of mobilizing so many reserves. At another meeting with Elazar, he asked: "And what if the Arabs don't open fire? When will the reserves be released?"

Elazar replied that he wanted to be sure first that Arab war plans had been cancelled.

"But what will happen if at midnight it turns out that there's no war?" pressed Dayan.

"The men won't be released for forty-eight hours," said Elazar.

"A hundred thousand men will hang around for a full day before they're sent home?" asked Dayan.

"They won't hang around," replied the patient chief of staff. "They'll go down to the front. If it turns out that there's no war, we'll release them within forty-eight hours."

The time was about noon, Saturday, October 6, Yom Kippur—two hours from war.

• •

CAIRO

At 1:30 PM, Anwar Sadat, smartly dressed in crisp military uniform, was driven in a Jeep the short distance from Cairo to Center Ten, the

139

modern headquarters of the Egyptian forces located deep underground in the desert. In the complex was the the operations center, a large, brightly lit room with walls covered by maps and clusters of desks representing all branches of the armed forces. Each group had its own tactical maps and communications to its field units. The main body of the room was taken up with a dais with places for Sadat, War Minister Ismail, Chief of Staff Saad Shazly and his deputy, Gamassi. On the wall was the strategic map of the battle area. Covering the map were glass panels showing the disposition of the troops and their movements on land, sea and air.

As Sadat took his place, the map showed Egypt with frontline troops of 200,000 men in two field armies, including five reinforced infantry divisions, 2,000 artillery pieces and 1,700 tanks. The Third Army, commanded by General Abdel Moneim Wassel, had responsibility for the northern sector stretching from Qantara to Deversoir at the northern end of the Great Bitter Lake and was comprised of the 18th, 2nd and 16th divisions. The Second Army, led by General Saad Din Mamoun, had responsibility for the rest of the canal to the south of Deversoir with the 7th and 19th divisions. The "seam" between these two armies, a separation of twenty to twenty-five miles that was left improperly guarded, was a fatal flaw in the Egyptian plan and would later cause the Egyptians no end of grief. But this would not become clear for many days.

Across the canal were 451 Israelis, mainly inexperienced reservists from Jerusalem, in twenty of the manned forts. The frontline troops were backed up by 18,000 men in a division of three armored and two infantry brigades with 290 tanks and 70 guns stationed in the center of the Sinai. Major General Avraham ("Albert") Mandler was in charge.

The vast Sinai Peninsula, covered by sand dunes and marshes in the north and stark mountains in the south where Moses was said to have received the Ten Commandments, was essentially empty of civilians. It presented a picture of timeless nature, of eternal forces indifferent to man.

The scene along the canal this historic day was deceptively peaceful. The Egyptian platoon commanders and their men had been officially informed only six hours before that war was to start. The lateness of the advisory was part of Egypt's successful deception plan. To keep the war plan secret, not even divisional commanders had been told of the time and day until October 3; brigade commanders were informed the next day and battalion and company commanders only on the 5th.

Despite the knowledge that war was to start in a few minutes, Egyptian soldiers maintained a studied routine of calm. Some fished in the canal, others did laundry. Some sat on the bank and drank coffee and chatted with friends. They wandered around without battle kits, without any apparent concern. On the Israeli side, religious Israelis observed the holy holiday and non-religious soldiers played soccer, sunned themselves and went about their normal chores. The panic being experienced by the Israeli high command had not yet filtered down.

Suddenly, at 1:45 PM, all went quiet on the Egyptian side. Soldiers disappeared. Muzzle covers over the barrels of artillery pieces and camouflage nets began to be removed. Out of sight, the operations room at Center Ten was abuzz with the clatter of telexes, the ringing of telephones, the scurrying of messengers and the issuing of orders and reception of reports. Anwar Sadat puffed on his pipe and sipped tea.

The soccer games on the Israeli side continued.

• •

THE SINAI

At 1:55 PM, under a clear Middle Eastern azure sky, the combined armies and air forces of Egypt and Syria flung themselves against Israel.

Air strikes by about 250 planes opened the assault at the Suez Canal by hitting radar sites, airfields, electronic jamming stations and command posts in the Sinai as well as the stronghold at Sharm el Sheikh at the strategic Straits of Tiran. At the same time, a thundering bombardment was opened by 2,000 high trajectory mortar and artillery pieces and another 2,000 flat trajectory cannons, mainly tank guns firing directly into the Bar-Lev Line. In the first minute, this massive attack unleashed an awesome 10,500 shells, varying in size up to 240mm, on Israeli positions. Several Frog missiles were also fired at targets deep in the Sinai.

Under the murderous bombardment, which lasted for an hour, reconnaissance teams and commandos furiously paddled across the canal to check that the fire devices had indeed been neutralized by the previous evening's raid and to lay ambushes for Israeli tanks racing to the combat area. At the same time, a thick smoke screen was laid down on the canal, obscuring its waters from the Bar-Lev Line. Twenty minutes after the start of the bombardment, the 4,000 men of the first Egyptian assault wave boarded 720 dinghies and disappeared into the smoke screen, rowing to the rhythmic chant of "Allahu Akbar," "Allahu Akbar"—god is great.

At a stronghold overlooking the Firdan Bridge north of Ismailia, an Israeli lookout identified only as Mordecai was stationed on a high observation tower when he felt a tremendous explosion that knocked out one of the four legs of the tower. The structure tilted precariously and Mordecai had

141

to hang on for dear life as he witnessed scores of Egyptian soldiers scale the rampart and assault the fort. Beneath him, the battle unfolded, men firing and dying, bombs exploding, machine guns clattering. But Mordecai heard none of it. He had been rendered deaf by a near explosion.

In the compound below Mordecai, Private Avitan watched the Egyptian assault with horror. The Egyptian troops, clad in grey uniforms, assaulted the wire fences, spraying the compound with flame throwers. Bullets and bombs were raking the area. "One man simply exploded and vanished before my eyes." An Egyptian soldier fell across the barbed wire, twitching and jerking as he bled to death. But still the Egyptians came.

The crossing and landing were an extremely intricate operation, involving twelve waves with a total of 32,000 assault troops. The danger of boats getting lost and units mixed up was great. Although enemy fire was kept to a minimum by the intense bombardment, the hundreds of boats had to navigate through the blinding clouds of the smoke screen in conditions of high danger and excitement. Landing sites had to be clearly marked and paths through the water rigorously adhered to in order to keep unit integrity. One man in each boat carried a large sign with the illuminated number of his vessel. Once ashore on the east bank, the numbered sign was stuck in the sand as a landing marker for following waves. Landing sites were separated by 25 yards within each company; there were gaps of 200 yards between companies, 400 yards between battalions, 800 yards between brigades. Gaps of as much as six miles separated divisions.

The first Egyptian flag was planted in the Sinai at 2:30 PM. Others soon followed, sending a surge of encouragement through the troops waiting to cross. At the same time, engineer platoons began ferrying across the high pressure pumps to scour the necessary passages through the rampart. By 2:45 PM the second wave of assault troops was across, landing 4,000 more men on the east bank. Succeeding waves crossed every fifteen minutes. At first, most of the troops moved directly into the Sinai, bypassing the forts, leaving them isolated behind the rapidly emerging Egyptian battle line beyond the Bar-Lev Line and ripe for picking.

The first fort fell at 3 PM. Before nightfall, nearly half of the forts were in Egyptian hands. Among the first Israeli prisoners taken was Lieutenant Shimon Tal, an engineer officer who had been sent to the Bar-Lev Line to explain to the troops how to operate the devices for setting the canal afire.

Israeli tanks, which inexplicably had been held far back by Southern Command commander General Shmuel Gonen rather than deployed for attack, now roared pell mell toward the canal to reinforce the embattled forts on the Bar-Lev Line. They were subjected to furious attacks. The Egyptian infantrymen blasted the tanks with hundreds of missiles—Saggers, Snappers and RPG-7s. The ferocity and destructiveness of these infantry weapons was a complete surprise to the Israelis, who had been trained in the conventional doctrine that held that the most deadly enemy of a tank is another tank, and the next most lethal weapon an anti-tank gun. Only after destroying these threats would tankmen bother firing at infantry. But the effectiveness of the Egyptian infantry missiles turned this doctrine upside down.

"I looked around and saw burning fireballs dancing through the air towards our tanks," said Barry Shamir, a loader-radio operator in an Israeli tank company speeding toward the canal. "I didn't yet grasp what was happening. Only later I understood these were missiles....All that day, I watched fireballs waltzing around the desert and being fired out of the sand dunes." Shamir's tank company was badly mauled by the missiles. Many of the tanks were knocked out of action, including Shamir's.

Repeatedly the Israeli tanks, totally disorganized, charged toward the besieged forts, desperately trying to save the men trapped by the invading Egyptians. Pitiful cries for help and reinforcements rose from the forts, but most of the dispersed Israeli armor was destroyed or repelled in ambushes by missile-carrying infantrymen. Those tanks that did manage to penetrate to the canal were met with a withering fire from Egyptian guns on the other side of the waterway. Within the first few hours, a battalion commanded by Lieutenant Colonel Yomtov had lost all but three of the twenty tanks it had set out with.

Throughout the early days of the war the screams and pleas of the entrapped men, many of them wounded, desperately trying to hold out in the forts would haunt the Israeli commanders. But in these early hours their plight still was not appreciated and they were refused permission to abandon their position.

• •

The effectiveness of the infantry missiles and the ability of the Egyptians to control them proved to be the biggest surprise of the war. The Sagger, dubbed the "suitcase missile" because its carrying case looked like one, had a range of up to 3,000 yards, better than a mile and a half, and traveled at 150 yards a second. It was guided by a hair-thin wire through which the operator controlled the missile's flight, meaning an infantryman had to expose himself for a half minute or so to aim and guide his missile in the daunting face of a tank armed with machine guns and a cannon. It took an extreme act of bravery to remain exposed in order to guide the missile the whole way to its target while a roaring tank charged.

143

The Sagger's high explosive shaped warhead was hollow and lined with copper. When it hit a tank, the shell in effect imploded, melting the copper which then spewed out in a molten jet that burned its way through armor. Even in cases where the jet stream did not penetrate, its searing heat of 1,000 degrees often was enough to set off fires inside the tank, incinerating the crew. The Snapper and the RPG-7 (for rocket propelled grenade) carried a similar warhead but had less range than the Sagger. The Snapper, also wire controlled, was effective up to 2,000 yards; the RPG-7 only to 450 yards. As its name indicated, the "bazooka" RPG was a missile fired from a hollow tube on an unguided trajectory.

These missiles were potent enough to penetrate even the frontal armor of Israel's Patton and Centurion tanks, which made up the major portion of its armor. All together, Israel had about 1,900 tanks, including 700 British Centurions, 450 U.S. M-48 Pattons, 250 Ben Gurions (modified Centurions), 250 Super Shermans, 150 U.S. M-60s and 100 captured Soviet T-54s and T-55s. All Israeli tanks fired a 105mm gun equipped with an American computerized fire control system that assured a high ratio of single-shot kills.

Only Israel's M-60 tanks had armor strong enough to withstand the shaped warheads of the missiles. But these tanks, the latest in the U.S. inventory, had vulnerabilities that the Egyptians soon discovered, no doubt much to the delight of the Soviets. The turret of the M-60 was activated by an inadequately protected hydraulic system (unlike the Centurion, which used a geared motor), and the fluid burned at a low temperature. When hit, it exploded into flames, incinerating the four-man crew inside. Another fault was in the design of the storage areas for ammunition and fuel. They had been located too close together, with the result that the combination often exploded under the impact of a missile that had not even penetrated the armor.

• •

It was not until 4 PM that Israeli air strikes in force hit the Egyptian positions along the west bank of the canal. The Israeli planes came under murderous fire from Egypt's dense antiaircraft screen. During the first attack at least half of the Israeli jets were blasted from the sky.

A U.N. observer, stationed along the canal as part of the observer corps put in place at the end of the 1967 war, reported that in another attack four out of five Israeli planes were hit. The Egyptians reported downing twenty-seven Israeli planes that day with a loss of eight of their own. When Israel countered that it had downed thirty Egyptian planes and lost only four of its own, one Israeli soldier on the front line in the Sinai where Israeli planes were plunging from the sky was heard to remark: "We have taught the Egyptians how to fight, and they have taught our radio announcers how to lie." Whatever the truth of the conflicting claims, the fact is that before the day was out Israeli pilots were ordered to stay a minimum of ten miles from the canal to avoid the deadly missiles.

By 5:30 PM, the twelfth wave of Egyptian assault troops was across the canal, making a total of 32,000 men facing Israel's disorganized and understrength forces. The Egyptians quickly established five bridgeheads, each about five miles long and three miles into the Sinai. In addition, a special amphibious brigade equipped with PT-76 light tanks had crossed the Great Bitter Lake and made a dash to the Giddi and Mitla passes. Some of the tanks had got within range of the passes when the Egyptian force ran into a reserve Israeli brigade rushing to the Bar-Lev Line. The Israeli unit had M-60 tanks and Centurions and mauled the thinly armored PT-76s, forcing the Egyptians to withdraw to the Egyptian lines at Great Bitter Lake.

As dusk fell, fifty helicopters filled with Egyptian commandos infiltrated deep into Sinai near the Giddi and Mitla passes in the central sector. In the north, other commandos were infiltrated by boats to the region east of Budapest, the northern most of the fortresses, where they could intercept Israeli reinforcements pouring into the battle zone over the seacoast road.

At 6:30, the first breach in the rampart was opened. Thirty-one ferries were by now ready to begin floating tanks and other vehicles across the canal. Some 15,000 engineering troops had erected ten dummy bridges at ten-mile intervals with decoy trucks on them. Egyptian pilots claimed they could not tell the difference between the dummies and the real bridges. These were made of metal pontoons of various types although they had been modified to make them all interchangeable. Here, in the contrast between the various models of bridges, the reasons for Sadat's demands on the Soviets for more and better weapons were well highlighted. Some of the bridges, such as the old Soviet World War II TPP (Tyaxheli Pontonnyi Park), were cumbersome, required as many as 150 vehicles to carry them and took up to at least a minute to erect four feet. By contrast, the modern Soviet PMP (Pontonno Mostovoy Park) bridge could be carried in only 40 vehicles and erected at the rate of 15 feet a minute, but the Egyptians had only three of these. All told, the convoy carrying the bridging equipment extended 185 miles.

The first bridge was opened at 8:30 PM and a stream of Egyptian tanks began pouring into the Sinai. By then, sixty passages had been scoured through the rampart. Within the next two hours, all of the ten heavy bridges were open to armored traffic except three in the Third Army sector in the south. In that area, clay mixed with the sand had turned into a viscous mud under the pounding of the high pressure pumps and had delayed the scouring operation. In addition to the heavy bridges, four light bridges for use by infantrymen had also been constructed. The way to the Sinai was now wide open.

Operation Badr had been a stunning success.

The crossing that everyone claimed could not be made was well underway. Not only that, but the casualties had been almost insignificant compared to what Egyptian planners had anticipated. They had feared that the crossing would cost as many as 30,000 casualties. But at the end of October 6, Egyptian losses were only 208 dead.

As military historian Trevor N. Dupuy summed up: "The combination of thorough and efficient planning, careful security, the achievement of complete surprise, and the highly efficient execution of carefully prepared plans, resulted in one of the most memorable water crossings in the annals of warfare. As with the planning, no other army could have done better."

• •

THE GOLAN HEIGHTS

On the Golan Heights, frontline dispositions pitted 60,000 Syrian soldiers in three infantry and two armored divisions, nearly 1,300 tanks and 600 guns to Israel's 12,000 men in three armored brigades, 177 tanks and about 70 artillery pieces. The Golan was a desolate, windswept plateau of volcanic rock where the two armies were confined to a narrow area that provided little room for tank maneuvering. The plateau extended about 50 miles north to south and 20 miles east to west, lying directly across the ancient trade route from Damascus to Upper Galilee in Palestine. The terrain was rough, covered by old volcano cones and heaps of basaltic rocks, rent by deep wadis and thrusting cliffs and tels.

To the north soared Mt. Hermon, Jebel Sheikh to the Arabs, a 9,223-foot mountain topped by a strong fortress from where Israeli observers could look all the way to Damascus, thirty miles beyond the Purple Line. Since its capture in 1967, Israel had constructed its most important electronic listening post on this cloud shrouded peak that was often covered with snow. The Mt. Hermon base was heavily fortified and usually manned by about fifty Israelis. Because the snow lasted nearly year-around, Israel had also turned the slopes of Mt. Hermon into a ski resort complete with a ski lift. Within an hour's drive, Israelis could water ski on the Sea of Galilee and snow ski on Mt. Hermon overlooking the biblical sea.

The west of the plateau provided a view of all of northern Israel, explaining the strategic value of the Heights. It was a commanding panorama of villages and fields and fish farms that Israelis had developed in the Huleh Valley to supplement their diet with carp and other fish. Before the 1967 war, when the Heights were in Syrian hands, much of northeastern Israel lay exposed to Syrian guns. A small parcel of land, 66.5 square kilometers, at the base of the Heights had been designated a demilitarized zone in the 1949 armistice agreement between Israel and Syria, but Israel had slowly absorbed it against U.N. complaints. The Syrians had responded by shelling Israeli farmers whenever they tried to cultivate the disputed land, another constant irritant inflaming relations between the two countries.

The western edge of the plateau precipitously dropped to the Jordan Valley and the Sea of Galilee. The escarpment then twisted along the Yarmuk River, a tributary of the Jordan, to make up the southern boundary of the plateau and mark the frontiers between Syria, Jordan and Israel. From south to north, the plateau rose from 600 feet to 3,000 feet. On the east lay the Purple Line, the ceasefire line concluded at the end of the 1967 war, and the plains of Syria. On either side of the line were the armies of Israel and Syria, Israel to the west, Syria to the east. They were separated only by a no-man's land of a mile width that was patrolled by U.N. observers.

•   •

In the six years since the last war, Israel had emplaced strong fortifications on its conquered territory. An antitank ditch had been excavated the entire length of the Purple Line, varying in width from six to eight yards and about six yards deep. Gravel and stone from the ditch had been piled up on the western bank of the ditch to form a protective embankment. Mine fields covered both sides of the ditch.

Paralleling the ceasefire line, Israel had constructed seventeen heavily fortified observation posts to overlook the antitank ditch, many of them dug into volcano cones. Ten to thirty men were stationed in each bunker-like fort, which enjoyed clear fields of fire and were supported by three tanks each, mine fields and barbed wire.

Interspersed among the Israeli and Syrian positions on both sides of the Purple Line were U.N. observation posts, seven on each side manned by two officers at all times. Their duty was to report on ceasefire breaches, which, according to their commander, Colonel Keith Howard of Australia, occurred at the rate of about twenty a day. The observation posts had radios

147

and, through relays, could get reports to the secretary general in New York almost instantaneously.

Though there were a number of small villages on the Syrian side, there was only one Syrian city, Kuneitra, perched on the Heights. It had been largely destroyed and systematically plundered by Israeli troops in 1967 and now stood in Israeli territory as a curiosity for Israeli tourists. The Syrian villages on the occupied part of the Heights had been razed by the Israelis and their inhabitants scattered, leaving the Israeli area devoid of Syrian civilians. In their place now were more than twenty Jewish settlements that Israel had established since 1967.

Syria's forces on the Heights were strong and well equipped. Aside from five divisions, it also had a formidable antiaircraft network. It included 100 batteries of SA-2, 3 and 6 missiles with around 500 ready missiles and 162 guns, many of them the lethal ZSU-23/4s.

The Syrians, like the Egyptians, had prepared well for the war. Under chief of intelligence Brigadier General Gabriel Bitar, aggressive reconnaissance patrols behind Israeli lines had revealed detailed intelligence about the Israeli defenses. This information had been converted into large scale maps of each combat sector as well a detailed mock up of the strong Israeli fortress atop Mt. Hermon. Capture of the lofty strongpoint atop Mt. Hermon was one of Syria's prime war aims. Its strategic goal was to recapture the Golan Heights within thirty hours, about half the time the Syrians estimated it would take Israel to get reinforcements to the plateau.

Israel's three brigades of 12,000 men, 177 tanks and 70 guns on the Heights included one of the most storied units in the Israel Defense forces. This was the 7th Brigade, which had battled heroically at Latrun and the approaches to Jerusalem in 1948. In 1956, it fought its way to the Suez Canal and repeated the feat again in 1967. It was, said General Chaim Herzog, the former chief of military intelligence, "the elite of the armored forces." The 7th's commander was Avigdor Ben-Gal, a tall, blue-eyed aristocratic looking veteran who was destined to bring even greater glory to his brigade. The other brigades were the Golani and Barak.

On the day war erupted, the 7th Brigade was deployed from the slopes of Mt. Hermon south to Kuneitra. It faced a Moroccan brigade and the Syrian 7th Infantry and 3rd Armored divisions and elements of the 9th Infantry division, which was deployed in the central sector opposite Kuneitra. The Barak Brigade was opposite the Syrian 5th Infantry and 1st Armored divisions in the south and parts of the 9th in the center. All of the Syrian infantry divisions had four brigades, one infantry, one tank and two mechanized, making them in effect reinforced mechanized infantry divisions. One or the other of the Syrian armored divisions was to be held in strategic reserve. The Golani Brigade was also being held in reserve.

At 1:45 PM, the Israeli observers on Mt. Hermon noticed unusual activities in the Syrian army behind the Purple Line. "Look, they are removing the camouflage nets from the guns!" said an artillery officer nicknamed Bambi.

A few minutes later, an excited UNMO, a U.N. military observer stationed at Observation Post 3 on the Israeli side of the Purple Line, reported to his headquarters, code named Tango, at Tiberias on the Sea of Galilee: "Tango, Tango from OP three. Sitrep, over."

The reference to sitrep meant he had a situation report to communicate. This was a very formal and precise format for reporting the time, the country, the incident and comments on a ceasefire violation. But the UNMO, Captain Harry Bloom of Canada, was too overwhelmed by the amazing scene unfolding before his eyes to follow protocol.

"Syrian army moving," shouted Bloom. "Too numerous to count."

Commented observer commander Colonel Howard dryly, "This rather astonishing message was our first report that the war had begun."

• •

As in the Sinai, the Syrian attack opened just before 2 PM with a massive, hour-long artillery and air bombardment all along the Purple Line. About 100 planes took part in the attack along with hundreds of guns, which included 130mm and 152mm artillery pieces.

Under the protection of this heavy bombardment, the well-trained Syrian units moved on the offensive. "It was not like an attack, it was like a parade-ground demonstration," said one awed U.N. observer, Australian Major George Mayes. Flail tanks lashed the ground, exploding mines and making paths through the thick mine fields. However, confusion in their deployment left bulldozers caught in heavy traffic behind the frontline, meaning infantrymen at first had to brave murderous Israeli fire to fill in the antitank ditch by shovels. Finally, the bulldozers arrived and filled parts of the antitank ditch or gouged routes through its banks while other engineering units laid portable bridges across the ditch, allowing tanks to advance with the infantry.

Israeli resistance was fierce and at first effective.

In the north, as Syrian tanks of the 7th Division tried to thrust through a shallow valley toward a road linking Kuneitra and El Rom, several miles to the north, tanks of the renowned Israeli 7th Brigade repulsed them. The Israelis were in prepared ramps atop a low hill behind the road, looking

149

down on the Syrians. With their tanks hull down, the Israelis blasted the Syrian tanks as they gingerly navigated their way through defiles in the lava strewn terrain doted with volcano cones and wadis, picking off tank after tank at ranges of more than 2,000 yards. Tanks turned into bonfires; as many as sixty were knocked out.

It was a slaughter and the momentum of the Syrian northern attack was blunted. The 7th Division's infantrymen were forced to dig in on the bank of the antitank ditch for protection. Another attack after darkness was also repulsed with heavy Syrian losses. But the Syrians had not yet given up their determination to take the valley that became known to the Israelis as the "valley of tears" because of the slaughter there.

It was not only the 7th Brigade that was reporting heavy Syrian losses. Initial reports from the field indicated considerable success all along the line by the Israeli tankmen in destroying Syrian armor. The enemy tanks were being picked off "just like on the firing range," said one report.

But for the Israeli troops there was an ominous pattern developing in both the skies and on the ground. Israeli tank crews noted that as their air support roared in to knock out the Syrians, one after another of the planes was blasted from the air by the dense Syrian missile screen. As many as thirty Israeli planes were lost that afternoon. And, despite the horrendous losses, the Syrian tanks came on, a mass of armor and men never before seen by Israel on the Golan Heights.

In the central sector, the 9th Syrian Division crossed just south of Kuneitra, also with heavy losses, but unstoppable by Israel's meager forces. Its tanks broke through the Israeli line at Kudne and bypassed the strong fort there, called A6, rolling westward toward the main Tapline or Petroleum road, so-called because it paralleled the Trans-Arabian pipeline transporting oil from Bahrein and Saudi Arabia to Lebanon. The road led northward to the Israeli command headquarters at Nafekh, only several kilometers away.

The biggest breakthrough came in the northern section of the southern sector, where the terrain was better for tank maneuvering. The 5th Syrian Division penetrated through the defenses of the Barak Brigade at two fort positions designated A7 and A10, and surged toward the Tapline road. The steady combat chewed up the small force of Israeli tanks. By late evening the Barak Brigade's ninety tanks had been reduced to fifteen and the units manning the fortresses were surrounded. Three of the Israeli forts had to be evacuated and Syrian armor was marauding within six miles of the Jordan River.

Equally important, a Syrian ranger unit had succeeded in overwhelming

150

the Israelis at Mt. Hermon and capturing that important installation after bitter fighting. The force of 500 heliborne rangers charged head-on the well prepared concrete defenses connected by tunnels. They were cut down by heavy machines, halted a hundred yards short of their objective with the loss of more than fifty casualties. The rangers then worked their way around to the west and charged with the setting sun blinding the Israeli defenders. They overran all the outer positions and then scaled a high concrete wall protecting the main Israeli defensive position.

The Israeli defenders were killed or taken prisoner, and then the rangers moved to capture the vital communications center. It was protected by a heavy steel door. A prisoner was beaten until he revealed how to manipulate a series of electronic buttons to open the door. The few men inside surrendered and the Syrians found themselves the new owners of a sophisticated electronic intelligence and communication network. Later, the Syrians showed their gratitude for Moscow's friendship by turning the advanced technology over the Soviet Union, which had been unsuccessfully trying for several years to buy it in Japan, where it had been produced.

All told, only eleven of the fifty-five Israeli defenders managed to escape. All the rest were either killed, including Bambi who had first sighted the Syrians removing their camouflaging, or taken prisoner. The vital observation post was now in Syrian hands and would remain so until the last day of the war.

• •

AMMAN

King Hussein telephoned both Sadat and Syrian leader Hafez Assad when word of the fighting spread. Although he had in a general way known about the war plans, he had not been informed of its timing. Now he was told it was on. Both leaders urged him to join the war, opening a third front along the Jordan River. Hussein put his armed forces on full alert. But then he hesitated. The memory of his losses in 1967 was fresh. He decided to wait.

• •

TEL AVIV

At the outbreak of war, the Israeli general command moved into its war quarters, a deep underground facility dug in a bluff north of Tel Aviv near the Mediterranean beach. The labyrinth of rooms, halls and descending

151

staircases was appropriately called the Pit. Like its Egyptian counterpart, Center Ten, it was dominated by a war room with wall maps, communications equipment and scurrying messengers and staff officers. Chief of Staff Elazar has his own office, a small, cramped, windowless room outfitted with a cot. The sudden shock of the war brought a stream of retired senior officers to the Pit. They were anxious to offer advice, impatient to hear the latest battlefield reports. They crowded into Elazar's small room, their cigarette smoke fouling the close air, coming and going hour after hour as the chief of staff tried to understand the developments on the battlefield, which were by no means clear.

Defense Minister Dayan met with Elazar in the Pit Saturday evening and found the activity there "like a beehive, but without the honey." He was consistently less optimistic than the generals.

Reports from the field were contradictory. Several canal forts were first reported to have fallen; then the reports were denied. It was unclear whether Mt. Hermon had fallen or not. The attack of the Syrian 7th Division had been blunted in the north of the Golan Heights and as a result things there were judged "not terribly serious." The civilians in all the settlements had been successfully evacuated.

Reports of the fierce resistance by Israeli forces also tended to reinforce the idea that the battle was going as well as expected with the forces on hand. As late as 6:30 PM, the general staff believed that Israeli casualties were only fifteen dead and thirty-five wounded—"relatively light," observed Elazar. In fact, they were in the hundreds, but the command did not know that yet. As a result, the general feeling in the Pit that Saturday night was that "things aren't so bad."

That was the impression Elazar conveyed to the cabinet at an emergency meeting called at 10 PM. At that time, he reported, mistakenly, the Syrian attack had been halted. The Egyptians had been more successful, he said, since they had managed to cross the canal at several points and at least one fort had fallen. However, mobilized reservists would start arriving in the Sinai on Sunday and by the next day Israel should have 750 tanks operating in the south. By then, Israel would be able to go over from defense to offense.

Some of the cabinet members favored going on the offensive immediately and pushing the Egyptian tanks out of the Sinai. Dayan was disheartened by what he considered false optimism. He dourly noted that "they were seized by the optimism in the chief of staff's survey and above all by their own wishful thinking. We were not on the same wavelength." He warned the cabinet that the Egyptian and Syrian armies were "not the Arab armies we had known in 1967. They were good troops using good equipment and fighting with determination.''

At this point, it appeared to Dayan that the canal front was the more critical, although he thought that once reinforcements were in place the ''prospects for success were good.'' Nonetheless, he suggested that since the fighting in the Sinai was taking place in desert wastes where no strategic point was threatened, the thin Israeli forces should withdraw to a second line about twelve miles east of the canal. His cabinet colleagues did not think highly of Dayan's pessimistic suggestion, and Elazar took no action on it.

The first day of war ended with the Israeli cabinet and the general staff convinced that the battle was going about as well as could be expected and that ultimate victory was not far away.

• •

CAIRO

Anwar Sadat was as sanguine as his Israeli counterparts, but for better reasons. He had followed the crossing in Center Ten, marvelling that ''the whole thing was overwhelming—truly astounding. I followed up the action...in perfect peace of mind, with complete calm...and if anybody had penetrated my apparent outward tranquility they would have found me equally calm within. I had no anxiety of any kind; any worries that might have existed before were now entirely dispelled.''

The Egyptian leader was so confident, in fact, that he felt after five hours and forty minutes in the war room that he could leave the war to the generals. He gave lavish praise to all involved in the war and went to Tahirah Palace to meet with the Soviet ambassador. Sadat thought the envoy had an answer for him about his question of what the Soviet reaction was to the war. But he was in for a shock. Instead of news from Moscow, Ambassador Vinogradov had a stunning message from Damascus: Syria wanted a ceasefire. President Hafez Assad, apparently hedging his bets against a repeat of 1967, had asked the Soviets even before the war started to work for a ceasefire within forty-eight hours after the start of the war. It was within that time, of course, that the Syrian general staff had concluded it would reconquer the Golan Heights.

Sadat challenged the Soviet about this startling but believable news, saying he doubted it. But he added: ''However, I'd like to inform the Soviet leaders that even if Syria did demand it, I won't have a ceasefire until the main targets of my battle have been achieved.''

When the ambassador left, Sadat sat down and wrote Hafez Assad a message. He wanted to know if his Syrian ally really wanted a ceasefire. Certainly Egypt did not, not when the war was going so well.

• •

WASHINGTON

Optimism about Israel's position remained the general attitude in Washington. Even two hours after war had actually broken out, the combined intelligence agencies of the United States still did not believe hostilities were likely or the Arabs capable of such coordinated action. In a report to the hastily formed WSAG, the Washington Special Action Group presided over by Henry Kissinger, the intelligence agencies said: "We can find no hard evidence of a major, coordinated Egyptian/Syrian offensive across the canal and in the Golan Heights area....It is possible that the Egyptians or Syrians, particularly the latter, may have been preparing a raid or other small-scale action."

When a short time later it was finally confirmed that war indeed was raging once again in the Middle East, the general belief was that Israel had started it. Kissinger's immediate reaction was that "we had to assure the survival and security of Israel; we needed to maintain our relations with moderate Arab countries, such as Jordan and Saudi Arabia....From the first, I was convinced that we were in a good position to dominate events."

Kissinger himself was certainly in a dominant position, since now he was not only the the secretary of state but he also remained the national security adviser, the first person to serve in both of these powerful offices simultaneously. He completely dominated America's foreign policy. Richard Nixon was in a less enviable position. He was drowning in scandals. The first of a string of criminal indictments flowing from Watergate was just being handed down by the courts. Among others, Presidential counselor John Ehrlichman, once one of Nixon's closest advisers, had been indicted, and campaign worker Donald Segretti had pleaded guilty to playing "dirty tricks" in the 1972 campaign. Nixon's vice president, Spiro Agnew, was plea bargaining to escape prison for taking illegal payoffs while he was governor of Maryland.

As Nixon recalled: "The immensely volatile situation created by the outbreak of this war could not have come at a more complicated domestic juncture."

When war broke out, Nixon was licking his political wounds in his Florida retreat at Key Biscayne. He was to take little direct action in the pursuit

154

of U.S. policy during the war. That was left to his secretary of state, who accepted the responsibility with alacrity.

Kissinger's first assumption, like that of nearly everyone outside of the Middle East, was that Israel would quickly prevail over the Arabs. As he complacently said to Alexander Haig, Nixon's chief of staff, America should let Israel "beat them up for a day or two and that will quiet them down."

This belief was reinforced by the Israelis themselves. In a message from the Israeli government, relayed to Kissinger by Foreign Minister Eban, the United States was informed that "there are good prospects" that Israeli forces would repel the Egyptians and Syrians within three days. In a Saturday night meeting with the Soviet Ambassador, Anatoly Dobrynin, Kissinger said: "Our reading of the situation is that the Arab attack has been totally contained, that now they are going to be pushed back and this process will accelerate as the [Israeli] mobilization is completed which will be no later than Monday morning and after that we will see what we have seen before."

Kissinger had already decided on a diplomatic ruse to contain the conflict and, perhaps, distance the Soviet Union from its Arab allies. He proposed a joint approach to the U. N. Security Council by Washington and Moscow calling for an immediate ceasefire. Under his plan, neither superpower would assess blame. More significantly, he wanted the combatants to return to the lines they held at the outbreak of war—an astonishing proposal since it meant the Arabs would have to return to Israel whatever gains they had made in recapturing the territory they lost in 1967.

Not unreasonably, Dobrynin was not impressed with Kissinger's idea. He pointed out that the Arabs were trying to regain land that had been taken from them by force. "...for us to tell them you cannot free your land, it is ridiculous," he pointed out with reasonableness.

• •

It was only during the darkness of Sunday morning, the second day of the war, that the gravity of Israel's position began sinking in on Chief of Staff Elazar and the government of Prime Minister Golda Meir. But still no one could believe it. The country was in shock. Yet by this time the Syrians were threatening the very heartland of the Jewish state and the Egyptians were decimating Israel's forces in the Sinai.

CHAPTER XVII

October 7: Trial and Error

ISRAEL'S POSITION ON THE GOLAN HEIGHTS was extremely grave. Syrian forces were at the very entry to northern Israel, poised to roll down the Heights onto the Israeli towns and cities of Upper Galilee. It still was not appreciated by the Israeli general staff how bad things were in the Sinai, but that was almost a disguised blessing. It left the generals time to concentrate on the disastrously deteriorating situation in the north. They realized that Syria's thrust had to be contained at all costs. Syrian troops could not be allowed to penetrate into Israeli territory, only short miles away, for psychological reasons as much as military ones. That meant they had to be prevented at all costs from descending down the Heights. The decision was made that Sunday to concentrate on the defense of the Golan Heights.

However, one man, Moshe Dayan, had no illusions about Israel's perilous position. He was so distraught that he apparently believed the only thing that could save Israel was use of the nuclear bomb. Rumors, never documented but widely believed, swept Tel Aviv and Washington on this day that Israel had activated its nuclear weapons and was prepared for a time to use them.

• •

SUNDAY

THE GOLAN HEIGHTS

Israeli defenses in the southern front on the Golan Heights began collapsing during Sunday's early morning hours. All along the line, Syrian tanks penetrated, bypassing the helpless forts and moving straight to the north-

156

south Tapline road in daring night fighting. It was an unexpected move, since the Israelis had been informed that the Syrians were not trained for night fighting. But now Syrian tanks, equipped with night vision devices and glowing infrared reflectors, could be seen operating everywhere, their eerie lights "like hundreds of cats' eyes" probing the darkness.

In an effort to understand what was going on, Colonel Yitzhak Ben Shoham, commander of the Barak Brigade charged with holding the southern sector, moved his advance headquarters from Nafekh in the middle of the western Golan to Juhader, about six miles to the south, and discovered how precarious the Israeli position had become. When he attempted to link up with his 3rd Battalion's headquarters near Juhader he found it was surrounded. Radio reports from his units were discouraging. Casualties were high. Throughout the sector, Israeli forces were running out of ammunition. Most of their armor was either destroyed or out of operation.

A major Syrian breakthrough had occurred at Hushniyah, between Juhader and the Nafekh headquarters, and Syrian tanks were now operating west of the Tapline road, meaning the important passage was blocked and Ben Shoham himself surrounded. Exploiting the breakthrough, the Syrians committed the 1st Armored Division and a mechanized brigade of the 3rd Armored Division in the south, making the force there 600 tanks strong.

By now, the Barak Brigade had only twelve tanks left. The first Israeli reinforcements had started arriving only late the previous evening, seven tanks from the 17th Reserved Armored Brigade. They were immediately thrown into the breach but by early morning they had been wiped out. As other tanks arrived, they were committed piecemeal in twos and threes against the Syrians in a desperate effort to stem the advance. But against the massive weight of Syria's numbers they were having little effect. Worse for Colonel Ben Shoham, the major part of Israel's reserves could not be expected to start to arrive on the plateau until around midday.

Under pressure from the Syrian advance, Ben Shoham withdrew farther southward to the edge of the escarpment near Ramat Magshimim on the road leading down the plateau to Ein Gev. He discovered the Syrians had penetrated even this far westward. He could see Syrian armor close enough to the escarpment that the Sea of Galilee was clearly visible.

Alarmed by the increasingly desperate reports, Defense Minister Dayan flew to the Golan Heights at dawn and discovered that the Israeli brigade in the south had completely collapsed. Dayan was appalled. He ordered Major General Dan Laner to "go down and prepare the Jordan bridges for demolition!" Laner later observed: "I understood that to mean that we were going to come down from the Golan." When Laner checked the order with

Elazar, he was ordered "not to wire any bridges for demolition."
Dayan was so worried that he also personally called Benny Peled, the air force commander. Dayan told Peled that his planes had to desert standard doctrine, which dictated that antiaircraft missiles first be destroyed before hitting other targets, and instead directly attack the advancing Syrian armor. "Otherwise we would lose the southern half of the Golan....I realized that the only force that could hold up the enemy advance at this moment was the air force, and not a minute was to be wasted."

The planes came in fours. As the Skyhawks swooped in they were accompanied by the whoosh of Syrian missiles. "All four planes exploded in the air in full view of the hard-pressed troops," reported General Chaim Herzog. "Undeterred, a second flight of four planes flew in. Two exploded." Nonetheless, the Israeli air force bravely pressed its attack, having, in Dayan's words, "a decisive effect on the situation." During this critical Sunday and the next day Israel would lose at least thirty aircraft on the Golan. The sacrifice stemmed Syria's attack.

The ferocity of the fighting made it clear to Chief of Staff Elazar that the situation on the Golan Heights was so critical that he had to order the air force to devote all its energies to the Golan. He also committed the 14th Armored Division to the heights, rather than sending it to the Sinai as originally planned.

From her verandah in Tiberias on the Sea of Galilee, Joan Howard, wife of U.N. northern observer commander Colonel Keith Howard, could clearly see and hear the desperate battle. "Sounds of battle on the Golan," she recorded on notes made at the time. "Big tank battle. Heavy artillery. Air battles. Sighted burning aircraft falling into lake (near Capernaum) and others directly opposite our house. Can see the tank battle from Verandah. Therefore the Syrians are half way down the Golan on the slopes nearest the lake [Sea of Galilee]. Continual air strikes by Israelis."

• •

Colonel Ben Shoham could not link up with any of his besieged forces in southern Golan, which was now crawling with Syrian tanks. The Tapline road back to the Nafekh was cut off. As the enemy armor pressed toward his hideaway among the boulders around Ramat Magshimim, Ben Shoham had his tank and a following half-track descend from the plateau down to the Jordan Valley. From there, he worked his way north and reascended the escarpment, arriving at the Nafekh headquarters at 9 AM. His report was grim. Most of the Barak Brigade was gone, destroyed by the Syrian onslaught. All that was left were two small units, one blocking the Syrian advance northward along the Tapline road and another that was isolated at Tel Faris near the Hushniyah gap where the Syrians had broken through in force.

Ben Shoham decided to join the fight on the Tapline road. By midmorning he reported back to the Nafekh headquarters: "I must have knocked out eight tanks so far."

More Israeli reserve tanks arrived piecemeal during the morning. They were immediately formed into three-tank platoons, plugged into a communications network and sent into the battle against the Syrians on the Tapline road. By noon, the 2nd Battalion reported it was being attacked by eighty tanks against its six on a dirt track west of the Tapline road. Ben Shoham came on the air and urgently ordered the battalion to hold off the Syrians at all costs. Otherwise, he pointed out, they would reach the Nafekh headquarters. Silence followed. Syrian tanks were soon reported behind Nafekh.

Brigadier General Rafael Eytan, commander of the Golan defense, ordered Ben Shoham to leave the Tapline road and return to Nafekh to defend the vulnerable headquarters. On the way northward, Ben Shoham's tank knocked out at least five more tanks, the brigade commander standing upright in the turret firing a machine gun. Just short of Nafekh, Ben Shoham came across a Syrian tank lying in a ditch with smoke coming from its turret. It was by now a familiar sight and Ben Shoham's attention was elsewhere, searching the hills for active tanks. A burst of machine gun fire from the disabled tank caught Ben Shoham and he slid dead into his tank. Major Benyamin Katzin, the brigade's operations officer, was also cut down by the machine gun blast. Fighting was so heavy around the headquarters that it would be another day before their bodies could be recovered. The brigade had now lost its top three officers and was barely a fighting force any more.

Under the crash of artillery and with Syrian tanks of the 1st Armored Division advancing within view, General Eytan was forced to withdraw from the Nafekh headquarters at 1:15 PM. The first Syrian tanks were already flattening the camp's southern fence. On his way out, Eytan managed to knock out a Syrian tank with a bazooka. He re-established his headquarters in the open about three miles to the north.

The Israeli forces were being routed. The deputy commander of the Brigade District, Lieutenant Colonel Pinie Cooperman, was horrified at the sight of retreating troops. He stopped one fleeing unit by standing in the middle of the road and warning the officer in charge that death was the penalty for cowardice in the face of the enemy. Other commanders were equally shocked. "All signs pointed to a withdrawal motivated by panic: interspersed among the withdrawing administrative vehicles were artillery and tanks," observed Israeli military historian Chaim Herzog.

Major Dov, the intelligence officer of Barak Brigade and now its senior officer, swung his half-track across the Nafekh-Bnot Yaakov Road leading down to the Jordan Valley and shouted to the retreating men: "Now, this is where we stop running. Nobody is going to pass us here." At Aleika, just west of Nafekh, he organized the beaten soldiers into a local defense.

The tanks of the Israeli 679th Reserve Armored Brigade, freshly arrived, rumbled up to the Nafekh headquarters shortly after Eytan's withdrawal, providing the strength Israel needed at this desperate hour. The camp was a scene from hell. Dozens of tanks and armored vehicles lay smoking, dead and wounded covered the ground, ammunition was exploding everywhere and artillery shellfire relentlessly blasted the area, scattering lethal splinters of metal indiscriminately through the compound.

The 679th's tanks opened pointblank fire at the Syrian tanks marauding inside the camp, setting them afire one by one. Syrian reinforcements failed to arrive and slowly the fresh troops of the 679th Brigade gained the upperhand. By nightfall, the 679th had prevailed and the Nafekh headquarters was again in Israel's hands.

• •

Meanwhile, another desperate battle was raging at the edge of the escarpment in the south, a bare six miles from the Jordan Valley and Israeli villages. If the Syrians broke through, all of northern Israel would be open to them.

By now, the overall commander of the northern military district, Major General Yitzhak Hofi, had decided to split the Golan into two separate commands to counter the Syria advance. He made Brigadier General Eytan responsible for the sector north of the Bnot Yaakov-Kuneitra road, including the road itself, and Major General Dan Laner commander of the south. That left two major routes down the escarpment in Laner's sector, the Yehudia road leading to the Arik Bridge and the El Al road going down to the Yarmuk River.

One daring detachment of the Syrian 51st Independent Tank Brigade under the overall command of Colonel Hassan Tourkmani stunned the Israeli command by actually descending the Heights by dawn on Sunday. The force of fifteen T-55 tanks had worked its way down the escarpment to a sea-level valley less than four miles from the Arik Bridge before encountering Israeli tanks going up. All the Syrian vehicles were destroyed near the Kuzabia crossroads—probably the deepest penetration of the war. Laner, who had retired from active duty the previous February after a distinguished career, took up his position at the Arik Bridge, which was already under shellfire by midday Sunday. With the roads crammed with reservists pouring into the area in buses and civilian cars and long convoys of tanks, some traveling on their own tracks for lack of transporters, fuel and ammunition trucks, Laner urgently dispatched his forces up to the plateau without regard for organization or unit formation.

By late afternoon, the attack by the Syrian 5th Infantry and 1st Armored divisions had brought their forward units within ten minutes of the Jordan Valley. The situation was desperate. A break through now would certainly carry the Syrians into Israel itself. The Israelis made their stand at the last high ground east of the escarpment, furiously fighting to stem the Syrian attack. The Syrians were exerting tremendous pressure all along the line from the Bnot Yaakov road in Eytan's sector through all of Laner's southern sector.

Losses on both sides were horrendous. About 250 Syrian tanks, destroyed or damaged, littered the battlefield in the southern sector, most of them from the 5th Division commanded by Brigadier General Ali Aslan and the 1st Armored Division led by Colonel Tewfiq Juhni. Nonetheless, the two Syrian commanders pressed their attack relentlessly.

Since the humiliating defeat of 1967, the Syrian soldiers, from private on up to generals, had had it drummed in them that they would not retreat. This doctrine had the advantage of giving the Syrian attacks a certain inevitability, a momentum that was difficult to stop. But there was also a costly disadvantage in that the troops were so determined not to retreat that even when they encountered a strong Israeli position they refused to fall back to regroup and maneuver. Instead, they often flung themselves forward in needlessly suicidal attacks. The result was that Israeli troops were able to inflict extremely heavy losses on the stubborn Syrians.

Despite the near total destruction of the Barak Brigade's ninety tanks, the rapid build up of Israel's forces in the southern sector of the Golan Heights began telling in the late afternoon of October 7. Fresh Israeli troops continued to be thrown into the battle as soon as they arrived. As a result, although losses were heavy, Israel's strength steadily increased. Slowly the momentum of the Syrian thrust was contained by intense resistance.

Illustrative of the ferocity with which the Israeli defenders fought and of the legends created in these early hours of struggle was the saga of Lieutenant Zvi Greengold, known as Zvicka. He had been on leave from the Barak Brigade when war broke out and on his own he made his way back

161

to the Golan by late Saturday night. With the brigade in disarray and Syrian tanks marauding on the Tapline Road and westward, Zvicka was ordered to sweep the road in the pitch darkness. He climbed aboard a Centurion with a pick up crew of three and led another Centurion out onto the road south of Nafekh. Soon he realized he had come across a Syrian tank only about ten meters away. Zvicka tapped his gunner and the Syrian vehicle exploded with a tremendous shockwave. The repercussion knocked out all of Zvicka's communications and he quickly confiscated the other Centurion, ordering the evicted commander to "do as I do."

The other vehicle soon became separated in the night and Zvicka advanced alone southward several miles before he spotted more Syrians. Three tanks from the 51st Independent Tank Brigade, their sidelights shining, were rushing to exploit the penetration of the Israeli line. Zvicka's tank knocked out all three vehicles, turning them into bonfires in the darkness.

Zvicka now took up a static position off the road and waited for more Syrians. He did not have to wait long. A column of thirty tanks accompanied by trucks came along the road. Zvicka waited until the lead tank was twenty yards away and blasted it, stalling the column and sending it into disarray. Zvicka now played cat and mouse with the Syrian force, popping up on a hill, blasting another tank, then disappearing in the darkness only to pop up again. In their frustration, several tanks turned on their spotlights trying to locate Zvicka, offering excellent targets. Zvicka's tank destroyed or severely damaged ten more Syrian vehciles before the Syrian force finally retired.

Still, the night was not over for Zvicka. Israeli reinforcements in the form of eight more tanks joined Zvicka and they launched an attack in two columns. Syrian gunners hit eight of the nine tanks, including Zvicka's. His clothing caught fire and he and his crew had to desert their vehicle. Zvicka quickly commandeered the remaining tank and reported back to brigade headquarters that "Force Zvicka" was back in action.

The Syrians found themselves unable to overcome such desperate Israeli defense. By the end of Sunday, Israeli forces blocked the vital Tapline road and held all the routes leading down the escarpment. They had waged one of the greatest defensive battles in Israel's history and had prevailed by sheer desperation.

North of Kuneitra, the 7th Syrian Infantry Division remained contained after a full day of extremely heavy fighting. But its commander, Brigadier General Omar Abrash, who had been trained at the U.S. Army Command and General Staff College at Fort Leavenworth, Kansas, was one of Syria's top commanders and he continued to press his attack. He had already lost at least 200 tanks by the afternoon of October 7. The shallow valley his force was trying to cross, which the Israelis were calling the valley of tears with good reason, was littered with the dead and the debris of destroyed vehicles, exploding ammunition trucks and a malodorous haze.

Attacks across the valley throughout the day had been repulsed with heavy losses by Israel's 7th Brigade. That night, General Abrash, taking advantage of the Syrians' night vision devices, returned to the fray with a massive attack. With the help of the 85th Infantry Brigade and the 3rd Armored Division, he threw 500 tanks into the thrust against the 40 tanks left in Colonel Ben-Gal's 7th Brigade. The Syrians advanced under a heavy artillery barrage laid down by 400 guns, getting as close as thirty yards to the Israeli line before they were spotted. From their ideal defensive position on a ridge at the western edge of the valley, the Israeli tanks blasted the Syrians with everything they had. When the attack broke off early in the predawn morning the Israelis discovered 130 Syrian tanks had been knocked out and abandoned, some of them behind the 7th Brigade's line.

General Abrash retired to lick his wounds. But he would return to the attack. The Syrian army remained strong and determined. It had not penetrated beyond the Heights into Israel, but it had not yet given up trying.

• •

THE SINAI PENINSULA

From the beginning, Major General Shmuel Gonen, commander of the Southern Command, had been overly optimistic and repeatedly confused the general staff in Tel Aviv about the actual situation on the Sinai battlefield. Although Gonen was a daring officer who had commanded the fabled 7th Armored Brigade in its heroic exploits in 1967, this was his first command of a regional force and he seemed to have difficulty forming a clear picture of the battlefield. Throughout the predawn hours of Sunday, Gonen reported things were "looking up" and, at 5:30 AM, "everything is coming along fine." In fact, the Israeli position could hardly have been worse.

By 1 o'clock Sunday morning, the Egyptians had already managed to get 800 tanks and 3,000 pieces of other top priority equipment across the canal and into the combat zone. By 8 AM, the Egyptians declared the crossing won. They had put across the Suez Canal 90,000 men, 850 tanks and 11,000 vehicles, a masterly achievement. The five Egyptian divisions had pushed about five miles forward and now controlled all of the canal bank except for the few Bar-Lev Line forts still holding out, surrounded and impotent, more of a drain on Israeli morale than a battlefield asset.

163

Israeli forces were in chaos. Their armor suffered from failure to organize into large units. Instead, in the tradition of the Israeli Armored Corps, they were blindly charging pell-mell against the Egyptians. One and two tanks were throwing themselves at the advancing Egyptians, easy prey for the missile-carrying infantry.

Only 110 of the 280 tanks that Israel's Sinai forces started with were still in operation less than a day after the war started. Egyptian commandos were operating deep in Sinai and ambushing reserve units rushing to the battle on the northern coastal road. In one ambush alone on the El Arish road between Romani and Baluza the commandos knocked out four tanks and killed thirty Israelis speeding to the front. For all practical purposes, the vaunted Bar-Lev Line was by now annihilated and the way was open for Egypt to reinforce its units. Israel was in a grave position. But headquarters did not yet understand that.

• •

When Major General Bren Adan arrived in northern Sinai shortly after dawn Sunday morning at the head of his division, he concluded that "even in our worst dreams, nobody could have anticipated such a grim situation....Most of our regular tank units had been lost, and the strongpoints that were still holding out were calling for help that we could not provide." Adan, who at this time was in charge of Israel's Armored Corps, had opted to lead a combat division and was put in charge of defending the northern sector of the Sinai.

The quick arrival of the Adan Division was in part due to the fact that the reserves had been mobilized on Yom Kippur. On that day of prayer, the streets and highways of Israel were devoid of their usual traffic and reservists had been able to speed to their units. The advantage of surprise that the Egyptian planners had counted on by attacking on Yom Kipper had in turn become an advantage for the Israelis.

Already, however, the Sinai roads were packed with cars and trucks and armor and artillery winding its way to the battlefield. In addition to Adan's division, another division had been activated under the command of Arik Sharon. Disgruntled at not being made chief of staff, Sharon had retired during the summer and entered politics, handing over the southern command to Gonen on July 15. This meant that Gonen was now commanding two men who were not only his superiors in experience and seniority, but two comrades who did not particularly like or admire him.

Adan thought Gonen had a "tendency to see the situation over-optimistically," perhaps in part because he "held in deep contempt" the

164

Egyptians. He also had reservations about Gonen's reputation as a strict disciplinarian. "More than once I had seen him throw things, tear maps, shout at those around him, and rashly confine soldiers to jail, often acting on impulse." Yet, Adan noted, he was soft-spoken and self-disciplined when around his superiors. Adan considered Gonen a "bicycle rider—one who presses hard downward but is always looking upwards."

When Adan visited Gonen's well fortified headquarters at Um Hasheiba at the foot of the Mitla Pass on Sunday afternoon, his opinion of Gonen became even lower. He found the "war room jammed with staff officers and visitors. The place was a mess; you could barely find your own feet. Looking at maps and listening to transceivers, I tried to follow reports from our forces along the front, but in vain. So deafening was the noise in the room and so distorted the sound from the radio that it was impossible to understand anything....I could not help thinking that it had to be impossible to work out any coherent plan amidst such disorder."

Further complicating Israel's Sinai command was the fact that Adan and Sharon did not get along well either. There was to be friction among the three generals all through the war.

* *

In the Sinai, Sunday was a day of gathering strength and consolidating forces for both sides. The Egyptians continued to pour men and materiel across the canal. Within twenty-four hours of their opening assault, they claimed they had 100,000 men, 1,020 tanks and 13,500 vehicles in the Sinai. Shazly proudly proclaimed the achievement the "largest first day crossing in world military history." In fact, the chief of staff was so content that he took some time off to go home, the first time since October 1, for a nap and change of clothes.

Now that the Egyptians were in Sinai, another complex operation faced the general staff. The troops had to be fed, their ammunition replenished and their equipment refurbished. The soldiers had crossed with only water and food for a day and all the ammunition they could carry or drag in little carts. Most of the ammunition was quickly gone in the frenzied fighting. Water too was in short supply. There was no fresh water along the salty canal and the soldiers were rapidly dehydrating in the desert heat and under the severe stress of fighting.

An intricate logistics organization had to be established to supply the men. Water pipes had to be laid from the Sweet Water Canal on the west, ammo and food transported across the bridges and to the battlefield, and a formal supply routine established. This too the Egyptians accomplished with impressive efficiency.

General Gonen apparently did not yet appreciate the size and strength of the Egyptian force facing him. Throughout Sunday he continued to talk about counterattacking and crossing the canal into the heartland of Egypt. "Evidently he did not perceive our grave situation that afternoon as being one with deep ramifications for the present and future course of the war but as a minor hitch easily overcome, an idea coming, apparently, from the profound contempt he felt for the Egyptians," observed Adan. "He never stopped thinking about a crossing operation and counterattacks."

Dayan definitely did not share Gonen's optimism. The defense minister arrived at Gonen's headquarters in the late morning and, after a review of the battlefield, insisted that Gonen withdraw to a defensive line back from the canal. He also insisted that all the remaining strongholds be allowed to evacuate—if they could. Up to then, Gonen had continued to order the men in the forts to remain on the presumption that Israeli armor would soon be able to link up with them. Now it was too late for most of them and their cries for help would continue to stretch nerves and plague the Israeli units helpless to aid them.

Gonen, bowing to Dayan's will, began establishing a new line at Lateral road, the north-south artery that lay about twenty miles east of the canal. Adan was in the north, headquartered at Qantara, Sharon in the center at Tasa and Mandler in the south opposite Suez City.

The first one hundred of Sharon's tanks began arriving shortly after Dayan's departure in the afternoon. Gonen immediately suggested to Elazar by telephone that he launch them in a counterattack. Sharon, as usual, also wanted to go on the attack and supported Gonen. But the chief of staff impatiently observed that, before attacking, a strong defensive line had to be established first. Otherwise, if the Egyptians attacked, they could route the disorganized and still weak Israeli forces.

Rather than attack, Elazar told Gonen, the front line forces must fight a retreating battle, "just like in school—delay and retreat...."

This they did during the rest of Sunday.

• •

TEL AVIV

Moshe Dayan was horrified by what he had seen during his visits to the Golan Heights and the Sinai. As he had flown back from the Sinai, Dayan recorded in his memoirs, "I could recall no moment in the past when I had felt such anxiety....Israel was in danger, and the results could be fatal if we did not recognize and understand the new situations in time and if we failed to suit our warfare to the new needs.''

Dayan made no effort to hide his deep pessimism when he returned to Tel Aviv and met with Elazar and his senior staff in the Pit. His extreme concern was shocking to the general staff. It was like watching the ''collapse of an entire world view and with it the image of a leader who had embodied it with such charismatic power,'' wrote Elazar's biographer, Hanoch Bartov. ''Since 1967, Moshe Dayan had consistently and impressively expressed his belief in Israel's ability to deter her enemies....And suddenly here he is talking about the 'fall of the Third Commonwealth,' and the 'Day of Judgment,' with all their chilling connotations.''

In a meeting that afternoon with Prime Minister Meir and some of her ministers, Dayan conveyed his pessimistic views. He said: ''Golda, I was wrong in everything. We are heading towards a catastrophe. We shall have to withdraw on the Golan Heights to the edge of the escarpment overlooking the valley and in the south in Sinai to the passes and hold on to the last bullet.'' If the Arabs would consent to a ceasefire in place, he would agree, Dayan said.

''I listened to him in horror,'' recalled Meir in her memoirs. Privately, she remarked that if Dayan's report was true, her world would collapse and she would have no reason to go on living. Admitted Meir: ''I think that if I hadn't learned...how to be strong, I would have gone to pieces then.''

Dayan realized the prime minister and her aides did not like what he was saying. They were shocked, he thought, because he told them he did not believe Israeli forces could not presently throw the Egyptians back across the canal. ''That very morning the chief of staff had told the cabinet that we could.....It was clear from their critical cross-questioning...that they thought the weakness lay not in our current military situation but in my personal character, that I had lost my confidence, and that my evaluation was incorrect.''

Golda Meir called in Elazar, who was considerably less pessimistic. He outlined three possible strategies: Use the Lateral road defense line as a temporary jumping off place for a counterattack the next day or Tuesday; fall far back to a strong defensive line at the Mitla and Giddi passes; or gamble and cross over to the west side of the canal.

The last option was considered too risky by both Elazar and Dayan. They realized that if the crossing failed there would be barely any Israeli forces the whole way between the canal and Tel Aviv. Dayan denigrated the idea as ''Arik's brainstorm,'' since the impetuous Sharon was already urging that Israel counterattack across the canal.

Elazar favored the first option, a counterattack in a day or two, but he first asked for permission to visit the Sinai to look at the situation himself. Permission was granted and Meir went immediately to a meeting of her cabinet. Despite Dayan's report, she sought and received the cabinet's endorsement of an Israeli counterattack against Egypt the next day, on October 8.

Later she sent the calm and unflappable Haim Bar-Lev up to the Golan Heights to make a personal inspection for her. He reported back that the situation was serious but not hopeless. A fresh division would arrive overnight and a counterattack would begin the next day.

That same Sunday night, Dayan, apparently stung at the implied lack of faith in sending Bar-Lev north, entered the prime minister's office and said to her: "Do you want me to resign? I am prepared to do so if you think I should. Unless I have your confidence, I can't go on."

The prime minister refused. In her memoirs, Meir is silent about her reasons but presumably she appreciated his considerable talents and believed they were essential to meet the present crisis. As she wrote, "[Dayan] has his faults, and like his virtues, they are not small ones."

• •

THE SINAI

Shortly after 7 PM, Elazar, accompanied by former chief of staff Yitzhak Rabin, who had recently relinquished his ambassadorial post in Washington, met with Gonen and his senior commanders at the Um Hasheiba headquarters. Gonen proposed having Adan and Sharon launch attacks aimed at capturing Egyptian bridges and crossing to the west side of the canal.

Elazar, quite realistically, labeled this ambitious plan as "too pretentious.

"I would like to attack, if possible, but first we must make a stand in defense—a mobile defense—so that they'll attack us first. Then we'll smash their assault forces, and once they've been weakened, we'll turn around and attack them," said Elazar.

The plan agreed on was for Adan's division to attack the Second Army from north to south, staying away from the canal and Egypt's heavy antitank weapons.

Sharon's division in the center was to act as a reserve. If Adan's attack was successful, Sharon then was to attack the Third Army in the south.

Mandler's division, which was decimated from the first day's fighting, was ordered to remain stationary as a blocking force.

Only if there was a major success would an attack across the canal be considered.

As Elazar was leaving the Um Hasheiba meeting, Sharon finally arrived. The helicopter transporting him had been late. He told the chief of staff that he had just been talking by telephone with some of the men trapped in the canal forts and wanted permission to take a hundred tanks to rescue them. Elazar asked whether, if he undertook the rescue mission, Sharon would be prepared to launch an assault in the morning as well. When Sharon admitted he could not, Elazar refused to allow him to try to rescue the forts. It was an unpopular but prudent order, one that could not have been easy to make in the face of desperate cries for help emanating from the forts.

The generals scattered through the desert night back to their commands to prepare for Monday's counterattack. With reinforcements steadily arriving, the divisions of Adan and Sharon now had 170 tanks each. Somehow, General Gonen had calculated that they had somewhere between them 650 to 700. It was a total miscalculation.

The Israelis were about to suffer a defeat every bit as painful as the ordeal that the Barak Brigade had undergone that day on the Golan Heights.

• •

CAIRO

Anwar Sadat did not bother visiting Center Ten on Sunday. "...everything was going according to plan," he reasoned, "and the commanders were fully professional. War was their line of business."

Instead, he stayed at Tahirah Palace, where he met again that evening with Soviet Ambassador Vinogradov. Sadat told the envoy that he had an answer from Syria's Hafez Assad, denying that his country had requested the Soviets to get a ceasefire.

"His face went white," Sadat recalled in his memoirs. "'I've in fact called,'" Vinogradov said, "'to convey another message from the Soviet government, following another request by Syria for a ceasefire.'"

Sadat dismissed the matter. "This subject is closed; I don't want you to take it up any further with me." Instead, Sadat demanded the Kremlin supply him with more tanks so he could carry on the war.

The question of a Syrian request for a Soviet ceasefire motion in the U.N. Security Council came up repeatedly during the first days of the war. Assad apparently did make such a request, motivated, in the words of Mohamed Heikal, by the idea that "if the fighting was going Syria's way the resolution would not matter; if the fighting went Israel's way the resolution might

169

come in useful.'' Another consideration may have been that Syria had coolly calculated it could take the Heights in the first thirty hours of fighting but after that Israel's strength would become formidable.

Obviously, the Russians tended to agree with Assad's cautionary assessment of the Arabs' chances of success. Kremlin leader Brezhnev contacted Marshal Josef Tito of Yugoslavia, a long and close friend of Egypt, urging him to try to persuade Sadat to accept a ceasefire. Said Brezhnev to Tito: "By being so stubborn...President Sadat would precipitate a disaster for the Arab world, progressive regimes everywhere, and the world at large." But Brezhnev's efforts backfired. Instead of pressing Sadat to accept a ceasefire, Tito sent Sadat 140 tanks, all loaded with fuel and ammunition.

• •

WASHINGTON

The rosy picture of an early Israeli triumph still persisted in Washington throughout Sunday. It was reinforced by a stream of optimistic messages from Israel itself. At 9:30 AM, a cable from Golda Meir assured the White House that "with our reserves of men and equipment the fighting will turn in our favor."

The purpose of Meir's message was to ask Washington to prevent a vote in the U.N. Security Council until at least Wednesday or Thursday, time enough, it was thought, to repel the Arabs. "I would not have come to you if I did not think the situation would improve in the next few days." She also repeated Israel's request for emergency supplies, especially Sidewinder heat-seeking air-to-air missiles, which was approved.

Israel's requests for emergency supplies had begun the same day as the war. Although they later became strident, the requests at first were modest and had little urgency. Most U.S. officials thought the war would be over before any supplies could arrive in Israel and so the requests were not given priority consideration.

In fact, some officials thought the Israelis were taking advantage of the Arab attack to gouge additional aid from the United States. Defense Secretary James Schlesinger, for one, suspected that one of the reasons Israel had not launched a preemptive attack was so it could later lay claim for American aid. This was a shrewd assessment since it was one of the reasons repeatedly mentioned by Golda Meir to justify America's support of Israel. In her message that Sunday morning, Meir had pointedly written:

You know the reasons why we took no preemptive action. Our

failure to take such action is the reason for our situation now. If I had given the chief of staff authority to preempt, as he had recommended, some hours before the attacks began, there is no doubt that our situation would now be different.

When Kissinger met with Dinitz on Sunday night, the envoy had yet another arms request and argued to justify it by claiming Washington had a special responsibility. He pointed out to Kissinger that Israel had refrained from attacking first, and somehow concluded "that decision bestows a special responsibility on America not to leave us alone...." It was a weak argument, yet Kissinger regarded it "sympathetically." He promised to help. Although Kissinger recognized that a preemptive strike by Israel at the late hour it could have attacked would have probably been meaningless, he nonetheless agreed with the Israeli claim that the United States thereby owed Israel special support.

During the same meeting Dinitz relayed another optimistic appraisal of the war. Dinitz had just returned from Tel Aviv and his report was by now outmoded, though no one in Washington knew that as yet. "We are on the move in terms of optimum power on both fronts," he told Kissinger. He repeated an earlier mistaken Israeli claim that it had destroyed nine of what it thought were only eleven bridges across the Suez. And, finally, he confidently assured the secretary of state that the war would be won by Wednesday.

Kissinger also agreed with Golda Meir's request that the United States give Israel time to complete its mobilization by stalling in having the Security Council take up the issue of a ceasefire. He reported that Soviet Ambassador Anatoly Dobrynin telephoned and "provided the pretext for the diplomatic procrastination that both Israel and we considered in the common interest." The Dobrynin message was that the Soviet leadership was meeting on the question and would have a message for President Nixon within two hours. Nearly five hours went by before the message from Leonid Brezhnev finally arrived. It was a mild communication making it clear that the Soviet Union at this point did not want a ceasefire either. That should have warned Kissinger and the WSAG team that the Arabs were doing better than Washington and Tel Aviv thought. But it did not.

Another strong hint that the situation on the battlefield was far different than believed was provided that Sunday by a surprise message from Cairo. The message was signed by Sadat's security adviser, Hafez Ismail, and it offered to end the war if Israel withdrew without any preliminary negotiations from all Arab territory. The message promised that "we do not intend

171

to deepen the engagements or widen the confrontation." The purpose of the war, the message added, was "to show we were not afraid or helpless." "Until this message I had not taken Sadat seriously," Kissinger confided in his memoirs. "Sadat's ability from the very first hours of the war never to lose sight of the heart of his problem convinced me that we were dealing with a statesman of the first order."

• •

Significantly, the message from Cairo had not requested a ceasefire. That glaring fact, indicating strongly that the battle was going well for the Arabs, had little impact in Washington. The mistaken belief remained that Israel was on the verge of victory.

CHAPTER XVIII

October 8: Error and Trial

THE THIRD DAY OF THE WAR caught Israel and the United States still trapped in a time warp, their perceptions at disastrous odds with reality. On the one hand, the staggering achievements of the Arabs were at last beginning to sink in. But at the same time the sense of overwhelming Israeli superiority lingered. The result was confusion and disbelief, a fractured version of reality, a shattered mirror.

Despite contrary evidence, Israeli leaders were optimistic on Monday. Sunday's dark mood had evaporated with the rising sun and soaring expectations. The Israeli high command and the government were now upbeat. They counted their blessings: Mobilization was proceeding rapidly and strong Israeli forces on both fronts were about to go on the offensive with powerful American weapons against inferior Soviet ones. It was anticipated that soon the tables would be turned, that Israel would again assume its traditional role of attacker rather than defender. Israeli forces, it was widely believed, would break the back of the Arabs' attack and take the battle even farther inside Arab territory.

"We're past the critical stage," Chief of Staff Dado Elazar confidently declared to his staff that Monday morning.

In fact, for many, the most critical day of the war, and the most disastrous for Israel, was about to begin.

• •

MONDAY

THE SINAI PENINSULA

The agony of the Israeli warriors on the front was symbolized by the

173

men trapped in the forts of the Bar-Lev Line—their cries for help, their pleas for rescue, and then the sudden, shattering silence. It was shocking, sapping the morale of their comrades. It was against the hallowed tradition of the Israel Defense Forces to abandon men. Yet here were scores of men begging for help over open radio nets, cries that went unanswered. It was a stunning blow to the Israeli soldiers, a vivid demonstration of how successful the Egyptian crossing had been, of how helpless Israel now was.

Egypt had captured half of the twenty manned forts before dark on the first day of the war, and its successes multiplied. During Sunday, all the remaining garrisons in the north, except for Budapest, which became the only fort to hold out all through the war, were deserted or captured. The men from Orkal, Drora, Ketuba and Milan all tried to escape. Most of them were unsuccessful. They were either killed or taken prisoner. On that same day Lachitzanit, with its seventeen men, fell.

Arik Sharon talked with two of the remaining forts in his central sector Sunday night and early Monday morning. In one, codenamed Troublemaker, there was only one fighter left well enough to communicate. It was the fort's cook. "Troublemaker asking for support," he radioed desperately. "We have no strength. Please give me encouragement."

Sharon asked for artillery support, which was practically nonexistent, and then said to the cook: "Troublemaker, we hear you. The guns are firing on your positions. You'll get help."

"I know you. You're the previous CO Southern Command. I'm very grateful to you. Don't abandon me. Please talk to me all the time...."

There was despair in the Sharon headquarters. Talk was all they could provide Troublemaker. It was already understood how strong the Egyptian forces were around the forts. The night wore on, emotions taut. Then shortly before Monday's dawn, Troublemaker radioed: "Bombard the gateway to the stronghold. The Egyptians are there with bazookas."

Sharon: "You will shortly see our movement...."

Troublemaker: "I'm in total darkness."

Sharon, frustrated, under orders not to attempt rescue and too weak to try it anyway, nonetheless said: "We'll take care of you."

Troublemaker: "Send planes!"

Sharon had another conversation with another fort, Purkan, the big stronghold that Egypt's Chief of Staff Shazly had gazed at on the eve of battle. Its situation was more encouraging than Troublemaker's but just as frustrating. There were thirty-three men trapped in Purkan, but at least none of them were yet wounded or killed. But the fort was surrounded by Egyptian armor and infantry. Sharon once again promised he would get

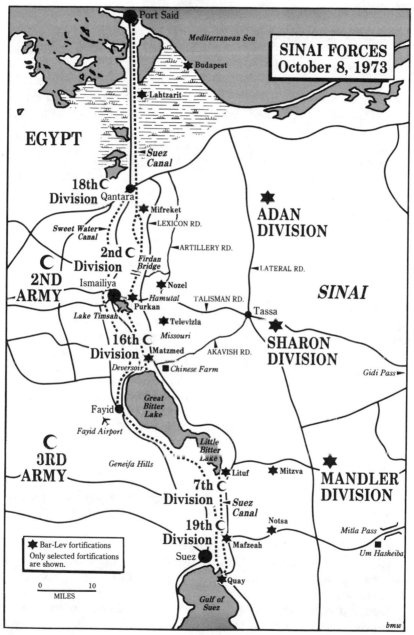

SINAI FORCES
October 8, 1973

Mediterranean Sea

Port Said

Budapest

Lahtzarit

EGYPT

Suez
Canal

18th C
Division Qantara

Mifreket

ADAN
DIVISION

Sweet Water
Canal

LEXICON RD.

ARTILLERY RD.

2nd C
Division

Firdan
Bridge

LATERAL RD.

2ND
ARMY

Ismailiya

Nozel

SINAI

Hamutal

TALISMAN RD.

Purkan

Tassa

Lake Timsah

Televlzla

SHARON
DIVISION

16th C
Division

Missouri

Matzmed

AKAVISH RD.

Deversoir

Chinese Farm

Gidi Pass

Great
Bitter
Lake

Fayid

Fayid Airport

Little
Bitter
Lake

3RD
ARMY

Geneifa Hills

Lituf

Mitzva

MANDLER
DIVISION

7th C
Division

Suez
Canal

Notsa

Mitla Pass

19th C
Division

Mafzeah

Um Hasheiba

Suez

Quay

Bar-Lev fortifications
Only selected fortifications
are shown.

0   10
MILES

Gulf of
Suez

bmw

175

the men out.

But he could not. The Purkan men were on their own. They would eventually make a dramatic escape. Not so Troublemaker and others. Troublemaker was never heard from again. The agony of his end echoed all along the line, all in the open over the radio waves, repeated time after time by other falling forts. It was a domino effect. At another fort, a laconic operator reported his stronghold was under attack by eight hundred Egyptians. Then he added: "The Egyptians are in the compound. I'm hiding. Give artillery on me."

Then he reported: "The Egyptians are coming in."

The battalion radio operator monitoring the report burst into sobs. Those were the fort operator's last words. "The sobs...could be heard from one end of the bunker to the other, and men hung their heads," reported a combat correspondent.

• •

CAIRO

Chief of Staff Shazly made his first visit to the front on Monday, leaving Center Ten early in the morning. He was satisfied with the troops' progress. Egypt's line now extended nearly ten kilometers into the Sinai and the bridgeheads of the five divisions were well established. As he drove along the canal, Shazly was pleased to note the obviously high morale of the Egyptian troops. "Many had not slept for two nights but, as ever, victory was a tonic," observed Shazly. "As I drove by, many of them, referring to my orders for the crossing, waved and shouted: " 'Directive 41, we did it.' "

• •

Anwar Sadat was in a ebullient mood too. Journalist Mohamed Heikal stopped by Tahirah Palace at dusk and found him in a "very happy and relaxed mood." Sadat took off his uniform, donned pajamas and the two men sat down to break the day's Ramadan fast. As they were eating, Soviet Ambassador Vinogradov telephoned with news that Moscow would soon start an airlift of resupplies. "Magnificent! Magnificent!" Sadat said in English, which the Russian also spoke well. "Tell Comrade Brezhnev I feel thankful to him from the bottom of my heart. Tell Brezhnev that it is Soviet arms which achieved the miracle of the crossing."

Sadat and Heikal chatted late into the night. After the journalist left, Sadat, still restless, watched a movie, a western.

176

• •

THE SINAI PENINSULA

The plan of the Israeli attack for Monday—for Bren Adan to assault north to south, stay away from the canal and make no effort to cross over unless unexpected success was achieved—somehow got completely altered during the night by General Gonen. Now Adan was to go to the canal, liberate the remaining forts and cross over at two points on Egyptian bridges at Purkan and Matzmed. Gonen had tried to give these new orders to Adan shortly before 4 AM, but the division commander was in the field on the northern Lateral road and radio communications were poor. Egyptian forces were jamming the airwaves. Unable to contact Adan, Gonen radioed Major General Kalman Magen at the headquarters at Baluza, which had a high antenna, and asked him to relay the orders to Adan. Fifteen minutes later, Gonen called Kalman again and said: "Cancel the crossing at Purkan. In crossing at Matzmed, take only one brigade. The liberation of the strongholds will be assigned to Arik [Sharon]."

It was only at 4:30 AM that Gonen and Adan finally managed to make direct radio contact. Gonen repeated his orders, but he expressed them in the form of questions, according to Adan. "Could you move to the Hizayon, Purkan and Matzmed strongpoints and link up with them while proceeding with your mission? Another possibility is that Arik will first link up with the strongpoints and return. Does that look simpler to you?"

Three minutes later, Gonen called Sharon and said: "Plan for the liberation of the strongholds in the morning, like Bren. It all depends on the enemy's position."

This confusion of communications and orders contributed heavily to the tragedy that befell Adan's division later in the day and became the focus of a bitter controversy after the war between Adan and Gonen and their supporters. Adan insisted that he was totally unaware that there was a change in the plan of attack. "My impression was that we were still speaking of moves included within the framework of the original plan. That is, I was being asked whether, as part of the plan to attack south to Matzmed while avoiding an approach along the entire water line, I could, nevertheless, move to the canal at certain points. My reply was perfectly simple: How could I know *now*?" Gonen insisted that he was only elaborating, conjecturing on the basic plan.

In a telephone conversation a short time later with Elazar, Gonen discussed the day's planned counterattack with the chief of staff. But either Elazar also failed to understand the changes planned by the southern com-

177

mander or they were not spelled out. Elazar was left with the impression that the original plan was operative. He had confidence in it and his optimism affected his staff. The mood in the Pit was euphoric.

But there were now basic misunderstandings that would make even worse the normal numbing confusion and chaos of warfare. These misconceptions existed right down the line: between the general staff in the Pit and the Southern Command at Um Hasheiba in the Sinai and between the Southern Command and its divisional commanders in the desert wastes.

• •

General Adan had three understrength armored brigades to launch his attack: Natke, Gabi and Karen brigades, named after their commanders, with a total of 183 tanks, only ten artillery pieces and no infantry. Even before the attack began at 8 AM, Natke brigade was already engaged in the north around Qantara with the aggressive 15th Egyptian Armored Brigade.

As Adan's tanks maneuvered over the sands, occasional pairs of Israeli planes flashed through the morning air against a blue sky. Needles of fire chased them, Egyptian missiles that were clearly visible to the troops on the ground. The Egyptian missile screen remained strong and lethal. It was obvious why the air support was limited and repeated requests for more strikes went unheeded.

From a sand dune 1,500 yards from Adan's force, correspondent Uri Dan, attached to Sharon's headquarters, watched the ground attack develop. "The tanks look like dots—black horses on the white desert background. From our observation point it seems to be a scene from a silent movie. We can see the sights, but can't hear the voices. Yet the mushrooms of black smoke constantly billowing up between the tanks tells us the intensity of the Egyptian artillery barrage on Bren's armor....Tanks maneuver between the black mushrooms, forwards and backwards, right and left—a macabre dance."

Dan added: "And it's all in vain. The direction of the attack is wrong...."

Indeed, several of Adan's battalions had started the attack too far east with some units as far as twenty-two miles away from the canal. To correct this error, they had to move westward—directly into the entrenched Egyptian positions. The north to south direction of the attack was completely askewed. Egyptian tanks and infantrymen armed with antitank weapons joined the Egyptian artillery, which early took its toll of Adan's force. Battles quickly erupted all along Adan's advancing line.

Gonen repeatedly radioed Adan, urging him to press the attack southward, to move "like a current." At 10:05 AM, Gonen's deputy, Uri Ben-Ari, called Adan and said: "There are some slight indications that the enemy has begun to collapse, so it's very important, very important, to rush at maximum speed with all your forces along your entire axis from the north, from Qantara, to down below to make contact and destroy. Otherwise they're liable to get away!''

Ben-Ari was a veteran of the war of independence and was esteemed by Adan as a ''a serious officer. So, of course, I took what he told me seriously. I also knew that Southern Command had means to collect intelligence from sources unavailable to me.''

But to carry out the order, Adan would have to pull out Natke brigade around Qantara, leaving his rear vulnerable. The brigade had already fought two battles with the 15th Brigade and the Egyptian unit remained a threatening force. It was equipped with modern T-62 tanks, the latest model in the Soviet armory, and it was full of fight. Adan suggested he leave part of Natke brigade at Qantara and be given one of Sharon's battalions. Ben-Ari refused.

Adan went over his head and took his request to Gonen, pointing out that the battalion he had in mind was idle. Gonen agreed and Adan detached a battalion from Natke brigade to protect Qantara and ordered the rest of the brigade to move southward toward the Firdan Bridge in the central sector and cross to the east bank.

Despite the rosy view of the high command, Adan could not find any evidence around him that the Egyptians were crumbling as the battle developed. He asked Colonel Gavriel (''Gabi'') Amir, whose brigade was heavily engaged in combat near the Firdan Bridge, if he had sufficient forces to cross the canal.

''No! I have just come under heavy artillery fire and am engaged with enemy tanks and missiles. I have already suggested getting Sharon's battalion which is deployed behind me doing nothing. And I need more artillery and strong close air support.''

Despite the Egyptians' vigorous defense, a stream of overoptimistic orders continued to flow from southern headquarters, much to Adan's mounting frustration. Adding to his discomfiture was the fact that Sharon was refusing to give up his idle battalion in spite of Gonen's order.

In a radio conversation with Gonen at 10:45 AM, Adan complained about not getting the Sharon battalion.

''Fire the battalion commander and appoint his deputy!'' shouted Gonen.

But the unit remained with Sharon. ''The situation was nerve-wracking,'' recalled Adan in his memoirs. ''Gabi's brigade, thrashing about under heavy artillery fire, was awaiting reinforcement. Southern Command had given its approval; the battalion was deployed at Havraga; and the battalion

179

commander was ready to join up with Gabi, but Sharon would not approve.''

·When Gabi Amir personally pleaded with the battalion commander, he was informed he could not without permission.

"You are arguing...and meanwhile my men are being killed," Amir shouted.

Sharon never did release the battalion. Instead, under orders from Gonen, he began moving his entire division southward toward the Third Egyptian Army in a fruitless maneuver that would waste the division's day. Worse, by withdrawing, Sharon deserted vital high ground at Hamutal, Machshir and Hamadia just east of the Artillery road, and, farther south, at the vital areas of Missouri and the Chinese Farm, destined in the days to come to become two of the bloodiest battlefields. More immediately, Sharon's withdrawal dangerously exposed Adan's southern flank just at a time when Egyptian forces were increasing their pressure on him.

• •

By noon, Adan's position was desperate. Near the Firdan Bridge, just north of Ismailia, Gabi brigade's left flank battalion was pushing toward the Bar-Lev Line when hundreds of Egyptian infantrymen emerged from the sand dunes and blasted the unit with antitank weapons. Twelve Israeli tanks went up in flames and the battalion commander was wounded. Before the unit managed a hasty withdrawal the guns on the opposite bank also opened up on them. Shells, missiles and small arms fire riddled the area. Tanks were burning and crewmen running around seeking safety. By the time the unit extricated itself, it had lost eighteen of its twenty-five tanks. Twenty men had been killed, including two platoon commanders, and dozens were wounded.

At his observation point on a high dune at Zrakor, nearly five miles from the canal, Adan heard the frantic radio traffic from the beleaguered Gabi battalion near the Firdan Bridge. There were desperate calls for heavy air support and messages of burning tanks and crewmen being cut down. Adan immediately asked headquarters for urgent air support but was told that it was unavailable. Then, shockingly, he was asked: "What's happening with your advance southward?"

Obviously, Gonen still did not appreciate how badly the battle was developing. The reports by the laconic Adan did not enlighten him. This false impression was further clouded by an erroneous report that some of Adan's forces had crossed to the west bank.

The misunderstanding apparently came about when shortly after noon,

Nathan ("Natke") Nir radioed Adan: "What I don't understand is whether we have forces on the other side?" Adan denied it, but a headquarters operator monitoring the network apparently heard only part of the exchange and concluded that the crossing had taken place. The rumor quickly found its way to the Pit in Tel Aviv, adding to the confusion among the general staff of what was actually happening in the Sinai.

Adan, under severe pressure, now over-reacted. Still trying to carry out the mission he later claimed was imposed by Gonen—of capturing several Egyptian bridges and crossing the canal—he ordered a two-brigade attack against the 2nd Egyptian Infantry Division in the Firdan Bridge area. The Natke and Gabi brigades were by now both understrength with only two reduced battalions apiece containing only about twenty tanks in each battalion. The promised air support did not appear, and Adan had only three reduced batteries of artillery to support the assault against the well-prepared Egyptian positions. Nonetheless, at around 2 PM, Adan gave the order to charge.

From his observation post atop Zrakor, Adan could follow the early part of the attack through binoculars. The commander of the Egyptian 2nd Division, Brigadier Hassan Abu Saada, could also see the attack developing and his men were ready.

"As soon as the Israeli tanks crossed the camouflaged infantry trenches the infantry jumped out of the trenches like devils and began to attack the 190th [Natke's] Brigade," said Saada. "Our tanks and all the anti-tank equipment concentrated in the area operated against the enemy and destroyed him. In three minutes the 190th Israeli Armored Brigade was destroyed."

The battalion commanded by Lieutenant Colonel Assaf Yaguri had impulsively flung itself upon the Egyptians without waiting for other units of the attacking force. The battalion was immediately cut down. Commander Yaguri was blown from his tank and taken captive. Natke desperately ordered a retreat.

"What happened, why are you withdrawing?" radioed Adan.

"If you continue to ask me questions there will be nobody left to answer in a few minutes," replied Natke, a veteran fighter whose right leg had been badly crippled in the 1967 war.

Only nine of the twenty-five tanks in Yaguri's battalion returned. Yaguri, his deputy, two company commanders and many platoon leaders were all missing. Before the day was out, Natke's brigade reported fifty-four men missing in action. Yaguri was later displayed on Egyptian TV as a prisoner-of-war and identified as a full colonel in charge of a brigade.

Gonen only realized in mid-afternoon that the progress southward of Sharon's division was so slow that he could not hope to attack across the southern canal in daylight. In addition, it was becoming clear the Egyptians were preparing for a major counterattack. Gonen decided near 3 PM that Sharon should return to the area he had just that morning deserted. The day so far had been a complete waste of time for Sharon's division— marching aimlessly without any significant fighting. And now the Egyptians were massing for a strong counterattack in the northern sector.

At the same time, Adan was faced with another emergency. Colonel Aryeh Karen, commanding his brigade to the south around Nozel near the Artillery road, reported that he was facing a serious threat from thousands of Egyptians advancing northward over the positions deserted that morning by Sharon's division. Aryeh was fearful of being cut off and he wanted permission to redeploy, which was granted. At that moment, Adan's advance headquarters at the Zrakor observation post came under a terrific artillery bombardment. The communications officer was killed and several others wounded. Adan and his aides fled, taking up a new position just to the south on top of a dune at Havraga.

Adan's difficulties, and Gonen's too, were increased by constant Egyptian jamming of radio waves. Under any circumstance, it was hard to follow the course of the battle, but now the confusion was magnified by the lack of clear communications.

The radio nets were a nightmare of shouting voices, static and jamming noise, of men pleading for help and commanders issuing orders, a babel of life and death. Adan could not get a clear picture of the battle. Radio reports were fragmentary and muddled. He could see his forces were dispersed, unorganized and ineffective, and that he was losing control. Also by now, it was clear, Karen was engaged in very heavy combat and his force was in danger of being cut off from the road leading back to Tasa. "...I knew I had to tighten my control, but I felt there was no way to do it by radio."

In desperation, Adan ordered Natke Nir and Gabi Amir to meet him at the junction of the Hazizit-Haviva roads north of Nozel to hear from them personally what was happening in their sectors. When he took his radio headset off, Adan was "astonished to find that the crash of exploding shells was more pleasant to my ears than the noise of the radio set that had been drumming into my ears for so many hours."

All three men were dead tired. They had not slept for three days and during that time they had engaged in some of the heaviest combat they had

182

ever experienced. Now they were involved in another hard fight whose outcome was by no means clear. Before they had a chance to compare notes, stiff attacks were launched at both of the colonels' brigades just south of Adan's Havraga advanced headquarters and they had to rush back to their units. The Egyptian 2nd Infantry Division was attacking straight ahead from the west and the 16th Infantry Division northward from the south, through the area left unprotected by Sharon's division.

Adan was near despair. "At about 1700 my division was in real trouble, and I was undergoing the worst crisis I have experience in four wars," admitted Adan. Nir reported that his position was under attack by at least a hundred tanks. Amir added: "They are coming on a very broad front at [Nir] and at us, and in large numbers. They are moving straight ahead, across the whole front. Give us air support, because we don't have enough forces."

Nir broke in: "They are coming in masses, they are coming in masses. We have to have planes right away, because we don't have enough strength."

Adan's entire division was now under heavy attack from west and south. "From each direction came thousands of enemy infantry accompanied by scores of tanks, while we were few, worn down, disorganized," Adan observed to himself. "Should I give the order to retreat?"

"There is no choice," Adan said aloud to his command group. "We must retreat."

Between 5 and 5:10 PM, Adan ordered Nir and Amir to withdraw.

About the same time, units of Sharon's division began arriving from their futile drive southward. Adan suddenly felt a flash of hope.

"Gilad," he said to his operations officer, Gilad Aviram, "ask Natke and Gabi if they can hold their present positions until Sharon arrives."

Both brigade commanders replied they could. "Meanwhile, we are setting them afire!" they reported.

"I love you!" shouted Aviram.

Astonishingly, Sharon refused to attack from south to north to relieve Adan's hard-pressed forces. Gonen did not push him because he finally was beginning to understand the truely frightful dimensions of the Israeli predicament at that time. Instead he ordered Sharon to return to Tasa and set up a strong defensive line to protect against an Egyptian breakthrough.

"At that time," recalled Gonen, "if the Egyptians should break through Adan, Sharon was all that I had left between them and Tel Aviv."

Meanwhile, the terrible destruction being inflicted by Nir's and Amir's brigades began having an effect. The Egyptians were being worn down,

183

their forces dispersed. The battle began slowly turning in Israel's favor, aided by the approaching darkness. The blinding sun that had been shining straight in the Israelis' eyes began setting and the troops could sight their guns better. Their deadly fire blasted tank after tank, turning them into bonfires. Smoke, dust, flaming tanks and fleeing troops covered the whole line, a confusion of death and destruction.

The Egyptians were steadily being fought to a standstill. Israeli morale began perking up, and with it the fierceness of the troops' determination. After dark, illumination shells lit up the battlefield, now a ghastly sight of dead and wounded, of smoldering tanks and armored personnel carriers. The flares revealed starkly that the Egyptian advance had been halted.

But the day's fighting was not yet over for Adan. Karen's brigade was still deeply engaged in a fight around Hamutal, which the Egyptians had captured before sunset. In a fierce counterattack by two battalions with twenty-five tanks to retake the long, flat dune bisected by the important Talisman road, the Israelis fought hard but failed. Battalion commander Lieutenant Colonel Dan Sapir was killed in the attack and Lieutenant Colonel Amir Joffe, another battalion commander, had his tank hit three times and its gun barrel explode. Still he charged using his machine gun and tried to crush the Egyptian infantry with his tank tracks. In the end, however, the Israelis had to withdraw with a loss of seven of the twelve tanks in Joffe's group and at least two in the other battalion.

Still the day was not done. As they were withdrawing from Hamutal, the Israelis discovered a concentration of tanks to the east attacking toward Hamutal. It was a brigade from Sharon's division returning to the positions it had left that morning, completely unaware that Adan's forces were on Hamutal.

"With no little irritation," Adan said, he managed to keep the two Israeli units from fighting each other.

• •

Finally, an hour after dark, "We realized we were no longer under attack," wrote Adan. "The main problem I faced now was to enable my division, which had been cut to pieces, to lick its wounds and reorganize for further fighting."

Of the 183 tanks he had started the day with, Adan now had only a hundred left. Hundreds of his men had been killed, wounded or captured, many of them officers.

It had been the worst defeat in the history of the Israeli army.

Nonetheless, the Israelis had stopped the Egyptian attack.

184

Sharon's division, by contrast with Adan's battered force, was still fresh. It had frittered the day away in its useless lunge to the south and then its return to where it started, all without engaging in any serious combat. Worse for the Israelis, Sharon's refusal in the morning and then again in the evening to come to Adan's aid had completely soured relations between the two generals. They would fight the rest of the war barely talking and deeply suspicious of each other.

• •

THE GOLAN HEIGHTS

For the Israelis on the Golan plateau, Monday started off no better than the previous day. Northern Command leader Major General Hofi, acting on rumors that there were still Israelis alive in the Mt. Hermon fortress, sent a relief force to rescue them. Troops of the Golani Infantry Brigade attempted to scale the slopes at dawn in a right flanking movement toward the crest but were repulsed in heavy fighting. Another attempt to the left was equally unsuccessful. The Syrians were well dug in and full of fight. The Israelis gave up the attempt after suffering heavy casualties. Twenty-five Golani troops were killed and fifty-seven wounded in the ill-fated assault. No more attempts to retake the fortress would be made until the last day of the war.

• •

The battlefield was still confused and fluid. Israel was throwing its might into a counterattack in the southern sector of the Heights in an attempt to push the Syrians back across the Purple Line. The Syrians, for their part, were still trying to break through in the northern sector and also trying to dash down off the plateau and maraud inside Israel. Neither side displayed an overwhelming advantage.

The Israelis now had two full divisions in the southern half of the heights, Major General Peled in the southernmost sector and Major General Laner on his left, but still the fighting was slow and grinding as the Israelis counterattacked all across the south. Syrian infantry armed with RPGs and Sagger antitank missile took their toll, blunting the Israeli attack. The 679th Israeli Armored Brigade alone suffered the loss of three of its battalion commanders and five of its nine company commanders in the day's hard fighting.

The Syrian 1st Armored Division, under Colonel Jehani, was proving to be an aggressive, formidable foe. Jehani's 91st Brigade commander, Col-

185

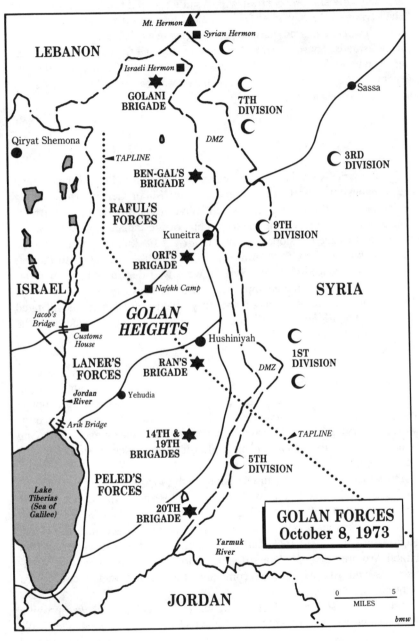

LEBANON

Mt. Hermon

Syrian Hermon

Israeli Hermon

GOLANI
BRIGADE

7TH
DIVISION

Sassa

Qiryat Shemona

TAPLINE

DMZ

3RD
DIVISION

BEN-GAL'S
BRIGADE

RAFUL'S
FORCES

Kuneitra

9TH
DIVISION

ORI'S
BRIGADE

ISRAEL

Nafekh Camp

SYRIA

Jacob's
Bridge

GOLAN
HEIGHTS

Customs
House

Hushiniyah

1ST
DIVISION

LANER'S
FORCES

RAN'S
BRIGADE

DMZ

Jordan
River

Yehudia

Arik Bridge

TAPLINE

14TH &
19TH
BRIGADES

5TH
DIVISION

PELED'S
FORCES

Lake
Tiberias
(Sea of
Galilee)

20TH
BRIGADE

GOLAN FORCES
October 8, 1973

Yarmuk
River

0   5
MILES

JORDAN

bmw

onel Shafiq Fiyad, led his powerful unit with dash and imagination. When he encountered strong Israeli forces at the recaptured Nafekh headquarters, he boldly bypassed them and made a run down the Damascus Highway that carried his advance units to the main Israeli supply depot at Snobar and all the way to the Customs House, only about three miles from the Bnot Yaakov (Jacob's) Bridge—one of the deepest Syrian penetration of the war. Determined fighting by Israeli troops holding the vital center subdued the Syrians, but the professionalism of the 91st Brigade earned the reluctant admiration of the Israelis.

In the north, Colonel Ben-Gal's 7th Brigade grimly held out against the relentless attacks by the Syrian 7th Infantry and 3rd Armored divisions across the shallow valley that by now was truly a valley of tears. His few tanks had inflicted devastating damage on the Syrians, yet they continued to press forward. The Israeli brigade had already lost fifty dead and was down to forty tanks and the troops were bone tired. They had been fighting without let up since the war started and there was no relief in sight.

As dusk descended Monday, Syrian Brigadier General Omar Abrash prepared his 7th Division for yet another attack against the 7th Brigade. Night vision devices gave his troops a decided edge, which Abrash capitalized on to the full. He was one of Syria's best generals and his leadership had been outstanding in the hard fight in which both Syria and Israel suffered many casualties.

Now, as he readied his tanks for another onslaught, Abrash was touring the grim battlefield, preparing for more death. Suddenly, his personal tank was hit and burst afire. Abrash was killed. His loss was a major blow to the Syrians. The planned attack was postponed until morning, giving Ben-Gal's battered force a badly needed respite.

• •

TEL AVIV

False optimism continued to pervade the Pit. Even Dayan had emerged from his deep pessimism of the previous day. There were reports that the Egyptians were collapsing, the Syrians suffering heavily. Chief of Staff Elazar decided around noon to fly up north to look at the situation on the Golan Heights firsthand. As he was leaving the bunker, another upbeat report from Southern Command repeated that a unit of Adan's division had penetrated to the other side of the Suez Canal. A short time later, Elazar was asked for permission to allow General Gonen to order Arik Sharon to cross over and capture Suez City. Elazar agreed. Everything seemed to be going well as far as the general staff could tell.

At General Hofi's Northern Command headquarters, Elazar found the fighting satisfactory but he was concerned by the build up of the Syrian 7th Division's forces for another attack. He recognized the Israeli forces were exhausted and their equipment limited. One breakthrough would bring Syrian forces onto Israeli soil. When he returned to the Pit, Elazar ordered all tanks and antitank weapons that could be found to be sent up north. "We must take these few dozen tanks and, before anything else, establish a fallback line....I want to create a terraced effect on the Golan Heights."

Elazar also slowly became aware that the counterattack in the Sinai was not going anywhere nearly as well as had been thought. Large Egyptian concentrations were reported at four points and Egyptian troops continued to flood across the canal.

"You can hardly say they've collapsed," observed Elazar with understatement.

Monday night, in his first press conference since the start of the war fifty-two hours earlier, Elazar sounded a considerably more upbeat note than either the facts or even his limited information justified. But, concerned about national morale, he said: "We have begun to destroy the Egyptian Army....We are advancing on all fronts....This war is serious, the fighting is serious. But I am happy to tell you that we are already at the turning point, that we are already moving forward."

Then he added: "We shall strike them, we shall beat them, we shall break their bones."

When he returned to the Pit, Elazar discovered that Israel's losses in airplanes were tremendous—forty-four in only two days of fighting. At that horrendous rate, Israel would soon be short of warplanes. It was one more worry pressing in on the beleaguered general.

• •

WASHINGTON

Henry Kissinger and the officials making up WSAG, the Washington Special Action Group monitoring the fighting, remained convinced that Israel was on the verge of winning the war. CIA reports reflected similar optimism. So too did Israeli Ambassador Simcha Dinitz. Kissinger met twice with him that Monday and found the envoy exuding optimism.

"This morning, our attacks on both fronts were successful," Dinitz told Kissinger shortly before 7 PM. By this time, it was already known in Israel that the fighting was not going well at all but obviously the word had not

188

OCTOBER 8: ERROR AND TRIAL

yet gotten to the envoy. "In Syria, they are pushed out of the heights except Mt. Hermon area....At the Egyptian front, we succeeded in destroying part of the Egyptian forces."

Dinitz even went on to speculate that Israel might want to capture more Arab territory than it already had. Kissinger warned against that course. But he promised that Israel could have any American supplies it could load on its own El Al planes to make up for its war losses.

Kissinger was somewhat puzzled by this time why the Arabs and the Soviets were not demanding an immediate ceasefire. But, in the face of all the optimism, he was not concerned. After all, it was in Israel's interests to prevent a ceasefire until the Arabs had been beaten, and so Kissinger continued to hold off the U.N. Security Council from making such a demand.

Confident that Israel would score a decisive victory within the next forty-eight hours, Kissinger took the time that evening to deliver a major speech at the Pacem in Terris conference in Washington. Later he went to bed "expecting a repeat of the Six Day War of 1967."

• •

In the Sinai and on the Golan Heights, the armies of Israel, Egypt and Syria girded themselves for more combat. There were still more than two weeks of war ahead.

CHAPTER XIX

October 9: Reality Emerges

BY THE FOURTH DAY OF THE WAR both sides were exhausted. Many of the troops and officers had not had more than cat naps, a few minutes of uneasy sleep caught in the pauses between fighting and maneuvering, hiding and seeking. Some had had no sleep at all for three days and nights, days of tension and terror. Yet the fighting went on.

It was only in the first hours of Tuesday that Chief of Staff Dado Elazar and his general staff finally learned the true dimensions of the failure of General Bren Adan's counterattack the day before. Said Elazar's deputy, Yisrael Tal: "The ninth of the month was the worst day of the war because it was then that the full extent of the debacle on the eighth became known to us."

· ·

TUESDAY

THE SINAI PENINSULA

Elazar and Defense Minister Dayan flew to the Sinai at midnight to meet with Southern Commander leader Shmuel Gonen in his advance headquarters at Um Hasheiba. It was a doleful meeting. From reports by Adan, Sharon and Gonen, it became painfully clear that Adan had suffered a stunning defeat. Sharon's day had been wasted in futile maneuvering. There had been no gains made at all. Quite the reverse. Nearly a hundred tanks had been lost and hundreds of men as well, all without inflicting any significant destruction on the Egyptian army.

Elazar officially gave Brigadier Kalman Magen responsibility for holding the northern sector above the Titur road, leaving Adan in the north center, Sharon in the south center and Avraham Mandler in the south. Since Sharon's division was the freshest, he was ordered to prepare for a crossing of the canal, the timing to be decided later.

For the moment, the concentration would remain on the Golan Heights, Elazar said. He ordered the Sinai forces to go on the defense, to prevent any Egyptian advances and avoid attrition of their own forces while they waited to build up strength. There would be no search for contact, no initiation of combat. The building up of strength was the prime immediate goal. Only after Syria had been fought to a standstill and more forces could be moved to the south would the offensive begin, Elazar decreed.

• •

During the dark, the thirty-three men trapped in the Purkan fort finally slipped away and carefully worked their way toward Israeli lines. Colonel Amnon Reshef, a brigade commander in Sharon's division, volunteered to rescue them in the early morning darkness of Tuesday. He formed a small force of three tanks and five armored personnel carriers and made his way toward Hamutal, where a fierce battle was still raging. Heavy Egyptian artillery was blasting the scraggly area and it was filled with Egyptian infantry. There was no way to find the stranded men in all the confusion, so Amnon radioed the Purkan group to set off a green flare to mark their position. Heading toward the flare, the Israeli force fell into an ambush. A sharp fight broke out.

With combat raging, one of the Israeli tanks spotted the Purkan survivors and went to their rescue. All thirty-three men squeezed aboard the tank.

"While we fought this infantry—with everything around burning, men screaming and soldiers racing to rescue crews of hit tanks—I saw something that I couldn't grasp at first," said Reshef. "A monster tank. It took a few seconds before I understood that scores of men were clustered all over it....They were hanging from the deck, the turret and any possible projection, while their rescue vehicle crawled eastward amid burning wreckage."

Casualties among the rescuers were heavy. Four of the APCs had to be left behind, but the men of Purkan had been saved.

Later that morning, the Egyptians finally overwhelmed the Matzmed fort, capturing its thirty-two men. Now there were only two manned forts left, each at the extreme end of the canal—Quay or Pier in the south and Budapest in the north.

TEL AVIV

By 3 AM, Elazar and Dayan were again airborne, returning from Sinai to the Pit to brief the general staff. Dayan's mood was again deeply pessimistic. It had been a day "wasted, frittered away, leaving in its trail disappointment, casualties and retreat." He told the stunned officers he thought the Southern Command had to make a major withdrawal and form a defense line, perhaps between El Arish and Sharm el Sheikh. In the north, there could be no retreat beyond the slopes of the Golan Heights. The IDF, the Israeli Defense Forces, had to fight to the last man there.

Then Dayan dropped a bombshell. He suggested that matters were so grim that the general staff consider an emergency mobilization of Jewish youth throughout the world as well as elderly men, youngsters below draft age and those who had been exempt from service. His piece said, Dayan walked out of the Pit, leaving the staff officers stupefied at the depth of his pessimism and the grave implications of his recommendations.

Elazar opposed emergency mobilization but he agreed with Dayan that the situation was critical. Yet, he reasoned, why voluntarily give up territory? One can always retreat, but there was no point in doing it on one's free will. He informed his staff that the Sinai force would rest up and gather strength while the main might of Israel concentrated on Syria. He ordered air strikes against strategic targets deep in Syria, including Damascus itself, and heavy ground attacks, both to bring Damascus to its knees and, equally important, to deter Jordan's King Hussein from entering the war. "I don't want Hussein to come in with four hundred tanks and force us to fight thirty kilometers from Jerusalem," Elazar said. "That's the last thing we need."

Dayan met later that morning with Golda Meir and found her morale good but her fatigue obvious. "It was pretty certain that she had not had a moment's sleep—though one could not say the same about cigarettes and coffee...."

He explained his dark view of the war and she was concerned enough to suggest that she should fly to the United States and personally brief President Nixon of the enormity of Israel's predicament. When this panicky idea was communicated to Washington, Henry Kissinger suspected that the "proposal could reflect only either hysteria or blackmail."

He prudently pointed out that such a trip could not be kept secret and, if revealed, would be a "sign of such panic" that it might bring into the war other Arab states, like Jordan, which were still hesitating to commit their resources. The Meir trip was not approved.

THE GOLAN HEIGHTS

Despite the loss of General Abrash, the Syrian 7th Division launched its delayed attack at dawn against Colonel Ben-Gal's weary and stunned 7th Brigade. The unit's losses had been heavy and its men under constant pressure ever since the war had begun. They were battle worn, numbed by the steady pounding of artillery shells and Katyusha rockets, the repeated attacks by armor and infantry over the valley of tears. The men were hoarse, disheveled, hollow-eyed, unshaven and filthy from the sweat and dust and grim of three solid days of heavy fighting. Now a hundred tanks accompanied by large numbers of armored infantry and a dense artillery bombardment were pressing toward Ben-Gal's position. As Syrian tanks were knocked out they were quickly replaced. The attack pressed relentlessly forward, forcing Ben-Gal to withdraw from the high ground to escape the devastating artillery barrage and weight of advancing armor. Syrian tanks quickly occupied the Israeli positions, others rolled on, pressing in on the desperate Israelis who now found themselves surrounded on all sides.

Dust, smoke and flames covered the battlefield, limiting visibility, adding to the confusion of lumbering tanks, exploding shells and the cries of the wounded. Syrian and Israeli tanks were so mixed up together that control and identification became impossible. Every tank was now fighting its own war, groping through the haze, seeking to separate enemy from friend.

At about 10 AM, Ben-Gal felt he could no longer hold on. His force was being systematically destroyed and the Syrians kept coming. He radioed the sector commander, General Eytan, and said he would have to retreat. Eytan was desperate. A breakthrough by the Syrians would create a gap through which they could go clanking down the Damascus road right into Israel. "For God's sake, Avigdor, hold on!" he urged. "Give me another half hour. You will soon be receiving reinforcements. Try, please, hold on!"

At that moment, the remnants of the battered Barak Brigade, now down to eleven tanks from its original ninety, moved into the sector. Eytan instantly dispatched it to Ben-Gal. By now, Ben-Gal had only thirty-two operating tanks out of his original force of 120 and ammunition was extremely low. Despite the reinforcements of the Barak tanks, he still thought he would have to withdraw.

But the Syrian momentum had run out of steam in the face of the fierce Israeli resistance. While Ben-Gal's forces had taken painful losses, so too had Syria's. Its fighters were exhausted and dispirited. The attack had been

193

ferocious, the fighting gruelling, the destruction frightful on both sides. Then, as so often happens in a battle, the Syrian offensive collapsed. The balance tipped and the Syrians suddenly stopped. Their losses were too horrendous. They could no longer go on.

A report from the Israeli fortress at A3 near the Purple Line, which had continued to hold out, reported that the Syrian supply vehicles were starting to withdraw. The Syrian tanks soon followed. The battle was over.

"You have saved the people of Israel," Eytan radioed exultantly to Ben-Gal.

On the battlefield of the valley of tears death hung in the air. Strewn across the black basaltic terrain were nearly 300 Syrian tanks, 200 other armored vehicles and hundreds of bodies. Intermingled among them were the losses suffered by the Israelis.

The Golan Heights had seen its last major battle although much hard fighting remained.

• •

TEL AVIV

A telephone call from air force commander General Benny Peled at 10 AM brought the first unalloyed good news of the war for Elazar. Peled reported that his planes had finally been able to breach the Syrian missile wall and destroy it. This was a significant development, for it meant that at long last Israel would be able to employ its superior air force. Its planes would be able to operate unopposed in supporting ground attacks on the Golan plateau, a strategic advantage. Elazar telephoned Northern Command commander General Haka Hofi, excitedly telling him: "Listen, Haka, if they've truly finished off the missiles, we're giving you the air force to operate freely."

Elazar's renewed optimism was for once justified. The Syrians were out of missiles and the Israeli air force was now in a position to turn the tide of battle on the Golan Heights. This it soon did, allowing Hofi's three divisions on the heights to mount a heavy counterattack that day that carried the Israeli forces back toward the Purple Line where they had started the war.

Heavy air attacks, personally approved by Prime Minister Golda Meir after Syria had ineffectually fired some FROG missiles into northern Israel, hit Syria during the day. The Syrian Defense Ministry in downtown Damascus was bombed as were other nearby areas, including the Soviet cultural center and a district housing embassies and foreign residents. Six Russians were reported killed along with twenty-four other civilians. Also hit by Israeli air strikes were the large refinery at Homs, which was set afire, and a radar station south of Beirut that was capable of tracking Israeli planes overflying Lebanon on their way to Beirut.

"Things are going beautifully in Syria," Elazar was able to exult by midday.

• •

THE SINAI PENINSULA

But things, as usual, were not going well in the Sinai. Against direct orders, Arik Sharon was attacking toward the canal. His reconnaissance unit had discovered there were very few Egyptians in the area around the northeastern shore of the Great Bitter Lake. Sharon wanted to attempt a crossing. He asked Gonen for permission to penetrate into mainland Egypt. The southern commander was appalled at the idea. Gonen had finally understood the strength of the Egyptian force and the relative weakness of his own units. He ordered Sharon to return to his previous position and instructed him to obey orders not to launch attacks that day. To make sure the impetuous Sharon understood, Gonen flew to Sharon's post and personally ordered him to avoid combat.

But Sharon was determined. When Gonen returned to his headquarters at Um Hasheiba, Sharon picked up the telephone and called a friend at the Pit, Brigadier General Dov Sion, the husband of Dayan's daughter, Yael.

"I have my feet dipping in the waters of the Great Bitter Lake," Sharon said. He asked Sion to try to persuade the general command to go over Gonen's head and approve a crossing.

Meanwhile, to create a diversion away from his presence at the Great Bitter Lake, Sharon ordered one of his brigades to attack at Missouri, known as Talata to the Egyptians, south of Timsah Lake. Again Gonen was forced to fly to Sharon's headquarters. He ordered the attack halted. But it went on, with Sharon's tank losses eventually estimated as high as fifty.

A visitor to Sharon's headquarters, retired Major General Avraham Joffe, once Sharon's commander, cracked: "The question is whether you are fighting the Arabs or the Jews."

At times in the coming days of fighting there was no clear answer to that question.

195

• •

TEL AVIV

Elazar had taken out three hours for his first sleep since the start of the war, but when he awoke and heard of Sharon's attacks he was furious. "Get him out of there!" Elazar shouted to Gonen during a telephone call. "I tell you he is not to cross! Not to cross! Not to cross!"

Gonen urged that Sharon be relieved of his command. But that could not be easily done. Sharon was widely admired in the army and by Dayan personally, who considered him Israel's best field commander. Although he had a reputation for bullheadedness and exceeding orders, that was more than offset by his tactical brilliance and aggressiveness in the field. Moreover, anything affecting Sharon's fate was ladened with political overtones. He was one of the leading opposition candidates in the upcoming elections and any action against him would be charged to political motives.

Already his division was being called the "Likud Party Division," after the political bloc he had formed with Menachem Begin, because many suspected he was intent on burnishing his reputation in the field in order to enhance his political fortunes. The same motive was ascribed by his critics to his repeated efforts to cross the canal, since the first Israeli on the other side would obviously become an instant hero.

If Elazar could do nothing about Sharon, he nonetheless was by now determined to straighten out the messy command structure in Southern Command. Tensions between Gonen, Adan and Sharon were so great that they were interfering with the war; communications were bad, and there was a sense of drift and disorganization about the whole command. Elazar asked Minister of Trade and Tourism Haim Bar-Lev whether he would consider putting his uniform back on and taking over Southern Command. The former chief of staff agreed, but only on the condition that it be clear he was in full command. To save face for Gonen, it was decided to announce Bar-Lev's appointment as being that of the personal representative of the chief of staff.

Now Elazar had the touchy task of informing Gonen, whom he continued to admire but felt had not had enough time to mature in his command before the war broke out. Gonen exploded when Elazar telephoned him with the new arrangement at 8:30 PM. Gonen accused Elazar of lacking faith in him and threatened to quit. Elazar tried to pacify the upset general.

"We're not talking about a commander of parallel rank but of an ex-chief of staff, a lieutenant general. And he's not coming down to you and on you because matters have been managed badly but because we're trying

196

to pull together all the talent at our disposal everywhere, so that things will be better.''

Reluctantly, Gonen accepted the new arrangement, quipping to his staff: "In this war I will have a private chief of staff of my own.''

• •

Moshe Dayan held a private briefing for top newspaper editors that Tuesday evening, telling them candidly that Israel at the moment remained too weak to push the Egyptians back across the canal. The IDF was on the defensive in the Sinai, he said, and probably would remain so for several more days. He doubted the war would be over within ten days. Dayan's words, while reflecting the reality, were bleak, his manner pessimistic, and the newspapermen were stunned. When he informed them that he planned to go on television that same evening to report to the Israeli people, the editors were appalled. Said one: "If you tell the public today on television what you have told us, this means an earthquake in the nation's consciousness and in that of the Jewish people and of the Arab people.''

One of the editors immediately telephoned Prime Minister Meir with his apprehensions, and she talked Dayan into cancelling his TV appearance.

• •

CAIRO

In his diary, Chief of Staff Shazly noted on Tuesday: "The enemy has persisted in throwing away the lives of their tank crews. They have assaulted in 'penny packet' groupings and their sole tactic remains the cavalry charge....In the last two days the enemy has lost 260 tanks. Our strategy always has been to force the enemy to fight on our terms; but we never expected them to cooperate.''

• •

The Soviet Union was less optimistic. It was aware by that evening that the war had turned dramatically against Syria with the unleashing of Israel's air force. Ambassador Vinogradov called on President Sadat at the Tahirah Palace, where he was monitoring war reports. Again the Soviet envoy asked whether Egypt wanted a ceasefire. Sadat hotly replied in the negative. Told that Syria still did, Sadat said President Assad had denied it to him in a recent message. It was a tense meeting and Vinogradov left frustrated.

Later that night Journalist Mohamed Heikal called on the Soviet ambassador. Heikal found Vinogradov in the residency, darkened because of

197

the general blackout, playing Rachmaninov's Second Piano Concerto in a room lit only by a candle.

"In times of tension this is really the only way I can relax," explained Vinogradov. He then described his difficult meeting with Sadat. It was an impossible situation for Moscow, he said, because one of its friends, Syria, wanted a ceasefire and another, Egypt, did not. "We can do anything, but we must know exactly what it is we are being asked to do."

Afterwards, Heikal telephoned Sadat and told him the Soviets thought Egypt was making a major mistake in not pushing to the Sinai passes and capturing them. Sadat disagreed. "As I told Hafez Assad, territory isn't important; what is important is to exhaust the enemy. I don't want to make the mistake of pushing forward too fast just for the sake of occupying more territory. We must make the enemy bleed."

• •

WASHINGTON

Word that all was not as encouraging as supposed finally seeped through to Ambassador Dinitz early in the morning Tuesday. He was so distraught about the news and Tel Aviv's increased demands for U.S. supplies that he twice woke up Henry Kissinger at the personal direction of Prime Minister Meir. In telephone calls at 1:45 AM and 3 AM, the Israeli envoy demanded urgent resupplies.

Kissinger was puzzled. He still had the impression that Israel was triumphing handily, and so he could not see the need of urgency or Dinitz's repeated calls—"unless he wanted to prove to the cabinet that he could get me out of bed at will...." Kissinger suspected there might be another reason: "The unworthy thought crossed my mind that perhaps the Israelis wanted to commit us to a schedule of deliveries now before their probable victory removed the urgency."

The two men, along with Israeli military attache Mordecai Gur, met in the White House at 8:20 AM. The grim news that Gur brought staggered Kissinger. Israeli losses were forty-nine airplanes, including fourteen Phantoms, and 500 tanks. All this in just two and a half days of fighting.

"So that's why the Egyptians are so cocky," exclaimed Kissinger, the reality finally sinking in.

Suddenly, he was extremely concerned. He promised Gur and Dinitz that he would have an answer for them on their requests for all types of military equipment that same day. When Gur asked for intelligence information, Kissinger instructed an aide to "give them every bit of intelligence we have.''

It was obvious to Kissinger and the Israelis that El Al's tiny fleet of seven civilian airliners would not be able to handle the volume of heavy military equipment that soon would be flowing to Israel. Yet the administration did not want to draw undue attention to its efforts to help the Jewish state by sending materiel in U.S. planes. This was especially true because Saudi Arabia's King Faisal had warned both Nixon and Kissinger that a public massive supply effort for Israel by the United States put irresistible pressure on his country to impose an oil boycott.

For the moment, Kissinger decided that unmarked El Al planes would be used, but he promised that if there was an emergency then ''we will get the tanks in even if we have to do it with American planes.'' No commitment could have been stronger, or politically riskier, in the face of the threatened Arab oil boycott.

But unlike Kissinger, other senior members of the administration remained suspicious that the Israeli government was using the war as a way to squeeze additional aid, both material and symbolic, out of the United States. At a special WSAG meeting of senior officials that morning, CIA Director William Colby voiced the suspicion that ''Israel was simply trying to obtain the maximum military aid from us before victory....'' The state department shared Colby's suspicions, and Defense Secretary James Schlesinger generally remained skeptical. Everyone, except Kissinger, agreed that there was a difference between helping Israel maintain its 1967 prewar frontiers and helping it to retain its conquests from that war. ''My own view,'' recalled Kissinger in his memoirs, ''was that events had gone beyond such fine-tuning.'' In the end, his view prevailed.

He conferred with President Nixon that day—Nixon at the time was anguishing over how to announce the resignation of his Vice President, Spiro Agnew, because of plea bargaining over charges that he took kickbacks when Maryland's governor—and later was able to assure Dinitz of bountiful resupplies. The Israelis would get just about everything they wanted—planes, tanks, jamming equipment, Sparrow and Sidewinder missiles and a blanket promise that all their losses would be replaced. They could begin picking up the materiel the next day in their own planes at Oceana Naval Air Station at Virginia Beach, Virginia.

When this generous promise was relayed to Tel Aviv, Chief of Staff Elazar exclaimed: ''We got everything!''

By then, it was known that earlier reports that the IDF was running out of tank shells were unfounded. This fear had added to the urgency of some of Israel's earlier requests to Washington. But the fact that there actually was no shortage apparently was never relayed to Washington.

To be sure that Israel's needs could be promptly communicated, Kissinger had installed in Dinitz's office at the Israeli Embassy a private, secure telephone line that directly linked the secretary of state with the ambassador, a unique privilege for a foreign country. But by this time there appeared to be no difference in Kissinger's mind between the identities of Israel and America: "I never doubted that a defeat of Israel by Soviet arms would be a geopolitical disaster for the United States."

CHAPTER XX

October 10: A Time of Decision

TUESDAY'S BREACH OF THE SYRIAN MISSILE screen had been a decisive turning point. The unsheathed might of the Israeli air force devastated Syria's armor and allowed Israel's three divisions slowly to roll back the Syrian forces. By midday Wednesday, all of Syria's troops had been pushed back behind the Purple Line they had crossed in such force four days earlier. Left behind were 867 tanks and thousands of vehicles, guns and stores of ammunition. Despite such losses, the Syrians were by no means defeated. Unlike 1967, the army had not collapsed—a source of pride in itself and a morale booster for the troops. It remained a strong fighting force, facing Israel across the ceasefire line in heavily fortified positions.

The sudden fortuitous turn of events on the Golan Heights faced Israel with its most momentous decision of the war—what to do next. Out of the swirl of events and numerous balancing factors, Israel's government now had to decide on a strategy for the rest of the war. Should it attack across the Purple Line and threaten Damascus? Should it keep its forces at the line, which was the best defensive position with its forts and antitank ditch, and transfer a division to the south? Or should it attack immediately in the south, hoping to score a psychological victory by grabbing some of the west bank of the canal?

Complicating these questions was the factor of time. If a ceasefire were called for by the United Nations now, Israel would have nothing to bargain with, no gains to show for all its fighting. It had not succeeded in destroying either the Syrian or Egyptian armies. Nothing had been gained on the Golan. And in the Sinai, Egyptian troops were firmly lodged on the east bank, a victory of Arab arms. The Egyptians certainly would not give back what they had retaken unless Israel achieved some gains it could use in a barter.

Then there was the painful factor of casualties. As of noon, Tuesday, after three days of fighting, incomplete figures showed Israel had lost 310 men dead, 100 missing and 1,150 wounded. This was already more than had been lost in the 1956 war, in which 189 were killed and 899 wounded, and was fast approaching the 983 killed in the 1967 war. Yet no one doubted that Tuesday's figures did not reflect the full story. The actual casualties were almost surely higher but in the pressure of combat a complete list had not yet been reported. Was it really worth fighting more and suffering more casualties?

These basic questions consumed the attention of Israel's generals and government leaders most of this fateful day. On their decision would hang the lives of Israelis and Arabs alike and the outcome of the war.

• •

WEDNESDAY

THE GOLAN HEIGHTS

Chief of Staff Elazar flew up to Northern Command late in the morning to get a reading of the situation on the ground. It was encouraging. Six Syrian planes had already been shot down that morning and no Syrian troops were west of the Purple Line. But there were also worrying signs. Part of the Syrian missile screen was back in operation and several missiles had been fired that morning. There were reports that the Soviet Union was about to begin its resupply effort with twenty-one giant Antonov planes, carrying among other things surface-to-air missiles.

U.S. intelligence had picked up the indications that same morning. (To hinder their landings, Israeli jets that day bombed the runways of the airports at Damascus and Aleppo as well as the ports at Homs, Latakia and Tartus.) Also, an Iraqi armored division with 300 tanks was reported moving toward the Syrian border, apparently to join the fight. Would that pull Jordan into the war?

In northern commander Hofi's opinion, the Syrians were not about to collapse. They had only about 350 to 400 tanks left out of their original 1,300 to 1,400, but they could quickly reinforce with another 200 and they showed no indication of retreating without a stiff fight.

Whatever was decided for the future, one thing was clear to Elazar. His troops badly needed a rest. Many of them had not slept in four days. Colonel Ben-Gal reported that whenever his men of the 7th Brigade stopped moving they instantly fell asleep. Division commander Dan Laner added that it was hard to get tanks moving because no one heard the command. They were all asleep.

Elazar ordered the troops on the Golan to stand down for the day, to "sleep, rest, grease, repair their machinery, take a breather." Since the rising sun shone in the Israelis' eyes, they could have until 11 AM Thursday before going back in action with the sun innocently overhead.

At last, a blessed silence descended on the scarred and littered Golan Heights.

• •

THE SINAI PENINSULA

The fighters in the Sinai were bone-weary too. At a meeting of brigade commanders and their staffs in Adan's war room tent shortly after midnight Wednesday, Adan noted that most of them had not slept for ninety-six hours. They were "grimy, unshaven, with bloodshot eyes and hoarse voices....At best, I thought, they would be able to catch an hour's sleep."

Although the Israelis remained on static defense, gathering stheir strength, the Egyptians were active and firefights erupted at all hours. Extremely heavy artillery duels raged all along the line. In Adan's division alone, his thirty-two artillery crews fired that Wednesday 4,700 shells. This equalled 250 tons that had to be unloaded from 50 trucks and then loaded in the guns, a draining physical burden.

Thousands of Egyptian infantrymen repeatedly attacked Israeli tanks, causing Adan to bemoan Israel's lack of armored personnel carriers. He and his predecessor as head of the Armored Corps, Yisrael Tal, had long disagreed about the need of APCs. Tal, who was known as Mr. Armor because of his strong advocacy of the tank, opposed the purchase of large numbers of APCs, arguing that their high cost detracted from the country's ability to buy tanks. He also did not believe armored infantry had a major place in today's battlefield. Adan disagreed, pointing out that armored infantry was another aspect of an integrated battle group that gave it flexibility and increased fire power which tanks alone could not match.

Egypt's tactics in using its infantry to fight tanks was now proving that Adan had the better part of the argument. Tank crews, shut in with limited vision and a lone machine gun, were unable to fight off infantry attacks supported by antitank missiles. For that, other tactics were needed employing armored infantry that could speed through the battlefield and spray it with withering machine gun fire. Though Israel was short on APCs, Adan and other Israeli commanders now began developing the tactics that eventually would become highly effective against Egypt's tank battling infantry.

• •

Haim Bar-Lev arrived in the Sinai that Wednesday and took over command of the southern forces. By all accounts, after some initial edginess, he and Gonen worked well together for the rest of the war. Bar-Lev's arrival had a soothing effect on the command, except perhaps for Sharon, who was a political foe and who did not believe Bar-Lev was aggressive enough. That evening Bar-Lev met with the division commanders, filled them in on what was happening in the north and said the south would remain on the defensive for the time being. Sharon again wanted permission to attack across the canal. But it was noted that the Sinai force still had only about 600 tanks, not nearly enough for a cross-canal trust. For that it was considered 1,000 tanks would be needed.

As Adan left the meeting late Wednesday, he felt "the worst of the crisis was behind us...." Adan returned to his sector for yet another meeting, this one with his brigade commanders. "I couldn't remember if or when I had slept or dozed—perhaps I had learned to live without sleep....Perhaps, I thought, it's possible to get along without sleep after all—but only on condition that things aren't dull. Dull it certainly was not."

• •

That same evening the Egyptian 1st Infantry Brigade attacked southward toward Ras Sudar, getting out of range of its protective SAM missile screen. It was a fatal mistake. Once exposed, Israeli warplanes swooped in and decimated the unit, knocking it out of action for several days. "The decisiveness of the encounter was a reminder, if we needed one, of how open our ground forces were to air attack the moment they left our SAM umbrella," observed Chief of Staff Shazly.

It was a reminder that would be driven home even more forcefully three days hence.

• •

CAIRO

Mohamed Heikal was worried about the Soviet criticism of Egypt's failure to advance beyond the canal area expressed the previous evening in his meeting with Ambassador Vinogradov. The journalist telephoned Marshal Ismail to repeat Vinogradov's remarks. "You know," Ismail replied, "that had been my intention. But in view of the deteriorating situation on the

Syrian front, we must revise our plans. Should the enemy turn and concentrate all his attacks on us we must at all costs avoid being dangerously extended.''

• •

TEL AVIV

The discussion on war strategy among Elazar and his staff that began in the morning and had been going on all day continued into the evening. Elazar had to report his recommendations to the prime minister later in the night. There had been many small fights but no major event during the day affecting the situation. All the confusing elements and options remained the same. But by now some aspects had become clearer. If Israel went on the defensive in the north, it would take four to five days to transfer a division to the Sinai. By that time a ceasefire might have been imposed and Israel would be left with little bargaining room. This was unacceptable to all of the leadership.

"The war should not be stopped at the present military lines," said Dayan, expressing the general view. "...I felt we should do whatever we could to prevent an immediate ceasefire decision."

On the other hand, the Purple Line on the Golan was the best defensive line. "And if we can't secure a better line, we might just as well save blood and armor and stay right where we are," commented Elazar. "That's the problem."

Another part of the problem was that the Syrian army remained strong. Israel could not expect it to collapse in the face of an attack.

The same was true in the south. The Egyptian army was too strongly dug in to hope that it could be dislodged before a ceasefire.

"We find ourselves in a situation whereby I doubt whether we can conclude the war without losing any territory," noted Elazar.

Therefore the best solution might be to "end up with mutually altered lines—we have changed the line in Syria and they have changed it in Egypt."

Elazar came to the conclusion that the best strategy was to hit hard at Syria by penetrating the Purple Line and advancing toward Damascus, only thirty miles away. If Israel could bring the capital city within range of its artillery, the Syrians might press for a ceasefire and accept a deal whereby it would get its land back to the Purple Line in exchange for Egypt surrendering its gains. Another advantage in hitting Syria was that it could be done the next day before Syria could substantially reinforce its Purple

205

Line troops. As Dayan later explicated: ''[The Syrians] would then come to realize that by launching war upon us, not only would they not gain the Golan Heights or defeat the Israeli army, but their own armies would be routed and their capital...endangered.''

But Elazar's deputy, Major General Yisrael Tal, disagreed. He favored a limited feint in the north with the major effort coming in the Sinai. Tal's suggestion was that Bar-Lev's forces retire deep into the desert, thereby luring the Egyptians out from under their missile umbrella. When they became exposed, Israeli air and tanks would deliver them a crushing blow.

Thus still disunited, the generals and Dayan went to Golda Meir's Tel Aviv office at 9:30 PM. Once again, the arguments and counter arguments washed back and forth, the advantages and disadvantages toted up, the contingencies calculated, the imponderables speculated upon. The meeting went on until after midnight, by now consuming at least nine hours of Elazar's busy day. In the end, it was finally decided to follow Elazar's recommendation to try to threaten Damascus. The prime reason for taking that course was not military but diplomatic. Israel had heard the Soviet Union was now pressing for a ceasefire in-place.

But, observed Meir, it was important for Israel to score a gain before that happened. ''If it is within our power to deal a crushing blow to the Syrians and force them to plead for a ceasefire, that will be a tremendous achievement.''

• •

WASHINGTON

Henry Kissinger heard of the start of the Russian resupply effort to Syria early that Wednesday morning. At the same time, he had a telephone call from Ambassador Dobrynin. The Soviet Union, the envoy said, ''is ready not to block adoption of a ceasefire resolution in the Security Council.'' He indicated Egypt was ready to acquiesce to a ceasefire. To Kissinger, it was clear that what the Soviets were talking about was a ceasefire in-place, not one with a return to the prewar ceasefire lines.

The proposal came in ''the worst possible circumstances for our strategy,'' Kissinger recalled in his memoirs. ''If the Soviets pushed their proposal at this juncture, it would have had nearly unanimous backing, including by our European allies. On the other hand, Israel, with the prewar situation not yet restored, would have refused.'' Even if Israel agreed, he reasoned, ''the war would have ended in a clear cut victory for the Soviet-supplied Arab forces.'' Kissinger's response was to stall while at the same time informing the Israelis of the Soviet message and urging Israel to "make the maximum military effort in the next forty-eight hours."

It was this news that decided Israel to accelerate the fighting and pursue its strategy to attack Syria the next day.

Kissinger also decided to try to hire private charter planes to transport supplies to Israel. This was an effort to keep U.S. involvement in a low profile and not raise Arab emotions in order to avoid King Faisal's threatened oil boycott.

Despite his busy schedule, Kissinger was in constant communication with Ambassador Dinitz throughout the day. That evening, they had an hour and fifteen minute meeting in the White House at which the Israeli envoy hotly opposed a ceasefire. Kissinger and Dinitz agreed to meet again at 7:45 AM the next day.

Throughout the day, Kissinger also called Dobrynin, offering one excuse after another why the United States could not respond to his offer of a U.N.-sponsored ceasefire. "You are playing quite well," the veteran Soviet diplomat remarked. But "don't overplay the theme of Russian irresponsibility."

It is doubtful that even if Kissinger sincerely wanted the President's decision on a ceasefire if he could have gotten it that day. Vice President Agnew resigned in the early afternoon, absorbing Nixon's attention and further weakening his bloodied presidency.

• •

In the Middle East, where it was already Thursday, Israel was about to launch its new strategy and attack toward Damascus, the first time the Jewish state would directly threaten an Arab capital with a land assault.

CHAPTER XXI

October 11-13: Attack in Syria

FOR THE FIRST TIME since the start of the war, Israel moved to extend its conquests beyond the ceasefire line of 1967 in Syria. While the Sinai Peninsula was now quiescent, all attention was on the fight with Syria and the effort to establish a salient inside that country before an anticipated ceasefire, expected within perhaps the next forty-eight hours. The expectation was wrong, but it nonetheless provided the impetus for Israel's race against time. In addition, it was certain now that an armored division from Iraq was approaching to do battle and it looked like King Hussein was going to join the war, at least in a limited way. (In fact, Iraqi units had started crossing into Syria on October 9. But when an Iraqi officer went to Damascus for instructions he discovered his unit had not been expected and there were no orders for it. He was told simply to "go forward and fight," the direction being vaguely indicated to the south.)

Another factor, the Soviets' intentions, was becoming increasingly complex and dangerous. Moscow was obviously mounting a major resupply effort to the Arabs. Its initiation of the effort the previous day had been met with a bold riposte by Israel. Israeli planes launched heavy raids on Syria's airfields, successfully causing some of the Soviet cargo planes to land in Hungary for lack of Syrian runways. The small Israeli navy was now also busy, blasting Syrian ports to prevent Soviet resupply by ships. On Thursday, the Soviets extended their efforts by starting to resupply Egypt too. The Kremlin was obviously determined that Soviet arms would prevail, as they had in Vietnam and in the recent Indian-Pakistani wars.

Israeli leaders were concerned by the increasingly hard Soviet actions, realizing, as Defense Minister Dayan observed, that "we had to be very careful to prevent the bear from getting out of the forest."

That too was becoming an increasing concern in Washington. Detente had obviously reached its limits. Now the superpowers were slowly being sucked into confrontation.

• •

THURSDAY/the 11th

THE GOLAN HEIGHTS

The Israeli attack was not easy. The ground over which it had to advance was well prepared for defense, sown with mines and antitank ditches and crisscrossed by integrated concrete emplacements connected by trenches and screened by wire. As the Israelis had on their side, the Syrians had been working on the defensive grid since 1967. They had anchored it on their right to the rugged slopes of Mt. Hermon and on the left at the impassable Yarmuk Canyon.

The Israeli plan was to try to break through on the Syrian right along the foothills of Mt. Hermon with General Eytan's division. This would protect the left flank of Dan Laner's division to the south, which would carry the main thrust of the attack straight up the Damascus-Kuneitra road to the gates of Syria's capital. The major objective was the capture of the charming village of Sasa, twenty-two miles southwest of Damascus and within artillery range of the capital.

The capture of Damascus was presumably not sought at any time, according to Israeli officials. The plan was limited, aimed at getting to within artillery range so that Syria would be cowered into seeking a ceasefire, thereby freezing that front and allowing Israel to concentrate its energies against Egypt.

General Eytan's 7th and Barak brigades, both now brought back up to strength after their initial heavy losses, opened the attack at 11 AM along the Syrian right flank at Mt. Hermon. Facing them were the Moroccan Brigade and the 68th Syrian Brigade, one of the remnants of the shattered 7th Infantry Division. After negotiating the thick mine fields along his front, Colonel Ben-Gal's 7th Brigade smashed toward the Hader crossroads through the 68th Syrian Brigade, commanded by a Druze, Rafiq Hilawi. The Syrian unit broke, allowing the 7th Brigade to reach the Hader junction, about three miles east of the Purple Line. The Barak Brigade on the south managed to penetrate several miles farther, capturing the Druze village of Horfa.

But the going was slow and the fighting tough for both brigades. The terrain was rough, covered with broken lava boulders, and the Syrian resistance remained stiff. Syrian infantrymen hid among the boulders and effectively employed Sagger antitank weapons and the Syrian air force repeatedly ventured into the battle, even though Israel enjoyed air superiority, which it exercised lavishly.

• •

Two hours after Eytan, General Laner attacked eastward on the heavily fortified Damascus road against elements of three Syrian infantry divisions, the 7th, 5th and 9th, from north to south. Immediately his 17th Brigade's reconnaissance unit came under terrific artillery bombardment and lost seventeen tanks. Syrian infantry swarmed in the area, firing RPGs and Saggers. As the 679th Israeli Brigade rushed to the rescue, a determined effort by the 17th punched a hole in the Syrian defense and several tanks managed to reach the Khan Arnaba junction, less than five miles from the Purple Line. With this breakthrough, General Laner urged the two brigades, plus the 19th, to exploit the opening by thrusting to high ground eastward and southward beyond the Khan Arnaba junction.

But then the Israelis discovered they had moved into a trap. The Syrian forces bypassed at Khan Arnaba closed in, blocking the highway and isolating Laner's forces east of the junction. They were unable to evacuate their wounded or receive supplies and the area became, in the words of General Chaim Herzog, ''a virtual death trap for Israeli tanks....'' The men had to be rescued by a parachute battalion, which eventually succeeded in taking the vital Khan Arnaba junction, but not without a long and bloody fight.

As darkness fell, Damascus was no where near being threatened and the Israelis had managed to penetrate only a few miles beyond the Purple Line. But they were important miles. Now Israel could bargain with additional Syrian territory, and it planned to try to get more.

• •

CAIRO

The mood at Tahra Palace was euphoric. Mohamed Heikal was sitting with Anwar Sadat in the presidential office when Marshal Ismail entered, looking cheerful. He had just received a message that the Syrians were containing the Israeli attack. "I knew it was good news as soon as I saw the expression on your face," said Sadat, who was wearing striped grey pajamas.

Then the telephone rang. It was President Houari Boumedienne of Algeria, commenting on Elazar's boast about "breaking bones." "It seems to me that when they start talking like this they are losing their nerve," he said.

Next came word that Abu Dhabi had contributed $100 million to the Egyptian war effort, Libya pledged weapons and oil and Jordan indicated it would send troops to help Syria. All this came on top of a personal pledge by King Faisal of Saudi Arabia of $200 million. He had made the pledge, which was in addition to his financing of Egypt's arms needs, two days after the war started, saying, "You have made us all proud. In the past we could not lift our heads up. Now we can."

Reported Heikal: "The atmosphere in Tahra Palace was optimistic, and the talk was about what we were going to do when the battle was over."

• •

THE SINAI PENINSULA

Chief of Staff Shazly made his second tour of the Bar-Lev Line on Thursday. He had a personal pledge to keep. He planned to visit the mighty Purkan fort that he had gazed at from across the Suez Canal on the eve of the war. Then it had appeared so looming, so powerful. Now it was in Egyptian hands, as he had predicted. "What a strange feeling it gave to enter it at last," he observed. Then he said: "Alhamdu Lillah, Allahu Akbar," thanks be to God, God is the greatest.

After inspecting Egypt's fortified positions along the canal, Shazly found himself satisfied, "...calmer than I had been since our assault began." Although Israel's strength was daily growing stronger as its mobilization began smoothly to go into high gear, Shazly was confident. "We had a foothold in Sinai. It was not impregnable....But ours was so defended that, to dislodge us, Israel would have to pay a price they would almost certainly find unacceptable."

• •

At the Israeli line about ten miles east of the canal, General Adan had just received word that the general staff had approved the start of planning for a crossing operation north of Deversoir at the Great Bitter Lake. The day was the anniversary of the Festival of Tabernacles, the celebration of

211

Moses' leading of the Jews out of Egypt more than three thousand years earlier. That biblical event had occurred over the same sands of the Sinai that Israeli and Egyptian were now fighting over. It had also led to the original establishment of Israel.

In the afternoon, Adan received the encouraging news that Israeli forces were attacking past the Purple Line in Syria. He happily passed the word to his brigade commanders by radio. Then, elated at the push against Syria, he relaxed. It was the first day in which he had not been not under constant Egyptian attack and the veteran warrior suddenly vented his emotions. Addressing the Egyptians on his radio net, he said: "Oh Egyptians! If you are listening to us, then listen carefully, you sons of bitches: Your turn is coming!"

• •

WASHINGTON

Henry Kissinger was peeved at the Israelis for announcing on Thursday that their troops were advancing toward Damascus. Defense Minister Dayan had contentedly pointed out: "The same road that leads to Tel Aviv leads to Damascus." The public boast was actually exaggerated, as Israeli claims consistently were about its Golan activities, which were never as great as Tel Aviv insisted. Nonetheless, the boast put Kissinger on the spot since, as he admitted, "...we had been stalling the Soviets for twenty-four hours on a ceasefire in place—a position we could hardly maintain if Israel announced that it was advancing on the capital of a Soviet ally." He voiced his complaint that Thursday morning to Mordecai Shalev, the deputy chief of mission at the Israeli embassy. "How can we get the UN to slow down when you make this kind of announcement by your defense minister....This looks like the most extreme form of collusion and bad faith."

Despite the obvious collusion, Kissinger continued to stall Soviet Ambassador Dobrynin and the Security Council. There would be no ceasefire that day.

• •

Israel's demands for resupplies became louder as the war lengthened. The instant need for ammunition was repeatedly put forth. Kissinger was accused of deliberately stalling on the matter as a way to exert pressure on Israel to limit its attacks, a charge he hotly—and almost certainly truthfully— denied.

The fact was there had been little sense of urgency at first, and much

212

suspicion about whether the supplies were needed at all. Moreover, there was great concern within the administration that an open resupply effort would force the Arabs to retaliate by imposing an oil boycott. To avoid that, the administration had at first opened its arsenal to what could be carried on El Al's seven Boeing 707 civilian airliners. When they proved inadequate to transport the abundant materiel, the administration attempted to hire U.S. charters to undertake the task. But it discovered none of them wanted to get involved in a war zone, or in the Arab-Israeli conflict. All this took time to sort out, but meanwhile Israel's supporters were becoming impatient, along with Ambassador Dinitz.

Senator Henry Jackson, a Democrat and one of Israel's strongest champions, was persistent in demanding that the resupply begin immediately. He repeatedly telephoned Kissinger. So too did others from Capitol Hill. The media began taking up the chant, so much so that beleaguered President Nixon, correctly suspecting Dinitz of encouraging the stories, told Kissinger on Thursday night to warn the envoy that the President would personally hold him responsible if the hostile news stories continued.

The aggressive Israeli diplomat was not deterred. He was now thinking of "going public," that is, galvanizing the Israeli Lobby to exert its full force on the administration through its significant influence in the media, business and Congress. At a time when the President was reeling under the assaults of Watergate and the Agnew resignation, the threat was not an idle one.

Later that night, Kissinger received a message from King Hussein saying Arab pressures were such that King Hussein of Jordan had to make at least a token contribution to the war. He would not open a third front along the Jordan Valley but instead would send a brigade into Syria to coordinate with its forces. He requested Israeli acquiescence or at least an assurance the Jewish state would not use his move as a reason to attack Jordan. Israel naturally refused officially, but privately it could not help but be relieved that it would not face a third front.

• •

FRIDAY/the 12th

CAIRO

Though the Israelis were not able to cause the collapse of the Syrian army—quite the reverse, it was fighting with great determination—the pressure was nonetheless severe enough to make Damascus plead with

213

Egypt for help. The request was for Egypt to press its attack eastward from the canal to engage the Israelis and relieve pressure on the Golan Heights as well as dampen the heavy air strikes that were hitting deep inside Syria. Though desirable from Syria's perspective, an attack in open desert was the most perilous course Egypt could possibly take. The best strategy was for the Egyptian troops to stay right where they were, to be, as General Ismail said, "the rocks upon which the Israeli waves would be shattered"— which they had been during the first days of the war. But now other considerations were involved.

Chief of Staff Shazly argued hotly against the attack with Ismail. Shazly pointed out what had happened to the unfortunate 1st Infantry Brigade when it had ventured out of the umbrella of the Egyptian missile screen two days earlier. "It was routed by air attack alone," Shazly protested. But in the end Ismail insisted the attack must be launched. He explained: "It is a political decision."

To accomplish the attack, Egypt would have to commit the major portion of its strategic reserves, the 4th and 21st Armored divisions. The two divisions, with a total of 330 tanks, had remained on the west bank of the canal to cover an Israeli counter-thrust to the west bank and for emergency plugging of any Israeli penetrations of the Bar-Lev. Now all but a brigade of the reserves were ordered across the canal for the attack. That left only one hundred tanks in reserve on the west bank. As Shazly later observed: "It was a grave mistake."

But, in context, the decision appeared unavoidable. The last thing Sadat now needed was to have Syria sue for a ceasefire. That would allow the full force of Israel to be concentrated against Egypt.

• •

THE GOLAN HEIGHTS

During his tours of the Golan while the fighting raged, Moshe Dayan was struck by the bleakness of the landscape. "The part of Syria stretching northward from Kuneitra...was a bare expanse of black basalt rocks, unmarked by tree or bush. In the distance I could see miserable dust-laden hamlets, their houses scrambled together with black unhewn stone...the scene was studded with burned out tanks, shattered vehicles, and smoking ammunition trucks, while along the side tracks streamed columns of fleeing villagers, their donkeys laden with bedding, their wives carrying large bundles on their heads and infants in their arms. In the fields, between the exploding shells, frightened old men and children led their wretched flocks.''

Israeli forces trying to reach Sasa found it hard and slow going over this woeful landscape. Sasa lay at the northern debouchment of steep ridges bordering both sides of the Damascus road. To the southwest, Tel Shams, sited on a high hill, commanded the highway and the entry into the Sasa defile, a stepping stone to the capture of Sasa.

Northern commander Hofi ordered Colonel Ben-Gal to take Tel Shams early in the morning with an attack across the difficult terrain by his Barak force operating south of the 7th Brigade. Three times a Barak battalion tried to mount an attack along Damascus road, but Syrian infantry hidden among the volcanic boulders blasted the Israelis to a halt. Around noon, Ben-Gal tried a deep flanking attack that was also fought to a standstill. The Syrians claimed that by this time they had knocked out forty Israeli tanks.

Ben-Gal moved his advanced headquarters to Hales, just to the west of Tel Shams, and took over a Druze house with a balcony. He ordered Barak's commander, Lieutenant Colonel Naty Yossi, to meet with him so they could study the terrain and lines of approach to the dominating feature of Tel Shams. While they sat on the balcony gazing through binoculars and study ing aerial photographs, they were stunned when a Druze approached and, with traditional Arab hospitality, offered them Turkish coffee. As they sipped the welcome drink, the two officers plotted out a path through the volcanic landscape.

Ben-Gal decided to attack again about 4:30 PM. As he watched the lead company reach the slopes of Tel Shams, the attack looked as if it was going to be successful. At the last moment, however, four of the remaining six attacking tanks were knocked out by antitank missiles. An attempt to send in a rescue force of tanks failed. The Israeli wounded had to be evacuated by foot and Syria retained control of the village.

• •

While Ben-Gal was being repulsed, General Laner was attacking in a sweeping movement to the south in an effort to take the Sasa defenders from behind. Standing on the high ground at Tel Shaar, just east of the Khan Arnaba junction, Laner was surveying the battlefield through binoculars shortly before 2 PM when he saw a mass of armor about six miles to the southeast. At first, he thought they must be Israeli, perhaps from General Peled's division, which was to operate on the Israeli right flank. But a call to headquarters informed him that Peled was still stuck at the Purple Line and had not yet moved. Laner suddenly realized that he was about to be attacked on his exposed flank by a force of 100 to 150 tanks.

They were from the Iraqi 3rd Tank Division. The Iraqi units had come into Syria in scattered sequence, the 8th Mechanized Infantry Brigade arriving October 9 followed the next day by the 6th Tank Brigade and, on the night of the 12th by the 12th Tank Brigade.

Before the two forces could organize themselves for a major confrontation, night fell and quiet descended on the battlefield.

• •

Although major battles still lay ahead and Chief of Staff Elazar repeatedly urged the northern forces to press forward to Sasa, Syrian resistance proved too great. No further large territorial gains were made by Israel in Syria and Sasa was never taken.

The Israeli advance in Syria was now essentially halted. Token forces from Jordan, Kuwait and Saudi Arabia moved onto the plateau during the next week, adding to Israel's problems. But coordination among the volunteer Arabs forces and Syria was almost nonexistent and their major contribution was to keep the Israeli forces frozen in their positions from October 12 onward.

Israel had penetrated to a line stretching at its furthermost from Kfar Shams on the southeast, about fifteen miles east of the Purple Line, to Mazrat Beit Jan in the northeast, located some ten miles from the Purple Line. It failed to get within artillery range of downtown Damascus itself although its long range guns were able to bombard the city's southern outskirts and Damascus International Airport.

Israel's important fortress atop Mt. Hermon remained in Syrian hands. That would have to be recaptured. But now all of Israel's attention began swinging toward the vast Sinai Peninsula where evidence was mounting that Egypt was about to make its long anticipated attack. That Friday night, the Israeli cabinet formally decided that if Syria pressed for a ceasefire in place it would accept.

• •

TEL AVIV

Israel's leadership was now presented with yet another grave question on which the outcome of the war would likely pivot: What strategy to adopt in the Sinai? The options were limited, but all carried fateful implications.

Israel's forces could withdraw to a strong defensive line and dig in, waiting for the Egyptians to try to break out of their bridgeheads; they could attack the Egyptians head-on at the canal, or they could try a daring crossing of the canal. But because of their lack of bridging equipment their supply route would be based on only one area in defiance of accepted doctrine, making it an extremely risky venture. This was particularly so since Egypt's five divisions dug in on the east bank remained strong and two other divisions continued waiting in reserve just across the canal.

In a meeting with Dado Elazar and his senior aides, Dayan again was in one of his funks, not enthusiastic about any of the choices. Certainly he was not impressed with the general consensus for an immediate crossing. He doubted that it would bring about a collapse of the Egyptian army or even an acceptance of a ceasefire. Instead, the war would drag on, he predicted, and months would go by before Israel could gather enough strength to achieve a victory.

Later Friday evening, Dayan, Elazar and other top commanders once again went before Prime Minister Meir and her close advisers to argue out what strategy should be chosen. By a coincidence, while they were discussing their future strategy, reports began arriving that the Egyptians were beginning at last to make their long anticipated transfer of the two reserve divisions over to the east bank.

Egypt was obviously about to try to make a breakout. It was the best of all options for the Israelis. If they could lure Egyptian armor out from its missile umbrella, Israeli air could decimate it and Israeli tanks could then crush it. Now no decision on the various options was necessary. Israel would await the outcome of the battle before deciding what to do next.

• •

THE SINAI PENINSULA

Arik Sharon was furious at the general staff's decision to await an Egyptian attack. He wanted to attack immediately across the canal. "They've got no guts," he complained to his staff at his Tasa headquarters. "They know neither the terrain nor the enemy. They're holding us up all the time. I tell them it is possible to cross. I'm prepared to go and do it, but they just sit there and decide it can't be done.

"I must talk to Moshe [Dayan]."

Sharon telephoned Dayan's Tel Aviv home and found himself talking to the defense minister's daughter, Yael. She did not believe he would be home until the next morning.

"What's happened, he's sleeping out again?" joked Sharon, referring to Dayan's widespread reputation as a womanizer. Yael was not amused, but Sharon continued. "Listen, if you talk to him tell him that the whole division here is champing on the bit. My horses are ready for war. You remember the picture—like the eve of the Six Day War. Explain that to him. He must understand that there is enough initiative here to bust up this Egyptian business."

• •

WASHINGTON

Richard Nixon was totally absorbed Friday with the selection of his new vice president to replace the dishonored Spiro Agnew. That left Henry Kissinger in charge of foreign affairs. He had been informed in the morning that Israel, having advanced beyond the Purple Line, was now amenable to a ceasefire. But instead of rushing forward, Kissinger took the time to query what Israel's preferred time for a ceasefire would be. The answer he received did not reflect the usual positions between a superpower and a client nation.

"...Israel would prefer—but did not insist—that the resolution not be put to a vote until the afternoon of the following day, Saturday," Kissinger reported. "However, we could start the process of consultation at our discretion." The new secretary of state accommodated the Israeli instruction. After receiving the concurrence of Foreign Minister Abba Eban, who was at the United Nations, Kissinger followed Israel's bidding to see that no vote would be taken by the Security Council before late the next day.

That same morning, Kissinger received intelligence that the Soviet Union had put on alert seven airborne divisions, not three as first reported. Additionally, the Soviets' airlift to Syria and Egypt since Wednesday now totaled eighty-four planes. Clearly the limits of detente were being stretched.

At his first news conference of the war, held the same morning, Kissinger showed that he was prepared not only to risk detente but an oil boycott too in his efforts to help Israel. "We have made a very serious effort, in this crisis, to take seriously into account Arab concerns and Arab views," he said. "On the other hand, we have to pursue what we consider to be the right course; we will take the consequences...."

Afterwards, Kissinger had lunch with Ambassador Dobrynin, who warned that the Soviet Union was not ready to sit by idly and watch Israel threaten Damascus. According to Kissinger, Dobrynin added ominously: "If Israel continued its advance, matters might get out of hand."

Kissinger passed on the warning to Dinitz, who a few hours later told the secretary of state that Israel was "very concerned" about the Soviet threat. It no doubt influenced Israel's decision to limit its military activity on the Golan Heights. Prime Minister Meir had also cabled that if Kissinger thought it wise he should submit a ceasefire resolution that same evening. But he believed that action would look too weak in the face of the Soviet threat and demurred. However, he could not stall the Soviet Union much longer.

Then came more Soviet warnings. Dobrynin passed on a Kremlin message in the evening assailing the "barbaric bombings by the Israeli aviation of peaceful population centers in Egypt and Syria, Damascus included...." Darkly, it added that "Israeli population centers would not remain immune indefinitely." It also charged that Israeli torpedo boats had attacked a Soviet merchant ship in a Syrian port and warned: "The Soviet Union will of course take measures which it will deem necessary to defend its ships and other means of transportation."

The Soviet message ended on a conciliatory note. It reiterated the Kremlin's willingness to pursue a ceasefire.

Kissinger's response was to relay immediately the messages to Dinitz. He promised the Israeli diplomat that the United States would send an additional aircraft carrier to the Mediterranean and then he made an extraordinary commitment—pending Nixon's approval, which at this point must have seemed automatic. The United States, Kissinger vowed, would intervene if "any Soviet personnel, planes or ground personnel appear in the area."

Kissinger barely had enough time to fill in Dinitz before he had to attend a White House function at 8:30 PM. It was for Nixon's announcement of his new vice president, Congressman Gerald R. Ford of Michigan.

Afterwards, at 11:20 PM, Kissinger met with Dinitz in the White House. The Israeli envoy was angry once again. He had met with James Schlesinger a few hours earlier and the defense secretary had generously offered him an immediate $500 million aid package. But still the Israeli was outraged, or pretended to be, both because Schlesinger refused, in deference to Arab sensibilities, to commit U.S. military aircraft to transport the materiel and because the package included only sixteen F-4 Phantoms.

Dinitz's session with Schlesinger had ended with a cold handshake. Dinitz, in his later meeting with Kissinger, appeared still upset. He emphasized to Kissinger that Israel was desperate because it was running out of ammunition. (Although it had been known since early Wednesday morning in Israel that there was adequate ammunition, no one apparently

219

bothered telling Dinitz or U.S. officials.) He referred sarcastically to the number of Phantom aircraft being offered as "a mockery to the poor." Then he threatened: "If a massive American airlift to Israel does not start immediately then I'll know that the United States is reneging on its promises and its policy, and we will have to draw very serious conclusions from all this."

The Kalb brothers, who interviewed Dinitz extensively for their biography of Kissinger, observed of this remark: "Dinitz did not have to translate his message. Kissinger quickly understood that the Israelis would soon 'go public' and that an upsurge of pro-Israeli sentiment could have a disastrous impact upon an already weakened administration."

Despite this implied blackmail, or perhaps because of it, Kissinger telephoned Schlesinger and the two men agreed on an emergency interim operation to meet what they thought to be Israel's urgent ammunition needs. They would immediately send ten C-130 cargo planes loaded with materiel to the Azores, where the Israelis could pick it up without having to fly the far longer route to the United States. Then, Kissinger promised Dinitz, a more organized operation would be worked out. Israel could count on receiving all American supplies it needed, and more.

That same day it was reported that Americans had already pledged to buy $128 million in Israeli bonds. Outright contributions were pouring in at such a rate that a spokesman for United Jewish Appeal said, "We're so swamped we can't count it."

.   .

Amid all the frantic events of the day, an important letter arrived at the White House for President Nixon. It was signed by the four chairmen of Aramco's controlling companies. Its warning was explicit: Increased military aid to Israel "will have a critical and adverse effect on our relations with the moderate Arab countries."

.   .

SATURDAY/the 13th

WASHINGTON

Kissinger met with President Nixon early in the morning and received permission to send three giant C-5A cargo planes directly to Israel. "Do it now!," Nixon instructed. It was a perfect opportunity for the wounded

President to appear strong and in control. He gave no indication that he thought at all about the warning of an oil boycott or the consequences of his rash action.

At a meeting of senior security officials convened by Kissinger a short time later, it was also decided to accelerate greatly the transfer of F-4 jets. Ten would be sent to Israel by the next day, four more on Monday—and many more later. One of the largest airlifts ever undertaken was about to begin. No European nation wanted to risk the ire of the oil nations and thus they all prudently denied permission to the United States to land or even over fly their air space. This difficulty was overcome by pressuring Portugal into allowing U.S. planes to refuel at the leased American base at Lajes in the Azores.

As a symbol of Washington's renewed concern, an SR-71 "Black Bird," America's most advanced high-flying reconnaissance plane, was sent over the Suez battlefield that day. But the battle lines were fairly static on Saturday and its information added little to Washington's knowledge. In addition, U.S. spy satellites at the time were in the wrong orbits for observing the Middle East, so for the most part Washington had to rely on Israeli reports of what was actually happening.

Ambassador Dinitz remained skeptical even after Kissinger telephoned his in the afternoon and assured him the airlift was soon to begin. A short time later the worried envoy telephoned Brent Scowcroft, Kissinger's top NSC aide, and warned that if the planes were not headed to Israel by sundown Saturday he could only conclude that there was a "crisis in Israeli-American relations," and it had been caused by the United States for failing to keep its word.

At 3:30 PM, Scowcroft telephoned Dinitz and assured him there would be no crisis in the two countries relations. Three C-5As had just taken off loaded with weapons and ammunition and they were headed directly to Israel.

· ·

VIENNA

By coincidence, a meeting of OPEC, the Organization of Exporting Countries, and the major oil companies had been going on since October 8 at OPEC's modest headquarters at No. 10 Doktor Karl Lueger Ring. Purpose of the conference was to discuss a rise in oil prices. The era of $2-a-barrel oil had passed. Libya's Muammar Qadhafi had boldly breached that level.

221

Now the Arab oil countries wanted the price to move above the current $3 price to over $5 a barrel. It was an enormous boost. The oil companies were ready to grant as much as a one-dollar increase, large enough in itself, but nowhere close to the figure that the Arabs were demanding. After four days of fruitless bargaining, George Piercy of Exxon, who was co-head of the oil companies' bargaining unit, admitted that such a dramatic increase would require consultations with headquarters and the government. He asked Saudi oil minister Ahmed Zaki Yamani, who was representing the Persian Gulf members, including Iran, for a two-week recess.

Yamani did not like it. He wanted to tie up the price level immediately. News reports of repeated Egyptian and Syrian victories in the war had excited all the Arab delegates and their mood was euphoric. They were not about to tolerate any stalling by the oil companies and they were ready to take unilateral action. "They won't like it," Yamani warned Piercy.

The Saudi then telephoned the Kuwaiti delegation in Vienna's Intercontinental Hotel, where the Arab groups were staying. Afterwards, he told Piercy: "They are mad at you."

The next morning, Piercy telephoned Yamani as the Saudi was preparing to fly back to Riyadh. The Exxon executive wondered what was going to happen next.

"You can hear it on the radio," Yamani replied coolly.

The meeting was the last time OPEC nations and the oil companies, which for so long had been so powerful, were ever to meet in consultation to determine oil prices. The oil countries no longer needed the companies. The Arabs were now about to embark on an independent course that would bring them wealth unknown even at the peak of the glory of the Islamic Empire.

• •

CAIRO

The British ambassador, Sir Philip Adams, called on Anwar Sadat early Saturday to inquire whether Egypt was ready, as claimed by Moscow, to accept a ceasefire. This was the day before Egypt's major move in the Sinai, and Sadat remained adamant.

"I haven't agreed to a ceasefire proposed by the Soviet Union or any other party," he told Adams. He added he would accept a ceasefire only "if Israel agrees to withdraw from the occupied Arab territories."

That Israel was unwilling to do.

THE SINAI PENINSULA

The Israelis trapped in the fort at Quay, at the southern end of the Bar-Lev Line opposite Suez City, were finally given permission Saturday to surrender. Their ordeal had been prolonged and painful. They had been under severe attack since the first day of the war when thousands of Egyptians surrounded their position and showered it with flame throwers and hand grenades. Four Israeli tanks tried to rescue the thirty men inside but the tanks were knocked out and twelve of their crewmen also became trapped.

By the end of the first day of the war, there had been fifteen wounded men in the fort, one of whom soon died. Within three days, the fort's doctor, Nahum Verbin, had used up all of the morphine and the groans and cries of the wounded became shrill. When one soldier was wounded by a bazooka shell, Verbin had to perform a tracheotomy without any anesthetic. By Saturday, five of the men were dead and fifteen wounded remained. Verbin was almost out of bandages and the soldiers were down to twenty hand grenades and a few belts of ammunition for light machine guns.

Shortly before the surrender, Southern Command asked the men if they wanted anything.

"To go home," exclaimed Lieutenant Shlomo Ardinest, the only one of five officers unwounded.

"We'll see you on TV with your heads up," radioed headquarters. "Tell your men to hold their heads up, and smile."

"We're all proud of everything," concluded Ardinest. "Give my regards to Tel Aviv."

With the International Red Cross acting as mediator, the men emerged from their dusty and squalid fortification at 11 AM. Ardinest saluted the waiting Egyptian officer and surrendered the fort's flag. The Egyptians then ceremoniously raised the Egyptian flag over Quay.

Now there was only one Israeli fort left, Budapest, in the north. It would hold out through the war.

• •

Chief of Staff Elazar, accompanied by former air force commander Ezer Weizman, now retired, flew to the Sinai late in the morning to discus tactics for the approaching battle. The two men, along with Bar-Lev and Gonen, observed the battlefield from a helicopter. Israel's strength was now impressive. Thousands of tanks, half tracks, APCs, trucks, ambulances and

223

other vehicles crammed the roads and desert expanses. The Sinai was alive with men and equipment.

As they flew along, Gonen was talking on the radio to General Avraham ("Albert") Mandler, trying to agree on a place where they could meet later. During the conversation Mandler gave Gonen his precise location so they could coordinate better. Suddenly, the radio went dead. "Ezer, Albert has been killed," exclaimed Gonen.

"What nonsense, you ass," said Weizman.

"If Albert doesn't answer me on the radio he can only be dead," said Gonen.

When they landed at Sharon's headquarters at Tasa, they learned that Mandler had been killed when his armored command vehicle took a direct missile hit near the Gidi pass.

Gonen, stricken by his friend's death and perhaps guiltily worried that their conversation had allowed the Egyptians to zero in on Mandler, went to the same spot the next day where Mandler had been killed. Standing completely exposed, he repeatedly announced his position over the radio. "Gonen stood for a few minutes, upright and motionless, as though inviting Albert's fate," reported an Israeli journalist. "Nothing happened. No missiles and no shells. Only then was General Gonen at peace with himself."

Elazar immediately promoted Brigadier General Kalman Magen and gave him Mandler's command in the southern sector. Then the generals decided that they would wait for a major Egyptian attack until the next evening, at which time their forces would attempt to cross the canal.

When he returned to Tel Aviv, Elazar reported to his staff that the men in Southern Command had high morale. "They're on top of things now. They know what the Egyptians are up to and have an answer for everything. The repair shops are working. The tanks are fine. There's ammunition there."

• •

THE GOLAN HEIGHTS

The Iraqi division south of General Laner on the Golan Heights began moving north toward Sasa shortly at 3 AM. Laner had positioned his division's tanks in a horseshoe shaped ambushed. The moon was bright. As the Iraqis advanced straight into his trap, Laner ordered his forces to hold their fire. All the division's tanks guns and artillery were pointed into the killing field. The Sherman tanks of Laner's 19th Brigade opened fire just as the first hint of dawn appeared. The range was 200 yards. The result was awesome. Eighty Iraqi tanks were left in the field with no Israeli losses.

This was welcome news to Elazar, but still he and Dayan remained unhappy with the failure of the Golan forces to advance toward Sasa and within artillery range of Damascus. Both men felt the Golan troops were not being aggressive enough, so Elazar ordered an infantry attack against Sasa. He planned to travel to the north to direct the operations personally shortly after midnight.

Meanwhile, the latest casualty count had been completed. It was distressing. It showed that about 600 Israelis had already been killed and 2,400 wounded so far in the war.

The numbers would surely, perhaps dramatically, increase because tomorrow it looked like there would be a major battle in the sands of Sinai. For the first time since the war began, Elazar approved informing families of their fallen sons and fathers.

CHAPTER XXII

October 14: Egypt Gambles

EGYPT'S LUCK CHANGED ON SUNDAY. Instead of letting the Israelis break themselves on the rocks of the Egyptian defensive positions, Egypt launched its long anticipated attack out from under its missile umbrella, with predictable results. That same day, the massive U.S. airlift brought the first American cargo planes to Israel. The planes were crammed with weapons—and a powerful symbolism. Their presence signalled to all that the United States stood firmly behind Israel. These two events marked a major turning point of the war and would trigger an economic earthquake in every country of the world.

• •

SUNDAY

THE GOLAN HEIGHTS

Chief of Staff Elazar arrived at Northern Command just after midnight only to discover that the planned attack could not take place. Syrian reinforcements were pouring onto the plateau and Israeli forces were spent. Brigadier General Yehutiel Adam, the command's chief of staff, told Elazar that he believed the Israeli forces "have enough strength to wear the enemy down but not to defeat it."

Despite the bloodying of the Iraqi division administered the day before, only minor progress had been made in extending Israeli lines. An attack by paratroopers had finally managed to take Tel Shams, but Sasa remained under Syrian control and beyond Israel's grasp. The troops, Elazar was told, were too tired after eight gruelling days of fighting and needed rest. Elazar agreed that the men should rest. He returned to Tel Aviv, where he managed to get two hours of sleep himself before the anticipated major battle in the Sinai.

That day a token Jordanian force, the 40th Armored Brigade with 4,000 men and 150 old Centurion tanks, entered into Syria at El Hara, south of Dan Laner's division. Its presence added to the significant defensive line that was containing the Israeli forces.

• •

THE SINAI PENINSULA

During the past two days, the Egyptians had carefully prepared the battle-field. They had moved fourteen SAM batteries, including six mobile SA-6 batteries, across the canal; artillery and mortar units had moved forward, and major elements of two reserve divisions had been transferred to the east bank. The Israelis estimated they faced 900 Egyptian tanks against 750 of their own while the Egyptians made an almost exactly opposite estimate: 780 Egyptian tanks against 900 Israeli.

Whatever the precise numbers, as Dado Elazar pointed out to the cabinet, "It is obvious the Egyptians do not really enjoy any numerical advantage as they attack and the IDF is deployed for defense." Simply on the basis of the numbers alone, military doctrine decreed that, as Elazar predicted, the Egyptian attack was "doomed to fail."

• •

The Egyptian plan of attack involved in its opening phase 400 tanks in four armored and one mechanized infantry brigades making four independent thrusts. The main aim of the attack was to reach the Gidi and Mitla passes, less than twenty miles from the canal. In the south, an armored brigade was to fight toward Mitla and the infantry brigade toward Gidi. In the center, two armored brigades were to attack toward Tasa and in the north another armored brigade was targeted on Baluza.

The battle opened at 6:15 AM with a heavy bombardment by 500 guns and simultaneous air strikes all along the line. Fifteen minutes later, the barrage halted and the brigades moved out into the open desert. The result was predictable and devastating.

As the Egyptian troops passed beyond their missile umbrella, Israeli warplanes tore them up. Then Israeli tanks hidden in the folds of the desert, hulls down, waited until the Egyptians approached to within close range and blasted them with concentrated fire. Israeli infantrymen also made good use of the newly arrived U.S. Tow antitank missile, a tube launched, wire

227

guided weapon much like the Russian Sagger.

The attack in the north toward Baluza in the Egyptian 18th Infantry Division's sector ran into the combined might of Brigadier General Yzhak Sassoon's division—he had replaced Kalman Magen in the north—and Bren Adan's forces. The Egyptian brigade was repulsed with heavy losses, including fifty tanks.

The two brigades attacking out of the 21st Division's sector against Sharon's division at Tasa fared ever worse. The two brigades lost at least eighty tanks. Sharon repeatedly pleaded with Southern Command to be allowed to counterattack but was denied permission, much to his frustration. He groused about the general command's lack of aggressiveness, its worry that the Egyptians might break through to Tel Aviv. "Anyone who visualized them running for Tel Aviv was daydreaming," he declared. "The Egyptians have lost all their taste for it. Today it's clear the Arabs were dreaming—together with a few Jews who turned into Arabs. In my opinion there was never any fear of it."

Bar-Lev told Elazar of Sharon's request to attack, saying pointedly he considered the general "a divisional commander who is a politician." Elazar endorsed Bar-Lev's refusal to go on the attack. Why should Israel risk losses when it could lure the Egyptians out of their strong defenses and chew them up in the desert?

In the south, the two attacks from the Egyptian 7th and 19th division sectors gathered the greatest momentum and penetrated nearly to the Lateral road. But Magen's division, reinforced by paratroopers, stopped the Egyptians with an Egyptian loss of about sixty-five tanks.

By noon, the worse was over. Most of the Egyptian forces were battered and in disarray, stunned under the burning sun. They were at last ordered to break off contact and withdraw.

The most they had penetrated was about twelve miles into the Sinai, far enough to get out from under the protection of their SAM missiles but not far enough to achieve anything but their own destruction. As they staggered back to the safety of the Egyptian bridgeheads, they were mercilessly harassed by Israeli warplanes.

• •

At the height of the battle, Chief of Staff Shazly tried calling Second Army commander Saad Mamoun only to be told that he was "having a rest." This struck the veteran paratrooper as strange during a major battle, but he did not insist. When he was ordered by Anwar Sadat later in the day to boost the men's morale on the front, he went to Mamoun's headquarters on the west bank of the canal. There he discovered the truth: Mamoun was gravely ill and bedridden. "As news had come all morning of the repelling of the attack and the mounting losses among his men, he had found each report harder to bear," reported Shazly. "Suddenly he had fainted. He had been in bed ever since, conscious but quite unable to discharge his responsibilities." He was replaced the next day by Major General Abdul Monein Khalil, who had been commanding the Cairo Military District. The collapse of the Second Army's commander at this critical hour no doubt contributed to the lackluster nature of the Egyptian attack; the delay in appointing his successor would also negatively influence the army's reaction to Israel's counterattack.

• •

At the end of the day, the Egyptian losses were 250 tanks. Israel claimed it suffered only six tank losses, but it has since been generally agreed it was much higher than that—Adan alone admitted to having twenty-five tanks hit. Shazly's estimate of fifty Israeli tank losses was probably closer to the mark. But by now Israel's repair shops were working at top efficiency and most of its damaged tanks could quickly be put back into operation, a capability that the Egyptians were unable to match.

One reason explaining the comparatively low Israeli losses was the successful tactic worked out to combat the Egyptian infantry antitank missilemen. This was done by coordinating tank movements with armored personnel carriers and artillery. APCs went into battle with one or two tanks. With their superior visibility and abundant machine guns, the APCs kept look out for missilemen, spraying machine gun fire in their direction when they exposed themselves to aim and guide their weapons. The fusillade was usually daunting enough to make the missilemen duck, thereby losing control of their missiles. Artillery was similarly used to suppress the mounted version of the Sagger. When an armored carrier—Egypt deployed both the Soviet BMP and BRDM-2—stopped to aim its mounted Sagger missiles, Israeli artillery blanketed the area, forcing the vehicle to speed away for safety.

These tactics helped Israel score a notable victory, even though Egypt had not pressed its attack with massive reinforcements as Elazar had hoped. Had Egypt done that, Israel's gains would no doubt have been even greater.

That night Bar-Lev telephoned Golda Meir and reported: "It's been a good day. We are back to being ourselves and they [the Egyptians] are back to being themselves."

Up to this day, Israeli military communiques had generally distorted the

229

actual situation on the battlefield and the Egyptians' had been more realistic. After this bloody Sunday, the Egyptian communiques became more exaggerated and Israel's more realistic.

• •

TEL AVIV

Elazar went before the cabinet Sunday night to receive official approval for an attack across the canal at Deversoir. The timing was for the next night. As he explained to the ministers:

> The Egyptians' position has already been undermined. Of the approximately 2,000 tanks at Egypt's disposal when the war broke out, about 1,300 were transferred to the east bank, and about 600 of these have been lost to date. In all of Egypt— including the Nile Valley, the 'palace guard' in the Cairo area and the forces in the southern part of the country—there is no more than a total of 700 tanks. That is not a very imposing force, so that we will be in a better position on the west bank than in the Syrian salient, where we've had to break through a defensive disposition that the enemy has spent more than ten years building. Only by sending their armor back over the canal can the Egyptians constitute a threat to the crossing forces. But then we'll be in an even better position than we were when the war broke out. I wish matters would come to that.

Added Elazar to the skeptical ministers: "Based on my knowledge of the facts, I believe that the chances of failing are pretty meager and the odds on success are good. How great that success will be, I can't say; but it may be very big."

At the end, shortly after midnight, the cabinet voted to approve the crossing. It was scheduled to start at 5 PM on Monday. Its code name: Stouthearted men.

• •

The first of the three giant American C-5As packed with emergency supplies landed at Lod Airport outside of Tel Aviv on Sunday amid much publicity, fanfare and symbolism. It was a dramatic demonstration that Israel enjoyed America's full support. With such mighty backing, there could be no question any longer about the fate of the Jewish state. It would

230

survive no matter what the Soviet Union did. This message was clear to all, and it provided a tremendous boost to Israeli morale. When she heard the first plane had landed, Prime Minister Meir cried in joy and relief. "The airlift was invaluable," wrote Meir in her memoirs. "It not only lifted our spirits, but also served to make the American position clear to the Soviet Union, and it undoubtedly served to make our victory possible."

• •

WASHINGTON

When Kissinger went to Richard Nixon on Sunday to suggest that the airlift to Israel be openly military, without any effort at disguising America's involvement, the President's response was enthusiastic. "We are going to get blamed just as much for three planes as 300," he said.

Now deep in the quagmire of Watergate, Nixon's prime attention was riveted on the unfolding scandal, as his memoirs attest. Nonetheless, he personally endorsed the airlift by U.S. military planes, probably for a variety of complex reasons extending from his sincere support of Israel to the hope that the airlift would divert attention from his personal problems. Whatever the nexus of motives, he was aware of the implications of his action, as he showed when he earlier told Schlesinger to facilitate the airlift regardless of concerns about an Arab oil boycott. "I assured him that I was fully aware of the gravity of my decision and that I would accept complete personal responsibility if, as a result, we alienated the Arabs and had our oil supplies cut off."

Kissinger, who now was essentially running U.S. foreign policy while the President fought the courts, the press and his abundant political foes, decided that the airlift would be "at maximum capacity and exclusively with American military planes." Kissinger was determined to show the Arabs and the Soviets how tough the United States could be. "We would pour in supplies," he decided. "We would risk a confrontation." He ordered that the airlift not only match the tonnage being provided by the Russians but exceed it by twenty-five percent.

Despite such strutting, the new secretary of state was cautious enough to write a letter to King Faisal explaining the reasons for the U.S. airlift. The leader of Islam was not impressed, and the United States and the rest of the world were soon to pay dearly.

CHAPTER XXIII

October 15-17: Battle for the Chinese Farm

THE ISRAELI PLAN OF ATTACK across the Suez Canal de-
pended on timing and surprise. If Israel could move its troops quickly before
the Egyptians figured out what was happening, the crossing could be accomplished with little loss. As Sharon explained to his staff: "The major
problem is to reach the water and set up the bridgehead before dawn—so
that the Egyptians will not discover the plan and meet us with massed armor
on the west bank."

But there was a problem. The Egyptians had established an extremely
strong defensive position at an oddly named point called the Chinese Farm.

• •

MONDAY/the 15th

THE SINAI PENINSULA

The daring Israeli operation was to commence at dusk on Monday with
a diversionary attack to fool the Egyptians into believing that Israel was
launching a major assault against its forces on the Bar-Lev Line. Then
Sharon's division, reinforced by a paratroop brigade, two engineering battalions and three reduced infantry battalions, would attack north from the
Akavish road, which led from Tasa to the Great Bitter Lake, just south
of the planned crossing site opposite Deversoir. The area between the
Akavish road up to Ismailia was strongly defended by the Egyptian 16th
infantry and 21st armored divisions.

They were dug in at two vital positions—Missouri, near the Televizia

232

fort south of Ismailia, and the Chinese Farm, so-called by the Israelis because it had been a Japanese experimental farm before the 1967 war and Israelis coming across it thought the Japanese writing was Chinese. The farm was crisscrossed by irrigation ditches and, unknown to the Israelis, had been turned by the Egyptians into an extremely strong defensive position. The irrigation ditches provided perfect protection for Egypt's infantry, which was equipped with numerous antitank weapons and backed up by tanks. To the south was the Great Bitter Lake and the seam between the Third and Second armies, which was devoid of Egyptian troops.

Branching off of Akavish Road was Tirtur, an unpaved east-west road that led to the main crossing area at the Matzmed fort. Tirtur road sliced through the center of the Chinese Farm and had been especially constructed for a crossing operation when Sharon was commander of Southern Command. Just south of the road's terminus at the canal, two miles north of Akavish at this point, a large compound, the "yard," had been constructed years earlier and camouflaged to serve as a marshalling area for heavy equipment and bridging parts. It was from this pre-prepared, 200-by-500 yard position, just north of where the canal joins the Great Bitter Lake, that the crossing was planned.

Sharon's mission was to secure both the Akavish and Tirtur roads as well as a bridgehead encompassing Missouri and the Chinese Farm up to a distance of three miles to the north. This was much smaller than doctrine called for, which normally was a bridgehead large enough to put crossing bridges out of artillery range. The shorter bridgehead would at most prevent Egyptian flat trajectory and light mortar fire, but it was considered acceptable because of the feared losses that would have to be suffered if Israeli forces attacked the dug-in Egyptians head-on all along the canal.

The time schedule of the crossing was vital to achieve surprise and avoid a build up of Egyptian forces on the west bank. The first actual crossing was assigned to a paratroop brigade, which was scheduled to get over in collapsible rubber boats by 8:30 PM Monday. The first rafts to transport individual tanks were slated to enter the water an hour later. Then Sharon, with 240 tanks, would erect two bridges across the canal and cross over, followed by Adan's fresh division with about 200 tanks.

Southern Command optimistically estimated that Sharon would be able to secure the bridgehead and construct the bridges during the first night of the attack. By 5 AM Tuesday both divisions were scheduled to be over. Tuesday would be dedicated to lightning ground attacks on Egypt's antiaircraft missile sites on the west bank to open up safe flight paths for Israeli warplanes and within a day after that Suez City would have been captured

233

and both banks mopped up.

But the Israeli planners underestimated Egyptian resistance, which quickly became clear during the dark hours of Monday night at the Chinese Farm.

• •

The attack got off to a good start as the sun began setting. A brigade struck westward toward Missouri in a diversionary feint while a strong armored brigade led by Colonel Amnon Reshef swung southwest to the Great Bitter Lake and then moved northwest up to the yard near the terminus of Tirtur road. It made its movements deep behind Egyptian lines and went without serious opposition by the surprised troops. The Matzmed-Tirtur crossing area was easily secured and the plan at first achieved its hoped for surprise. There was no opposition at all at the pre-prepared yard, not even artillery attacks.

By 9 PM, however, the Egyptians recovered from their shock and, full of fight, opened a devastating counterattack with tank guns and Sagger missiles in the Chinese Farm at the vital junction of Tirtur and the north-south supply road known to the Israelis as Lexicon, about a kilometer from the canal. The desert night was suddenly lit by the flashes of guns and the burning of tanks and vehicles. Egyptian infantry were hidden throughout the area, along the irrigation dikes at the Chinese Farm and in the ditches along the road. Israeli tanks attempting to avoid them by getting off Lexicon road hit mines. Others suffered withering assaults by antitank missiles.

The combat became so close that tanks often could not identify each other, causing anxious seconds in which they could not decide whether to fire or not. One of Reshef's battalions lost ten tanks almost immediately. Another battalion escaped with only six of its original twenty tanks. An attempt by an Israeli paratroop company to open the junction was roundly defeated, with all of its tanks destroyed, the commander killed and nearly everyone else killed or wounded.

Repeated attacks to open the vital junction were repulsed. The Israeli losses mounted alarmingly. Colonel Reshef's brigade was more than decimated. He lost sixty of his original one hundred tanks, with more than 120 men either dead or missing.

But still, the Egyptians did not yet recognize that this was an attempt to cross the canal, falling instead for the ruse that the Israelis carefully nurtured that they were trying to roll back the Egyptian positions in a south-to-north assault. As a result, the crossing point remained quiet and the opportunity still existed for the Israelis to make an unopposed crossing.

The paratroop brigade assigned the initial strike across the canal ran into repeated troubles. First, the sixty half-tracks promised to brigade commander Colonel Danny Matt did not arrive. He had only thirty-two. This was solved by one of his resourceful battalion commanders. He sent thirty drivers and his headquarters commander in the general direction of the major supply depot in the middle of the Sinai at Bir Gifgafa, Refidim to the Israelis, to scrounge up as many half-tracks as they could find. The officer discovered twenty-six half-tracks lined up outside a canteen at Refidim, the drivers all inside having refreshments. He found the officer in charge and learned that the half-tracks were to be delivered to another division. "I'm the man you are waiting for and I don't need your drivers," Matt's man said. The commander acquiesced and Matt now had fifty-eight half tracks, enough for the attack to cross.

But there was another hitch. The inflatable rubber boats had been promised for 10 AM but they had not arrived and were hours late. They were only discovered at the last minute at another rendezvous where they had been delivered by mistake.

Then the timing went totally awry. When Matt's brigade moved out from his staging area twenty miles east of Tasa, it found traffic control totally broken down. The road was packed with vehicles. Matt's brigade moved less than fifteen miles in two and a half hours westward to Tasa and then it found even worse traffic on the single four-meter wide Akavish road leading to the Tirtur terminus. It was the only paved road from Tasa, and it was packed. Hundreds of tanks, jeeps, bulldozers, buses, armored personnel carriers, mobile work shops, guns, tank transporters and vehicles hauling ammunition, fuel and engineering equipment were literally stuck bumper to bumper for fifteen miles. It was near complete gridlock. Vehicles trying to bypass the traffic skidded off the macadam and became stuck in the sand dunes which bordered the road, rendering even the shoulders impassable.

It took the brigade two hours to go less than three miles on Akavish. It was only at 9 PM—a half hour after the crossing had been scheduled to start—that the brigade arrived just west of Tasa. It was there that the boats promised them eleven hours earlier were finally found. By shortly after midnight, Egyptian fire forced them to move off the road and make their way laboriously through the steep sand dunes. They were still two miles away from the canal.

By this time, Bar-Lev wondered if the whole operation should not be put off for twenty-four hours. He consulted with Sharon, but was assured that the operation could proceed. Dayan too had his doubts, but in the end he, Elazar, Bar-Lev and Gonen all agreed it should go forward. It was likely that Sharon's optimistic reports during this terrible night of battle contributed heavily to the distrust that was increasing between him and Southern Command.

• •

TUESDAY/the 16th

THE SINAI PENINSULA

Colonel Matt's brigade worked its way slowly to the yard. Finally, at 1:25 AM, nearly five hours behind schedule, the first Israeli rubber boat slipped into the water and began its trip across the narrow canal. By 3 AM, Matt's brigade was across, completely unopposed. It had made the crossing without losses. "Acapulco!" Matt radioed, meaning Israel at last had a hold on the west bank of the Suez Canal. It was the first time Israeli forces had ever crossed the canal.

Excitedly, Chief of Staff Elazar, who was following the progress of the Israeli attack at Southern Command headquarters, radioed Matt. "Everything is all right," said Matt. "We are in Africa."

• •

But everything was not all right. Had the attack kept to its planned timing, both Sharon's and Adan's division could have sped across the canal under cover of darkness and landed without resistance. Instead, the schedule was now hopelessly botched up. The unexpectedly heavy Egyptian fighting at the Chinese Farm was holding up movement to the crossing point and the incredibly heavy traffic jamming the main Akavish road was delaying the arrival of the bridges to the yard embarkation point.

One of the bridges was an immensely cumbersome contraption called a roller bridge. It weighed 400 tons, extended for 180 yards—nearly the length of two football fields—and had to be towed by eighteen tanks. The monster repeatedly broke down or crushed the shoulders of the narrow road and slipped off. On a downslope east of the Artillery road in the dark hours of Tuesday, the tanks towing the bridge were unable to brake its acceleration and it broke away. The bridge ended up stuck at the bottom of the hill. It was feared that it would take as long as a day to repair it.

Israel had two other kinds of bridges, both also snarled in the heavy traffic. One type was called Gilois, which were large mobile units. Three of

236

them could be linked together to form a raft capable of transporting one tank, or a large number of them could be attached to form a bridge. The other apparatus was a unifloat, which was an iron box measuring 5 x 2 1/2 x 1.2 yards and weighing three tons. The unifloats also could serve as individual rafts. Now sixteen of the Gilois and eight unifloats were slowly trying to work their way through the stifling traffic.

The self-propelled Gilois were the first to reach the yard at 4 AM. With them were two bulldozers, which immediately began demolishing the artificial earth embankment that Sharon had earlier marked out for easy breaching. Still, it was not until 6:52 AM Tuesday that the first Israeli tank reached the west bank, far behind schedule. Instead of having two divisions with more than 400 tanks across by this time, Israel had only one paratroop brigade and one tank in "Africa." Yet the crossing area remained free of opposition. The Egyptians still had not caught on to the Israeli plan. The west bank remained wide open for the Israelis. But the unifloats and the roller bridge were still solidly stuck in traffic and the Tirtur-Lexicon junction in the Chinese Farm remained in Egyptian hands.

Elazar was frustrated. He complained to his staff about the delay in getting the bridges to the canal. "The Egyptians didn't understand what was happening. They didn't read the attack correctly; they thought it was some kind of a raid, so they didn't call for reinforcements to dam up the breach....The shore was absolutely deserted....There wasn't any disposition facing us....It makes your heart ache. If the bridge had been up by ten, Bren could have gone in and wreaked havoc. If ever there was a golden opportunity, this is it."

• •

Dawn revealed a horrid scene around the Tirtur-Lexicon junction at the Chinese Farm. The desert floor was a picture from purgatory. Scores of burning tanks, twisted guns and smoking vehicles lay everywhere. Dead infantry and charred tank crews still covered the ground. The desert sand was a junkyard of every conceivable type of military equipment, from mobile kitchens to huge transporters with SA-2 missiles. Egyptian and Israeli tanks were mixed up in no apparent pattern, sometimes within scant yards of each other.

As General Bren Adan stood on a hill overlooking the devastation around the Chinese Farm, he could see a column of Israeli tanks and half tracks moving west on the Akavish road. "...I suddenly saw four tanks begin burning within seconds," he reported. "The column was caught by surprise. Many things then happened at once. We saw crews jumping out of tanks

237

starting to run in our direction, half-tracks halted as the troops abandoned them to lay down on the ground and other half-tracks turning around and moving back....It was now clear that the Akavish road was totally blocked.''

Israel's losses were already 200 men dead and fifty tanks lost. And the battle was far from over.

Arik Sharon repeatedly underestimated the strength of the Egyptian resistance, in part perhaps because the embarkation point, where he had his advance headquarters, remained free of any hostile activity. There was no shelling on the site and Egypt's main resistance remained focused to the east, at the Chinese Farm. But rather than concentrating his forces to clear the Akavish road, Sharon was intent on crossing the canal. He was determined to get as many of his tanks across the canal in as rapid time possible.

By Tuesday noon it was clear to General Gonen, and the general staff as well, that the Egyptian resistance on the east bank had to be crushed before the planned operation could proceed. Egyptian planes had appeared over the west bank bridgehead and any hope that surprise could be maintained was rapidly evaporating. Gonen was worried that without a secure supply route the paratroopers would get stranded. He ordered Sharon not to transfer any more tanks across on rafts until the Akavish road was cleared and the bridges constructed over the canal. There was no point in risking more tanks on the other side, Gonen believed.

Instead of sending more tanks across, Sharon was ordered to concentrate on clearing out the Egyptians from their strong positions in the Chinese Farm and the southern sector of Missouri; Adan was ordered to clear the Akavish road so the bridging equipment could get to the Tirtur terminus. The order infuriated Sharon, although all these objectives had been included in his original orders. He tried to go over Gonen's head by calling Bar-Lev, but he too believed it too risky to pump more troops over before a bridge was up and a supply route secure. Sharon argued that the first priority was to exploit the west bank breakthrough and pump as much force as possible across before the Egyptians gathered strength on the west bank, but he got nowhere.

As Dayan observed, "There was an absence of mutual trust" between Sharon and his superiors. "Arik was convinced that they discriminated against him and did not place full confidence in his reports on the battle situation and on his actions. His superior officers, for their part, argued that he did not carry out their orders, that in his activities he was guided by personal motivation—placing himself and the achievements of his unit in the limelight—and that he broke the elementary principles of discipline,

238

telephoning his friends and public figures in the rear...and involving them, unlawfully, in military affairs."

Dayan himself had mixed emotions about Sharon but not about his fighting capabilities. "I do not know a better field commander than Arik," he wrote in his memoirs. "This is not to say I never had cause to criticize him. When I appointed him commander of the special paratroop unit, Force 101, I told him that it was not enough to know how to beat the Arabs; one must also know how to live with the Jews. We also had our quarrels. But even when I feel like 'murdering' him, at least I know he is somebody worth 'murdering.'"

After being ordered to send no more tanks across the canal, the silver-haired Sharon delivered a mocking monologue to his amused staff. "Am I surrounded or surrounding? Danny Matt is encircling the Egyptians but according to you they're encircling him. Amnon [Reshef] is surrounding the enemy—but as you put it, the enemy is surrounding him. We're cut off, but we're cutting off the Egyptians. When will you finally understand that in mobile desert war, at one stage you encircle, and at another you are encircled?"

Sharon's monologue touched on an intriguing question of perception, the difference between a genius on the battlefield and an incompetent, a Napoleon or a Custer. It was a question that dogged the Israeli commanders throughout the war, with Sharon consistently on the side of greater aggressive efforts. Unfortunately, it was a question that was never adequately answered during the war, with the result that afterwards there was endless controversy in Israel over whose perception was correct.

• •

Sharon pleaded for a delay in opening his attack against the Chinese Farm, saying his tanks had "empty bellies," they were out of ammunition and fuel after fighting all night. Permission was granted. But then Sharon disappeared from the radio and could not be found for many hours. Gonen, who by this time was completely mistrustful of Sharon, suspecting he was seeking glory by trying to get across the canal first, contacted one of Sharon's brigade commanders and warned him not to cross over without personal permission from Southern Command. This was, as Adan observed, a good indication of "the mistrust that had developed between him and Sharon."

Adan, meantime, was completely stymied in his attempts to open Akavish road. Every time his tanks ventured forward, showers of antitank missiles greeted them from hidden Egyptian infantry. There were also strong Egyp-

239

tian armor forces to the north, which maneuvered incessantly in an apparent attempt to lure Adan's forces into a trap. The Israeli commander finally concluded that the only way to open the road was to root out the Egyptians with Israeli infantry in a night attack. Meanwhile, the Akavish road remained blocked and the bridges stuck miles from the crossing area.

• •

TEL AVIV

Golda Meir made a truculent speech before the Israeli Knesset at 4 PM Tuesday, several hours after Anwar Sadat had addressed the People's Assembly in Cairo. He had repeated his call for a ceasefire linked to a complete Israeli withdrawal to the June 4, 1967 frontiers. Meir rejected this as "ridiculous." Apparently, she added, the Arabs have "not yet been beaten enough to evince any desire for a ceasefire [which] will come about only when the Arab armies are defeated."

Then, to the consternation of her military commanders, the prime minister boasted: "Right now, as we convene in the Knesset, an IDF task force is operating on the west bank of the Suez Canal."

Now any hope of keeping the crossing operation a surprise was gone.

Moshe Dayan was distressed. At this point, he noted to the general staff, all that had been accomplished had been merely a raid across the canal. Unless there were radical changes on the battlefield, the best course would probably be to take the paratroopers out of the west bank. Now that was impossible, because "...after the prime minister's superfluous announcement, [it] would be an admission of failure that the Egyptian propaganda machine will know how to exploit only too well."

• •

CAIRO

Shortly after Golda Meir's speech, Mohamed Heikal telephoned Anwar Sadat. He wanted to know about the Israeli presence on the west bank, but the President said "he had no information that would bear out her claim." However, Sadat was concerned enough to telephone General Ismail, who assured him that only "three infiltrating Israeli tanks" had crossed the canal. By this time Israel actually had twenty-eight tanks across, not a substantial force but enough to give the Egyptian command far more concern than it displayed. Apparently Sadat's personal interest alerted the Egyptian high command because by the next day the west bank bridgehead, and soon the east bank bridgehead too, came under heavy artillery fire that increased to murderous proportions in the days ahead. A precious advantage on the field had been squandered for political gain by Golda Meir, not necessarily an overly cynical action. Sometimes, as numerous leaders have discovered, homefront morale is as important as battlefield achievements.

• •

Soviet Premier Aleksei Kosygin arrived in Cairo in the evening for a four-day visit and immediately met with Sadat, urging him to accept a ceasefire. The high rate of losses on the battlefield was very risky, he warned. But Sadat refused.

"I am not prepared to have a repeat of the 1948 'truce' which was behind our loss of the war," said Sadat.

"We'll come in here and guarantee nothing of the sort would happen," said Kosygin.

"With Israel, you can't guarantee anything," the Egyptian leader replied.

• •

KUWAIT

The OPEC producers who had failed to convince the major oil companies to approve a price increase in their meeting in Vienna the previous week now gathered again on their own at the Sheraton Hotel. They made a historic decision. They unilaterally raised the price of a barrel of oil a stunning $2.11, a jump from $3.01 to $5.12, the largest increase ever. It was their declaration of independence. Never again would the Arab oil states bargain with the companies. From now on they would set the price of oil as they liked. The Arab members rejected a total embargo but they did decide to imposed an immediate 10% cut in production, with further cuts of 5% a month until the Arab-Israeli conflict was settled. The Arabs were in a perfect position. With the 70% price increase, they could slash production by nearly half and still not lose any revenues.

• •

WEDNESDAY/the 17th

THE SINAI PENINSULA

An elite paratroop battalion under Colonel Uzzi Yairi was ordered to clear the Egyptians away from the Chinese Farm. Yairi was told by Bar-Lev that the success of the crossing operation depended on his mission. If the roads could not be opened, the operation might have to be dropped and the paratroopers on the west bank withdrawn.

The necessity of clearing up the traffic became immediately obvious to Yairi. It prevented him and his men from reaching Adan's advance headquarters south of the Chinese Farm until well after dark on Tuesday night. With no chance to study the terrain, Yairi had to depend on a briefing by Adan to get a sense of the lay of the land. Adan was not much help.

As he confessed to Yairi, "It was unclear exactly where the enemy was deployed and in what strength....The main problem lay in the broad irrigation ditches that extended southward from the farm to the area between the Tirtur and Akavish roads, and also south of Akavish toward [the Great Bitter Lake.] The soldiers of the Egyptian 16th Division were making good use of the ditches, which provided cover for crews equipped with Sagger missiles. It was extremely difficult to pinpoint the locations of these units because the ditches crisscrossed such a broad area."

Yairi's force set out at midnight, already too late to clear out the entire area, so Adan ordered him to clear Tirtur road only. The unifloat rafts were just west of the Akavish-Tirtur junction, tantalizingly close to the embarkation point but idle because of the blocked road.

Near 3 AM Wednesday, Yairi's forces began taking fire on Tirtur road east of the Lexicon junction. The Israelis threw themselves in the numerous irrigation ditches and fierce fighting broke out at close quarters. Flat trajectory weapons, mortars, machine guns and hand grenades lit the night. One of Yairi's companies tried a flanking movement, but the Egyptians were deployed in depth and most of the company's officers and non-coms were wounded or killed.

Fire was so heavy that the paratroopers could not disengage, could not get their wounded out.

It was not until dawn that a tank battalion was able to try to extricate the paratroopers. The tanks charged the Egyptian positions, running over infantrymen in their ditch trenches, only to be beaten back by a hail storm of missiles. Within four minutes, the battalion had five tanks hit by Saggers and was forced to withdraw, having suffered ten men killed, four missing and fifteen wounded in the unsuccessful thrust. Now even more wounded had to be rescued.

Adan finally had to commit four armored battalions along with a Sharon brigade into the raging fight. It was only slowly, painfully with dogged fighting that the Israelis were able to press the tenacious Egyptians north, away from the vital Akavish-Tirtur road. Adan officially declared the road open at 11 AM. Yairi's paratroop battalion had lost forty killed and twice that number wounded.

The battlefield was a graveyard of men and machines. All told, about 250 tanks had been destroyed in a day and a half of fierce fighting, about two-thirds of them Egyptian.

When Moshe Dayan visited the area later in the day, he was visibly shaken at the evidence of the bitter fighting. "What you people have done here," he murmured. "I am no novice at war or battle scenes," he confessed in his memoirs, "but I had never seen such a sight, neither in action, nor in paintings nor in the most far-fetched feature film. Here was a vast field of slaughter stretching all round as far as the eye could see. The tanks, the armored personnel carriers, the guns and the ammunition trucks crippled, overturned, burned and smoking were grim evidence of the frightful battle that had been fought here."

Meanwhile, under the diversion of the heavy fighting, Adan had taken a gamble. He began moving forward the bulky unifloat pontoons, afraid that another day might go by without a bridge across the canal. The move was successful. The Egyptians were totally absorbed by the battle with the paratroops and the bridge sections arrived undamaged at the yard at just after dawn, at 6:30 AM. Now, at last, the Israelis had the equipment necessary to support a major crossing. They were already more than twenty-four hours behind schedule but so far the terminus had remained blessedly free of artillery attacks.

Within a half hour, however, Egyptian artillery began ranging in on the yard, unleashing a terrible bombardment from at least 144 guns, not counting mortars and Katyusha rockets. Egyptian planes also attacked the yard, further delaying the construction of the unifloat rafts into a solid bridge.

This was the opening of a major Egyptian counterattack against the bridgehead by elements of the Second and Third armies. The 116th Infantry Brigade attacked south in the morning but was beaten off with heavy casualties. On the west bank, the 21st Division also struck south. In a sharp clash near Serapheum, twelve Israelis were killed and twenty-two wounded. But this attack too got bogged down. Nonetheless, the Egyptians obviously by now were taking seriously Golda Meir's announcement of the previous day that Israeli forces were operating in the west.

• •

There was still a basic disagreement between Sharon and the other generals on the importance of a secure bridge and the pace of moving forces to the west. In a meeting at Adan's advance headquarters on the hill at

Kishuf, south of the Akavish road, Sharon, Adan, Dayan, Elazar and Bar-Lev gathered to argue out the issue. Sharon asserted that everything must be done faster, that it was a waste of time to wait for the construction of the pontoon bridge. More armor should be sent across on the rafts. If the Israeli force on the west was quickly strengthened, the Egyptians would collapse. It was useless to fight with the Egyptians on the east bank, Sharon said.

Adan took the opposite view, arguing that all Israel now had was a toehold, not a bridgehead. Egyptian forces were still so close that they were shelling the yard area with ease. In addition, the unifloat pontoon bridge had still not been constructed and the huge roller bridge was still tied up in traffic on the Akavish road. Until these problems could be sorted out, no more forces should be sent westward, he said.

The other generals supported Adan. "There is no resemblance between our aims and what has actually happened," complained Bar-Lev. Relations between him and Sharon were now so bitter that the two men could barely stand the sight of each other.

"I don't accept the judgment that expectations have not been fulfilled," responded Sharon. He was furious at the charge and later admitted: "I almost slapped Bar-Lev's face."

"What can I say," replied Bar-Lev. "Nothing has worked out. The bridgehead hasn't been consolidated and there was no Egyptian collapse."

Sharon said sarcastically: "Any minute now you'll tell me I didn't take part in this war at all."

There was also argument about which division would go over first once a bridge was up. Sharon wanted the honor but Adan objected, arguing that they should stick to the original plan which called for him to cross in force. Bar-Lev came up with compromise idea in which parts of both divisions would go over, but Elazar forcefully ruled that out.

"I have decided," said Elazar. "Sharon will continue with the task of consolidating the bridgehead, and Bren will cross westward according to the plan."

Turning to Sharon, Elazar added: "Arik, complete the task assigned to you and then you can cross too."

At that point Adan had to leave the meeting because the 25th Egyptian Independent Armored Brigade was moving northward from the Third Army with a strong force of late model T-62 Soviet tanks toward Akavish. This was the third prong of the Egyptian counterattack that had been launched without effect that morning. The 25th brigade was to have attacked simultaneously with the two units, but it had been delayed and was now entering the battle zone only in the afternoon after the other trusts had already been beaten off.

Adan quickly deployed two brigades commanded by Colonels Natke Nir and Aryeh Karen in an ambush east of the Great Bitter Lake. Other tanks swung southward to get behind the Egyptian column while still others were positioned in the north. When the Egyptian column arrived it discovered it was in a box. The battle was no contest. The Israelis, operating from dominating positions, set tank upon tank on fire, blasting the column into a confused mass of armor roaring aimlessly in the killing field.

By the time the fight was over, Adan's troops had destroyed fifty to sixty Egyptian tanks as well as APCs, guns and many supply vehicles. Adan's only losses were two tanks that had blundered into an Israeli minefield and one that was hit by a Sagger missile. It was a perfect ambush and earned the praise of Elazar.

"He's worth gold, that Bren," said Elazar. "That's really a strategic achievement."

Indeed, following the heavy losses Egypt suffered on the fourteenth and during the past two days, its armored strength on the east bank was now substantially weakened. In addition, its troop concentrations in the Chinese Farm began withdrawing during the night into strong positions just to the north in Missouri.

As far as Elazar was concerned, this destruction was justification of his policy not to follow Sharon's plan to pour armor across the canal. He correctly pointed out to his staff:

"It's good that Bren was still east of the canal when the 25th brigade came up from the south. It's good that Bren was on the east bank when the assault by the Second Army hit us from the north. If we had advanced and crossed, we might have achieved a greater victory in the west, but we could have lost the east."

• •

Meanwhile, the difficulties with Sharon continued. He had promised to replace Colonel Gabi Amir's brigade, temporarily attached from Adan's division, with one of his own in the combat area north of Tirtur road. But by late afternoon he had still not done it despite repeated complaints by Adan to Southern Command. The pontoon bridge across the canal had finally been completed at 4:15 PM and Adan was scheduled to go over immediately. But he could not pull Amir's brigade out of the line for fear that the Egyptians would again overrun Tirtur road.

After repeated failures to get Sharon on the radio nets, Elazar finally contacted him at 4:45 PM and emphasized that his prime responsibility was to keep open the Tirtur-Akavish roads and replace Amir's brigade. Sharon promised but nothing happened.

At 5:30 PM, Dayan returned to Southern Command from a visit with Sharon at the yard. He was clearly upset. He wanted Adan to get moving. "The option you asked for from the cabinet is now in your hands," he said. "With every hour that passes the Egyptians will organize better."

"I have ordered Bren to move," said Elazar, "and Arik told me that he would replace Bren within minutes."

Said Dayan: "Replace or not replace, they have to speed to the bridge, the bridge is ready for a crossing."

Sharon too joined the chorus. Over the radio he asked: "The bridge is ready, why isn't Bren crossing?"

Adan was extremely frustrated. All his tanks had to be refueled and rearmed so they would cross ready for combat. But in the dark and with Egyptian artillery pelting the area, reloading the tanks was a slow, two to three hour process. And still Sharon had not relieved Amir's forces. He did not do so until 8 PM.

When Bren Adan's blacked out armored division arrived at the bridge at 10:40 PM on Wednesday night, the scene was peaceful and quiet. Bright moonlight reflected from the serene waters of the canal. The pontoon bridge stood there, floating ponderously, ready to transport his forces over into the heart of Egypt.

Shortly before midnight Adan's division at last began crossing, two days behind the original schedule and with only one bridge yet constructed. But the mass of armor now made the Israeli bridgehead on the west bank secure for the first time—if the bridge could be kept open.

• •

As Elazar prepared to return to Tel Aviv from Southern Command, Bar-Lev turned to him and said only in half jest: "If you go back north without solving the Arik problem, I'm going with you." Then he said seriously: "If I were in your place, I would dismiss him."

But that, Elazar felt, he could not do. The effect on morale would be too great and the political upheaval would be endless. He returned to Tel Aviv, leaving Bar-Lev behind and the "Arik problem" unresolved.

• •

WASHINGTON

A delegation of Arab foreign ministers from Algeria, Kuwait, Morocco and Saudi Arabia, in New York for the U. N. General Assembly session, called on Nixon and Kissinger to support the Arab cause. The President promised them that the United States would launch a major diplomatic effort after a ceasefire. "You have my pledge," he said. "I can't say that we can categorically move Israel back to the 1967 borders, but we will work within the framework for Resolution 242."

He then volunteered Kissinger as the negotiator. "Some of you may accuse him of being a Jew. He is but he's an American too and he serves me well. I'm sure his feelings as a Jew won't interfere with his loyalty to America or his loyalty to me. Mrs. Meir once told our ambassador in Israel: 'Now you and we both have Jewish foreign secretaries, the only difference being that our foreign secretary [Abba Eban] talks better English than yours does.'"

Kissinger noted in his memoirs that the Saudi Foreign Minister, Omar Saqqaf, turned the comments about his Jewishness "deftly aside: 'We are all Semites together.'"

Saqqaf painted the Arab position in moderate tones. "Israel is not being threatened by the Arabs with annihilation," he said, adding that there was no reluctance in accepting its existence. "We want no more than a return to the 1967 borders and respect for the rights of refugees to return to their lands or be compensated for what they have lost. This would be enough to guarantee the stability and integrity of Israel."

In a separate meeting with the Arab officials, Kissinger told them: "We know Israel is not prepared to accept any of the present Arab ideas. The Israeli prime minister said so yesterday....If you insist on everything as a precondition for a ceasefire, then the war will go on."

In his memoirs, Kissinger reported: "I cannot say that these observations evoked wild enthusiasm; but neither were they rejected. The four foreign ministers urged me to involve myself despite all my reservations...."

• •

In the afternoon, Kissinger held a meeting of the Washington Special Action Group. The atmosphere was relaxed. "I complacently observed that the mood of the Arab ministers seemed to confirm that there would be no immediate oil embargo."

247

CHAPTER XXIV

October 18: Israel in Africa

ISRAEL'S PLAN FOR A MASSIVE CROSSING of the canal was now nearly two days late, mainly because of unexpectedly stiff Egyptian resistance but also in large part because of Israel's failure to control traffic on the clogged roads. While the traffic jam impeded Israel's counterattack, it was also something of a hidden blessing. The mass of vehicles was a dramatic symbol of Israel's growing strength while Egypt's was slowly draining away. Now the two countries were in the climactic phase of the war. Egypt remained firmly installed on the east bank of the canal, a force too strong to defeat without horrendous losses. But Israel was shrewdly gambling that a dramatic thrust into Egypt's heartland would counterbalance that achievement by giving it more Egyptian territory to barter with and perhaps cause, as Sharon kept predicting, the collapse of the Egyptian army.

• •

THURSDAY

THE SINAI PENINSULA

Gripped by the excitement of the moment of at last invading the heartland of Egypt, Adan radioed his troops: "The great moment has arrived and we are crossing to Africa." As his APC rumbled across the bridge, Adan was handed a bottle of whiskey by one of his crewmen. Waving it high, he shouted: "To the breakthrough in Africa! L'chaim!"

The celebration was soon chopped off. Egyptian artillery ranged into the bridgehead and shattered the quiet of the early hours of Thursday. A tremendous bombardment began. Then more bad news. Only three tanks had crossed the bridge before it snapped, trapping a tank. The other tanks would have to cross on the Gilois rafts until the bridge could be repaired, no easy job in the hellish bombardment that was increasing in intensity. Shells and flights of Katyusha rockets exploded in blinding fireballs with ear-splitting thunderclaps, raising showers of sparks and the stench of roasting flesh and of an iron foundry as shrapnel splattered against armored vehicles. One scored a direct hit on a raft, sending the tank and its crew trapped by the closed hatch to the bottom of the canal.

By now it was after midnight and still the bridge remained broken. Time was running out. Daybreak would come in another five hours and with it increased accuracy by the Egyptian gunners.

Through the rain of artillery shells, Adan's tanks were frantically ferried by ones and twos across the canal, where bodies floated in the shifting tides and would continue to do so through the war, a ghoulish, bobbing spectacle to both Israelis and Egyptians gazing at the once peaceful waters.

• •

TEL AVIV

Chief of Staff Elazar was still holding meetings in the Pit early Thursday. He told his staff of his plans to enlarge the bridgehead, which he complained was "still just pint-sized." His order was for part of Sharon's division to cross the canal, attack northward to the sand rampart opposite the Second Egyptian Army and from this high point bombard Missouri. The heavily defended position just north of the Chinese Farm, which by now had been deserted by the Second Army, was still held by Egyptians. From it they continued to rain murderous artillery fire on the crossing area.

"If we can capture Missouri, which is the high ground northeast of the bridgehead, we'll finally have a bridgehead worthy of a self-respecting army," concluded Elazar. This had been Sharon's responsibility since the beginning. But as hard as the fighting was for the vital position, his main interest focused on the west bank.

• •

ON THE WEST BANK

It was not until 1:35 AM that the unifloat pontoon bridge was repaired and the crossing of Adan's division could resume at full speed.

By 5:15, Thursday, fifteen minutes before daybreak—and two days to the hour after they had been originally scheduled to arrive—Adan's division of two brigades with seventy tanks each was over. Now, for the first time,

249

Israel had a respectable force in "Africa."

Adan's intent was to strike south and west beyond the Sweet Water Canal. It brought water from the Nile and paralleled the Suez Canal by a distance of about a mile. Along its banks, for distances varying from a hundred yards to several miles, fellahin cultivated orchards, fields of grain and vegetable gardens. The belt of green in the tawny desert was muddy and had heavy undergrowth, ideal for infantry but not tanks.

The desert surrounding the green belt, called the Plains of Aida in this region, was dotted with military camps and storage areas and was ideal maneuvering ground for tanks. To the southwest were the Geneifa Hills, which dominated the plains, and was the site of many of the sixty-one SAM installations. Adan's mission was to maraud southward, to destroy missile sites so safe corridors could be opened for Israeli planes and to envelope the rear of the Third Army. The antiaircraft screen made it impossible for Israeli planes to provide ground support in this region, thus its destruction would add enormously to Israel's strength.

Adan had expected Sharon's paratroopers to establish their bridgehead to the edge of the desert, west of the green belt along the Sweet Water Canal. Instead, they had pushed only to the eastern bank of the Sweet Water Canal in Adan's sector. As a result, Egyptian armor and infantry had been able to move into the western part of the green belt, hidden among buildings and ditches, a potent antitank force to stem the Israeli break out into the open desert.

In addition, by now other Egyptian forces were moving into the region, the 23rd Armored Brigade and the 150th Paratroop Brigade, both from the Egyptian headquarters reserves at Cairo, about eighty miles to the southeast. From the south, the Egyptian high command sent the 2nd Armored Brigade of the 4th Division. The Egyptians were clearly at last very concerned and making a supreme effort to staunch the invasion.

Beyond these measures, Egypt now committed its air force against the bridgehead. In three separate attacks this day, Egypt lost at least fifteen MiGs and a number of helicopters trying to knock out the bridge. With Egyptian planes in the air, the SAMs could not be fired and so the Israelis were able to commit their own air force. Furious dog fights resulted. Adan and his men could clearly witness these air duels, many of which took place directly above them. One attack involved twenty Egyptian planes. "Every time a burning torch spiraled earthward, we literally held our breathe until we received verification that it was Egyptian," recalled Adan. Then two slow Egyptian helicopters appeared, one of them dropping a barrel of napalm which failed to explode but nearly landed on Moshe Dayan who, as Adan reported, "was wandering around the area, scraping at the ground looking for antique shards." The two helicopters were shot down. In total, Egypt lost seven helicopters and sixteen jets that Thursday. Israel lost six planes.

• •

Instead of breaking out immediately as planned, Adan and his force had to fight hard all day long to clear out routes through the green belt. Although Colonel Natke Nir managed to break out fairly quickly and capture a warehouse on a fortified hill at Arel overlooking the main north-south Ismailia-Suez road, Colonel Gabi Amir's brigade got bogged down in heavy fighting in the green belt. It was slow, bloody fighting against small clusters of Egyptian infantry hidden in the thick foliage, which the Israelis soon began calling "the jungle."

When the two brigades were finally both out, they then faced counter-attacks from the north and south by Egyptian tanks. A strong defensive position at the crossroads of Tsach, south of the Arel fortified hill on the junction of the Ismailia-Suez and Deversoir-Cairo roads, kept the Israelis constantly under fire. These battles consumed more time and caused many casualties. Adan pleaded for air support, but he was denied it on the basis of the presence of SAM sites in the area. His answer was to send out two armored battalions that, standing off at long range, were able to blast the comparatively defenseless bases. One SAM base in desperation even lowered its antiaircraft missiles and futilely fired them in flat trajectories against the tanks.

The raids against the missile sites paid important dividends. They had begun as soon as Danny Matt's paratroopers had crossed two days earlier and their growing frequency caused the Egyptians apprehension. Because the sites were essentially without defenses against tanks, many were ordered to move westward away from Israel's forces, thus opening to some extent the skies to Israeli warplanes. The Israeli general staff estimated—too optimistically, as it turned out—that of fifty-four sites in the immediate area, only twenty were left and air support was now at last possible for the ground troops.

• •

The stiff Egyptian resistance against Adan's force had consumed the whole day on the west bank. By late afternoon, Adan's tanks were out of fuel and ammunition. It would not be until the next day, Friday, that he would launch his massive breakthrough in lightning raids out in the countryside.

Meanwhile, Sharon's forces on the west bank—Colonel Matt's paratroopers and others who had been slowly moving over—were running into tough resistance. One force trying to penetrate north between the Sweet Water Canal and the north-south railway that ran just west of the canal hit an Egyptian strongpoint near Serafeum. A bitter fight raged all day at hand grenade range. One commander, Captain Asa Kadmoni, reported shooting scores of Egyptians as they repeatedly assaulted the house he had taken refuge in. When a relief force finally extracted the besieged unit, the Israelis had suffered eleven killed and twenty-seven wounded.

Other elements of Sharon's division remained on the east bank, containing the Egyptian Missouri stronghold. But still he had not taken the position and heavy artillery attacks from Missouri continued to rake Israel's bridgehead, making it a slaughterhouse. In one night alone forty-one men were killed by the Egyptian fire; ultimately a hundred would be killed and many hundreds wounded in the exposed compound.

• •

TEL AVIV

Elazar estimated that Egypt lost 150 tanks during the fighting Thursday on both sides of the canal, as against several dozen Israeli tank losses. In giving those figures to the cabinet, the chief of staff added: "I believe things will improve tomorrow. There are no drastic developments as yet, but we can see realistic developments, battles in which we gain the upper hand, though we're doing so at a slow pace, and we're paying for that."

Israel's casualties so far in twelve days of fighting were reported as 906 dead, 266 missing, 4,204 wounded; 77 others had been taken prisoner. These were comparable to what had been lost in the 1967 war (983 killed, 4,517 wounded) but in no way reflected the true dimensions of the blood already shed. Egyptian casualties were not available but were estimated at several times those of Israel.

• •

CAIRO

Soviet Premier Kosygin remained in Cairo, holding daily talks with Sadat, some of them bitter and acrimonious. The Soviet official continued to urge that Egypt accept a ceasefire in place but Sadat refused. He disliked Kosygin intensely, calling him in his memoirs "aggressive and a bureaucrat" with a "vicious side." On the evening of Adan's crossing, "[Kosygin] came to see me with gloom written all over his face, and said: 'With all this counterattacking you have finally been checked....A threat is now posed to Cairo.'"

Sadat's response was a counterattack of his own: "I'm sorry to disappoint you," he snapped, "but no threat will ever be posed to Cairo. However, where are the tanks I asked you for?...You send the tanks and I'll deal with the counterattacks."

To that end, Sadat dispatched Chief of Staff Shazly to the Second Army's rear headquarters on the west bank. By now relations between the hot tempered chief of staff, Sadat and War Minister Ismail were extremely tense. On this day, in his memoirs, Shazly referred to both officials as "neither particularly competent military men." He wanted to withdraw armored forces from the east bank in order to meet the Israelis on the west bank, but they feared that such a move might undermine morale and cause a rout similar to 1967. Shazly's orders were to see that the Second Army was not allowed to be surrounded. He left unhappy and filled, he later said, with foreboding.

· ·

WASHINGTON

The Kremlin was not only pressing for a ceasefire in Cairo but in Washington too. On Thursday night Chairman Brezhnev sent a message to the White House proposing a ceasefire in place, Israeli withdrawal to the 1967 lines in accordance with Security Council Resolution 242 and consultations. The proposal placed the administration in an awkward position. If it did not work in conjunction with the Soviet Union, then Moscow could just as well go it alone. Its proposal would probably be accepted by the Security Council and then on what basis would the United States veto it? And, noted Kissinger, "If we vetoed, we would be alone in the crisis that followed, tempting Soviet threats, European dissociation, and Arab radicalism." In addition, only that day Golda Meir had sent a message saying Israel opposed accepting a ceasefire linked to Resolution 242.

At the same time, a message arrived from Saudi Arabia's King Faisal, saying that prolongation of the war would help Moscow and that Israel must return to the 1967 lines. He warned: "If the United States continues to stand by the side of Israel, then this [U.S.-Saudi] relationship will risk being diminished." Also that day Riyadh increased the size of its reduction of oil production to 10%, instead of the previously announced 5% OPEC

253

agreement, and threatened a total embargo to the United States unless there were "quick, tangible results."

Despite the Soviet overture and the Saudi warning, Kissinger concluded that a way must be found for Washington to dominate the negotiations and "to gain a little more time for Israel's offensive...." At the same time, he sent a less than sincere message to Sadat, urging him to accept a ceasefire: "[You] know the importance we attach to a prompt end to the hostilities...."

CHAPTER XXV

October 19-21:
Oil Embargo

NEVER HAD THE ARAB OIL STATES been in a better position to exercise their precious natural resource as a political weapon. World consumption of oil had been rising dramatically since 1962. The average annual increase was 7%, a rate that equalled a doubling of consumption in ten years. Americans alone consumed energy at a rate equal to 200 fulltime servants for each American. Demand was reflected in the rise of prices, from $1.70 a barrel in 1950 to the $5.12 level imposed just three days earlier by OPEC. For the first time the Arab nations could not only reduce production and still retain revenues at current or higher levels, but they were free to impose whatever prices the market would bear. It was a powerful weapon and now they were determined to wield it.

The Soviet Union too was becoming more active. It was reading the battle correctly, and it recognized that the Arabs were slowly losing what they had gained. Although the Syrians continued to block the Israelis from getting within artillery range of downtown Damascus, as they had hoped, the combined Arab force on the Golan Heights was nonetheless also unable to push the Israelis back to the old ceasefire Purple Line. Thus the Israelis occupied more ground than they had started with, thereby denying the Syrians from profiting by waging war. In the Sinai, the major Israeli crossing meant that Egypt's achievements were now also being undermined. Each advance there meant one less political asset for Egypt and the Arabs in general. It was obvious from the Kremlin's view that a ceasefire was needed as quickly as possible, both to preserve what was left of Arab gains and to avoid a clash with the United States, which loomed as the two countries vied to resupply their clients. To that end Moscow now embarked on an unconventional diplomatic strategy.

. .

FRIDAY/the 19th

WASHINGTON

The Kremlin's sense of urgency was demonstrated in the morning with a highly unusual message from Brezhnev to Nixon:

Since time is essential and now not only every day but every hour counts, my colleagues and I suggest that the US Secretary of State and your closest associate Dr. Kissinger comes in an urgent manner to Moscow to conduct appropriate negotiations with him as your authorized personal representative. It would be good if he could come tomorrow, October 20. I will appreciate your speedy reply.

The message also contained a subtle warning by noting that the war was becoming so dangerous that it could even "harm" relations between the two superpowers.

This Soviet gambit unintentionally carried the potential of actually playing into Israel's hands, as Kissinger and Nixon were quick to perceive. The long transit time to Moscow and back would mean that any U.N. action would be delayed and "would gain at least another seventy-two hours for military pressures to build," as Kissinger put it. More than that, the secretary of state was being hosted at a large dinner that night by the Chinese ambassador, prior to his planned trip later to China. It would bring more delay since he could hardly break it in order to travel to the capital of China's most powerful enemy. Thus he informed Soviet Ambassador Dobrynin that he could not leave earlier than Saturday morning and would not be ready to start negotiations until Sunday. The conditions were acceptable to Moscow, an indication of how badly Moscow wanted a ceasefire by this time.

Before he left, Kissinger briefed Israeli Ambassador Dinitz and asked him to send detailed military reports to him in Moscow. He also assured the envoy that he would support Israel by rejecting the basic Arab and Soviet position that a ceasefire should be linked to a near complete Israeli withdrawal under Resolution 242.

• •

That same Friday, Nixon, now reeling from the repeated revelations of Watergate and desperately in need of all the support he could get, submitted a $2.2 billion special appropriations request for emergency aid to Israel. Aside from actually committing U.S. troops to Israel's cause, there was nothing he could have done that would be more provocative to the Arabs. They reacted with fury.

• •

RIYADH

King Faisal was in his Riyassa Palace office when he received word of Nixon's action. He was furious. From his view, the United States had repeatedly spurned his warnings, flaunted its support of Israel and was flagrantly, provocatively lining itself up against the whole Arab nation. He decided that night that some drastic action had to be taken. It would be announced the next morning.

• •

TRIPOLI
Muammar Qadhafi was also furious. He announced that Libya was immediately cutting off all oil shipments to the United States, about one percent of U.S. consumption, and raising the price of its premium oil to other countries from $4.90 to $8.25 a barrel, another rise of almost 70% above the one imposed by OPEC only three days earlier.

• •

THE SINAI PENINSULA

The evacuation of the Egyptian 16th and 21st Divisions from the Chinese Farm during the night of October 17-18 had allowed Israeli engineering units to sweep clean the mines cluttering the Tirtur road so that the mammoth roller bridge could finally move forward. It arrived at the Tirtur terminus, about a mile north of the pontoon bridge, and was floated at midnight and in service by Friday's dawn. It was just in time because nearly all of the Gilois rafts had already been sunk by Egyptian artillery, which continued to plaster the bridgehead. Now with two bridges in operation, Israel's growing forces on the west bank could be assured delivery of the huge amounts fuel and ammunition their tanks needed.

Nonetheless, traffic jams persisted because of the incessant Egyptian bom-

257

bardment. During the dark hours the snarls became worse. When shelling intensified, the drivers of the fuel and ammo trucks fled for cover as far from their dangerous loads as possible. It took endless time for them to find their vehicles and move out again.

• •

ON THE WEST BANK

By dawn Friday, Karen Magen's division had crossed over, meaning there were now three divisions operating on Egyptian territory never before penetrated by Israel. Sharon's division, part of which remained on the east bank, was attacking northward around the green belt and now Adan was prepared to break out and attack southwest across the Plains of Aida toward Suez City; Magen stood in reserve on his right rear flank.

This was the moment for which the tankmen had been waiting. For the first time, they would be able to fan out and maneuver, marauding as they sped over the ideal tank terrain. Adan felt his heart skip as his division raced across the flat plain. "It was as though the armored forces, which had fought so hard to break out of the green belt, had achieved the prize of the freedom to maneuver they so much wanted."

At 9 AM, the division ran into an Egyptian artillery brigade with dozens of guns and reinforced by tanks and infantry in the area around Hushana, southeast of the northern tip of the Great Bitter Lake. Colonel Natke Nir's brigade charged full speed, overrunning the brigade and scattering fleeing Egyptian infantrymen across the desert.

As Adan watched the battle with his small command group from the Hills of Geneifa the Israelis were again witnesses to dogfights between Israeli and Egyptian jets. MiGs were swooping in low to attack the Israeli bridgehead. As one flight of two MiGs roared over the command group, one of Adan's crewmen fired at it with a machine gun. The two jets broke off their bridgehead attack and threateningly began circling the command group. Suddenly, four bombs began arcing through the sky toward the group.

Adan reported: "Sudden fear—what to do—stay in the Zelda [the M-113 APC] or jump out and look for shelter? Some jumped, most stayed in the vehicles. Tension was high as the bombs made their seemingly interminable descent; would they hit us?" They missed. But then the jets began strafing the Israelis with rockets and machine guns, wounding two of them.

While the jets attacked, the Israelis fired everything they had at them, knocking down one. The pilot bailed out and was captured. He claimed that he had been unaware that Israeli forces were operating so deep inside Egypt. This was a good sign to Adan, who concluded that "disarray in the Egyptian camp was growing."

By the end of the day, Adan's force had penetrated twenty miles southwest of the green belt, destroying about ten SAM sites and an artillery brigade.

• •

Sharon's division ran into heavy resistance in its efforts to push northward. Attempting to overrun an Egyptian commando battalion four miles north of Sarafeum, Colonel Amnon Reshef's brigade was fired on by an advance platoon of the Egyptian battalion. They fought fiercely, and to the last man. Reshef called in reinforcements for the assault on the heavily fortified main position on a hill. There was a radar station there with bunkers and a radio interception station equipped with an Israeli receiver. The battle raged through the day in trenches and fortified positions. When it was over, there were three hundred Egyptian bodies, a testament, as General Herzog observed, "to their extremely obstinate and brave stand."

Despite this hard fight, Southern Command was angry with Sharon. He had again failed to take the Missouri area on the east side with its murderous artillery and now General Gonen again wanted him dismissed for insubordination. Chief of Staff Elazar decided to visit Sharon's advance headquarters on the west bank. Sharon admitted to Gonen: "I have fought for twenty-six years. But I must say that all the others were only battles. This was a real war." This was a sentiment shared by most Israelis. Adan had earlier confided to his troops that since 1948 Israel had fought only "deluxe wars" compared to the current one.

Elazar was moved by Sharon's description of the hard fighting by his division on both sides of the canal. Nonetheless, he still wanted Missouri captured. He later remarked that he had yet to see any sign that the Egyptian army was about to collapse. For that, he estimated much fighting would be needed.

By now, Friday evening, it was known that the Soviets were pressing for a ceasefire and that Kissinger would soon be on his way to Moscow. The estimate was that there were only three to five days left to enlarge Israel's gains on the west bank. Israel's objectives would be to establish strong lines and to annihilate as much of the Egyptian army as possible. In addition, Defense Minister Dayan warned Elazar that before any ceasefire took place, Israeli forces must recapture the vital Mount Hermon fortress, which was valuable both as a listening post and as a symbol. The Syrians must not be allowed to retain any gain from the war.

CAIRO

The unpleasant visit of Premier Kosygin ended with Sadat declaring to the departing Soviet: "I won't have a ceasefire until the final stage of my war plan has been carried out. I hope this is clear for you."

• •

Sadat had another unpleasant meeting that day. Chief of Staff Shazly had returned from the Second Army certain that the only way the Israeli invasion could be turned back was by withdrawing four armored brigades from the east bank. Ismail refused. Even though it was 10 PM, Shazly was so angry that he insisted Sadat be summoned to Center Ten to make the decision personally. According to Shazly's version, Sadat refused to speak to him but was told by the commanders of the air force and other services that the situation was grave. Nonetheless, Sadat said: "We will not withdraw a single soldier from the east to the west."

According to Sadat, Shazly was "a nervous wreck" when he returned from the Second Army and he secretly fired him that night.

• •

SATURDAY/the 20th

RIYADH

At 9 PM local time, Saudi Arabia announced it was imposing a total oil boycott against the United States, an economic jihad, in retaliation for its unlimited support of Israel. The Kingdom would no longer sell the average of 638,500 barrels daily it had been providing America during the past ten and a half months. This equalled less than 4% of U.S. daily consumption, which came to seventeen million barrels, but it nonetheless was a severe jolt from this normally cautious and compliant country. Worse, it had a domino effect on other Arab oil producers—Abu Dhabi, Algeria, Bahrain, Kuwait and Qatar—who quickly followed suit, causing economic chaos around the world.

• •

CAIRO

After his unpleasant confrontation with Shazly late Friday night, Anwar

Sadat stayed around the operations room at Center Ten to catch up on the latest battlefield reports. What he saw obviously gave him no pleasure for by the time he left during the early morning hours on Saturday he had decided that the moment had come for a ceasefire.

He returned to Tahirah Palace and had the Soviet ambassador summoned. While he waited, he sent a message to Syrian President Assad explaining his decision. He charged that because of the massive American airlift, which was continuing at a heavy rate, he was in effect not only fighting Israel but all the sophisticated weapons of the United States too. "To put it bluntly, I cannot fight the United States....My heart bleeds to tell you this, but I feel that my office compels me to take this decision."

When Ambassador Vinogradov arrived, Sadat officially informed him that Egypt would accept a ceasefire within the existing lines, meaning his troops would continue to occupy the Bar-Lev Line but Israeli troops would hold portions of the west bank. How large the Israeli salient would be would depend on when Israel accepted a ceasefire too.

Henry Kissinger was determined that would not be too soon.

• •

EN ROUTE TO MOSCOW

Secretary of State Kissinger was flying to Moscow, concentrating on his scheduled negotiations with Chairman Brezhnev when he was suddenly horrified. The cause was a copy of a letter that Nixon was sending to Brezhnev, assuring the Soviet leader that the secretary of state had "full authority" to make commitments, which would have "my complete support." One of Kissinger's negotiating styles was to claim the need to check with the President before conceding a point, thus gaining time to stall and maneuver. Now that excuse was gone. Kissinger expressed his distress in his memoirs: "'Full authority' made it impossible for me from Moscow to refer any tentative agreement to the President for his approval—if only to buy time to consult Israel. Moreover, the letter implied that the Soviets and we would impose an overall Mideast settlement on the parties and that I was empowered to discuss that subject as well....[I]n a situation in which time was our most important ally, it deprived me of the opportunity to procrastinate, hence of maneuvering room."

Kissinger soon became even more horrified when he received another message, this one directly from Nixon. Although the President was by now in the midst of what became known as the "Saturday night massacre"—that traumatic evening when he fired special Watergate prosecutor Archibald

Cox with the result that his own attorney general and deputy attorney general resigned in protest—Nixon nonetheless took the time to suggest a bold solution to the Arab-Israeli conflict. Kissinger was impressed by its cogency, if not its import, recognizing it as "a remarkable feat of concentration considering the Watergate storm raging around him." Nixon wanted Kissinger to discuss with Brezhnev what the Soviet leader had suggested at their San Clemente meeting in June: an imposed settlement by the two superpowers. Said the President's message:

> The Israelis and Arabs will never be able to approach this subject by themselves in a rational manner. That is why Nixon and Brezhnev, looking at the problem more dispassionately, must step in, determine the proper course of action to a just settlement, and then bring the necessary pressure on our respective friends for a settlement which will at last bring peace to this troubled area.

Nixon went on to point out to Kissinger that even Israel's best interests would be served if the United States now used "whatever pressures may be required in order to gain acceptance of a settlement which is reasonable and which we can ask the Soviets to press on the Arabs." What was holding back an agreement, Nixon said, was Israel's intransigence, the Arabs' refusal to bargain realistically and America's "preoccupation with other initiatives." Referring euphemistically to the Jewish vote, Nixon added: "U.S. political considerations will have absolutely no, repeat no, influence on our decisions in this regard. I want you to know that I am prepared to pressure the Israelis to the extent required, regardless of the domestical political consequences."

Kissinger called this thoughtful and brave message "an unnerving surprise" that caused him "extreme displeasure." His response was to completely ignore it, thereby missing the Nixon Administration's one realistic chance where a full peace may have been achieved in the Middle East.

• •

ON THE WEST BANK

The Egyptians were throwing all they could into a desperate effort to contain the Israeli thrust out of its bridgehead on the west bank. They had by now committed in a broad arc around the Israeli forces four reduced armored divisions—the 3rd, 6th and 23rd mechanized and the 4th armored,

262

extending from Ismailia south and to west of Suez. This arc of Egyptian troops screened Cairo from the Israeli force and prevented any consideration by the Israeli general staff of mounting an attack on the capital—although Bar-Lev is reported to have worried that Sharon might try to make just such a daring raid. "I lived in fear of Sharon running to Cairo," he said, according to journalist Uri Dan, who was no friend of Bar-Lev's.

Adan's forces continued to advance southward on Saturday, destroying a number of SAM bases on the way. By noon they managed to capture the old airfield at Fayid, midway down the west bank of the Great Bitter Lake. It was an important catch, because as Adan's lines grew so too did his logistical problems. But Egyptian resistance around the airfield remained too strong for Israeli planes to use the field that day.

He also tried to secure a land route, the main north-south road between Ismailia and Suez, called Havit by Israelis, which ran through Fayid. But in that too he failed that day. Repeated attacks were beaten back by Egyptian tanks and infantry with antitank missiles. By the end of the day, Adan concluded, "We felt we had been blocked...and would have to fight even more resolutely the next day."

Nonetheless, his forces had managed to penetrate another twelve miles southward into the Egyptian heartland, destroyed many missile sites and had managed to cut the Asor road, the northernmost of the two main east-west highways between Suez and Cairo.

* *

In the north, Sharon's troops continued to find tough going in trying to press toward Ismailia against entrenched Egyptian paratroops and commandos through the green belt. Sharon launched a three-brigade attack toward Ismailia but came up against the hardened troops of the 182nd Paratroop Brigade from the Second Army, which stopped the attack just south of Lake Timsah. The Egyptians had blown up the water conduits, flooding the area and making progress through the mud slow. The day's fighting had brought Sharon's forces gains of only about two to three miles. But now Israeli artillery could interdict the main Ismailia-Cairo road.

Sharon's troops on the east bank once again made no headway in their efforts to silence the potent artillery in the high ground at Missouri. It continued to blast the bridgehead and its troops showed no indication of collapsing. Southern Command was impatient. It ordered that Missouri finally had to be taken. In the evening, Sharon was informed that the next day he should place the "stress...on Missouri. You'll get all the air support you want." But Sharon's eyes continued to be directed toward the west bank and

Ismailia—and, who knew, perhaps a dramatic dash toward Cairo.

• •

The gains by Adan and Sharon on Saturday increased the Israeli zone on the west bank to an area equal to about twelve miles westward and thirty-five north to south, a threatening bulge but still faced with sizable Egyptian defenders.

• •

SUNDAY/the 21st

ON THE WEST BANK

Much of Sunday was squandered in uselessly enervating arguments between Sharon and Southern Command over the wisdom of renewing the attack to take Missouri. Sharon continued to maintain that capturing the strong position would be too costly in casualties and not pay the dividends that the encirclement of Ismailia would. But Elazar and Southern Command wanted the artillery on Missouri muted and the bridgehead finally secured.

In the morning, Gonen radioed Sharon: "You must transfer your main effort to Missouri...."

Sharon replied: "All you need is to have the air force attack there without let up."

After he was informed that the air force was already in action, Sharon promised to attack .

Although the air attacks were heavy and prolonged, the Egyptian defenses remained strong. When Gonen telephoned this information to Elazar, the chief of staff exploded. The attacks had been going on for six days, he pointed out. "Must we blast out a hole the size of a lake so that the Egyptians will drown in it?" he asked.

When a short time later Gonen learned that Sharon had still not made any preparations for attacking, he called Sharon again but the burly general only repeated his argument that it was a waste of manpower. Bar-Lev had to fly to Sharon's headquarters on the west bank to get his agreement. Bar-Lev explained: "The little time left to us before the anticipated ceasefire makes it imperative that we secure the northern flank of the bridgehead. That's the most important thing."

Sharon agreed to attack at 2:30 PM. But forty-five minutes later, the attack had still not developed and Gonen again ordered him to move his forces. At last Sharon gave the order. Colonel Tuvia Raviv's brigade, which had been breaking itself for days on the Missouri defenses, tried once again. But by now his exhausted force had only forty-one tanks, including a reinforcement of only five provided by Sharon. It was too weak a force to overrun Missouri. The Egyptians smashed Raviv's assault. When he withdrew, he had only nineteen tanks left. In all, another twenty-four men, including eight officers, were lost.

Gonen ordered Sharon to try another attack that night but Sharon refused. "Bear in mind that this will be failure to carry out an order!" warned Gonen.

"Well, really," retorted Sharon, "don't bother me with things like that."

Sharon later telephoned Dayan in Tel Aviv and succeeded in having the defense minister cancel the order.

• •

During the day's fighting, ninety Israelis had been killed. Yet the only gain to show in Sharon's sector had been a northern advance of about a mile and a half.

Things had not gone much better in Adan's sector, although there had been two important achievements. The Suez-Ismailia road had been opened and the Fayid airport secured. These accomplishments now gave the Israeli forces in the south direct ground and air supply and evacuation routes to sustain their attack southward. They were an important part of the infrastructure to support a determined thrust the next day, which it was now recognized might be the day of the ceasefire.

• •

MOSCOW

Kissinger found the Soviet leadership impatient for a quick ceasefire, so anxious in fact that the two sides were able to agree to a U.S. formula within an unprecedented four hours. The three-point agreement called for a simple ceasefire in place. There was no mention of Israeli withdrawal to 1967 lines; it merely urged the parties to implement Resolution 242—a mandate, Kissinger observed, "sufficiently vague to have occupied diplomats for years without arriving at agreement." Its third point was equally vague. It required immediate negotiations "between the parties concerned" under "appropriate auspices."

When Brezhnev interpreted "appropriate auspices" as a peace imposed by the two countries—the approach Nixon had ordered Kissinger to pursue—the secretary of state rebuffed the Soviet leader. "I rejected the proposition,'' Kissinger reported. To Kissinger, the intricate wording of the third point meant that the Arabs would have to negotiate directly with Israel. Although he claimed that the Soviets accepted his interpretation, later Soviet actions indicated that the Kremlin leadership was far from agreement with Kissinger and continued to believe the superpowers should work together.

Kissinger and Brezhnev agreed they would request the Security Council to convene at 9 PM Sunday, New York time, and that the ceasefire would go into effect twelve hours after its passage. This arrangement, Kissinger believed, would help Israel by putting the ceasefire at least twenty-eight hours away, given the expected arguments in the council and other technical details. To make sure the Israelis got as much time as possible, Kisinger sent U.N. Ambassador John Scali a top secret cable noting that the "stress Soviets have put on speed. We do not have same interest in such speed."

He then drafted a message for Nixon's signature informing Prime Minister Meir of these arrangements, emphasizing that "there is absolutely no mention whatsoever of the word 'withdrawal' in the resolution...." He added: "Madame Prime Minister, we believe that this is a major achievement for you and for us and supportive of the brave fighting of your forces."

• •

TEL AVIV

Washington had flashed a message, arriving at 10:15 PM on Prime Minister Meir's desk, that a ceasefire formula had been agreed to by Kissinger and Brezhnev.

Golda Meir was exceedingly unhappy. The one thing all Israeli leaders had always feared most was collusion by the superpowers, whether they were Britain and France in the old days or America and Russia now, to impose a settlement on the Middle East. Inevitably, Israel could never come out of such an arrangement without losing some of the territory it already possessed, since by definition compromise meant giving up something. Thus an imposed solution was anathema to Israel, and an imposed ceasefire, although Meir knew it to be inevitable, was not much better. It might set a precedent for broader superpower cooperation.

The best Israel could hope to salvage from the situation was to make a dramatic display of its favored status with the United States. To that end Meir strongly hinted that if her country was expected to accept the ceasefire then Kissinger would personally have to stop in Tel Aviv and explain its terms. These were probably less important to her than the symbolism of having the American secretary of state detour to Tel Aviv on his return from Moscow. Nothing could more vividly demonstrate Israel's importance in the forming of U.S. policy.

Kissinger observed: "Delicately, Golda had not made Israeli acceptance of [a ceasefire] dependent on my agreeing to the visit." But the implication was clear. Although such a radical change in travel plans caused a logistical nightmare for Kissinger's party—among other things permission had to be gotten to fly south over parts of the Soviet Union usually not open to foreigners—the secretary of state nonetheless acceded to Meir's request. If there remained any lingering doubts in the Arabs' minds about the extent of U.S. support for Israel, they were now irrevocably dispelled.

When Sadat learned of the visit, he too invited Kissinger, no doubt trying to counterbalance the symbolism. But Kissinger refused.

• •

Now, with Kissinger's visit impending—and thus the full backing of the United States highlighted—Israel prepared its forces to conquer as much Egyptian land as possible in the climactic spasms of the war.

CHAPTER XXVI

October 22-23: Ceasefire

AFTER ONLY TWO HOURS AND FIFTY-TWO MINUTES of debate, the U.N. Security Council passed Resolution 338 at 12:52 AM on Monday, October 22. It was a call for a ceasefire, and it represented major diplomatic gains for Israel. The brief resolution directed the parties to stop fighting and to start negotiating to find a "just and durable peace." This wording in essence demolished the Arab argument, made since the 1967 war, that the terms of Resolution 242—the return of Arab lands—should be implemented before negotiations. From now on, Israel and the United States would insist that 338 meant what Israel had claimed all along: Negotiations should be held on the basis of 242, the implication being that 242 could not be carried out without talks. The negotiation clause also meant that for the first time in Israel's history Arabs would agree to talk directly with Israeli officials.

By working together, the United States and the Soviet Union had taken the first step to stop the fighting. But in the days ahead this momentary harmony among the superpowers would be shattered and the specter of nuclear war would haunt the world.

In the Middle East, it was already 6:52 AM at the time of the resolution's passage, meaning the ceasefire would go into force as night fell twelve hours later. One span of daylight was left for fighting.

• •

MONDAY/the 22nd

TEL AVIV

Chief of Staff Elazar appeared at a cabinet meeting shortly after midnight,

268

before the passage of Resolution 338 and before the ministers had decided whether Israel would accept it. Elazar's message was grim, and serious. He pointed out that the Arabs might agree to cease firing only for the purpose of getting time to reorganize and re-equip before launching another sharp attack and inaugurate another depleting war of attrition. The lines that Israel now occupied were not the best for defense, and Arab forces both in the Sinai and on the Golan Heights remained substantial. If the Arabs had a week or ten days to install new missile systems it would pose severe problems for Israel. By way of illustration, Elazar told the cabinet that the air force flew 500 sorties on Sunday and lost only three planes. This was because of the earlier destruction of the missile sites—quite a contrast to the total of 102 planes lost so far, mainly in the early days due to missiles.

As the cabinet knew, Prime Minister Meir had done all she could to persuade Nixon to give Israel more time. But he had been adamant. There was nothing left but to accept—or risk the wrath of the President of the United States. Despite Elazar's somber warning, the cabinet decided at 3 AM to agree to a ceasefire.

• •

THE GOLAN HEIGHTS

The symbolic and practical importance to Israel of recapturing Mt. Hermon—"the eyes of Israel"—was great. It was the one tangible profit Syria had obtained from the war, and it was a significant one. Under no circumstances was Israel prepared to allow Syria to keep this highly symbolic, highly practical intelligence gathering station. Elazar ordered a strong attack against the fortification starting Sunday evening with the aim of capturing the fortification.

Two full brigades, the Golani and the 31st Paratroop, were invested in the attack. They were to coordinate, with the paratroops staging a surprise nighttime assault to capture a Syrian fortress, "Syrian Hermon," to the north; the Golani troops were ordered to wait in the foothills to see how that operation went. If at dawn it was determined that the momentum of the paratroopers' attack could carry them onto Mount Hermon from the unexpected northern direction, they would take the fort and the Golani Brigade would act as a blocking force.

Almost immediately, coordination between the two brigades broke down. The paratroop attack went off without a hitch and the Syrian position was found deserted. But instead of urging the paratroops to press on to the fortress, the Golani Brigade launched a frontal attack straight up the steep and

269

boulder strewn mountain. It was the predictable approach, and the Syrians were ready. Syrian snipers were hidden among the rocks and riles, and they put their night vision telescopic sights to effective use. They picked off Israeli after Israeli.

Fighting was fierce, with artillery, mortars and automatic weapons lighting up the chill night. All attempts during the night to take the fortress were repulsed. The brigade commander was wounded, as were seven of eight tank commanders and numerous other officers and soldiers. Israeli casualties were soon so great that the men to carry them to medical aid down the mountain could not be spared.

As dawn broke, the Israelis found themselves still several hundred yards from the fortress and intermingled with deeply entrenched Syrian troops. The situation was grim. But the fighting had taken a heavy toll on the Syrian defenders too. In midmorning. the Israelis regrouped and in a final all-out charge the Israelis smashed through the Syrian defenses. At 11 AM, Golani troops finally re-entered the fortress they had lost seventeen days earlier.

The cost to the Golani Brigade had been high: fifty-five killed and seventy-nine wounded.

• •

TEL AVIV

Henry Kissinger arrived in Israel at 1 PM, directly from Moscow. He was taken to a meeting with Israel's top leaders—Meir, Dayan, Elazar and others. He found them exhausted. "Weariness, physical and moral, was stamped on each face," Kissinger observed. "The characteristic Israeli show of bravado was not absent, but it required so much effort that it seemed to exhaust the participants rather than armor them. They spoke of imminent victories but without conviction, more as if to prop up the image of invulnerability. There were grumbles about how Egypt's Third Army might have been fully encircled and destroyed in another three days of fighting."

Observed Kissinger: "But these were the same leaders whose repeated predictions—'we need three more days'—had consistently been proved overoptimistic."

The Israelis were suspicious that Kissinger had made a secret agreement to impose a settlement, suspicious the Arabs would not maintain a ceasefire, suspicious the Arabs would not return Israeli prisoners. He tried to reassure them. In order to mute their complaints about the lack of fighting time left, Kissinger said: "...I would understand if there was a few hours' 'slippage' in the ceasefire deadline while I was flying home...."

Kissinger later claimed this was a mistake because the Israelis took him at his word. Over the next three days, Israel repeatedly violated the ceasefire with the understanding that it had Kissinger's private approval. In fact, Kissinger had earlier calbed Ambassador Dinitu in Washington assuring Israel that "we would understand if Israelis felt they required some additional time. . . ."

While they ate lunch, a message arrived that Egypt had accepted the ceasefire, to go into effect at 5 PM. The timing confused Kissinger and the Israelis since it was two hours ahead of time. He asked if perhaps Cairo was in a different time zone. None of the Israelis knew. The problem was finally solved by a call to the state department in Washington, which assured the negotiators Tel Aviv and Cairo were in the same time zone. It was later agreed that the ceasefire would begin that same day at 6:52 PM, October 22.

Five hours after his arrival, Kissinger was on his way back home, a ceasefire agreement in his pocket and a pledge by Israel to honor it—or so he pretended.

• •

ON THE WEST BANK

Even before Kissinger had arrived in Tel Aviv, Israel's pre-ceasefire attacks were well underway. At 5:10 AM, Bren Adan, who had received word of the pending ceasefire, radioed his daily report to his units: "Karish here. Today is Monday, 22 October, the eighteenth day of the war. On this day the Levites would chant in the Temple: 'And you shall strike the Egyptians and pursue them to the end.' Strike them thoroughly and quickly. Should it come to pass that you do not hurry, you will not finish the task!"

This his division was to do in a daring day of maneuver and battle, a day that would finally cause the rout of some, but by no means most, Egyptian units.

Adan's reinforced division of 175 tanks was deployed in an arc swinging from Panara on the south of the Great Bitter Lake westward to the dominating Geneifa Hills to just above the Sarag Cairo-Suez road on the south. Sarag was the last major artery open between the capital and the Egyptian Third Army, which was deployed on both sides of the canal from south of the Great Bitter Lake to the Gulf of Suez.

The day's objective was to attack to the Zidron area on the canal at the southern end of Little Bitter Lake. Simultaneously, another attack was planned for the east bank to push the Third Army southward. Its objective was also to reach Zidron, meaning there would be a link up between the

Israeli forces on both banks of the canal. If the Israelis could join at Zidron, they would control a strip of both sides of the canal stretching from the bridgehead south of Ismailia to south of Little Bitter Lake, a significant bargaining chip in any diplomatic talks.

For Adan's forces, to get to Zidron meant a thrust of fifteen miles eastward and twenty miles southward right through the rear area of the Egyptian Third Army. It was filled with camps and troops of all types. The distance was great. Tanks had to travel over broken terrain against stubborn opposition by strong elements of the Egyptian Third Army's 4th Armored and 6th Mechanized divisions, as well as small units of Palestinian and Kuwaiti troops.

Before the Israelis could attack, the Egyptians launched a counterattack. The Egyptians opened with artillery barrages at 4 AM, followed by infantry and armored attacks at dawn. The fighting was hard, fierce at times, all along the line. It was not until about 9 AM when Israeli air support began slow—because of identification problems—but destructive ground support that the Egyptians began breaking.

By 9:30, after several worried calls from Southern Command about the lack of progress, Adan's division at last was able to begin advancing. It was a methodical advance, movement and fire, movement and fire, dispersing infantry and intimidating armor. Air attacks against the reluctantly withdrawing Egyptians were heavy, and getting heavier by the minute, yet the Egyptians fought back.

Under air attack, reported Adan, Egyptian "crews could be seen evacuating the tanks, running off, and then returning. The same was the case with the antiaircraft units (23mm guns) that were deployed near the tanks. The Egyptians' staying power was surprising." Yet the Israeli pressure, with the support of air attacks, was relentless.

Shortly before 11 AM, General Abdel Moneim Wassel, commander of the Third Army, radioed Minister of War Ismail and reported: "Sir, the situation is fluid, the enemy is breaking through." Wassel was at his headquarters on the Sarag road west of Suez within sight of the advancing Israeli force. The headquarters was buried deep in bunkers but nonetheless was under air attack. Already the communications system had been hit, damaging the headquarters' command and control capacity. With increasing reports coming in that the Israelis were pushing toward his headquarters, Wassel ignored warnings about Israeli tanks in the area and went above to survey the scene himself. It was not a happy sight. Hundreds of Egyptian infantrymen were fleeing on foot and the Israeli attack was pressing forward without pause.

Before Adan's units reached the Third Army headquarters, however, Southern Command, worried about the approaching ceasefire and the lateness of the hour, ordered Adan to break off his southern movement and attack east to try to reach the canal before darkness.

At 3 PM, Radio Cairo officially announced that Egypt would accept the ceasefire. This was the first public announcement, and up until now the Israelis suspected that Egypt would renege on its private assurances and refuse. Now it was more urgent than ever to get to the canal, although the general staff had already ordered that any attack in progress at the start of the ceasefire should continue to its conclusion.

The Egyptians were fighting with tenacity, holding up the Israeli advance. Adan's units were engaged in local mopping up actions in all sectors against Egyptian infantry and tanks. Mines were blowing up during the maneuvering and the Israelis were taking casualties in nearly every battalion.

By 4 PM, the Israelis had fought their way out of the hilly and fissured terrain to the Plains of Aida, ready to start their wild dash to the canal, bypassing as much as possible strong defensive points in order to gain as much ground as possible. As the mass of Adan's tanks rumbled across the hard, arid earth, raising clouds of dust amid the thump of artillery and the roar of engines, a confusion of battles broke out and the Egyptian infantry in the way scattered.

"Thousands of Egyptians, I was told, were fleeing every which way but were not throwing down their arms." It was unclear whether the infantrymen did not know that to surrender they should throw down their arms or whether they were simply fleeing and planning to fight elsewhere. Adan advised his men to exercise caution but not to shoot blindly. "We had no interest in preventing surrender and in arousing resistance that would only end in more casualties...."

In the dark, the Israeli charge finally reached the environs of Zidron and the canal. Adan, in his memoirs, claims that the position was achieved just before 6:52 PM.

Cost of the day's fighting: thirty-two tanks, five half-tracks and three M-113 APCs hit; five men killed and forty-eight wounded. Egyptian losses were estimated at many times more.

• •

Adan's force, in four days of fighting, had penetrated about forty miles southward and twenty miles westward. However, many pockets of Egyptian units still existed and in the green belt along the Little Bitter Lake the Israeli and Egyptian units were badly intermingled. The 30,000-man Third Army with three hundred tanks was still a fighting force, although its position was grave. But it had not collapsed, nor was it surrounded. Nor had Israeli forces managed to link up on both banks of the canal. An attempt on Monday to push the Third Army southward on the east bank so that Israeli forces would face each other over the canal at Zidron had failed.

It was a highly unsatisfactory situation for Israel, particularly if the ceasefire did not hold.

• •

In the north, Sharon's division had no luck at all. A last gasp effort to capture Ismailia failed in the face of stern resistance by Egyptian paratroopers. The Israeli thrust was halted south of the city at the time of the ceasefire. Sharon made no effort that day to capture Missouri on the east bank, which also remained in Egyptian hands at the ceasefire. Reported Adan: "The general feeling in Sharon's division was that they were just worn out."

• •

All in all, it was an indisputable achievement for Israel, but an unsatisfactory one. As matters stood, the ceasefire had come with the battlefield at an inconclusive stage. In the north and on the west bank, Sharon's division was stymied and in Adan's sector Israeli and Egyptian forces were hopelessly intermixed. There was no clear victory by either side.

It was a prescription for instability, nervousness and—more fighting.

• •

TUESDAY/the 23rd

ON THE WEST BANK

Bren Adan was anxious to keep fighting. "I wanted to complete the encirclement of the Third Army come hell or high water....There can be no doubt that many commanders of all ranks felt as I did." When General Magen gently tried to nudge Southern Command to relent on the ceasefire, General Gonen replied: "We in the army take orders. It was the Government of Egypt that decided to launch this war, and the Government of Israel that decided on the ceasefire. And we in the army accepted both orders."

Despite this answer, Adan had informed Gonen late Monday that there were local violations of the ceasefire by the Egyptians and that "I was going to continue fighting on the following day." He did not find Gonen's response "a negative one." In fact, he was finding considerable vagueness among senior commanders in their attitude toward the ceasefire. "...conversations at all levels were ambiguous. Maintain the ceasefire but...should the enemy violate, etc." As a result, he added in his memoirs, "I planned to mop up the area we had captured, hope that the enemy would violate the ceasefire, thus leading to an expansion of the fighting so we could complete our task of encircling the Third Army."

Adan's forces began mopping up operations at first light and soon enough there were reports of Egyptian resistance. Adan was obviously delighted, because when Colonel Natke Nir hesitated to fire, the division commander ordered: "The enemy has opened fire, and we are responding. If they have opened fire on you, fire back. Take up positions and fire back! Don't make me any armistice here—fire back and go into action!"

The Israeli forces began moving en masse. They overran the numerous camps in the area and in several hours the division had rounded up 4,500 prisoners, a potent chip in the propaganda war as well as in the diplomatic bargaining ahead.

The momentum of Adan's fighting infected headquarters.

Elazar and the members of the general staff had been unhappy with the failure to score a clearcut victory against the Third Army at the end of the fighting Monday. When they received reports Tuesday morning that there were attacks in the sector they were not unhappy. Elazar telephoned Dayan and reported: "Last night they destroyed nine of our tanks, and now they're attacking in a number of places, trying to wrest territory back from us. I want to tell Southern Command it's free to act in the Third Army's sector." Dayan gave his approval.

By 10 AM, Gonen ordered General Magen, whose division was blocking to the west, to attack southward to complete the encirclement of the Third Army. But Magen was spread too thin to be ready before the middle of the afternoon. Gonen then radioed Adan and told him to lead the attack south. The attack, Adan was promised, would be supported by heavy air raids. (Before the first full day of the ceasefire was out, the Israeli air force had flown 354 sorties, most of them in Adan's sector.) The Israeli objective was to get to Suez City and the Gulf of Suez, about ten miles away across flat desert terrain. The aim was to reach Suez, which would finally isolate the Third Army.

Adan's force rampaged through the countryside in a wild charge, scattering bewildered Egyptian troops who were under the illusion that there was a ceasefire. Thousands of Egyptians fled and abandoned their equipment in the face of the massive Israeli charge. Adan did not stop to take prisoners.

He urged his force on, determined finally to cut off the two Egyptian divisions on the east bank, the 7th and 19th. An hour after darkness, one of Adan's units captured the fertilizer plant on the outskirts of Suez. The port of Adabiya, south of the city, was captured at 11 PM. The encirclement was now at last complete—a day after the ceasefire.

•   •

WASHINGTON

Henry Kissinger was back in his office Tuesday morning, only to find complaints that Israel was violating the ceasefire. At about 10 AM came an urgent message from Chairman Brezhnev, charging Israel with "flagrant deceit" and warning that breaking of the ceasefire was "unacceptable." The Soviet leader suggested the Security Council convene in two hours' time to reconfirm the ceasefire resolution.

The secretary of state correctly concluded from the urgency of Brezhnev's message that the Egyptian Third Army was in desperate straits. He also recognized that the Israeli attack put the United States in an extremely awkward position. As he noted: "If the United States held still while the Egyptian army was being destroyed after an American-sponsored ceasefire and a secretary of state's visit to Israel, not even the most moderate Arab could cooperate with us any longer."

When he telephoned Ambassador Dinitz to ask what was going on, the envoy told him that on behalf of the prime minister he could be assured "personally, confidentially and sincerely that none of the actions taken on the Egyptian front were initiated by us."

Not even Kissinger, with all his admiration for Golda Meir, could swallow this: "I thought she was imposing on my credulity...."

As the crisis atmosphere heated up, the messages to Kissinger escalated into a snowstorm. In response to U.S. demands for clarification, Prime Minister Meir called shortly after 11 AM, assuring him personally that Egypt had started the fighting. At 12:36, another message arrived from Brezhnev, again denouncing Israeli "treachery" and suggesting the two powers jointly take the "most decisive measures" to reimpose the ceasefire.

In a return message, Kissinger, in Nixon's name, assured the Soviet leader that the United States would "assume full responsibility to bring about a complete end of hostilities on the part of Israel."

After two more telephone conversations with the Soviet embassy, Kissinger received another message from Brezhnev, this one accepting a formula that the ceasefire be reconfirmed and a demand made that the parties return to the lines occupied at the time of ceasefire.

Then came what Kissinger characterized as a "blistering communication" from Meir. She complained bitterly that the United States was cooperating with the Soviet Union. She declared Israel would not accept a new Security Council resolution. Indeed, she asserted, Israel would not even talk about it.

At 3:15 PM, there came an urgent message from Sadat. He proposed an extraordinary course. The United States should stop the fighting even if it meant sending troops into the region to face the Israelis. Sadat added: "What is happening now, in the light of your guarantees, does not induce confidence in any other future guarantees." Kissinger replied that Washington was urging the Israelis to stop; he also recommended that Egyptian forces maintain the ceasefire.

By 8:30 PM, Golda Meir had cooled off and Dinitz telephoned to say that Israel would respect the ceasefire if Egypt did.

The Security Council that same evening passed Resolution 339, reconfirming the ceasefire. It also "urged"—not demanded, wording insisted on by Kissinger—the parties to return to the previous lines of Monday night. But Israel had no intention of stopping fighting yet, much less withdrawing.

277

CHAPTER XXVII

October 24-25: Nuclear Alert

THE UNITED STATES WAS PLACED in an awkward bind by Israel's breaking of the ceasefire. Secretary of State Kissinger had in effect pledged America's word to the Soviet Union that Israel would abide by the agreement. Yet to all appearances Washington was now reneging. The bounteous U.S. resupply effort continued unabated, giving Israel the means to break the agreement, and Kissinger's maladroit comments in Tel Aviv—he would understand Israeli "slippage" in obeying the ceasefire—all conspired to make the United States appear in collusion with Israel. The Russians were furious, the Egyptians desperate, the Arab world up in arms. Every post-ceasefire Israeli gain was an implied challenge to Moscow's power and influence, an embarrassment to the Soviet Union's relations with the Arabs. From the Kremlin's view, it was intolerable. More specifically, Chairman Brezhnev was being made to look the fool even among his own colleagues, not all of whom were his friends. Under the prod of even more Israeli breaches of the ceasefire, he acted forcefully.

• •

WEDNESDAY/the 24th

ON THE WEST BANK

Having broken the ceasefire in a massive way, Israel's leadership decided to keep on fighting for its maximal goals even if that meant going beyond the start of the new ceasefire, which both Israel and Egypt had agreed would start at 7 AM. General Adan's orders for Wednesday were to cut off the water and fuel pipes leading from the west to the Egyptian Third Army on the east bank, thereby literally leaving its troops high and dry; to mop up throughout his whole sector, and, most boldly of all, to capture Suez City, "provided it does not become a Stalingrad situation."

As Adan observed in his memoirs:

"The entire operation was in the nature of a last-minute, grab-what-you-can action...I decided to launch our attack at dawn...so that when the ceasefire did become effective we would already be engaged, and it would take time—perhaps even some hours—until the troops could hold their fire...."

Suez was a city of a quarter of million people before the War of Attrition had driven out the civilians. Now it was being held by a commando battalion and the remnants of the 4th and 6th Divisions. There was also a missile company in the city that had been transferred from the 19th Division on the east bank. The downtown area of Suez was densely built up with buildings two to five stories high, some taller, and traversed by the Sarag-Suez-Cairo road. It was a two-lane strip divided by a railroad down the center. A concrete curb about ten inches high ran on both sides of the railway, just high enough to make vehicle maneuvering difficult.

The capture of Suez, one of Egypt's major cities, was meant to be a searing symbol of Israel's military prowess. Instead, it turned into a disaster.

• •

Unknowingly, Adan was now about to embark on one of his worst operations of the war, reminiscent of his ill-fated attacks on October 8 when he and other Israeli commanders still underestimated the fighting capabilities of the Egyptians. Despite all the evidence to the contrary since then, that haughty disregard for the Egyptians had crept back into Israeli thinking. Adan admitted in his memoirs, "...we envisioned the collapse of the Egyptian forces [in Suez] based on our experience of the mass surrender of the past two days. Therefore I assumed that we would encounter no particular difficulties in capturing the city."

A heavy air bombardment was scheduled to precede the ground attack, but Dayan, who flew to Adan's headquarters that morning to watch the breaching of another ceasefire, warned that the air attack must stop at the 7 AM ceasefire deadline. That way Israel would appear to be abiding by the new ceasefire. But the ground assault would be allowed to continue under the rubric that the combat had begun earlier and could not easily be disengaged.

Right from the beginning, the attack got off to a bad start. Morning mist covered the area until 6:30, limiting the air attack to bombing runs by four squadrons, perhaps as many as eighty planes. This was a powerful force but obviously nothing compared to what Israel had planned since Adan complained that the air assault had amounted to "a pretty poor softening up."

For the ground assault, Adan committed two armored brigades reinforced by paratroopers. As the Israeli tanks and armored personnel carriers loaded with infantry advanced into the seemingly deserted city, they began taking fire. "They aren't giving up," said Colonel Aryeh Karen in an early report. "They're still fighting."

Shortly afterwards, one Israeli battalion, commanded by Nahum Zaken, reached a downtown junction of Sarag road surrounded with buildings six and seven stories high. The column was stretched out over a mile and a half and contained twenty-one tanks and fifteen armored vehicles. Suddenly it came under withering fire from flat trajectory weapons, antitank missiles, machine guns and hand grenades tossed from balconies. As was their habit, the Israeli tank commanders had kept their hatches open and were standing in the turrets when the fire fight erupted. Within minutes twenty of the twenty-four commanders were hit and only four officers were left.

The column went out of control. Tanks and APCs could barely maneuver in the confusion. The tanks discovered they could not mount the low concrete curb paralleling the railroad and some turned down side streets, never to be heard from again. Some crews and paratroopers leaped from their damaged vehicles and sought cover in buildings. One group of seventy paratroopers became entirely cut off in the center of the city at a triangle junction. In all, the battalion suffered eighteen dead and about forty wounded in the lightning ambush.

The fighting had just begun for Suez.

A paratroop battalion following Zaken's in nine APCs and three commandeered buses halted at the sound of fire and the troops dismounted. But the fighting was a quarter mile away and they were ordered to remount quickly to drive to the battle. Precious time was lost in this futile exercise and when they arrived at the junction Zaken's battalion was already in disarray and they too came under very heavy fire. Three men were killed instantly and others were wounded, including battalion commander Yossef "Jossi" Yafeh.

The brigade's intelligence half-track with nine officers and sergeants fled through a side street, never to be seen again. The other paratroopers deserted their vulnerable vehicles and took up positions in a nearby police station that was two stories high and surrounded by a twenty-inch thick stone fence.

Around the police station were buildings four and five stories tall, from which came relentless sniping and grenade attacks. Repeated efforts by other Israeli units to relieve the paratroopers were beaten off by the determined Egyptians hidden throughout the built up area.

Now Adan not only had many casualties to evacuate but he also had two separate groups of paratroopers entrapped in the city, the seventy troops from Zaken's battalion at a triangle junction in the center of the city and ninety men from Jafeh's battalion trapped in the police headquarters. All together, there were seventy to eighty wounded with the two groups.

Their problem was acute. They had no maps of the city and therefore they could not get artillery or air support for fear of being hit themselves. Although some of the wounded were extricated during determined raids, the besieging Egyptians remained strong. Attack after attack to rescue the trapped units was repelled by the Egyptians. Only a determined effort by reinforcements from Gabi's brigade finally extricated the paratroopers besieged at the triangle junction in the city around noon.

But still the eighty men in the police station remained surrounded and unable to move. It was concluded the only hope for the besieged Israelis lay in waiting for darkness and then extracting themselves—if they could find their way through the city's mazes.

The group had twenty-three wounded, including battalion commander Jafeh. A lieutenant, Dudu, had taken over the unit and in a radio contact with headquarters he expressed grave reservations about venturing out in the unknown streets. Gonen broke into the radio conversation and asked the lieutenant to describe in detail his surroundings. Headquarters then was able to locate the position from an aerial map of the city and describe a precise route for the unit to escape. After much planning and hesitations, this they finally did without getting lost or taking any more casualties. The last paratrooper arrived back behind Israeli lines at 4:45 AM Thursday.

The attempt to take Suez was a total failure, and a costly one: eighty dead and one hundred twenty wounded, all after the second ceasefire had begun. Adan himself later wondered about the wisdom of what he called such "last-minute 'grabs.'" He was of mixed emotions. "Undoubtedly," he wrote in his memoirs, "it is best to refrain from them, and well-prepared operations are always to be preferred." But he added: "At the same time, anyone who foregoes such 'snatches' is also foregoing taking advantage of his success and is reducing his achievements."

In the end, and despite the debacle at Suez, the additional day of fighting after the ceasefire significantly solidified Israel's hold of Egyptian territory and hardened its clamp on the encircled Third Army, much to the concern of Leonid Brezhnev.

281

WASHINGTON

When Kissinger arrived at his office at 8 AM, a message was already awaiting him from Egypt complaining that Israel had again broken the ceasefire. He checked with Ambassador Dinitz, but he assured Kissinger that Israel was merely defending itself against attacks by the Third Army. Noted Kissinger: "I cannot say that I gave Dinitz's report credence equal to my affection for him."

Then a message directly from Anwar Sadat to President Nixon arrived, seeking American help. He again suggested U.S. forces "intervene, even on the ground, to force Israel to comply with the ceasefire."

Kissinger telephoned Ambassador Dobrynin and said: "The madmen in the Middle East seem to be at it again."

A short time later, Dobrynin called with a message from Brezhnev to "Mr. President," dropping the "Esteemed" the Soviet leader had used the previous day. The letter spelled out in detail Israel's violations of the ceasefire and ended menacingly: "I wish to say it frankly, Mr. President, that we are confident that you have possibilities to influence Israel with the aim of putting an end to such a provocative behavior of Tel Aviv."

Another telephone call was made to Dinitz, urging Israeli restraint. But Israel replied again that it was the Egyptians who were attacking. Israel had not tried to advance during the day and it had no plans to do so, Dinitz insisted.

At a WSAG meeting that morning, Kissinger heard worrisome details about Soviet military moves. Five or six Soviet transport vessels had sailed into the Mediterranean that day, bringing to an unprecedented high of eighty-five Russian ships in the sea.

By 1 PM, the White House sent a soothing message to Brezhnev, summarizing the Israeli assurances. A similar message went to Sadat, just as another message from the Egyptian leader was received, this one extremely disturbing to the administration. Sadat again asked for U.S. troops and then added a bombshell: He was also asking the Soviet Union to send in troops. Almost simultaneously, Cairo publicly announced it was calling for a meeting of the Security Council to request U.S.-Soviet forces to police the ceasefire.

This the administration vehemently opposed, even to the point of open hostilities. "We were determined to resist by force if necessary the introduction of Soviet troops into the Middle East regardless of the pretext under which they arrived," Kissinger recalled, adding sourly: "We had not worked for years to reduce the Soviet military presence in Egypt only to cooperate in reintroducing it as a result of a UN resolution.''

In midafternoon, another Soviet message arrived, this one from Foreign Minister Gromyko complaining again about Israeli violations, and was shortly followed by a 4:15 PM visit to the state department by Ambassador Dobrynin. He was without new instructions from Moscow, where it was nearing midnight, and he and Kissinger discussed ideas for a peace conference. Kissinger found the atmosphere calm and felt a crisis had been averted, at least for the day.

But then, at 7:05 PM, already 2:05 AM Thursday in Moscow, came the stunning news in a telephone call from Dobrynin that the Kremlin had decided to support the idea of having the Security Council call for a joint U.S.-Soviet force to be sent to the Middle East. Kissinger warned that the United States strongly opposed such a course.

But before the secretary of state could elaborate, Watergate intruded. Kissinger had to interrupt his talk with Dobrynin to take a call from the President. Nixon was ''as agitated and emotional as I had ever heard him,'' recalled Kissinger.

Talk of impeachment was growing, and the wounded and battered President had been driven into torment. He believed his enemies were out to destroy him, perhaps even kill him. ''I may physically die,'' Nixon exclaimed. Kissinger tried to console him but Nixon was beyond consolation. ''What they care about is destruction,'' Nixon said, referring to his enemies, which by this time were as real as he always suspected they were. ''It brings me sometimes to feel like saying the hell with it.''

He pleaded with his secretary of state to inform congressional leaders of the ''central, indispensable role'' he as President had played in the Middle East crisis, although in fact he had taken little direct action over the past three weeks of bloody war and diplomatic maneuver.

After listening for ten minutes to the rantings of his distraught and discouraged Chief Executive, Kissinger hastily returned to the accelerating crisis that was pressing in on him from an entirely different direction. The Soviet Union was embarked on a dangerous course, one that could bring a direct confrontation with the United States. Under no circumstances would the administration sit by and watch Soviet troops enter the Middle East. The Kremlin at the end of the wars of 1956 and again in 1967 had similarly urged joint U.S.-Soviet action in the Middle East and had been flatly turned down by Washington then. There was no reason to change policy now. The Soviet ploy was obviously meant as the first step in a process aimed at involving the United States in a joint effort to impose a settlement. This

283

Kissinger had no intention of doing. In a return call to Dobrynin, he warned that if the Soviet Union moved to have its troops sent to the region under U.N. auspices, the United States would veto the effort.

There now followed a series of frantic actions to try to derail any effort in the Security Council, meeting again in emergency session, to pass a resolution calling for creation of a U.N. force including Soviet and American troops. Egyptian Ambassador to the United Nation Mohammed Zayyat that evening made a speech endorsing the idea, although not submitting it in the form of an official resolution. Next the Soviet ambassador, Yakov A. Malik, told the council that Egypt's request was justified but, cautiously, he declined for the moment to commit his government publicly to the proposal.

Then, at 9:35 PM, 4:35 AM Thursday in Moscow, came a hurried call from Dobrynin. He had a message from Brezhnev for Nixon so urgent it had to be read on the telephone to Kissinger. It lacked the usual niceties of communications between the two leaders, starting out simply: "Mr. President" and concluding with a request for an "immediate and clear reply." It was, in Kissinger's estimation, an ultimatum, a judgment that may have been influenced by the highly emotional atmosphere in the Watergate-shaken White House that Wednesday evening.

> "It is necessary to adhere [to the ceasefire] without delay. I will say it straight that if you find it impossible to act jointly with us in this matter, we should be faced with the necessity urgently to consider the question of taking appropriate steps unilaterally. We cannot allow arbitrariness on the part of Israel...."

Kissinger's reaction was to lash back sufficiently strong to "shock the Soviets into abandoning the unilateral move they were threatening—and, from all our information, planning." When he tried to telephone Nixon with Brezhnev's message, he was told the President had retired for the night. Kissinger suggested Nixon be awakened, but the presidential chief of staff, Alexander Haig, curtly refused. In his memoirs, Kissinger recalled: "I knew what that meant. Haig thought the President too distraught to participate in the preliminary discussion....From my own conversation with Nixon earlier in the evening, I was convinced Haig was right."

Kissinger called an emergency meeting of the Washington Special Action Group and, while he was waiting for its members to gather at 10:30 PM, he again telephoned Dobrynin.

"I just wanted you to know if any unilateral action is taken before we have had a chance to reply that will be very serious," Kissinger warned.

"Yes, all right," said Dobrynin.

"This is a matter of great concern," said Kissinger. "Don't you pressure us. I want to repeat again, don't you pressure us!"

"All right," calmly replied Dobrynin again.

• •

When the senior security officials of the administration—Defense Secretary Schlesinger, CIA Director Colby, Joint Chiefs Chairman Moorer, the NSC's Scowcroft and Haig—met with Kissinger at the White House, they were given copies of all recent Brezhnev messages. They concluded that the tone of the latest note was "totally different," "harsh" and "blunt." As the evening wore on and more intelligence arrived, they also concluded that there was a "high probability" of some kind of "unilateral Soviet move." They expected that this might be an airlift of alerted Soviet airborne troops from East Germany to Egypt at dawn, by this time barely two hours away.

Kissinger and his group agreed that some dramatic action should be taken to demonstrate unequivocally to the Kremlin that the United States would not tolerate unilateral moves. The course chosen was certainly dramatic: a worldwide alert, issued at 11:41 PM to all U.S. military forces, including nuclear units. Their readiness status was raised from DefCon IV (for Defense Condition) to DefCon III, a state of readiness short of a determination that war was likely; DefCon II meant war was likely and DefCon I meant war. Most U.S. forces were usually kept at DefCon IV, which was a heightened alert during peace; DefCon V was peace. It apparently had never been invoked worldwide since World War II.

They also took a number of other measures designed to increase military communications traffic that could be detected by the Soviets. The 82nd Airborne Division was alerted to be ready to move out, B-52s based on Guam were ordered to return to the United States, the aircraft carrier *Franklin Delano Roosevelt* was ordered to move from Italian waters to the eastern Mediterranean where the carrier *Independence* was already stationed and the carrier *John F. Kennedy* was ordered to steam at full speed from the Atlantic to the Mediterranean.

Dobrynin was once again warned that the Soviet Union should not take any action until a reply was drafted to Brezhnev's message, and Sadat was urged in a message drafted over Nixon's name to rescind his request for

285

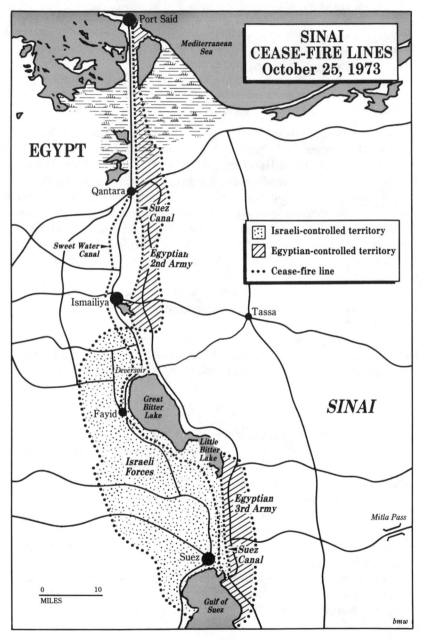

SINAI
CEASE-FIRE LINES
October 25, 1973

Port Said

Mediterranean
Sea

EGYPT

Qantara

Suez
Canal

Sweet Water
Canal

Egyptian
2nd Army

Israeli-controlled territory

Egyptian-controlled territory

••• Cease-fire line

Ismailiya

Tassa

Deversoir

Great
Bitter
Lake

Fayid

SINAI

Little
Bitter
Lake

Israeli
Forces

Egyptian
3rd Army

Mitla Pass

Suez

Suez
Canal

0   10
MILES

Gulf of
Suez

bmw

Soviet troops: "I ask you to consider the consequences for your country if the two great nuclear countries were thus to confront each other on your soil."

It was decided to postpone answering Brezhnev until 5 AM to give time for these various actions to percolate, actions taken without direct consultation with the President.

With the alert and various other measures, the American side had done all it could, or thought it should. Now it was up to the Soviet Union to respond, to determine by its reaction whether the crisis would deepen or disappear. The fat, as President Eisenhower used to say, was really in the fire.

• •

THURSDAY/the 25th

WASHINGTON

At 5:40 AM, the reply to Brezhnev was finally delivered by messenger to the Soviet embassy. It was, as Kissinger and his group wrote it to be, both strong and conciliatory at the same time. The message warned that unilateral action would end detente and be a "matter of the gravest concern involving incalculable consequences;" it added that joint action was "infeasible" and "not appropriate to the situation." Instead, it offered a compromise. A small number of U.S. and Soviet personnel should go to the region, not as military units but as U.N. observers to help keep the peace.

Kissinger awoke after three hours of sleep at 6:30 AM, only to discover to his chagrin that news of the alert had already leaked to the press. The crisis was worldwide headline news, and there was more than a little skepticism—inevitable but unjustified in this case—that the alert had been fabricated as a way to divert attention from Nixon's Watergate troubles. Now, with the sensational details leaking out, the Kremlin's prestige was on the line and in public. An acute concern was whether Moscow might harden its position, if for no other reason than to save face in public.

• •

As so often happens in international crises, the nuclear alert crisis dissipated just as quickly as it had erupted. A combination of factors contributed to its resolution, ranging from a cautious prudence on all sides, a thoughtful diplomacy that allowed both superpowers to compromise without humiliation, strong steps by Moscow and Washington that con-

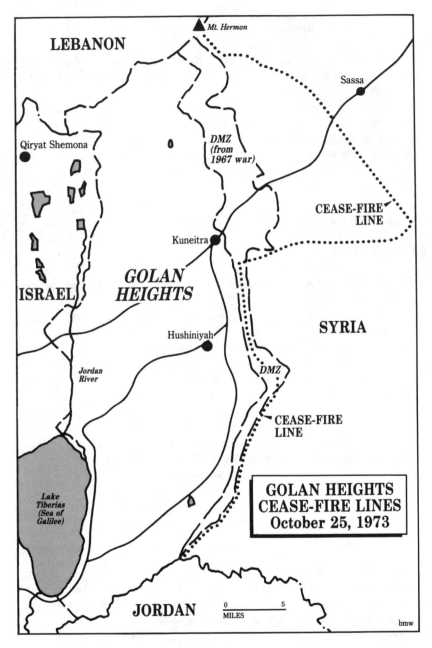

Mt. Hermon

LEBANON

Sassa

Qiryat Shemona

DMZ
(from
1967 war)

CEASE-FIRE
LINE

Kuneitra

GOLAN
HEIGHTS

ISRAEL

SYRIA

Hushiniyah

Jordan
River

DMZ

CEASE-FIRE
LINE

Lake
Tiberias
(Sea of
Galilee)

**GOLAN HEIGHTS
CEASE-FIRE LINES
October 25, 1973**

JORDAN

0   5
MILES

bmw

vinced both countries that the other meant business and, finally, what might be considered a dash of good luck—under heavy U.S. pressure, Israel did stop its ceasefire violations.

In addition, despite the leaks about the superpower confrontation, which may have been deliberately planted by foes of detente to worsen relations between Washington and Moscow, the Soviet leaders prudently swallowed their pride and ignored the public uproar, a significant action in helping to defuse the crisis.

Good news began coming in shortly before 8 AM Thursday. Messages from Egypt informed the administration that Cairo would withdraw its request for a joint U.S.-Soviet force and asked instead for an international peacekeeping force. This effectively meant an end of the joint force idea since, without Egyptian support, Moscow could not successfully push it in the United Nations nor move unilaterally on Egyptian soil without Sadat's concurrence.

In the afternoon, at 1:10, a message from Sadat officially accepted an international force composed of only nonpermanent members of the Security Council, meaning neither Americans nor Russians. A few minutes later, U.N. Secretary-General Kurt Waldheim informed Kissinger that the Soviet Union would support the Egyptian proposal.

Resolution 440 was passed in the afternoon, demanding—no longer "urging"—an immediate ceasefire and the return to the positions occupied by the parties at 16:50 GMT October 22. It also established a peacekeeping force of nonpermanent members of the Security Council to separate the sides and increased the number of observers to report on violations.

At 2:40 PM, Dobrynin telephoned, saying he had Brezhnev's answer to Nixon's early morning message. The Soviet leader said he agreed to act jointly in sending seventy "representatives" to Egypt to observe the ceasefire. He made no mention to the tense hours earlier. The message seemed to indicate that as far as the Kremlin was concerned, there was no crisis.

Equally good news was that there were no reports during the day of major ceasefire violations by Israel or Egypt or Syria.

Quite suddenly, the nuclear crisis, and the war, were over. The DefCon III alert was canceled at midnight and the world returned to its state of precarious peace known as DefCon IV.

CHAPTER XXVIII

Shuttle Diplomacy: 1974-5

WHEN THE CEASEFIRE FINALLY TOOK HOLD ON OCTOBER 25, the battlefields in both the north on the Golan Heights and the south on both sides of the Suez Canal remained volatile. Strong forces faced each other threateningly on the two fronts and no one side could claim to be the decisive victor, although Israel obviously enjoyed the upper hand on the Golan. But the situation was much more confused in the Sinai. At the start of the first ceasefire on October 22, Egypt had been in a fairly good position. Now, however, Israel stood tantalizingly at the edge of a major triumph against the trapped Egyptian Third Army, a victory it desperately wanted to avenge the Arabs' surprise attack.

Resolution 440 demanded that the parties return to the lines of October 22, but Israel refused to budge. Its strong lines on the west bank of the Suez Canal completely cut off the 20,000 troops of the Egyptian Third Army on the east bank. Old biblical sentiment for revenge, for an eye for an eye or even ten eyes for an eye, was high in Israel, and particularly in the army. Israeli passions seethed with the desire to destroy the encircled Egyptian army or at the very least to force it into a humiliating surrender. But this Henry Kissinger was determined not to allow to happen. Such slaughter or humiliation would spark new fighting and outrage the Arab world. It could be such a blow for Anwar Sadat that he might be toppled.

Day after day Israel resisted U.S. pleas to ease its stranglehold on the Third Army and to withdraw to the lines of October 22. Increasingly desperate requests came from Anwar Sadat to allow a convoy with non-military supplies such as water, food and medicine to reach the Third Army. The water lines Adan's division had cut off on October 24 remained severed and there were no streams or wells on the east bank. The Third Army's plight was extreme. It had no more than a week's supply of food and water.

Soon its troops would begin dying of thirst under the scorching desert sun. After three days of Israeli resistance, the administration finally lost its patience. It laid down the law in no uncertain terms. In an almost unique display of determination, the administration, in the words of Dayan, informed Israel that "if you don't allow the Third Army to receive civilian, not military, supplies—food and water—if you bomb them and force them to surrender, then we, the United States, will send our planes, our helicopters, to bring them supplies and you will be in trouble with us."

That kind of unusually blunt language from Washington was so rare that the Israelis could not ignore it. On Monday, October 29, a convoy was allowed through Israeli lines and the parched members of the Third Army finally started getting a regular supply of food and water.

As a result, the army never did surrender, nor did any other major Arab unit. On the other hand, neither did the Israelis withdraw to the October 22 lines even though the European Community, in one of its rare unanimous declarations on the Middle East, strongly urged Israel to withdraw.

The supplying of the Third Army was highly unpopular in Israel, where the terrible toll of the war had finally begun to become clear. Dayan had to explain the government's reasons in the Knesset on October 30. "[It] was not," he emphasized, "a humanitarian gesture." Rather, Israel had had to yield under U.S. pressure. He admitted: "We had no choice....the alternative to allowing food and convoys was much worse."

As the Soviet and Arab leaders had contended all along, if the United States really wanted to influence Israeli policy it had the power to do so, a message Israel did not want to be reminded of and did everything it could to hide from the rest of the world. So too did Kissinger, who worried that once it was perceived that the United States could facilely extract concessions from Israel, Arab demands would escalate. "Then we would be blamed for Israel's failure to meet Arab terms, which would be raised with the ease of their accomplishment," observed Kissinger. "Our strategy depended on being the only country capable of eliciting Israeli concessions, but also on our doing it within a context where this was perceived to be a difficult task."

The problem with this strategy, of course, was that it was self-fulfilling. Israel resisted automatically almost all U.S. advice and in most cases could only be persuaded with the commitment of yet more American aid and diplomatic support. This had been the pattern of all negotiations between the two countries. Kissinger was now about to suffer the consequences of his strategy as he pursued exhaustively a series of limited agreements between Israel and its neighbors.

With the Third Army's welfare secured, direct talks between military officers from Egypt and Israel soon began on a daily basis at Kilometer 101 on the west bank of the canal. It was the first time the two sides had met since the disengagement talks that ended Israel's war of independence a quarter century earlier. Diplomacy was at last being given a chance.

Kissinger thought he had a strategy that would work, soon dubbed step-by-step diplomacy. He had always opposed the idea of seeking a comprehensive solution, which he considered a "mirage," unattainable and counterproductive. One of his main reasons was a reflection of the depth of sympathy he shared for Israel. He believed that applying the needed pressure on Israel to make it give up its conquests might, as he explained in his memoirs, cause the "psychological collapse" of Israel and destroy the essence of the Jewish state. Thus a comprehensive settlement should be resisted even though Washington was repeatedly on record as promising the Arabs that it favored near-total Israeli withdrawal from its 1967 conquests. Instead, to avoid traumatizing Israel, Kissinger would try achieving finite pacts between Israel and its neighbors, one step at a time.

During the first half of November, Kissinger visited the Middle East for five days, stopping in Morocco, Algeria, Egypt, Jordan and Saudi Arabia. He bypassed Israel since he had been there a fortnight earlier. It was his first visit to any Arab country and his first meeting with Anwar Sadat. He was impressed. "...from that time onward, I knew I was dealing with a great man," Kissinger recalled. "Sadat was neither starry-eyed nor soft. He was not a pacifist. He did not believe in peace at any price. He was conciliatory but not compliant. I never doubted that in the end he would create heroes [that is, launch a new war] if no other course he considered honorable was left to him."

In talks in Cairo between November 7 and 8, Kissinger quickly perceived that Sadat was ready to take considerable risks for peace. The Egyptian ruler let it be known that he wanted to enlist America's help in finding an agreement with Israel. To that end, he agreed to a resumption of the diplomatic ties which had been severed since 1967 and assented to a six-point plan that, in effect, bypassed the prickly issue of the October 22 lines and aimed at talks toward a larger withdrawal; Israel signed the agreement on November 11. From Egypt, Kissinger traveled for brief visits to Jordan and Saudi Arabia, where he received the blessings, reluctantly in Jordan's case, of the monarchs of those two countries for his step-by-step diplomacy.

Kissinger's next maneuver was to give an international framework to the peace process. This would be done at a conference in Geneva with the two superpowers acting as co-chairmen under the auspices of the United Nations and with the attendance of both Arabs and Israelis. As originally perceived by the Soviets and Arabs, the conference would discuss a comprehensive peace settlement. From the Arab and Soviet viewpoint, it would give Moscow the opportunity to champion the Arabs' maximum demands. But Kissinger had other ideas. He wanted the conference as a symbolic umbrella lending legitimacy to the peace process, but privately he was determined to keep Geneva an empty shell.

Kissinger's hidden plan, if that is what it could be called, was probably far more ad lib and based on a much more complex of motives than generally assumed. Foremost, there was Nixon's Watergate tragedy, which was destroying his presidency and with it Kissinger's own reputation and ambitions. This reality, more than the Middle East, was the encompassing framework in which the harassed secretary of state had to operate. It was a political and intellectual morass, and Kissinger brought to the problem his remarkable agility that left his admirers doting and his detractors more than suspcious of his sincerity and honesty.

By using the forum of an international conference as a way to trick Moscow out of a substantive role in Middle East diplomacy, he played to Nixon's—and his own—natural constituency, Democratic as well as Republican, the "military-industrial complex," those national hardliners who prosper on international unrest. By his gyrations of travel and media coverage, he diverted attention away from his embattled president and onto his own admitted craving for the spotlight. By this time, Kissinger had become the nation's media star. He had so enchanted the press corps assigned to the state department, and the reporters' editors, that the usually cynical journalists were acting more like his cheerleaders than his monitors. And, finally, by playing a devious game against Moscow, Kissinger averted the one thing that he, and Israel, feared most: an imposed solution.

Underlying Israeli policy over the years, and American policy, had been the realization that any agreement imposed by the superpowers in the Middle East would have to involve some flexibilty by Israel. If the superpowers were ever able to come to terms on the Middle East, it would certainly have to include the withdrawal of Israel from at least part of the occupied territories. This would, in effect, prove the justness of the long standing policy of the Soviet Union in the Middle East, which had consistently been, however sincerely, that the acquisition of territory by force was unacceptable. This was an affirmatiion of Soviet policy that Washington was not anxious to grant. Moreover, Kissinger was determined to upstage Moscow and in this way demonstrate that it was Washington which was the key

293

player in the Middle East.

Beyond all of these considerations, of course, was the basic realization that Israel and its supporters in the Congress would fiercely resist any policy that sought major concessions by Israel. With Nixon's Watergate weakness, there was no realistic hope that the administration could confront Israel head-on and prevail.

Thus Kissinger pursued the easiest course, which he argued was the only course available, and continued his step-by-step strategy. It was a dangerous game, since the Soviets and the Arabs were not long fooled, and in the end his strategy accomplished far less than Kissinger pretended or the American media asserted. But for the next year Kissinger vigorously pursued this scheme, perhaps missing the one chance in that period when cooperation by the superpowers would have been able to bring about a giant leap in solving the conflict.

Kissinger's progress in convening Geneva was mired in a swamp of Israeli and Syrian conditions for attending the conference. Israel, always suspicious, did not want any representation by Palestinians, it opposed a strong role for the United Nations and it refused to have its representatives sit in the same room as Syrians before Damascus made public a list of the Israeli prisoners it held from the October war. For its part, Syria, equally suspicious, refused to provide such a list or to attend the conference before Israel agreed to withdraw totally from the Golan Heights. Kissinger was left with the prospect that he might call a conference and no one would come.

To break the impasse, he made his second tour of the Middle East in mid-December, traveling to Algeria, Egypt, Israel, Jordan, Lebanon, Saudi Arabia, and, for the first time, Syria. Egypt was the easiest of his stops. Sadat had already agreed to attend Geneva and, in nine hours of talks with Kissinger on December 13 and 14, he made clear once again that he wanted peace. Kissinger, in his memoirs, said Sadat told him: "I could tell Golda Meir that he genuinely wanted peace but not at the price of 'my' land."

In Damascus, Hafez Assad was less accommodating. The Syrian president greeted Kissinger in his modest official home on December 15, the first secretary of state to visit Syria since John Foster Dulles twenty years earlier. They were in a room dominated by a painting depicting the conquest of the last Crusader strongholds by Arab armies. As Kissinger noted, "The symbolism was plain enough; Assad frequently pointed out that Israel, sooner or later, would suffer the same fate." Assad, Kissinger found in this first meeting with him, was of medium height with flashing eyes and an expressive face. "He spoke in a quiet but firm voice, with a kind of rough shyness; he was as intense as Sadat was remote, as literal-minded as Sadat was reflective—the two men were similar only in their passions," observed Kissinger.

Assad was a shrewd and hard bargainer, but not unrealistic. In the end, Kissinger came to have a high regard for him. "In the Syrian context he was moderate indeed," Kissinger recalled. "He leaned toward the Soviets as the source of his military equipment. But he was far from being a Soviet stooge. He had a first-class mind allied to a wicked sense of humor....Assad never lost his aplomb. He negotiated daringly and tenaciously like a river-boat gambler to make sure that he had exacted the last sliver of available concessions."

At their first meeting, which lasted nearly seven hours, Assad was not willing to make any concessions. He wanted a prior commitment that Israel would withdraw from Syrian territory, meaning surrender of all of the Golan Heights, before committing himself to Geneva. As intransigent as this position sounded, Kissinger was pleased to note that at the same time Assad indicated he would not oppose the opening of the conference and might participate later in Kissinger's step-by-step negotiations. This stand, Kissinger realized, "hid a major breakthrough. In his convoluted way, Assad was in fact blessing the peace process and our strategy." By not attending the opening session, Israel's demands on the prisoner of war issue would be academic and other issues like the Palestinian representation could more easily be finessed.

Kissinger's visit to Israel December 16-17 was his most difficult. Israeli refusal to come to a decision to attend had already caused a postponement from the originally scheduled opening date of December 18. "All our sympathy for Israel's historic plight and affection for Golda were soon needed to endure the teeth-grinding, exhausting ordeal by exegesis that confronted us when we met with the Israeli negotiating team," recalled Kissinger.

Even though President Nixon had sent Golda Meir a toughly worded letter on December 13, demanding that Israel commit itself to participating in Geneva or risk losing U.S. support, the Israelis still had a number of points they wanted cleared up. In particular, they refused to have any mention made of Palestinians in the letter of invitation for the conference. Kissinger agreed. But still the Israelis wanted more: a secret memorandum of understanding promising, among other concessions, that the United States would use its veto if necessary to prevent an invitation to the Palestine Liberation Organization. This Kissinger agreed to also. At last, with these U.S. concessions, the Israelis consented to go to Geneva.

The conference formally opened on December 21 with the superpowers, the secretary general of the United Nations and Egypt, Israel and Jordan in attendance. An empty chair represented Syria's place, a symbol that Syria was entitled to a seat if it decided to exercise its option to attend at some future date. After a day of speeches, mainly for the TV cameras, the conference reconvened for twenty minutes on December 22 and then adjourned, presumably to reconvene at some future date for substantive talks. It never did. Nonetheless, Kissinger had his international umbrella, but his true efforts went into seeking bilateral agreements brokered step-by-step by the United States—without the Soviet Union.

• •

After the spotlight of Geneva, Kissinger immediately launched into a series of maneuvers to achieve bilateral agreements between Israel and its neighbors, Egypt and Syria. Egypt was the easiest and it came first. Between January 11 and January 17, Kissinger flew back and forth between Egypt and Israel in search of an agreement via what was to become known as his famous shuttle diplomacy. Bargaining was hard. Israel wanted Egypt to commit itself to a number of political conditions, including a pledge of nonbelligerency and the opening of the Suez Canal as well as limiting forces on its own territory. Sadat wanted Israel to withdraw east of the Sinai passes of Gidi and Mitla and to accept reciprocal limitations of forces. Though the positions of both sides were not too far apart, the bargaining was again arduous—one meeting with the Israelis lasting as long as nineteen straight hours.

Toward the end of the negotiations, on January 16, Sadat gave Kissinger a personal note to Golda Meir saying, "You must take my word seriously. When I made my initiative in 1971, I meant it. When I threatened war, I meant it. When I talk of peace now, I mean it."

In the end, it was only by Kissinger signing another secret memorandum of understanding with Israel that an agreement was achieved. The secret MOU contained ten detailed points ranging from U.S. affirmation that it considered Bab al-Mandab at the head of the Red Sea an international waterway to a far-reaching pledge that Washington would be responsive to Israel's defense needs on a "continuing and long-term basis."

Israel consented to disengagement on January 17 and the next day the accord was formally signed at Kilometer 101. That same day Kissinger had a return letter for Sadat from Gold Meir. It read, in part, "I am deeply conscious of the significance of a message received by the Prime Minister of Israel from the President of Egypt. It is indeed a source of great satisfaction to me and I sincerely hope that these contacts between us through Dr.

296

Kissinger will continue, and prove to be an important turning point in our relations. I, for my part, will do my best to establish trust and understanding between us.''

Though the withdrawal agreement was a modest achievement in terms of traversing the long road to peace, it was a major accomplishment, mainly because Kissinger had been able to overcome the highly emotional and suspicious atmosphere in both countries. Under the pact, Israel agreed to withdraw its forces in the west of the canal, thus liberating the surrounded Egyptian Third Army, and withdraw all its forces back fifteen miles from the eastern side of the canal to positions west of the Gidi and Mitla passes. Between the two armies would be stationed a U.N. peace force. Both sides also agreed to mutual force limitations.

•   •

An agreement between Syria and Israel was more difficult and complex, and consequently it took even greater exertions than the Israeli-Egyptian pact. On the Golan, the two armies were confined to a narrow area that provided little room for maneuvering, either military or diplomatic. Syrian leader Hafez Assad demanded that Israel not only give up what it had captured in 1973 but that it also withdraw some distance even beyond the 1967 ceasefire line. Golda Meir exploded at the terms. "In October we had eight hundred killed and two thousand wounded in Golan alone—in a war they started....[Assad] lost the war—and now we have to pay for it because he says it's his territory!''

The rub, of course, was that it was Assad's territory, all of it. But the reality was that Israel occupied it by force of arms and, unlike in the Sinai, it could continue to do so without excessive cost since fewer troops were needed to defend the narrow plateau. Perhaps because of this reality, Syria openly embraced U.N. Resolution 383, which meant that for the first time publicly it also accepted Resolution 242, an open announcement that Syria was ready to bargain with Israel.

Despite Israel's seeming strong bargaining position, there were urgent reasons for both sides to disengage. With the troops so close to each other the situation on the Golan Heights remained explosive. There were daily incidents, including exchanges of artillery fire, which took a steady toll. On one day alone, April 27, fourteen Israelis were killed in incidents on the Golan, bringing Israeli casualties since the war to 41 killed and 94 wounded.

Additionally, the political mood in Israel was ugly. The government of Golda Meir was under severe criticism for being unprepared for the war

297

and, in order to pacify the populace, it was anxious to stop the shooting and officially close out the war on the Golan with a formal agreement. Still, the return of land to the hated Syrians was not a popular prospect.

As usual, outside forces were at work. The major one affecting the United States was the continuing oil boycott. The Arab oil states, led by Saudi Arabia, made it clear that in return for lifting the boycott they expected the United States to achieve a Syrian-Israeli accord. The boycott was causing economic shockwaves around the world and its lifting was a powerful goad for the United States to mediate an agreement on the Golan. Nixon and Kissinger maintained publicly and privately that there was no linkage between the boycott and developments in the Middle East, but there can be no doubt it was a potent motivator.

It was, for instance, only after Nixon announced on February 19 that Kissinger was being sent back to the region to seek an Israeli-Syrian pact that the boycott was finally lifted on March 18, 1974.

With Israel, Kissinger's position was strengthened because the United States held a powerful lure to induce the Israelis to make compromises. This was economic aid. Nixon had the presidential prerogative to forgive as much as $1.5 billion of the $2.2 billion given to Israel in emergency aid during the war—ironically the aid package that was the final straw causing the Arabs to invoke the oil boycott in the first place. Also, at the same time, the 1975 aid package was being prepared by the administration. Thus, as one analyst observed, "Aid was clearly going to be an important adjunct of the Nixon-Kissinger diplomacy." This became clear when Moshe Dayan showed up in Washington on March 29 to discuss the Golan Heights. He brought with him, as usual, a huge weapons request. It included a request for one thousand tanks, four thousand armored personnel carriers and much more—but no real offer of Israeli flexibility in withdrawing on the Golan.

• •

Kissinger leaned on both sides throughout the winter to try to understand each other's psychology and domestic political pressures. Then, with the preparatory groundwork completed, he arrived in Israel on May 2 to begin a gruelling shuttle between the Jewish state and Syria. His task in Israel was eased by the fact that shortly before he left Washington the embattled President, now in the final agonies of Watergate, agreed to turn $1 billion of the emergency aid into grants, meaning Israel would not have to return it. (On June 30, he also forgave another $500 million, making Israel's windfall a total of $1.5 billion.) Nonetheless, it was not until May 29, after an exhausting schedule of flights back and forth between the two countries, that Kissinger finally achieved an agreement.

Under Kissinger's constant badgering, Israel reluctantly agreed to return roughly to the 1967 line with one major concession to Assad. It agreed to surrender Quneitra, the former provincial capital of the Golan, which lay about two miles inside Israel's captured territory. Although it was deserted and the Israelis had deliberately ruined many of its buildings by bulldozing them, the symbolism of achieving the return of a provincial capital as a result of the war was enough to convince Assad to agree. As in the Sinai, force reductions were imposed on both sides and a U.N. peace force was interjected between the two armies.

The agreement won Kissinger fulsome praise. Newsweek pictured him on its cover as a bespectacled Superman and Time called him a miracle man. As Kissinger himself recalled with evident relish in his memoirs, "Commentators described the shuttle as one of the greatest diplomatic achievements in history; there is no record indicating that I resisted the hyperbole."

No similar praise was given the Meir government by the Israeli public. Meir and her cabinet had resigned on April 11 under the unrelenting public outcry against their handling of the war. Leaving high office with Golda Meir was Moshe Dayan, once Israel's greatest and most revered war hero. Now he was almost universally reviled in Israel. On June 3, 1974, a new government headed by Yitzhak Rabin was sworn in. It was a weak coalition with strong competing personalities, especially Defense Minister Shimon Peres and Foreign Minister Yigal Allon.

• •

While Kissinger was now being hailed for the success of his step-by-step diplomacy, the natural question arose: what happens now? And here was the problem. Logically, it would be Jordan and Israel's relinquishment of the occupied West Bank. But this, Kissinger knew, was passionately opposed by powerful elements in Israel, some of whom resisted relinquishing the smallest slice of land they believed had been given to the Jews in the Old Testament. The other problem facing the cabinet was the fact that the issue was so explosive that Golda Meir had promised before her retirement that no agreement on the West Bank would be concluded without holding national elections first. Thus there would be a period of as much as six months before Israel could hold elections and form a new cabinet, a period in which nothing would happen.

In addition, there was the stark chance that Kissinger's own reputation might be soiled if he took up an Israel-Jordan shuttle and failed. In this

299

case, the concern transcended even Kissinger's well known arrogance. Failure could blunt his effectiveness as secretary of state. As he observed "In my view, the secretary of state should not, as general rule, go abroad on a serious negotiation unless the odds are heavily in his favor....A reputation for success tends to be self-fulfilling. Equally, failure feeds on itself: A secretary of state who undertakes too many journeys that lead nowhere depreciates his coin."

Beyond these concerns, there was Watergate. The President was under tremendous pressure, facing possible impeachment, leaving him hardly in a position to exert the kind of strong pressure on Israel that would be needed if an agreement with Jordan was to be achieved. "...a President facing impeachment was not in a brilliant position to insist on a negotiation that—if Israel resisted, as was nearly certain—would multiply his domestic opponents," observed Kissinger.

The result was, as Kissinger expressed it, that "I played for time...hoping that circumstance might resolve our perplexities." It did not. On August 9, 1974, at noon, Richard Nixon ceased to be president and was replaced by his vice president, Gerald Ford, who was a neophyte in foreign affairs. Then on October 28, 1974, the Arab states at a summit meeting in Rabat designated the Palestine Liberation Organization as the sole legitimate representative and spokesman for the Palestinians, sidelining the more moderate King Hussein from the West Bank diplomatic game.

With Israel adamantly refusing to even speak with the PLO, much less negotiate with it, and Kissinger unwilling to apply pressure on the Jewish state, any slim hope for an Israel-Jordan deal was crushed by Rabat. Still, Kissinger wanted another achievement and President Ford needed a foreign policy victory to help his chances for election to the high office that he occupied without ever campaigning for it. The logical choice to achieve this was in the Sinai, where Sadat was pressing for another Israeli withdrawal to free his oil wells around Abu Rudeis and in order to control the strategic passes of Mitla and Gidi. But the atmosphere in the Middle East was now not as conducive for negotiations as it had been in the spring.

Egypt was becoming slowly isolated because of its willingness to seek another Israeli withdrawal without gaining anything for the Palestinians. Syria's Assad was openly opposed to a second Sinai agreement, fearing correctly that it would split Egypt from Syria, thereby leaving Damascus to face militarily stronger Israel alone. This, in fact, was official Israeli policy as publicly detailed by Prime Minister Rabin in an extraordinary interview with Haaretz. Similarly, Moscow by now was resentfully aware that Kissinger's tactics were aimed at excluding the Soviet Union from the peace process and at limiting its influence in the Middle East. Syrian-Soviet opposition to another Sinai agreement was publicly displayed on February 1, 1975, when the two countries issued a joint communique calling for the reconvening of the Geneva Conference.

Despite this opposition, Kissinger flew to the Middle East in early February on an exploratory visit to see if the two sides might be able to reach an agreement. The sides were still far apart. Israel wanted to achieve its isolation of Sadat by making him pledge to conduct a policy of "nonbelligerency." Sadat could not go that far without losing even more support from other Arab nations. Nonetheless, back in Washington, Kissinger kept after both sides to reduce their differences. By March, he felt the chances of success were good enough to risk another shuttle.

• •

Kissinger began his second Israel-Egypt shuttle in Jerusalem on March 9. After a frustrating period of traveling back and forth between Israel and Egypt, Kissinger returned in defeat to Washington on March 24. Not even a sharp presidential letter from Jerry Ford on March 21 had been able to shake the Israelis from their refusal to soften their position. Said the letter, in part: "I am disappointed to learn that Israel has not moved as far as it might." It added that if Israel did not become more flexible then the United States would have to reassess its Middle Eastern policy, "including our policy towards Israel."

The ploy backfired. The Rabin government merely became more intransigent and the talks collapsed the next day, March 22, 1975.

On Kissinger's return to Washington, President Ford announced a major "reassessment" of U.S. policy for the Middle East. This was a thinly veiled effort to pressure Israel. To add to its impact, scheduled visits to Washington by Israeli leaders, including Defense Minister Peres, to discuss an Israeli request for $2.5 billion in aid were postponed, talks on supplying F-15s to Israel were suspended and deliveries of other military equipment were delayed.

Other events intruded. On March 25, King Faisal of Saudi Arabia was assassinated by a demented nephew, causing fears for the stability of the kingdom. Then on April 13, Christian gunmen opened fire on a busload of Palestinians, beginning a cruel and ceaseless civil war in Lebanon. Even events outside the area had an impact. On April 17, Phnom Penh fell to communist forces; on April 29, Saigon finally fell. Ford's presidency was being littered by crises and humiliations.

Meanwhile, Kissinger made a public display of reassessing U.S. policy in the Middle East. On April 1, 1975, he called together a prominent group of America's foreign policy establishment: George W. Ball, David Bruce, McGeorge Bundy, C. Douglas Dillon, Averill Harriman, John McCloy, Robert McNamara, Peter Peterson, David Rockefeller, Dean Rusk, William Scranton, George P. Shultz, and Cyrus Vance. Also in attendance were all the important U.S. ambassadors stationed in the Middle East.

Many of the men were openly critical of Kissinger's step-by-step diplomacy, Ball in particular. He criticized Kissinger for excluding the Soviets from Middle East diplomacy and accused him of trying to split the Arabs. Ball suggested that the United States should return to Geneva and, with the Soviets, work out a comprehensive plan that, if necessary, might have to be imposed on the region. Similar advice came from others at the meeting and, in subsequent weeks, from diplomats and eminent academics as well.

All this made Israel's many supporters in Congress suspect that the administration was about to exert maximum pressure on Israel. As a result, on May 21, 1975, seventy-six senators sent a letter to Ford urging that Washington be "responsive to Israel's economic and military needs." This bold display of strength convinced Kissinger—who probably did not need much convincing since he opposed the idea of a comprehensive settlement—and Ford that continued pressure on Israel would be counterproductive. Step-by-step seemed the only strategy that could receive congressional support and had a chance of succeeding.

Once again, Israel used its advantage to get more bountiful aid from America than it or any other country had ever received. Its requests for aid suddenly burgeoned to a total of nearly $3.5 billion by mid-August and demands for secret promises blossomed into gigantic proportions. One of Kissinger's aides said that if the United States had accepted all of the Israeli demands they would have amounted to a "formal political and military alliance" between the two countries.

With Israel now willing to make concessions in return for generous U.S. aid, progress was achieved in negotiating a second Sinai agreement. On August 20, Kissinger flew off on his final shuttle. After arduous bargaining over final details in Israel and Egypt, an agreement was finally achieved on September 1, 1975. Its price for America was high.

In a secret memorandum of understanding with Israel, Kissinger committed the United States to "make every effort to be fully responsive...on an on-going and long-term basis to Israel's military equipment and other defense requirements, to its energy requirements and to its economic needs." The memorandum officially committed American support against

302

threats by a "world power," meaning the Soviet Union. Among other promises:

* America would guarantee for five years that Israel would be able to obtain all its domestic oil needs, from the United States if necessary.

* America would pay for construction of storage facilities capable of storing a one-year's supply of reserve oil needs.

* America would conclude contingency planning to transport military supplies to Israel during an emergency.

* America shared Israel's position that any negotiations with Jordan would be for an overall peace settlement, that is, there would be no further attempt at step-by-step diplomacy.

There was still more. In a secret addendum to the secret MOU, Kissinger promised that the administration would submit every year to Congress a request for both economic and military aid for Israel. It also asserted that the "United States is resolved to continue to maintain Israel's defensive strength through the supply of advanced types of equipment, such as the F-16 aircraft." In addition, America agreed to study the transfer of "high technology and sophisticated items, including the Pershing ground-to-ground missile," usually used only to deliver atomic warheads.

In yet another significant secret memorandum, Kissinger committed America not to "recognize or negotiate with the Palestine Liberation Organization as long as the Palestine Liberation Organization does not recognize Israel's right to exist and does not accept Security Council Resolutions 242 and 338." It was also promised that the United States would coordinate fully on strategy for any future meetings of the Geneva Conference.

For all this commitment of U.S. wealth, prestige and diplomatic support, the Israelis agreed to withdraw between twenty to forty miles east of the Suez Canal, still leaving well over half of Sinai under its control. However, it did surrender Egypt's oil fields and withdraw east of the Gidi and Mitla passes, which were turned into observation posts. The United States once again paid the price by promising to set up stations manned by two hundred Americans to protect both sides from violations.

As Shimon Peres told Time: "The...agreement has delayed Geneva, while...assuring us arms, money, a coordinated policy with Washington and quiet in Sinai....We gave up a little to get a lot."

• •

The signing of the second Israeli-Egyptian accord essentially ended Kissinger's active involvement in Middle East diplomacy. Jordan, once again, was the big loser. Despite repeated pledges from Washington that it favored the return of its lands, Israel did not, and that firm rejection was enough to blunt any enthusiasm Kissinger might have had for trying to achieve another bilateral agreement.

During the rest of his tour as secretary of state, which ended with the defeat of President Ford in 1976, there were no more agreements between the two sides, nor did the pacts already achieved significantly improve the atmosphere between Arabs and Israelis. Mutual suspicions remained high and volatile, the region more dangerous than ever.

But Sadat had made a difference. Suspicions were so ingrained that it would take more of his courage and his vision to break the diplomatic impasse that once again descended on the region after Kissinger's shuttles. This he displayed with his dramatic and highly imaginative trip to Jerusalem in 1977. It was there in the city revered by the world's three great monotheistic religions that the Egyptian leader displayed the full greatness of his statesmanship.

Alone and against the advice of some of his closest advisers, Sadat stood in the "house of Israel," the Knesset, clearly nervous and sweating profusely, and boldly declared to the world his desire for peace.

"I have come to you so that together we should build a durable peace based on justice to avoid the shedding of one single drop of blood by both sides. It is for this reason that I have proclaimed my readiness to go to the farthest corner of the earth....today I tell you, and I declare it to whole world, that we accept to live with you in permanent peace based on justice."

Four years later, after concluding a separate peace treaty with Israel, Sadat was assassinated by Moslem fundamentalists. His death came on the eighth anniversary of the start of the 1973 war.

Epilogue

THE SIGNING OF THE ISRAELI-SYRIAN PACT officially ended the 1973 war. The costs to Egypt, Israel and Syria had been devastating. While Israel had repeatedly pleaded for just a few more days of combat and Kissinger had listened sympathetically, prolonging the fighting, the nineteen days of combat had cost Egypt 5,000 killed, 2,000 wounded and 8,031 taken prisoner or missing; Israel 2,838, 8,800 and 508, and Syria 3,100, 6,000 and 500. Equipment losses were just as staggering: Egypt lost 1,100 tanks and 223 aircraft, Israel 840 and 103 and Syria 1,200 and 118.

At the end of the fighting, the wide perception took hold in the west, particularly in the United States, that Israel, after recovering from its initial surprise, had thoroughly trounced the Arabs. That obviously was not the case. It had been a hard war, the hardest, as many Israeli generals admitted, that Israel and the Arabs had ever fought. The Arabs did not break and run, despite the best efforts by Israeli forces. On the contrary, the Arabs fought like the Israelis, with great valor, a display of courage worthy of the warrior traditions of both cultures, if not the traditions of humanism and enlightenment that distinguish the two peoples.

The Israeli crossing to the west bank of the canal was a dramatic achievement, but it was not in a class with the Egyptian crossing to the east, nor had it been a particularly successful venture up to the first ceasefire. Sharon's division was consistently unable either to widen the bridgehead in order to destroy the Egyptian artillery, which bombarded the crossing point right to the end of fighting, or significantly expand his sector on the west bank. Only General Bren Adan's forces scored notable gains.

But it was only in the two days after the first ceasefire that Adan made dramatic advances against the Egyptian Third Army while violating the ceasefire agreement. It was during the fighting on October 23-4 that Israel captured most of its Egyptian prisoners; Adan estimated the number taken in that brief time period at 6,000. It was also only in that period that Israel managed to encircle the Third Army.

305

While Israel paraded these gains as proof that it had "won" the war, the facts reflected a less decisive resolution. At the end of the war, Egyptian forces still occupied the much vaunted Bar-Lev Line and Israel had been unable to repulse them despite strenuous attempts. The Third and Second armies remained formidable forces with a combined strength of 70,000 men, 720 tanks and 994 artillery pieces, all still on the east bank when the war ended.

On the Golan Heights, the Israelis were never able to achieve their goal of capturing Sasa and thrusting to within artillery range of downtown Damascus. While the exact strength of the Arab forces on the plateau at the end of the war is not known in detail, they were significant and included strong units from both Iraq, with three divisions at war's end, and Jordan, with two brigades, as well as five Syrian divisions resupplied by 600 Soviet tanks; there were also token forces from Saudi Arabia and Kuwait. The Syrians claimed they were strong enough that they were planning a major counterattack with five divisions when, the day before its scheduled launching, the October 22 ceasefire was accepted.

As Yitzhak Rabin later admitted: "The Yom Kippur War was not fought by Egypt and Syria to threaten the existence of Israel. It was an all-out use of their military force to achieve a limited political goal. What Sadat wanted by crossing the canal was to change the political reality and, thereby, to start a political process from a point more favorable to him than the one that existed.

"In this respect, he succeeded."

• •

The traumas of the war would reverberate through history, profoundly affecting the future of the Middle East and its unhappy countries. Blood and treasury had been squandered, a nuclear confrontation risked, a disastrous oil embargo imposed and careers both made and ruined. While Sadat and Kissinger emerged as heroes, Golda Meir's government, never forgiven for not preventing the Arab surprise attack, fell and Dayan would never again enjoy the soaring reputation he had before October 6.

Everyone had suffered. There were few families in Egypt, Israel or Syria that did not mourn the loss of sons and fathers, uncles and cousins, or have friends who did. The experience had been searing, brutal.

Economically, people around the world suffered the repercussions of the war. Suddenly, whole ways of life had to be changed to accommodate to the soaring prices for oil that ran automobiles, heated homes, fueled industry, provided electricity and formed the base for products from wheels to water pipes. The manipulation of prices and production by the Arab oil states caused the greatest transfer of wealth in the world, in the greatest commercial coup of history. Every country was affected, the Arabs by an unheard of prosperity and the rest of the world by a dramatic reduction in wealth. The irony was not lost on many that the Arabs' new wealth came in large part as a result of Israel's existence.

• •

Henry Kissinger's highly publicized shuttles after the war seemed at the time to be major achievements for American diplomacy. But from the vantage of more than a decade, the judgment must be that his tactics achieved little that contributed to overall peace. His refusal to address the most difficult problem, Israel's continued occupation of the West Bank, allowed the occupation to continue with the result that the Palestinian guerrillas grew more extreme and the opposition to U.S. policy of other Arab states increased. Kissinger later explained in his memoirs his motives for not tackling Jordanian-Israeli negotiations. They are peculiar reasons for an American secretary of state, and they indicate what many suspected at the time: Kissinger's partisanship toward Israel apparently was so great that he could not bring himself to demand that it disgorge what it so passionately wanted to retain. Wrote Kissinger of attempting an Israeli-Jordanian agreement:

> I did not think it was achievable without demonstrating to Israel brutally and irrevocably its total dependence on American support. In my view, this would break Israel's back psychologically and destroy the essence of the state. It would also be against America's interest—not least of all because a demoralized Israel would be simultaneously more in need of American protection and less receptive to our advice."

The result of Kissinger's refusal to insist on Israeli flexibility and his determination instead to concentrate on dealing with Egypt left the Middle East in an even more dangerous mess than it was before his appearance on the scene. In fact, it is obvious now that his tactics directly led to the situation of today where Israel is more aggressive than ever and shows even less interest than in the mid-1970s in making any effort to return captured lands. As Assad and others suspected at the time, the effect of the second Sinai agreement was to split off Egypt from the rest of the Arab world. This was a major goal of Israeli strategy, but in terms of furthering the peace process it was a disaster and certainly against America's national interests.

As a result of Sinai II and the subsequent separate peace treaty Sadat signed with Israel in 1979, the Arab world today totally distrusts U.S. diplomacy and is becoming more radicalized than ever. There is a wide suspicion that extremists in Israel may one day complete what began in 1948 and drive all of the Palestinians out of their homeland and into Jordan. If this should happen, nearly 1.5 million more Palestinian refugees would come flooding into Jordan, a tidal wave that could wash Hussein from power and bring about another radical state on Israel's frontiers.

Finally, the loss of Iran to Moslem fundamentalists was at least in part caused by the stalemate in the Middle East. Now the poison of the fundamentalists is spreading throughout the Arab world. They are already well entrenched in Lebanon and they pose dangers to Arab regimes throughout the region. It was fundamentalists who, on the celebration of the eighth anniversary of the crossing of the canal, assassinated Sadat.

Kissinger's major effort to keep the Soviet Union out of the Middle East proved no more successful than his efforts to solve the Arab-Israeli conflict. Although Sadat did indeed renounce his treaty of friendship with Moscow in March 1976, the Soviet Union remained a major player in the region and has grown stronger since. It now has treaties of cooperation and friendship with Iraq and Syria; it is the patron of South Yemen, the only communist government in the Arab world; it arms Libya, which until 1969, the first year of Kissinger's presence in Washington, had been firmly in the Western camp; and it has recently established diplomatic relations with Oman and the United Arab Emirates. Jordan today is being completely spurned by Washington, with the result that it may draw closer to the Russians in order to receive the weapons it needs for its own defense. In addition, there have been some low key contacts between Moscow and Riyadh, and Saudi Arabia may be on the edge of establishing diplomatic relations with the Soviet Union, if for no other reason than to give it a superpower prop in the face of the total pro-Israeli tilt of the Reagan Administration and the Congress. Finally, Moscow plays a role in Lebanon, where civil war sparked in part at least by covert arms aid to the Christians by Israel—certainly with the knowledge and acquiescence of Washington—has taken an untold toll on life and property for more than a decade.

While Moscow was making these gains over the years, Washington lost its two major bases in the Arab world. Saudi Arabia refused to renew the U.S. lease on the Dhahran air base in 1961 and Libya did the same at Wheelus in 1970. The United States thus lost its largest base in Africa and its only base in the Persian Gulf.

In sum, then, Kissinger's diplomacy was fatally flawed. The Soviet Union is now a stronger force in the region and the United States, if not demonstrably weaker, then at the least less trusted and more clearly identified than ever as an enemy of the Arabs. As for Israel, which enjoyed the special concern of Kissinger, it is outwardly stronger than ever. But the reality may be far different. Its dependence on America is now nearly complete; it could not long sustain its level of strength nor could its citizens sustain their increasingly lavish lifestyle, without American support. That support is obviously not going to last forever. Some day there will be a true reassessment of U.S. policy. When that day comes, Israel will be faced with far graver problems than it faced in the mid-1970s. At that time, the Arabs showed themselves willing to seek peace. They may be less willing with an Israel that no longer is cocooned by the full diplomatic and military support of the United States.

The sad message of the 1973 war was that only violence succeed in spurring diplomacy. After all the deaths and all the suffering, after all the sacrifice and all the destruction, both sides were shocked—temporarily—into something approaching a sense of reality. Israel had been stunned enough to realize that it must negotiate, at least in the long run with Egypt; and the Arabs had recovered the measure of pride that would allow them to drop their haughtiness and talk with their Jewish neighbor. Both of these conditions had been needed to break the logjam that had persisted since 1967. Goodwill would have provided them peacefully. Lacking that, war was the only answer—a doleful comment not only on the peoples in the region but on the lack of imagination of the diplomats and politicians in Washington who had allowed the conflict to fester so long, so futilely. If they had sincerely wanted to influence Israel before the war, they could have, as the saving of the Third Army proved. But neither the courage, nor the will, nor the vision existed in Washington to protect Israel from its own worst instincts or discourage the Arabs from their ruinous rejectionist policies.

It was only the vision of one man, Anwar Sadat, that, through war, brought diplomacy to the Middle East. He too later would lose his way, but for the moment he was the man of the hour, the hero who saw and dared, gambled and won. Anwar Sadat, the much maligned black-skinned peasant from the Delta, the figure of derision and butt of jokes, had joined, at least for now, the pantheon of the pharaohs.

Notes

PROLOGUE

PAGE
5   Almighty and eternal: Beatty, Charles. *De Lesseps of Suez: The man and his times.* New York: Harper & Brothers, 1956, p.257.
5   As Monseigneur Bauer: Ibib., p.257.
5   "Henceforth, the Indian: Ibib., p.257.
6   "Egypt has no: Eban, Abba. *An Autobiography*, p.489.
7   On its side: Whetten, *The Canal War*, p.258.
7   The complex was: Ibid., p.272.
7   It was on: Badri, Hassan et al, *The Ramadan War*, 1973, p.72.
7   Twenty minutes later: Ibib., p.62.
7   Soon portable bridges: Ibib., p.62.
8   At 6:15 that evening: Insight Team, *The Yum Kippur War*, p.152.

CHAPTER I: The Death of Nasser

PAGE
13 It was 6 PM: Sadat, *In Search of Identity*, p.202. Though Sadat does not mention it, his wife Jehan says she accompanied him; see J. Sadat, *A Woman of Egypt*, p.246.
13 Cairo, a city: Nyrop et al, *Area Handbook for Egypt*, p.76; and US Embassy information sheet in Cairo.
13 Nasser, aged fifty-two: Heikal, *Autumn of Fury*, p.35
14 Nasser had died: Ibib., pp.208-15.
14 Sadat exclaimed to: Ibib., p.203.
14 General Mahmoud Fawzi: Stephens, *Nasser*, p.556.
14 The physicians, reportedly: Sadat, op. cit., p.203.
14 Formally, as vice president: Kissinger, *Years of Upheaval*, p.201.
14 Although he was: New York Times, 9/30/70.
14 The general judgment: Viorst, *Sands of Sorrow*, p.138.
14 Nasser himself had: Karen Elliot House, Wall Street Journal, 8/4/81.
14 At other times: Hirst and Beeson, *Sadat*, p.81.
14 According to a popular: Rubinstein, *Red Star on the Nile*, p.131.
14 According to journalist: Heikal, op. cit., p.34.
15 Turning to Heikal: Ibib., p.35.
15 "We should...follow: Ibib., p.35.
15 As Heikal put: Ibib., p.35.

NOTES

15   Conspicuous among the: Time, 10/12/70, p.23.
15   Otherwise Nasser had: Rubinstein, op. cit., p.129.
16   Westerners who dealt: Ibid., p.93; Nutting, *Nasser*, pp.307-8.
16   Years later Sadat: Sadat, op. cit., p.163.
16   As Heikal noted: Heikal, op. cit., p.36.
16   At the end: Ibid., p.36.
16   But first a red: Time, 10/12/70, p.29.
16   Then a tearful: Ibid., p.29. United Arab Republic was Egypt's official title at the time.
16   From loudspeakers atop: Ibid., p.22.
16   In Cairo, no: Ibid., pp.22-3.
17   On October 15: Heikal, op. cit., p.37.

CHAPTER II: Diplomacy vs Force

PAGE
18   As Time magazine: Time, 9/19/69.
18   In the jaundiced: *Arab Reports and Analysis*, Journal of Palestine Studies, Vol. XIII,   No. 3, Spring 1984, p.148.
18   Despite such stern: Facts on File 1970, p.988.
19   No one doubted: Israel captured 20,700 square miles, including the 2,100 square miles of the West Banki; Israel's prewar size was 8,000 square miles. See Nyrop (ed.), *Israel: a country study*, p.xix; Sachar, *A History of Israel*, p.667, and Fpp, *Whose Land is Palestine?* p.195. The original U.N. Partition Plan had awarded Israel 5,900 square miles. At the conclusion of the fighting that ended in 1949, Israel controlled 8,000 square miles. That figure grew to 28,700 square miles at the end of the 1967 war as a result of conquests in Egypt, Jordan and Syria.
19   The upwelling of: See, for instance, O'Brien, *The Siege*, p.503.
19   Although there were: Sachar, op. cit., pp.669 and 709.
19   Begin's Gahal opposition: Ibib., pp.708-9.
19   A month after: Nyrop, *Syria a country study*, p 41
19   A career military: Petran, *Syria*, p.28.
19   He was to bring: Ibid., p.182.
19   In the process: Wright, *Libya*, pp.119-24.
19   In his first: Facts on File 1970, Vol. XXX, p.650.
20   In 1969, Libya: Sampson *The Seven Sisters*, p 208 and Wright, op. sit., p.111.
20   He quickly recognized: Sampson, op. cit., p.211.
20   It made the price: Facts on File 1970, p.596.
20   A short time: Wright, op. cit., p.237.
20   Other oil firms: Ibid., p.238.
21   A water buffalo: Time, 10/12/70, p.25.
21   The average per person: Time, 5/16/69, p.37.
21   Foreign exchange was: Ibib., p.32.
21   The country's liquid: Sadat, op. cit., p.214. Also see J. Sadat, *A Woman of Egypt*, p.250.
21   Disenchantment was so: Time, 5/16/69, p.32.
21   The population had: Ibib. p.32; Nyrop and et al, op. cit., p.73.
21   At least half: Sheehan, Edward R. F. *The Way Egyptians See Israel, Uncle Sam, and the SAM's*. New York Times Sunday Magazine, 9/20/70.
21   By the time: Nyrop et al, op. cit., p.274; Time, 5/16/69, p.37.
22   He promised the: Rubinstein, *Red Star on the Nile*, pp.131-2. Also see Sadat, *In Search*

311

of Identity, p. 208; and Hirst and Beeson, *Sadat*, p.106.
22 He cultivated the: Sheehan, *The Arabs, Israelis, and Kissinger*, p.47.
22 He bearded his: Facts on File 1970, Vol. XXX, pp.747 and 826. He was installed 11/12/70.
22 The disgrace, the shock: Hirst and Beeson, op. cit., p.43.
22 Nasser never really: Nutting, *Nasser*; p.432.
23 Sadat in one: Sadat, op. cit., p.184 and 215.
23 These reminders of: J. Sadat, op. cit., p.282.
23 "Kosysin's message was: Heikal, *The Road to Ramadam*, p.217.
23 "Would it be: Heikal, Ibid., p.108.
24 The condition that: Ibid., 108.
24 Instead, he acquiesced: Facts on File 1970, p.815.
24 "We are not: Ibid., p.826.
24 At the end: Hirst and Beeson, op. cit., pp.106-7.
24 But underground his: Sadat, op. cit., p.206.

CHAPTER III: The Nixon White House

PAGE
25 There was a war: Heikal, *The Sphinx and the Commissar*, p.219.
26 The remark brought: Facts on File 1968, Vol. XXVIII, p.529.
26 Privately, Nixon was: Hersh, *The Price of Power*, p.214.
26 Nixon considered himself: Kissinger, *White House Years*, pp.559 and 564; also see Nixon, *The Memoirs of Richard Nixon*, p.481.
26 "One of the main: Nixon, op. cit., p.481.
27 At the beginning: See, for instance, Nixon's memoir comments on pp.481 and 787.
27 "I constantly wrote: Eugene Trone, interview, Washington, DC, 2/9/86.
28 "I did this: Nixon, op. cit., p.477.
28 Kissinger's ruthless infighting: Hersh, op. cit., pp.213-4.
28 As Kissinger himself: Ibid., p.589.
28 As a result: Ibid., p.349.
28 Part of his problem: A number of Rogers' former aides, while praising his intellectual powers, remarked in interviews on his disinclination to work long hours.
29 Henry Kissinger came: Kissinger, op. cit., p.341. In interviews, most U.S. diplomats and intelligence officials commented on how limited Kissinger's knowledge was in the early years about the region and particularly about the Arab countries.
29 He had never: Ibid., p.341.
29 Despite this, his: Kalb and Kalb, *Kissinger*, p.188. They report: "He never concealed his strong concern about the Jewish state."
29 At the end: The Kalbs, pp.31-5, say 12 of Kissinger's relatives were killed but Kissinger in *Years of Upheaval*, p.203, puts the figure at 13.
29 He remembered that: Kissinger, op. cit., p.188.
29 Observed one of: Sheehan, *The Arabs, Israelis, and Kissinger*, p.173.
30 When Jewish leaders: Ibid., p.173.
30 Kissinger shared Nixon's: Quandt, *Decade of Decisions*, p.79.
30 By contrast, experts: Ibid., p.79.
30 "I thought delay: Kissinger, *White House Years*, p.354.
30 Kissinger also disagreed: Ibid., p.563.
30 He blamed Arab: Ibid.; see pp.341-7 for a summary of his parochial views on the history of the conflict.

NOTES

30 In this, Kissinger: Ibid., p.564. Also see Nixon, op. cit., p.786.
31 "We have been: *White House Years*, p.564.
31 Kissinger saw Israel: Quandt, op. cit., p.121.
31 In the view: Ibid., p.121.
31 Khaled, a young: Facts on File 1970, Vol. XXX, New York, pp.637-8.
32 The third hijacked: Nyrop, *Jordan*, Washington, DC, The American University, 1980, p.40.
32 The jubilant Palestinians: Facts on File 1970, p.638.
32 All three jets: Kissinger, *White House Years*, pp.606-7.
32 "The government can: Sheehan, "In the Flaming Streets of Amman," New York Times Sunday Magazine, 9/27/70.
33 As a result: Kissinger, *White House Years*, p.608.
33 "My confusion as: Ibid., p.603.
34 Instead, the group: Ibid., p.604.
34 "In my view: Ibid., p.606.
34 In fact, as: Hersh, op. cit., p.237.
35 Hussein ibn Talal: Hussein's name means the son of Talal, the grandson of Abdullah, the great-grandson of Hussein, the Sharif of Mecca and keeper of the holy places, from the clan of Hashimi, indicating descent from the Prophet Mohammed.
35 His desert country: Manchester, *The Last Lion*, p.700. A no-doubt apocryphal story has it that some squiggly lines delineating the border with Saudi Arabia and called "Churchill's hiccup" were made by Churchill after a lavish luncheon.
35 According to U.N.: UN A/6797*, "Report on the Mission of the special Representative to the occupied territories, 15 Sept. 1967."
36 Friction between the: Hart, *Arafat*, pp.306-7.
36 The confrontation between: Kissinger, *White House Years*, p.609.
36 The consensus was: Ibid., p.611.
36 When they instead: Facts on File 1970, pp.669-70.
37 An amphibious force: Kissinger, *White House Years*, p.614.
37 On September 19: Ibid., pp.610-1.
37 Shortly after noon: Ibid., p.618.
37 In all, there: Kalb and Kalb, op. cit., p.200.
37 If Syria staged: Snow, *Hussein*, p.228.
37 "We could not: Nixon, op. cit., p.483.
37 The Soviet Union: Quandt, op. cit., p.124.
37 When the Sixth: Hersh, op. cit., pp.240-1.
37 Actually, it was: Ibid., pp.244-5.
38 There would be: Kissinger, *White House Years*, pp.605-6.
38 While Nixon kept: Ibid., p.620.
38 In other words: Ibid., p.611.
38 His extraordinary request: Quandt, op. cit., p.116; Kalb and Kalb, op. cit., p. 202; Snow, op. cit., p.228, and Kissinger, *White House Years*, p.621.
38 As the President: Kissinger, *White House Years*, p.622.
38 "King Hussein has: Rabin, *The Rabin Memoirs*, p.187. Kissinger's version of this conversation is considerably different, see him memoirs, vol. 1, p.623. He says he asked only for Israel to fly a reconnaissance flight, making no mention that Hussein had asked for an Israeli air strike. (Kissinger's reticence is explainable by the fact that a request for an Israeli strike is a touchy subject that remains sensitive in the Arab world today.) Rabin then asked, according to Kissinger, if the US would object to an Israeli air strike if the reconnaissance showed major Syrian advances. Kissinger replied that the US would like to make that decision after the results of the reconnaissance were in. "We were in the process of discussing this when I was handed another urgent message from the King...."

39 "You place me: Rabin, op. cit., p.187.
39 The Syrian vehicles: Ziegler, Col. William A. "United States Reaction to the 1970 Jordanian Crisis." Carlisle Barracks, PA: US Army War College, 1/29/73.
39 He approved an: Kissinger, *White House Years*, pp.621 and 623.
39 "Yes, subject to: Rabin, op. cit., p.187.
39 He promised that: Ibid., p.187.
39 ". . .Nixon gave his: Kalb and Kalb, op. cit., p.206.
40 Israel soon began: Kissinger, *White House Years*, pp.624 and 626. The Israeli increase in tank strength was dramatic, reaching 400 by 9/22; see Ziegler, op. cit., p.20.
40 "In short, American: Quandt, *Camp David*, p.119.
40 As Talcott W. Seelye: Seelye letter to the author, 10/27/87.
40 "Moscow's involvement: Seelye, op. cit.
41 Between September 25: Facts on File 1970, p.691.
41 "Hunger and thirst: Ibid., p.690.
41 It called for: The next day, as he was seeing off the kings and presidents of the Arab world, Nasser suddenly felt so tired that he could not walk. He was driven home at 3:30 PM where his wife and children were waiting for lunch with him. But Nasser said he was too tired and would rather lie down. He asked his wife for a glass of orange juice. He took one sip and then asked for a doctor. By 4 o'clock it was determined he had had a heart attack. There were now several doctors around Nasser. One massaged his heart. Another sparked an electrical current through his body. There   was no response. Nasser, the Arab world's greatest leader, was dead.
42 (When King Hussein: From a friend of the King's who declined to be identified.
42 "The President will: Rabin, op. cit., p.189.

CHAPTER IV: Sadat Offers Peace
PAGE
43 There had been: Kissinger, *White House Years*, p.378.
43 Yet Sadat was: Donald Bergus, telephone interview, 1/28/86. Also see numerous derogatory comments toward the Soviets in Sadat's memoirs as well as his wife's memoirs, J. Sadat, *A Woman of Egypt*, p.250. She reports Sadat "distrusted completely" the Soviet Union.
43 "It liked to: Sadat, *In Search of Identity*, p.221.
43 Repeatedly Sadat referred: Ibid., pp.218 and 222.
43 Sadat's first approaches: Heikal, *The Road to Ramadan*, pp.119-20, and Riad, *The Struggle for Peace in the Middle East*, pp.176-7.
43 On November 23: Quandt, *Decade of Decisions*, p.133.
43 "I want peace: Ibid., pp.133-4; also, Rubinstein, *Red Star on the Nile*, p.135. In an interview, 12/2/85, Washington, DC, Joseph Sisco denied knowing about this specific message but added: "When we dealt with Sadat we always felt he wanted peace." Various other officials of that period have made the same point in interviews. A similar message was also given Nixon by King Hussein in their meeting 12/8/70, see Riad, op. cit., p.176. Neither Nixon nor Kissinger mentions these Sadat messages in his memoirs.
44 Expressing the general: Kissinger, op. cit., p.1277.
44 The state department: Ibid., p.1277.
44 Even though self-determination: Facts on File 1970, p.909. It passed 47-22; 50 nations abstained, including Britain and France.
44 It was due: Sadat, op. cit., p.219.
44 Sadat, blaming Soviet: Ibid., p.219.

NOTES

44 "Are you *really*: Hirst and Beeson, *Sadat*, p.107.
44 Secretary of State: Rogers made the statement 1/11/71; see Quandt, op. cit., p.143.
45 Rogers also assured: Ibid., pp.134-5.
45 Egyptian Foreign Minister: Hirst and Beeson, op. cit., p.107.
45 The attention of: Ibid., p.108.
45 "We cannot, we: Ibid., pp.107-8.
45 He offered to: Moshe Dayan had been informally floating the idea of a canal withdrawal since late summer, 1970. But in his version there would be a thinning of forces on *both* sides of the canal. The difference between the Dayan and Sadat ideas was bluntly explained by Kissinger in the first volume of his memoirs, p.1280: "Egypt wanted an interim agreement as the first step toward a total withdrawal; Dayan put it forward as a means to forestall that prospect." In other words, the Dayan plan was aimed at defusing the canal zone and thereby blunting calls for Israel's total withdrawal. This was an eventuality feared by some Egyptian officials, including Sadat's foreign minister, Mahmoud Riad; see Riad, op. cit., p.187; also Rubinstein, op. cit., pp.137-8.
45 "The party that: Whetten, *The Canal War*, p.146-7.
46 He thus became: Quandt, op. cit., p.135.
46 None of his: The only diplomatic action in the immediate postwar period was the ineffective effort undertaken by the United Nations as a result of the November 22, 1967 Security Council Resolution 242. The resolution called for Israeli withdrawal "from territories"—not "*the* territories"—captured in the war and a "just and lasting peace." It also asked the secretary-general to appoint a special representative to go to the Middle East to help the peace process. The man chosen was Swedish diplomat Gunnar Jarring, an expert in Turkomanish languages and at the time ambassador in Moscow. Jarring had little political significance in the international scene and no bargaining power, and so not surprisingly was soon to be openly regarded with contempt by most of the nations involved. "What divisions, ships at sea, or missiles in the air does he have?" Soviet Foreign Minister Andrei Gromyko is reported to have sneered (see Aronson, *Conflict & Bargaining in the Middle East*, p.90). Israeli diplomat Gideon Rafael snidely observed that "it was far easier for [Jarring] to understand the fine nuances of Turkomanish dialects than the subtleties of oriental politics"; see Rafael, *Destination Peace*, p.193). With the superpowers locked at opposite poles, there was scant hope that Jarring could accomplish the fulfillment of the terms of Resolution 242,and he did not. By the end of 1968, he had been at his mission for a year and was no nearer success than at the start. In fact, he was probably worse off since by then the Arabs and Israelis had hardened their positions. Both sides remained fatally deadlocked and Jarring broke off his efforts temporarily on December 7, 1968. His mission resumed fitfully the next year and continued into 1971, when it finally ended (see UN document S/100/70, 1/4/71).
46 From Egypt he: Quandt, op. cit., p.135.
46 That said, Israel: Ibid., p.136.
46 The Heikal series: Rubinstein, op. cit., p.139.
47 He asserted the: Ibid., p.140. Heikal, reports Rubinstein, p.140, wrote that "the consequences of the 1948 aggression by removing Israel altogether" was not a realizable goal. This assertion bordered on heresy in the anti-Israel climate of the day.
47 "What we must: Ibid. p.141.
47 "Any effort by: Quandt, op. cit., pp.137-8; also Facts on File 1970, p.145.

315

CHAPTER V: Russia Becomes Suspicious

PAGE
48 "...they were still: Heikal, *The Sphinx and the Commissar*, pp.219-21.
48 Russia was at: Rubinstein, *Red Star on the Nile*, p.139.
48 "You come to: Riad, *The Struggle for Peace in the Middle East*, pp.191-2.
49 "Have you studied: Heikal, op. cit., p. 223
49 "Our people are: Ibid., p.224.
49 "I was livid: Sadat, *In Search of Identity*, p.220.
49 Russia never did: Sadat, op. cit., p.220.
50 At that, there: Heikal, *The Sphinx and the Commissar*, p.224.
50 "This does not: Facts on File 1971, p.161.
51 "Waiting for the: Hirst and Beeson, *Sadat*, p.110.
51 By March 16: Facts on File 1971, p.182.
51 On March 5: Heikal, *The Road to Ramadan*, pp.116-7.
51 He also pleaded: Quandt, *Decade of Decisions*, p.138.
51 Nixon was encouraged: Rafael, *Destination Peace*, p.259. Unless he is referring to an earlier
    letter unreported by anyone else, Rafael places receipt of this letter in early February.
    Neither Kissinger nor Nixon mentions a Sadat letter in this period.
51 They included, as: Quandt, op. cit., pp.138-9.
51 Menachem Begin's ultranationalistic: Ibid., p.139.
51 "As Abba Eban: Thomas L. Friedman, New York Times, 6/14/87.
52 He also repeated: Facts on File 1971, pp.181-2.
52 "At stake is: Ibid., p.204.
52 However, he added: Quandt, op. cit., p.139.
52 It was "the: Washington Post, 4/4/71.
52 The Israeli foreign: Facts on File 1971, pp.243-4.
52 As an inducement: Quandt, op. cit., p.139.
52 No Egyptian troops: Kissinger, *White House Years*, p.1282.
52 Nixon responded affirmatively: Quandt, op. cit., pp.139-40.
52 He rejected them: Ibid., p.139-40.
53 With Bergus, Sterner: Michael Sterner, interview, Washington, DC, 1/24/86.
53 At the end: Ibid. Also, Donald Bergus, telephone interview, 1/28/86.
53 This was the: Eugene Trone, interview, Washington, DC, 2/9/86. Trone was the CIA station
    chief in Cairo at the time.
54 Against Kissinger's wishes: Kissinger, op. cit., p.1282.
54 Now May was: Hirst and Beeson, op. cit., p.111, from an Al Ahram article by Mohamed
    Heikal, 4/30/71.
54 "The country which: Ibid., p.111.
54 Rogers found Sadat: Facts on File 1971, p.341; Quandt, op. cit., p.140
54 That was to: Heikal, *The Road to Ramadan*, p.132.
54 The Rogers-Sadat: Facts on File 1971, p.341; Quandt, op. cit., p.140
54 However, it now: Quandt, op. cit., pp.140-1.
54 There has been: Facts on File 1971, p.341.
54 "There is nothing: Washington Post, 6/17/71.
54 And feisty Foreign: Washington Post, 6/18/71.
55 Neither side was: Heikal, *The Road to Ramadan*, p.132.

NOTES

CHAPTER VI: The Soviet-Egyptian Friendship Treaty

PAGE
56 Sadat saw this: Sadat, *In Search of Identity*, p.222.
56 "Although I am: Ibid., p.222.
57 "President Sadat has: Heikal, *The Road to Rumadan*, p. 131.
57 The break came: Ibid., p.133. Sadat, p.223, gives the date as May 11, but such details in his memoirs are frequently wrong and most other writers have agreed with Heikal's date. On the other hand, Jehan Sadat uses May 11 but her version of this episode is almost totally different in detail if not substance; see J. Sadat, *A Woman of Egypt*, pp.264-5. Also see, Hirst and Beeson, *Sadat*, p.115.
57 What he heard: Ibid., pp.133-4.
57 The tapes revealed: Sadat, op. cit., p.223.
57 "It astonished me: Heikal, op. cit.
58 It was all: Ibid., p.134.
58 They had apparently: Ibid., p.135. Also, Sadat, op. cit., p.224.
58 It was, as: Heikal, op. cit., p.135.
58 Sadat's swift moves: Hirst and Beeson, op. cit., p.117. Heikal, *Autumn of Fury*, p.42, says Sadat changed the assembly's name while he was addressing the body by informing it of its new designation in a most undemocratic way: "I have decided to come to talk to you, the People's Assembly—by the way, your name is no longer the National Assembly, but the People's Assembly."
59 It was the: Rubinstein, *Red Star On the Nile*, p.147. A number of historians, including Rubinstein, have concluded that the Russians were upset by the fall of Ali Sabri's group and pushed the treaty on Sadat as a way to cement their interests in Egypt. Sadat himself later claimed this, although at first he said it really was at his initiative that the treaty was signed. It appears that his original version was the correct one, based mainly on convincing evidence by Mohamed Heikal, who was still very close to Sadat at this time. In both his *Road to Ramadan* (p.138) and in greater detail in *The Sphinx and Commissar* (pp.227-8), Heikal asserts that the treaty idea was first broached by Sadat in early April and agreed to in principle on May 1 by the Russians. The details Heikal provides, and the conclusions of U.S. officials involved at the time, leave little doubt that Heikal's version is the correct one.
59 The Russians still: Riad, *The Struggle for Peace in the Middle East*, p.205.
59 It financed, designed: Nyrop et al, *Area Handbook for Egypt*, p.387.
59 There were even: Heikal, *The Sphinx and the Commissar*, p.139.
60 Alienation from the: Lenszowski, *Soviet Advances in the Middle East*, pp.162-3.
60 It surpassed in: Rubinstein, op. cit., p.29-30.
60 Postwar, Soviet advisers. Ibid., p.30.
60 The first postwar: Whetten, *The Canal War*, p.395.
60 Three months later: Rubinstein, op. cit., p.46-7. Also see CIA, *Mediterranean Strategy and Force Structure Study (extract)*, 8/19/70, p.7.
60 They were granted: Ibid., p.108. The airfields were located at Cairo West, two in upper Egypt, two in the canal area and one in the Delta.
61 Thus Moscow finally: Ibid., p.109.
61 From 750 ship-days: CIA, op. cit., p.3. A ship-day equals one ship in the Mediterranean for one day whether at sea, in port or at anchor.
61 The number of: Ibid., p.2; also see Whetten, op. cit., p.391.
61 By late 1969: CIA, op. cit., p.7.
61 The Soviet Union: Ibid., and Whetten, op. cit., p.109. For a good summary of Soviet naval gains see Lenczowski, *Soviet Advances in the Middle East*, pp.154-8.
61 "The Soviet Mediterranean: CIA, op. cit., p.3.

WARRIORS AGAINST ISRAEL

61   From these harbors: International Security Affairs, Office Assistant Secretary of   Defense.
      US Policy and Strategy in the Mediterranean Basin, February 1970; secret, p.5.
61   "...the Soviets can: Ibid., p.6.
61   Rogers told Nixon: Kissinger, *White House Years* p.1284.
62   Rogers was strongly: Eugene Trone, interview, Washington, DC, 2/8/86.
62   "Rather than strengthening: Kissinger, op. cit., p.1284.
62   "Our strategy had: Ibid. p.1285.

                         CHAPTER VII: Kissinger Prevails
PAGE
63   Bergus found the: Donald Bergus, telephone interview, 1/28/86. Asked if he might have
      been motivated in part by a desire to buttress Rogers' position against Kissinger, fearful
      that Kissinger would use the negatively worded Egyptian draft as "proof" that there was
      no flexibility on the Egyptian side, Bergus said no. "I had the naive belief that we had
      a government—not two governments. I helped with the memo because I thought it was
      a great opportunity to find peace."
63   Bergus returned the: Ibid.
63   Bergus' action, although: According to Ambassadors Michael Sterner, who worked closely
      with Bergus during this episode, and Richard Viets, who served in Jordan and other posts,
      and other U.S. foreign service officers, it is not unusual for ambassadors and members
      of U.S. missions around the world to help host governments to penetrate the thickets
      of the Washington bureaucracy by unofficially suggesting the wording of messages and
      other communications for maximum impact. This is done on the most idealistic level as
      an effort to help U.S. policy by making the working relationship between two countries
      as harmonious as possible.
63   The result was: Kissinger, *White House Years*, p.1283.
64   "I was annoyed: Ibid., p.1284.
64   "They had reached: Rafael, *Destination Peace*, p.268.
64   By this time: Richard Helms, interview, Washington, DC, 6/16/83.
64   He felt quite: Kissinger, op. cit., p.1223.
64   The affair ended: Rubinstein, *Red Star on the Nile*, p.151.
65   He was in: Michael Sterner interview, Washington, DC, 1/23/86.
65   He complained that: Joseph Kraft, Washington Post, 6/27/71.
65   Actually, there could: Quandt, *Decade of Decisions*, p.142.
65   A lot of: Donald Bergus, telephone interview, 1/28/86.
65   By this time: Michael Sterner interview, Washington, DC, 1/24/86.
66   "He was absolutely: Ibid.
66   The most they: Ibid.
66   Senator Stuart Symington: Facts on File 1971, Vol. XXXI, p.167.
66   As early as: Jack Anderson, Washington Post, 1/20/70.
66   Columnists Rowland Evans: Evans and Novak, Washington Post, 6/4/71.
66   A short time: Ibid., 10/1/71.
67   On July 23: Quandt, op. cit., p.143.
67   At a meeting: Facts on File 1971, p.563.
67   At a meeting: Rubinstein, op. cit., p.156.
67   The 1,700 delegates: Facts on File, 1971, p.563.
67   He still felt: Sadat, *In Search of Identity*, p.226. Also, Rubinstein, op. cit., p.157.

                         318

NOTES

67 "It's too late: Rubinstein, op. cit., pp.154-5; Also, Heikal, *The Road to Ramadan*, pp.142-3.
68 "From Saigon I: Kissinger, *The White House Years*, p.737.
68 But, Nixon added: Quandt, op. cit., p.143.
68 Between July 30: Ibid., p.143. Also Facts on File 1971, p.607.
68 But requests for: Rafael, op. cit., p.269.
68 His talks were: Eugene Trone interview, CIA Cairo station chief at the time, Washington, DC, 2/9/86.
68 "[Nixon] was afraid: Kissinger, *Years of Upheaval*, p.196.
68 Rogers also urged: Quandt, op. cit., p.146. He wrongly gives the date as Oct. 14.
68 Nixon had stalled: Ibid., p.146.
68 The day after: Facts on File 1971, p.808.
69 A Memorandum of: Quandt, op. cit., p.146. The memo was signed 11/1/71. Also, see *US Assistance to the State of Israel*, Report by the Comptroller General of the United States, GAO/ID-83-51, June 24, 1983, US Accounting Office, the most comprehensive survey ever made of the extraordinary special arrangements provided for Israel's profit.
69 In addition, the: Rafael, op. cit., p.271.
69 This aircraft was: Steven, *The Spymasters of Israel*, p.219.
69 Although I had: Sadat, op. cit., p.226.
69 "We have heard: Riad, *The Struggle for Peace in the Middle East*, p.216.
69 Andre Grechko began: Ibid., p.217.
69 "The first two: Heikal, *The Road to Ramadan*, p.168.
70 At any rate: Riad, op. cit., p.217.
70 He then pledged: Riad, op. cit., pp.217-8.
70 With impressive insight: Heikal, *The Sphinx and the Commissar*, pp.234-5. Seeing US aims so clearly, it's amazing that Sadat later signed the Camp David Accords, which effectively achieved the first two goals of Israel that Sadat had outlined to the Russians.
70 At the end: Riad, op. cit., p. 218.
70 But the Soviets: Rubinstein, op. cit., pp.158-9.
70 The Soviets wanted a: Ibid., p.160.
71 Sadat claimed "there: Sadat, op. cit., p.227. Also, Facts on File 1971, p.802.
71 At any rate: Sadat, op. cit., p.227.
71 On November 11: Rubinstein, op. cit., p.161.
71 The next day: Ibid, p.161. Also, Facts on File 1971, p.902.
71 Washington responded the: Facts on File 1971, p.902.
72 Under the pressures: Kissinger, *The White House Years*, p.1289. Also, Quandt, op. cit., p.147.
72 "If the memorandum: Quandt, op. cit., p.147. Quandt says the agreement was for only 82 A-4s, but when the memo was signed 2/2/72 and announced three days later the figure as given as 90.
72 But by this: Ibid., p.147.
72 "By the end: Kissinger, *The White House Years*, p.1289.

CHAPTER VIII: Emergence of Black September
PAGE
73 Two young gunmen: Facts on File 1971, Vol. XXXI, pp.922-3.
73 He gleefully licked: Becker. *The PLO*. New York: St. Martin's Press, 1984, p.77.
73 It had been: Hirst, *The Gun and the Olive Branch*, p.273.
73 Underground factions like: Fatah is a double acronym for Harakat Tahrir Falestini, the

319

Movement for the National Liberation of Palestine. The initials FTH mean victory in Arabic; when reversed they mean death. According to Hart's biography, *Arafat*, p.67-9, which is the most complete yet written, Arafat was not born in Jerusalem, as many writers, including myself in *Warriors for Jerusalem*, believed. Instead he was born Mohammed Yasser Arafat (his first name was never used even in his youth) on 8/24/29 in Cairo where he lived until he was four, then moved to Jerusalem for four years and later returned to Cairo. His family on his mother's side was of the Abu Saud of Jerusalem, a distinguished family that claimed to trace its lineage back to the Prophet Mohammed. His father, Abdel Rauf Arafat, was from the Qudwa family of Gaza and Khan Yunis, of the Husseini clan, meaning Arafat was related to Haj Amin Husseini, who in 1922 was appointed Mufti of Jerusalem and thus was the leader of the Palestinians up to World War II.

74   Fatah began attacks: Hirst, op. cit., p.282.
74   As such, it: Yodfat and Arnon-Ohanna, *PLO Strategy and Tactics*, pp.24-5; also, Nyrop, Richard F., *Jordan: a country study*, pp.173-4, and Abu Iyad, *My Home, My Land*, pp.32-5.
74   The most important: Yodfat and Arnon-Ohanna, op. cit., pp.23-5. The groups were the Vengeance Youth, a branch of the Arab Nationalist Movement, which was headed by Habash; the Heroes of Return, a pro-Egyptian group; and the Palestine Liberation Front, headed by Ahmed Jabril, a former Syrian army officer. According to Hart, op. cit., pp.124-5, Habash was born in Lydda in 1926, son of a Greek Orthodox grain merchant. He is generally considered the most brilliant theoretician for Palestinian leftists.
74   Most significantly for: Yodfat and Arnon-Ohanna, op. cit., p.25.
74   It reversed the: Ibid., p.25.
74   "Unlike...some other: Cooley, *Green March, Black September*, p.135.
74   "The only language: Hirst, op. cit., pp.280-2.
74   "We do not: Time, 9/28/70, p.24.
74   Terrorism was necessary: Time, 6/13/69, p.42.
75   King Hussein's subjugation: Hart, *Arafat*,
75   On January 13, 1972: Facts on File 1972, vol. XXXII, p.27.
75   Indeed, the Soviets: Rubinstein, *Red Star on the Nile*, p.163.
75   To add to: Ibid., p.164.
76   They called the: Bartov, *Dado*, p.133.
76   Worse for Sadat: Facts on File 1972, p.27.
76   Nonetheless, he promised: Ibid., p.50
76   In an effort: Rubinstein, op. cit., p.177.
76   Finally, Sadat launched: Facts on File 1972, p.49-50.

CHAPTER IX: Israel Gets a New Chief of Staff

PAGE
77   Israeli jets bombed: Facts on File 1972, Vol. XXXII, p.27
77   That same month: Ibid., p.50.
78   "To make life: Bartov, *Dado*, p.113.
78   Shortly after the: Facts on File 1972, p.27.
78   When three Israelis: Ibid., p.140.
78   Under Elazar, such: During Elazar's tenure, Israel set a dubious record of being condemned or urged to cease its actions by the Security Council five times within 22 months: On 2/28/72, 6/26/72, 7/21/72, 3/21/73 and 8/15/73. Most of the actions centered on Israel's violation of its frontier with Lebanon.

NOTES

79   Skeleton crews manned: William Touhy, Washington Post, 2/20/69.
79   This was underscored: O'Ballance, *The Electronic War in the Middle East 1968-70*, p.43.
      The attack occurred 10/26/68.
79   Such heavy artillery: Herzog, *The War of Atonement*, p.6.
79   Major General Avraham: He began officially studying the problem in late 1968.
79   The consideration that: Bar-Siman-Tov, *The Israeli-Egyptian War of Attrition*, p.64.
80   "We faced a: Adan, *On the Banks of the Suez*, p.46.
80   One sensor at: Ibib., p.47.
80   Thus emerged the: Ibib., p.47.
80   The world's latest: There is considerable confusion about the number of forts actually built,
      partly because of military secrecy and perhaps because of confusion about what actually
      constituted a fort. Adan says (pp.47-8) his original plan called for twenty but that the
      Southern Command added forts at at least three points on the canal, and that the chief
      of staff then added "a few more at the northern and southern ends of the canal". Herzog,
      op. cit., p.12, says there were twenty-six; Dupuy (*Elusive Victory*, p.396) says there were
      thirty-three; O'Ballance (*No Victor, No Vanquished*, p.29), who counted them but may
      have been influenced by Herzog, says there were at least twenty-six while the Egyptians
      counted thirty-one; Bartov says in his biography *Dado* (p.149) there were thirty. I've
      used Bartov's figure because of private confirmation from an Israeli officer and because
      Bartov's research seems the most thorough.
80   Between thirty and: Herzog, op. cit., p.7.
80   To add to: Ibib., p.6.
80   A massive construction: Ibid., p.11.

CHAPTER X: Sadat Ousts the Soviets
PAGE
82   "In October you: Boris N. Ponomarev was a member of the Politburo and secretary general
      of the Soviet Central Committee; Heikal, *The Road to Ramadan*, p.158.
82   "They were not: Sadat, *In Search of Identity*, p.228.
82   "We got the: Facts on File 1972, p.85.
82   "Back in Egypt: Sadat, op. cit., p.228.
83   The Arab oil: Facts on File 1972, p.31.
83   Interior Secretary Rogers: Facts on File 1972, Vol. XXXII, p.308.
83   A nation with: Nixon, *The Memoirs of Richard Nixon*, p.082.
83   It was predicted: Ibid., p. 308.
83   Twice during the: Facts on File 1972, pp.350, 746 and 1047.
83   The Office of: Ibid., p.746.
83   President Sadat was: Heikal, op. cit., p.169. Also, Rubinstein, *Red Star on the Nile*,
      pp.182-3.
83   He was keenly: Rubinstein, op. cit., pp.182-3.
83   "Any new American: Heikal, op. cit., p.169.
83   He also brought: Ibid., p.169. For population figures, see Washington Post, 4/17/71, p.A20.
      The official Soviet census reported there were 2,151,000 Soviets Jews; Jewish sources
      claimed there were more than 3 million.
83   In 1970, only: Harry Trimborn, Los Angeles Times, 3/15/71.
84   The figure skyrocketed: Richard Homan, Washington Post, 3/5/72, and Ben-Sasson, H.H.
      (ed.). *A History of the Jewish People*. Cambridge, MA: Harvard University Press, 1976,

321

p.1073.
84 Noting the increased: Heikal, op. cit., p.167.
84 This the Soviet: Rubinstein, op. cit., p.168.
84 There was also: Ibid., p.238.
84 "Never did they: J. Sadat, *A Woman of Egypt*, p.285.
84 They were worried: Rubinstein, op. cit., pp.170-1.
84 The leak did: Heikal, *The Road to Ramadan*, p.167.
85 Then his visit: Rubinstein, op. cit., p.178.
85 The idea was: Sadat, *In Search of Identity*, p.229.
85 "Our enemies were: Rubinstein, op. cit., p.178.
85 The Soviet Union: Ibid., p.179.
85 They were, he: Sadat, op. cit., p.229.
86 It listed seven: Kissinger, *White House Years*, pp.1493-4.
86 "I sought the: Ibid., pp.1247-8.
86 "As far as we: Ibid., p.1247.
86 "In my opinion: Heikal, *The Sphinx and the Commissar*, p.241.
86 The Egyptians grumbled: Rubinstein, op. cit., p.195.
87 It was they who: Ibid., pp.180 and 195-6.
87 Sadat's continuing vacillation: Unsigned, Washington Post, 5/4/72.
88 His message was: Quandt, *Decade of Decisions*, p.151.
88 The expulsion of: Heikal, *The Autumn of Fury*, p.79.
88 It was not: In his memoirs, p.233, Sadat says the letter reached him July 6, which is technically correct. But Sadat "felt so tense" that he asked the ambassador not to call on him with the letter until the 8th, Heikal, *The Road to Ramadan*, p.174. Sadat also uses the 8th as the date of the letter's receipt in his 8/30/72 letter to Brezhnev, reprinted as Appendix I in his memoirs.
88 The Soviets reported: Sadat, op. cit., p.229.
88 Brezhnev urged Sadat: Heikal, *The Road to Ramadan*, p.171.
88 "I have decided: Sadat, op. cit., pp.229-30.
89 He "didn't believe: Ibid., p.230.
89 By the time: Facts on File 1972, p. 549.
89 "It was a total: Eugene Trone, interview, Washington, DC, 2/9/86.
89 "I had expected: Kissinger, op. cit., p.1296.
89 He thus decided: Heikal, *The Road to Ramadan*, p.141. In fact, so total was the Egyptian leader's disgust with the state department that he cut off all personal communications with it. When Joseph Greene Jr. replaced Donald Bergus at the beginning of 1972, Sadat refused to see Greene—and never did during his entire tour up to the 1973 war.
89 CIA station chief: Eugene Trone, interview, op. cit. Also see Heikal, *The Road to Ramadan*, p.140.
89 "The only barrier: J. Sadat, op. cit., p.283.

CHAPTER XI: Massacre in Munich
PAGE
91 Richard Nixon was: Isaacs, *Jews and American Politics*, pp.182 and 195.
91 Israeli Ambassador Yitzhak: Ibid., p.192.
91 Polls were showing: Stanley Karnow, Washington Post, 6/17/72. Also, Joseph Alsop, Washington Post, 11/3/72.
91 Then he riled: Stephen S. Rosenfeld, Washington Post, 7/14/72.

91   The uproar was: At least since 1967, it had become unusual to write anything critical about Israel since the media was generally silent about U.S. policy toward the region because of harsh denunciations by the Israeli Lobby that inevitably followed any critical examination. Von Hoffman paid for his boldness by quickly losing readers and support at the Washington Post, which he eventually left to become a successful syndicated columnist and writer.

92   But now, nearly: Anthony Lewis, New York Times, 12/23/82.

92   He had been: Kissinger, *White House Years*, p.1296.

92   The Washington Post: Hirst and Beeson, *Sadat*, p.138.

92   When Sadat vowed: Ibid., p.140.

92   A post-expulsion: Heikal, *The Sphinx and the Commissar*, p.246.

92   I would like: Sadat, *In Search of Identity*, Appendix I.

93   In concluding, Sadat: Ibid., Appendix I.

93   "Dr. Sidqi came: Ibid., p.237. The visit took place 10/16/72.

94   Jews were relentlessly: Facts on File 1972, p.567. Fifteen of the settlements were on the Golan Heights and the West Bank each and 14 in Sinai.

94   The twenty-hour: Hirst, *The Gun and the Olive Branch*, p.311.

94   The Olympic operation: Hart, *Arafat*, p.349.

94   On the morning: Hirst, op. cit., p.311.

94   Their orders were: Ibid., p.312.

94   "We do not: Ibid., p.312.

95   So too were: Ibid., pp.312-3.

95   But, in the end: Ibid., p.314.

95   A letter in: Time, 10/2/72.

95   In some cafes: Hirst, op. cit., p.314.

96   In response, Libya: Facts on File 1972, p.799.

96   The FBI, the: Ibid., p.798.

96   Two days after: Ibid., p.709.

96   Between two hundred: Hirst, op. cit., p.314.

96   Israel followed suit: Facts on File 1972, p.709.

96   On the same: Ibid., p.733.

96   The PLO claimed: Ibid., p.820.

96   "We are no longer: Ibid., p.819.

97   Former head of: Ibid., p.819. The reference work identifies Herzog as a former chief of staff, a position he never held.

97   Only Lebanon reported: Ibid., p.819.

97   The guerrillas placed: Ibid., pp.860-1.

97   "We have tried: Ibid., p.991.

97   At about the: Ibid., p.1038.

97   Renewal of its: Rubinstein, *Red Star on the Nile*, p.225.

CHAPTER XII: Nixon Searches for Peace

PAGE

99   K—you know my: Kissinger, *Years of Upheaval*, p.212.

99   Kissinger, after working: Ibid., pp.202-3.

100   "Though not practicing: Ibid., pp.203-4.

100   "The U.S. presidential: Sadat, *In Search of Identity*, pp. 232-4.

100   To his chagrin: Ibid. Sadat, p.234, gives the date as the 28th but as usual his figures are

suspect. Both Heikal, *The Road to Ramadan*, p.181, and Shazly, *The Crossing of the Suez*, p.172, give the 24th as the date.

101 Sadiq favored a: Heikal, op. cit., p.180.
101 Sadat was stunned: Sadat, op. cit., pp.235-6.
101 "We've completely exposed: Ibid., p.236.
101 "I'm sorry, but: Ibid., p.236.
101 The man chosen: His full name was Achmed Ismail Ali, but following frequent Arab custom he did not use his family name.
101 Ismail was a: Heikal, Ibid., p.180.
101 Best, from Sadat's: Dupuy, *Elusive Victory*, p.388.
102 "...I really wanted: Adan, *On the Banks of the Suez*, p.233.
102 Ismail and Shazly: Shazly, *The Crossing of the Suez*, p.183.
102 The troubles between: Ibid., pp.184-5.
102 The first task: Ibid., p.189.
103 As with any: Dupuy, op. cit., p.393.
103 During the day's: Facts on File 1973, Vol. XXXIII, p.11.
103 Syria charged that: Ibid., p.25.
103 Three days after: Ibid., p.25.
104 On February 21: Bartov, *Dado*, p.175. See International Civil Aviation Organization working paper "Report Concerning the Libyan Arab Airlines Boeing 727-224: 5A-DAH, (Sina-21 February 1973)."
104 Earlier that same: Facts on File 1973, p.137.
104 "...I want to tell: Bartov, op. cit., p.177.
104 Arab response to: Facts on File 1973, pp.137 and 160.
104 Nixon bridled at: Kissinger, op. cit., p.211.
105 King Hussein of Jordan: These secret meetings have long been rumored and have been confirmed by sources close to the Jordanian throne.
105 What was needed: Kissinger, op. cit., p.220.
105 Next to arrive: Ibid., p.213.
105 Privately, Kissinger felt: Ibid., pp.216-7; Heikal, op. cit., p.pp.202-3, and Quandt, *Decade of Decisions*, p.155.
106 Last to arrive: Rabin, *The Rabin Memoirs*, pp.153 and 208.
106 "We never had: Kissinger, op. cit., p.620.
106 It would get: Kissinger, Ibid., pp.220-2; Rabin, op. cit., pp.214-8. Rabin remarks in his report on this meeting how transitory power is. The next time the four were together Meir and Nixon were either out or about to be ousted from their high posts, Kissinger was secretary of state and Rabin was becoming the new premier of Israel.
106 Because of Arab: Kissinger, op. cit., pp.220-2.
106 When Nixon then: Heikal, op. cit., p.203; Quandt, op. cit., p.155.
106 Sadat was explicit: Hirst and Beeson, *Sadat*, pp.151-2.
106 During this same: Ajami, *The Arab Predicament*, p.95.
106 Nonetheless, Sadat kept: Facts on File 1973, pp.301 and 345.
107 When Golda Meir: Ibid., p.204.
107 Moshe Dayan urged: Ibid., p.267.
107 At about the: Ibid., p.346.
107 Moore, Noel and Ein: Ibid., p.177; Hirst, *The Gun and the Olive Branch*, pp.318-9. It was widely suspected, but never proved, that Yasser Arafat was at the other end of the radio in Beirut.
107 The terrorists surrendered: Facts on File 1974, Vol. XXXIV, p.511.
107 Israel struck back: Bar-Zohar, Michael and Eitan Haber. *The Quest for the Red Prince*. New York: William Morrow and Co., Inc., 1983, pp.174-5.

NOTES

108 Unknown to the: Abu Iyad, *My Home, My Land*, p.117-8.
108 All told, twelve: Facts on File 1973, p.285.
108 Elazar's mention of: Ibid., pp. 73, 122, 204, 347, 591 and 655.
108 More dramatic operations: Ibid., pp.653-4 and 674-5.
108 The incident brought: Eban, *An Autobiography*, p.491.
109 A choice was: Sadat, op. cit., p.241.

CHAPTER XIII: The Politics of Oil
PAGE
110 Nonetheless, he held: Newsweek, 9/21/70.
110 Faisal had never: Heikal, *The Road to Ramadan*, p.119.
110 It was in part: Lacey, *The Kingdom*, p.393.
111 It was in 1972: Ibid., p.398.
111 Faisal contacted other: Ibid., p.398.
111 "Only make sure. Ibid., p.401.
111 "Now they are: Rubinstein, *Red Star on the Nile*, p.229.
111 Despite his pledge: Facts on File 1973, Vol. XXXIII, p.329.
111 Yet it was: Lacey, op. cit., p.398.
112 "This should not: Ibid., p.399.
112 "Afterwards the oil: Ibid., p.399.
112 Although The Post: Washington Post, 4/20/73.
113 "He means what: Lacey, op. cit., P.400.
113 Israel's Foreign Minister: Ibid., p.400.
113 In May, Faisal: Sheehan, *The Arabs, Israelis, and Kissinger*, pp.66-7.
113 "It was ignored: Ibid., pp.66-7.
113 "You may lose: Lacey, op. cit., pp.401-2.
113 The oilmen tried: Ibid., pp.400-2.
113 The board chairman: Facts on File 1973, p.654.
114 Another oilman, Maurice: Ibid., p.780.
114 Throughout the summer: Sheehan, op. cit., p.67.
114 It was yet another: Ibid., pp.67-8.
114 When asked if: Facts on File 1973, p.741.

CHAPTER XIV: Confronting the Bar-Lev Line
PAGE
115 First, and most: Shazly, *The Crossing of the Suez*, p.8.
116 The final barrier: Ibid., pp.8-9.
116 Israeli Chief of: Badri et al, *The Ramadan War*, 1973, p.34.
116 Thus, as a starter: O'Ballance, *No Victor, No Vanquished*, pp.177-8; Whetten, *The Canal War*, p.249.
117 Counterbalancing this: Whetten, op. cit., p.258.
117 In all, there: Ibid., p.254.
117 In addition, the: O'Ballance, *The Electronic War in the Middle East 1968-70*, p.102.
117 The United States: Ibid., p.102; also Whetten, op. cit., p.246.
117 To overcome this: O'Ballance, *The Electronic War in the Middle East 1968-70*, p.110; Whetten, op. cit., p.274.

117   The most potent: Whetten, op. cit., p.258.
117   Equally important was: Ibid., pp.247 and 257.
117   Egypt's estimated 800: Ibid., pp.247-8; O'Ballance, *No Victor, No Vanquished*, p.282.
118   Foremost, concluded an: Badri et al, op. cit., p.19.
118   Major General Hassan: Badri, *The October War*, p.8.
118   Its standing forces: Badri et al, op. cit., p.19.
118   The Egyptian analysts: Ibid., p.19; Shazly, op. cit., pp. 25-6.
119   The superpowers would: Dupuy, *Elusive Victory*, p.389.
119   He instructed the: Badri et al, op. cit., p.19.
120   The disintegration of: Kissinger, *Years of Upheaval*, pp.105 and 110.
120   The President was: Woodward, Bob, and Carl Bernstein. *The Final Days*. New York: Simon & Schuster, 1976, p.36.
120   "For Nixon to: Kissinger, op. cit., p.298.

CHAPTER XV: Countdown to War

PAGE
121   Stories began leaking: Bartov, *Dado*, p.189.
121   Aviation Week, the: Ben-Porat et al, *Kippur*, p.117.
121   Moshe Dayan expressed: Bartov, op. cit., pp.189-90.
122   These reports, together: Ibid., pp.189-91.
122   Elazar ordered the: Ibid., pp.193 and 196.
122   Nonetheless, with increasing: Herzog, *The War of Atonement*, p.29.
122   With such divided: Facts on File 1973, p.366.
122   "Israel is today: Bartov, op. cit., p.216.
122   The Soviet Union: Ibid., p.194.
123   More public scorn: Ibid., p.191.
123   Complacency again set: Ibid., p.220.
123   "The balance of: Dupuy, *Elusive Victory*, p.406.
123   "Our military superiority: Pollock, *The Politics of Pressure*, p.132.
123   Arik Sharon, the: Eban, *An Autobiography*, p.488.
123   "Egypt has no: Ibid., p.489.
123   So confident were: Facts on File 1973 Vol. XXXIII, p.654.
123   An atmosphere of: Herzog, op. cit., p.29.
124   Over several years: Badri et al, *The Ramadan War*, p.35.
124   In war, "such: Shazly, *The Crossing of the Suez*, pp.54-5.
124   In war, "such: Shazly, Ibid., pp.55-6.
125   (In their own: O'Ballance, *No Victor, No Vanquished*, p.30.
125   The Egyptian engineer: Badri et al, op. cit., p.39.
125   The Egyptians had seen: O'Ballance, op. cit., p.45.
125   The Israeli fire: Shazly, op. cit., pp.56-7. Israeli spokesmen have repeatedly claimed that the system was tested in 1971 and was abandoned since it was found wanting because of the canal's tidal current. Herzog, however, admits in his *War of Atonement*, p.149, that two devices were installed; he says the other outlets were dummies. He adds Israel unsuccessfully tried to use the two devices during the invasion. O'Ballance, op. cit., p.45, who toured the line after the war, says, "I saw ample evidence of this secret weapon." He numbered the devices at 39. Whatever the facts, in Egyptian eyes the system existed and had to be overcome.
126   The solution: Little: Shazly, op. cit., pp.61-2.
126   To sustain the: Ibid., p.64-5.

NOTES

126 The final major: Badri et al, op. cit., p.48.
126 The timing of: Ibid., pp.47-50; Dupuy, op. cit., p.394.
127 The Israeli general: Bartov, op. cit., pp.207 and 213.
127 Nonetheless, Egypt correctly: Shazly, op. cit., p.75.
127 This was done: Dupuy, op. cit., p.392.
128 The aerial combat: Bartov, op. cit., pp.230-1.
128 Chief of Staff: Ibid., p.236.
128 "We'll have one: Ibid., p.239.
128 As the deadline: Ibid., p.243.
129 "Perhaps you have: Hirst and Beeson, Sadat, p.155.
129 But in the eyes: Bartov, op. cit., pp.241-3.
129 Only an American: Quandt, Decade of Decisions, p.160.
129 Then Sadat deliberately: Sadat, In Search of Identity, p.244.
129 This was emphasized: Facts on File 1973, p.614.
129 Probably as part: Ibid., p.815.
130 By then, the Central: Bartov, op. cit., p.244-5.
130 Interestingly, the CIA: The Pipe Report on the hearings of the House Select Committee on Intelligence, written in 1976 and published in the Village Voice, 2/16/76.
130 On October 4, some: Shazly, op. cit., p.75.
130 Diplomatic activity continued: O'Ballance, op. cit., p.43.
130 Hidden from view: Ibid., p. 45.
130 Sadat had secretly: Sadat, op. cit., Appendix II.
130 It came after: Ibid., p.246.
130 On the same: Bartov, op. cit., p.258.
130 With all this: Ibid., p.259.
130 If a mobilization: Ibid., p.260.
130 "The enemy must: Golan, The Secret Conversations of Henry Kissinger, p.36.
131 The other big: Facts on File 1973, pp.881 and 961. By mid-November, 13 more African nations had broken ties with Israel, leaving it practically isolated in the continent where it once had flourishing relations.
132 He found Kissinger: Eban, op. cit., 497.
132 "It seemed that: Ibid., p.498.
132 The next day: Sadat, op. cit., Appendix III.
132 Chief of military: Bartov, op. cit., p.264.
132 Not even a telltale: Shazly, op. cit., p.213.
132 That same night: O'Ballance, op. cit., p.45.
132 The war was: Bartov, op. cit., pp.207 and 213.
133 It was a stark: Beatty, Charles. De Lesseps of Suez: The man and his times. New York: Harper & Brothers, 1956, p.257.
133 The thirty-three men: Bartov, op. cit., p.283.
133 "The next time: Shazly, op. cit., p. 215.
133 That same night: Bartov, op. cit., p.267.

CHAPTER XVI: October 6—War

PAGE

137 At 4:30 in the: Bartov, Dado, p.273. The Israelis had probably broken the Egyptian or Syrian military codes and intercepted final orders as the Arabs counted down toward war. Former director of Central Intelligence Richard Helms, while disclaiming any knowledge of how the Israelis were so sure of war, noted that the information of an informant would

not likely have been considered solid enough because of fears of planted information, human error or being a double agent, etc. Much more credibility, Helms pointed out, would be given to radio intercepts, particularly if there were a number of intercepts with detailed information. Helms interview, Washington, DC, 11/28/85.

137   "This is it: Bartov, op. cit., p.273.
137   "No, it will: Herzog. *The War of Atonement*, p.54.
137   The error would: Bartov, op. cit., p.273. A number of authors have speculated that the Arabs advanced the attack time from 1800 to 1400 hours after getting warnings from the US not to attack. This seems farfetched, since changing the timing of such a massive operation at the last minute would be incredibly complicated. Among others, Bartov, who had unusual access to both Elazar and general staff records, seems to have it right, that it was an error in the Israeli chain of command.
137   The short period: Ibid., p.274.
138   Chief of Intelligence: Ibid., pp.276-8.
138   After all, on that: Time, 10/29/73, p.33.
138   Additionally, "I feared: Dayan, *Story of My Life*, p.461.
139   Instead of the: Bartov, op. cit., pp.284-9.
139   Meir next saw: Kissinger, *Years of Upheaval*, p.451.
139   As soon as he: Ibid., p.451.
139   "And what if: Bartov, op. cit., pp.294-5.
139   At 1:30 PM, Anwar: Insight Team, *The Yom Kippur War*, p.145.
140   As Sadat took: Shazly, *The Crossing of the Suez*, p.225. There is no Egyptian First Army. It originally had been meant to designate the Syrian army under the short-lived United Arab Republic in which the Egyptian forces were then designated the Second and Third armies.
140   The "seam" between: Ibid., p.236.
140   Across the canal: Dupuy, *Elusive Victory*, pp.401-3; Bartov, op. cit., pp.283 and 317. Herzog, op. cit., pp.151, says there were 436 soldiers in the forts, but Bartov's figures again appear more reliable. He gives a breakdown of the number of men in each of the 20 forts that were manned at the time: From north to south, Traklin, 6 men; Budapest, 63; Orkal I, 20; Orkal II, 7; Orkal III, 20; Lachtzanit, 17; Drora, 19; Ketubah, 21; Milan, 28; Mifreket, 16; Hizayon, 20; Purkan, 33; Matzmed, 33; Lakekan, 10; Botzer, 26; Lituf, 29; Maftzeach, 28; Nissan, 20; Quay, 30; and Egrofit, 5.
140   The scene along: Shazly, op. cit., p.211.
140   Despite the knowledge: O'Ballance, *No Victor, No Vanquished*, p.69. Ben-Porat et al, *Kippur*, p.42.
141   Suddenly, at 1:45 PM: Sadat, *In Search of Identity*, p.248; O'Ballance, op. cit., pp.68-9.
141   The soccer games on: O'Ballance, op. cit., p.69.
141   Several Frog missiles: Badri et al, *The Ramadan War*, 1973, pp.62 and 72. Frog is an acronym meaning free rocket over ground and is the NATO designation.
141   Under the murderous: Shazly, op. cit., pp.222-3.
141   At a stronghold: Ben-Porat et al, op. cit., p.34. Ben-Porat's book was published in December 1973, when Israeli censorship usually, but not always, prevented identification of troops under the rank of commanding officer.
142   In the compound: Ibid., pp.34-5.
142   The crossing and: Shazly, op. cit., p.227.
142   The first Egyptian: Badri et al, op. cit., p.62
142   The first fort: Ibid., pp.62-3.
142   Among the first: O'Ballance, op. cit., p.73.
142   Israeli tanks, which: Bartov, op. cit., p.297.
143   "I looked around: Ben-Porat et al, op. cit., pp.44-6.

NOTES

143 Repeatedly the Israeli: Adan, *On the Banks of the Suez*, p.22.
143 Throughout the early: Ibid., p.26.
143 The effectiveness of: O'Ballance, op. cit., pp.73-4.
144 These missiles were: Luttwak and Horowitz, *The Israeli Army*, p.346.
144 All together, Israel: O'Ballance, op. cit., pp.54-5; Whetten, *The Canal War*, p.246.
144 Only Israel's M-60: Insight Team, op. cit., p.171.
145 "We have taught: Dupuy, op. cit., p.419-21. Dayan, op. cit., p.495, admits in his memoirs that Israel lost 35 planes to missiles alone in the first 24 hours of fighting.
145 Whatever the truth: O'Ballance, op. cit., p.86.
145 By 5:30 PM, the: Dupuy, op. cit., p.416.
145 As dusk fell: Shazly, op. cit., p.229.
145 In the north: Adan, op. cit., p.30.
145 At 6:30, the: O'Ballance, op. cit., p.82.
145 These were made: Ibid., p.83.
146 Not only that: Ibid., pp.47 and 91.
146 As military historian: Dupuy, op. cit., p.417.
146 On the Golan: Dupuy, op. cit., pp.441, and pp. 444, Bartov, op. cit., p.296.
147 A small parcel: Bull, Odd. *War and Peace in the Middle East*. London: Leo Cooper, 1976, pp.49-51.
147 Paralleling the ceasefire: O'Ballance, op. cit., pp.121-2; Dupuy, op. cit., pp.437-8.
147 Interspersed among the: Keith Howard, letter, 3/1/86. Howard reports the posts on the Israeli side were numbered 1 to seven, north to south, although because of various moves the sequence was mixed, going 1, 6, 5, 2, 3, 4, 7. On the Syrian side, the posts were designated by the phonetic alphabet. According to international usage, three of the posts were named "whiskey, Yankee and Zulu." When U.N. Undersecretary Ralph Bunch heard of these designations, he objected on various grounds of sensitivity to national or moral concerns and insisted they be changed to "winter, yoke and zebra," causing no end of confusion to troops used to the international code.
148 Though there were: UN A/6797*, *Report of the Special Representative of the Secretary-General on His Mission to the Occupied Territories*, 9/15/67.
148 The Syrian villages: Observed by the author during a tour of the Golan Heights in 1975.
148 In their place: Kissinger, op. cit., p.937.
148 Syria's forces on the: Dupuy, op. cit., p.441.
148 The Syrians, like: Ibid., p.439.
148 Capture of the: O'Ballance, op. cit., p.123.
148 Israel's three brigades: Herzog, op. cit., p.65.
148 On the day: Dupuy, op. cit., p.443. O'Ballance, op. cit., p.124.
149 At 1.15 PM, Herzog, op. cit., p.72.
149 A few minutes: Keith Howard, letter to the author, 3/1/86.
149 As in the Sinai: O'Ballance, op. cit., p.125.
149 Under the protection: Asher, *Duel for the Golan*, p.90.
149 Flail tanks lashed: Ibid., p.125.
149 However, confusion in: Dupuy, op. cit., p.447.
150 It was a slaughter: Ibid., pp.447-8; Herzog, op. cit., pp.80-1 and 106.
150 It was not only: Herzog, op. cit., p.82.
150 But for the Israeli: O'Ballance, op. cit., p.128.
150 And, despite the: Herzog, op. cit., pp.78-9.
150 In the central: Ibid., p.82.
150 The biggest breakthrough: Ibid., p.84.
150 Three of the Israeli: Ibid., p.96.
151 All told, only: Ibid., pp.72-4.

329

151   King Hussein telephoned: O'Ballance, op. cit., p.170.
151   At the outbreak: Bartov, op. cit., pp.290 and 299.
152   Defense Minister Dayan: Dayan, op. cit., pp.478-80.
152   Reports of the fierce: Bartov, op. cit., pp.301-3.
152   That was the impression: Ibid., pp.306-8.
152   Some of the cabinet: Dayan, op. cit., pp.277-8.
153   Anwar Sadat was: Sadat, op. cit., p.215.
153   The Egyptian leader: O'Ballance, op. cit., p.123.
153   Sadat challenged the: Sadat, op. cit., pp.252-3.
154   "We can find: *Pike report on the hearings of the House Select Committee on Intelligence*, written in 1976 and published in the Village Voice, 2/16/76; also see Kissinger, op. cit., p.458.
154   When a short: See, among others, Quandt, *Decade of Decision*, p.170.
154   Kissinger's immediate reaction: Kissinger, op. cit., p.467.
154   As Nixon recalled: Nixon, *The Memoirs of Richard Nixon*, p.922.
155   Kissinger's first assumption: Kissinger, op. cit., p.472.
155   "Our reading of: Ibid., pp.474-5.
155   Not unreasonably, Dobrynin: Ibid., p.474.

CHAPTER XVII: October 7—Trial and Error

PAGE

156   However, one man: Time, "How Israel Got the Bomb," 4/12/1976, reported that Dayan personally received Meir's permission to use the bombs in the early hours of Oct. 9. There is little doubt that Israel had the bomb at the time and this may help explain Washington's determination to resupply Israel in order to prevent it from using the devices. Since at least 1968 the Central Intelligence Agency had concluded that Israel possessed nuclear weapons. According to records of a classified briefing given by ex-CIA official Carl Duckett in 1976, the agency informed President Johnson of its findings. Johnson's response was to order the CIA not to inform any other members of the administration, including Defense Secretary McNamara and Secretary of State Rusk (see unsigned, Washington Post, 3/2/78). Israel's efforts to develop a nuclear capability began in 1948 with the founding of the state. That same year the Defense Ministry set up the Research and Planning Branch to explore uranium resources in the Negev Desert. In 1952, Israel established its Atomic Energy Commission under the Israeli Defense Ministry. The next year it signed a nuclear cooperation agreement with France covering heavy water and uranium production. The agreement was modified substantially in 1957. Although the details were secret the agreement was believed to have provided Israel with a large (24-megawatt) reactor capable of producing one or two bombs' worth of plutonium a year in the form of spent fuel (see Spector, *Nuclear Proliferation Today*, p.119.). France also provided Israel with blueprints for a reprocessing plant for turning spent fuel into weapons' grade plutonium (see Spector, p.119.) It later withdrew its help, but the plant was believed to have been completed, probably sometime in the 1970s (see Spector, p.125.). (Charles deGaulle reveals in his memoirs that he ordered France's withdrawal from the project after Israel launched the 1967 war against his advice. "...French cooperation in the construction of a factory near Beersheba for the transformation of uranium into plutonium—from which, one fine day, atomic bombs might emerge—was brought to an end" [see deGaulle, *Memoirs of Hope, Renewal and Endeavor*, p.266.].)

Construction of Israel's major nuclear research facility began in the late 1950s at Dimona in the Negev desert and was kept completely secret from the rest of the world, including the United States. To those foreigners who noted the growing facility in the desert, Israelis explained that it was a textile factory. Its true nature was not determined until late 1960 when a U.S. spy plane reportedly photographed it and Israeli officials were presented with the evidence. The disclosure caused Senator Bourke Hickenlooper to explode: "I think the Israelis have just lied to us like horse thieves on this thing. They have completely distorted, misrepresented, and falsified the facts in the past. I think it is very serious, for things that we have done for them to have them perform in this manner in connection with very definite production reactor facility which they have been secretly building, and which they have consistently, and with a completely straight face, denied to us they were building" (see Spector, op. cit., p.121.).

Although Israel insisted the Dimona plant was dedicated to peaceful research, it refused repeated urgings by the United States to sign the Non-Proliferation Treaty or accept IAEA (International Atomic Energy Agency) safeguards. Egypt signed the Non-Proliferation Treaty in 1981, but Israel still refused—and has continued to refuse to this day. The plant started up in late 1963 or early 1964. By 1966, the U.S. Atomic Energy Commission determined that 382 pounds—it takes about 20 pounds to make one bomb—of highly enriched uranium that had been supplied to NUMEC, the Nuclear Materials and Equipment Corporation of Apollo, PA, were missing (see Associated Press, 2/26/82.). There was a "clear consensus" in the CIA that the uranium had been illegally shipped to Israel, according to Carl Duckett, who was the agency's deputy director for science and technology from 1967 to 1976 (see New York Times, 5/2/81.). However, although a number of investigations were launched, no criminal charges were ever filed in the case.

In its pursuit of plutonium, Israel is generally believed to have spirited away two hundred tons of processed uranium ore, yellowcake, in the late 1960s. Using intermediaries, Israel is reported to have arranged shipment of the yellowcake in November 1968 from Antwerp to Genoa, where the cargo, ship and its crew all disappeared. The yellowcake was abundant enough to produce several hundred kilograms of weapons quality plutonium (see Spector, op. cit., p.125. Also see Davenport, The Plumbat Affair.). Israel consistently denied that it had nuclear bombs and insisted it would not be "the first to introduce nuclear weapons into the Middle East." But on September 4, 1974, the CIA began circulating a report within the government stating: "We believe that Israel has already produced nuclear weapons. Our judgment is based on Israeli acquisition of large quantities of uranium, partly by clandestine means; the ambiguous nature of Israeli efforts in the field of uranium enrichment and Israel's large investment in a costly missile system [Jericho] designed to accommodate nuclear warheads" (see Spector, pp.128-9.). On July 31, 1975, the Boston Globe reported that Israel was believed by "senior American analysts in the American security community" to have more than ten nuclear bombs. An unnamed CIA official (see Spector, who identifies him as Carl Duckett, p.130.) revealed at a rare CIA briefing in February 1976 that Israel had ten to twenty nuclear bombs "ready and available for use" (see Arthur Kranish, Washington Post, 3/15/76). In its April 12, 1976 issue, Time magazine reported that Israel had thirteen bombs. In 1980, the former head of France's Atomic Energy Commission, Francis Perrin, said: "We are sure the Israelis have nuclear bombs....They have sufficient facilities to produce one or two bombs a year" (see Spector, p.132.). On 10/5/86, The Sunday Times of London, quoting a disaffected worker at Dimona, Mordechai Vanunu, reported that Israel had "at least 100 and as many as 200 nuclear weapons." It said Israel had been producing the weapons for twenty years and that it now was a leading nuclear power.

Israel has long been suspected of cooperating with South Africa in the development of nuclear weapons. On September 22, 1979, a U.S. Vela surveillance satellite detected an intense double pulse of light—the unique signature of an atomic explosion—off the

331

WARRIORS AGAINST ISRAEL

coast of South Africa. The Carter Administration claimed that the data was too vague to prove that a nuclear test had taken place, but numerous reports said it had and that it was a joint Israel-South African operation (see Spector, p.133. Also see Robert Manning and Stephen Talbot, *American Cover-Up on Israeli Bomb*, The Middle East, June 1980.). Israel could deliver nuclear warheads either on its 260-mile ballistic missile, Jericho, or by airplanes or artillery. Its efforts to get the U.S. Lance missile in 1975 were finally turned down because the Lance is mainly used to deliver nuclear warheads.

156 Israeli defenses in: O'Ballance, *No Victor, No Vanquished*, p.131.
157 But now Syrian tanks: Herzog, *The War of Atonement*, p.79
157 A major Syrian: Ibid., p.78.
157 By now, the Barak: Ibid., p.84.
157 Alarmed by the: Bartov, *Dado*, p.313.
158 Dayan was so: Dayan, *Story of My Life*, pp.481-3.
158 The planes came: Herzog, op. cit., p.87.
158 Nonetheless, the Israeli: Dayan, op. cit., p.483.
158 During this critical: Whetten, *The Canal War*, p.250.
158 The ferocity of: Herzog, op. cit., p.98.
158 From her verandah: Joan Howard, notes made 10/11/73 and lent to the author.
159 Ben Shoham decided: Herzog, op. cit., pp.88-9.
159 Brigadier General Rafael: Ibid., p.90.
159 The brigade had: Bartov, op. cit., pp.337-8.
159 Under the crash: Dupuy, *Elusive Victory*, p.454.
160 "All signs pointed: Herzog, *The War of Atonement*, p.94. Herzog identifies the colonel as only "Pinie." His full name can be found in Asher, *The Duel for the Golan*, p.165.
160 Major Dov, the: op. cit., p.94; Asher, op. cit., p.182.
160 The tanks of the: Asher, op. cit., p.170, identifies this unit as the 679th; he offers so much detail about it that I have used his designation even though Herzog, O'Ballance and Dupuy all refer to it as the 79th.
160 Meanwhile, another desperate: Dupuy, op. cit., 454.
160 One daring detachment: Asher, op. cit., p.154.
161 Laner, who had: Herzog, op. cit., pp.99-100.
161 Since the humiliating: Dupuy, op. cit., p.455.
161 Despite the near: O'Ballance, op. cit., p.138.
161 Illustrative of the: Asher, op. cit., p.129.
162 The other vehicle: Herzog, op. cit., p.85.
162 Zvicka now took: Ibid., p.86.
162 North of Kuneitra: Dupuy, op. cit., pp.457.
163 Attacks across the: Herzog, op. cit., p.107; Asher, op. cit., pp.194-7.
163 From the beginning: Bartov, op. cit., pp.310 and 312.
163 By 1 o'clock: Shazly, *The Crossing of the Suez*, pp.231-3.
164 Only 110 of: Adan, *On Both Banks of the Suez*, p.33. Bartov, op. cit., p.319.
164 When Major General: Adan, op. cit., pp.36 and 39.
164 Adan thought Gonen: Ibid., pp.33 and 155-6.
165 When Adan visited: Ibid., p.95.
165 In the Sinai: Shazly, op. cit., p.234.
165 An intricate logistics: Ibid., p.234.
166 General Gonen apparently: Adan, op. cit., p.111.
166 Dayan definitely did: Ibid., p.92.
166 Rather than attack: Bartov, op. cit., p.323.
166 Moshe Dayan was: Dayan, op. cit., p.494.
167 Dayan made no: Bartov, op. cit., p.326.

NOTES

167 "Golda, I was: Herzog, op. cit., p.116.
167 If the Arabs: Bartov, op. cit., pp.329.
167 "I listened to: Meir, *My Life*, p.428.
167 Privately, she remarked: Bartov, op. cit., pp.328-9.
167 Admitted Meir: "I: Meir, op. cit., p.429.
167 Dayan realized the: Dayan, op. cit., p.495.
167 Golda Meir called: Bartov, op. cit., pp.329-30.
168 Elazar favored the: Meir, op. cit., p.429.
168 Later she sent: Herzog, op. cit., p.118.
168 That same Sunday: Meir, op. cit., pp.429 and 551.
168 Shortly after 7 PM: Bartov, pp.335-6; Adan, op. cit., pp.98-9.
168 "I would like: Bartov, op. cit., p.335.
169 As Elazar was: Bartov, Ibid., p.336.
169 The generals scattered: Adan, op. cit., pp.108-9.
169 Anwar Sadat did: Sadat, *In Search of Identity*, p.253.
169 Instead, he stayed: Ibid., p.253
169 "His face went: Ibid., p.253.
169 The question of: Heikal, *The Road to Ramadan*, p.209. There seems little doubt that Assad played this duplicitous game, and probably for the reasons cited by Heikal. See Fahmy, *Negotiating for Peace in the Middle East*, pp.25-6, for more details.
170 Another consideration may: O'Ballance, op. cit., p.123.
170 Obviously, the Russians: Sadat, op. cit., p.254.
170 The rosy picture: Kissinger, *Years of Upheaval*, p.477.
170 The purpose of: Ibid., p.477.
170 Israel's requests for: Ibid., p.478.
170 In fact, some: Ibid., p.480.
170 You know the: Ibid., pp.477.
171 When Kissinger met: Kalb and Kalb, *Kissinger*, p.464.
171 Although Kissinger recognized: Kissinger, op. cit., p.477.
171 During the same. Ibid., p.485.
171 Kissinger also agreed: Ibid., pp.479-80.
171 Another strong hint: Ibid., p.482.
172 "Until this message: Ibid., p.482

CHAPTER XVIII: October 8—Error and Trial
PAGE
173 "We're past the: Bartov, *Dado*, p.348.
174 Egypt had captured: Badri et al, *The Ramadan War*, 1973, p.63.
174 During Sunday, all: Bartov, op. cit., p.342.
174 Troublemaker: "Send planes!: Dan, *Sharon's Bridgehead*, pp.29-30
174 Sharon had another: Insight Team, *The Yom Kippur War*, pp.10-2.
174 Then he reported: Ben-Porat et al, *Kippur*, p.86.
174 The battalion radio: Ibid., p.86.
174 Chief of Staff: Shazly, *The Crossing of the Suez*, p.238.
176 Journalist Mohamed Heikal: Heikal, *The Road to Ramadan*, p.213-4.
176 Sadat and Heikal: Ibid., p.214.
177 "Cancel the crossing: Bartov, op. cit., p.345.
177 "Plan for the: Ibid., p.346.

177 "My impression was: Adan, *On the Banks of the Suez*, pp.113-4.
177 In a telephone: Bartov, op. cit., p.347-8.
178 General Adan had: Adan, op. cit., pp.98 and 118-9.
178 Dan added: "And: Dan, op. cit., p.63.
178 Indeed, several of: Herzog, *The War of Atonement*, p.185.
178 "There are some: Adan, op. cit., p.123.
179 Ben-Ari was a veteran: Adan, op. cit., p.123.
179 "No! I have: Ibid., pp.124-5.
179 "Fire the battalion: Ibid., p.126.
179 "The situation was: Ibid., p.126.
180 "You are arguing: Ibid., pp.126-7.
180 By noon, Adan's: Herzog, op. cit., pp.185-8.
180 Before the unit: Adan, op. cit., p.136.
180 "What's happening with: Ibid., p.137.
180 The misunderstanding apparently: Dupuy, in his excellent *Elusive Victory*, incorrectly refers to Nir as Baram. When I questioned him about this, he replied: "All that I can be sure of is that the name that most people use when referring to this officer is Natke. I thought that his real last name was Baram. More than that I cannot say."
181 "What I don't: Adan, op. cit., p.138.
181 "As soon as: Herzog, op. cit., p.189.
181 The battalion commander: Adan, op. cit., p.140.
181 "If you continue: Herzog, op. cit., p.189.
181 Only nine of: Adan, op. cit., p.140.
182 Gonen only realized: Bartov, op. cit., p.360.
182 At the same: Adan, op. cit., pp.141-2.
182 "...I knew I: Ibid., p.143.
183 "At about 1700: Ibid., p.144.
183 Between 5 and: Ibid., pp.144-5.
183 "At that time: Dupuy, op. cit., p.432.
184 "With no little: Adan, op. cit., pp.147-8.
184 "We realized we: Ibid., p.152.
184 Of the 183: Ibid., pp.152-3.
184 It had been: Dupuy, op. cit., pp.433 and 434-5.
185 Twenty-five Golani: Bartov, op. cit., p.360.
185 The Israelis now: O'Ballance, *No Victor, No Vanquished*, p.138.
185 The Syrian 1st Armored: Herzog, op. cit., p.122.
187 In the north: Ibid., p.108.
187 Now, as he: Dupuy, op. cit., p.457.
187 False optimism continued: Bartov, op. cit., pp.358-9.
188 "We must take: Ibid., pp.360-1.
188 "You can hardly: Ibid., p.363.
188 Monday night, in: Insight Team, op. cit., p.191.
188 When he returned: Bartov, op. cit., p.367.
188 "This morning, our: Kissinger, *Years of Upheaval*, p.490.
189 Dinitz even went: Kissinger, , p. 490.
189 Kissinger was somewhat: Ibid., p.489.
189 Confident that Israel: Ibid., pp.490-1.

CHAPTER XIX: October 9—Reality Emerges

190 "The ninth of: Bartov, *Dado*, p.378.
191 Elazar officially gave: Ibid., p.372.
191 For the moment: Adan, *On the Banks of the Suez*, p.172.
191 During the dark: Herzog, *The War of Atonement*, pp.193-4.
191 "While we fought: Ben-Porat et al, *Kippur*, p.87.
192 Dayan's mood was: Dayan, Yael. *My Father, His Daughter*. New York: Farrar, Straus & Giroux, 1985; pp.213-4.
192 Then Dayan dropped: Bartov, op. cit., pp.373 and 399.
192 "I don't want: Ibid., pp.375-6.
192 He explained his: Dayan, *Story of My Life*, pp.500-01.
192 When this panicky: Kissinger, *Years of Upheaval*, p.493.
193 Despite the loss: Dupuy, *Elusive Victory*, p.458.
193 Dust, smoke and: Herzog, op. cit., p.111.
193 "For God's sake: Ibid., p.112.
193 By now, Ben-Gal: Bartov, op. cit., p.393; Herzog, op. cit., p.113, says there were only seven tanks left but Bartov's figures are generally more reliable.
194 "You have saved: Herzog, op. cit., p.113.
194 On the battlefield: Dupuy, op. cit., p.459.
194 "Listen, Haka, if: Bartov, op. cit., p.379.
194 Elazar's renewed optimism: Facts on File 1973, Vol. XXXIII, p.835.
195 "Things are going: Bartov, op. cit., p.383.
195 But things, as: It was on this same lake 28 years earlier that President Roosevelt met with King Abdul Aziz ibn Saud of Saudi Arabia aboard the USS Quincy and promised him that the US would do nothing to harm the Arab cause in Palestine. In a written commitment of that policy, Roosevelt wrote Saud on April 5, 1945: "Your Majesty will...doubtless recall that during our recent conversation I assure that I would take no action...which might prove hostile to the Arab people. It gives me pleasure to renew to your Majesty the assurances which you have received regarding the attitude of my Government and my own, as Chief Executive, with regard to the question of Palestine and to inform you that the policy of the Government in this respect is unchanged."
195 "I have my: Dupuy, op. cit., p.475.
195 Meanwhile, to create: Bartov, op. cit., p.386. Bartov later, p.401, says the true figure was 23. But Dupuy, op. cit., p.475, says Gonen told him the figure was 36.
195 A visitor to: Dan, *Sharon's Bridgehead*, p.76.
196 "Get him out: Bartov, op. cit., p.385.
196 Gonen urged that: Herzog, op. cit., p.194.
196 Sharon was widely: Y. Dayan, op. cit., p.215.
196 Already his division: Dan, op. cit., p.40.
196 "We're not talking: Bartov, op. cit., p.395.
197 "In this war: Herzog, op. cit., p.198.
197 Moshe Dayan held: Ibid., p.196; Bartov, op. cit., pp.390-1.
197 "The enemy has: Shazly, *The Crossing of the Suez*, p.240.
197 The Soviet Union: Sadat, *In Search of Identity*, p.253.
197 Later that night: Heikal, *The Road to Ramadan*, pp.218-20.
198 "As I told: Ibid., p.120.
198 Word that all: Meir, *My Life*, p.430.
198 Kissinger was puzzled: Kissinger, op. cit., p.491.
198 "So that's why: Ibid., p.492.
198 Suddenly, he was: Ibid., p.493.

199   It was obvious: Sheehan, *The Arabs, Israelis, and Kissinger*, p.69.
199   For the moment: Kissinger, op. cit., p.496.
199   But unlike Kissinger: Ibid., p.493.
199   He conferred with: Ibid., p.496. Kalb and Kalb, *Kissinger*, p.467.
199   When this generous: Bartov, op. cit., p.403.
199   By then, it: Ibid., p.399.
200   To be sure: Kalb and Kalb, op. cit., p.467.
200   But by this: Kissinger, op. cit., p.493.

CHAPTER XX: October 10—A Time of Decision

PAGE
201   By midday Wednesday: Herzog, *The War of Atonement*, p.127.
201   Despite such losses: Dayan, *Story of My Life*, p.518.
202   Then there was: Bartov, *Dado*, p.406.
202   U.S. intelligence: Kalb and Kalb, *Kissinger*, p. 468-70
202   (To hinder their: Bartov, op. cit., p.406.
202   In Northern Commander: Ibid., pp.404 and 414; Asher, *The Duel for the Golan*, p.254.
203   Elazar ordered the: Bartov, op. cit., pp.404 and 407.
203   The fighters in: Adan, *On the Banks of the Suez*, pp.193 and 196.
203   Although the Israelis: Ibid., p.200.
203   Thousands of Egyptian: Ibid., pp.206-13. Israel had only 500 M-113 Zelda APCs; however it had 3,500 half-track vehicles, less effective than the M-113 but eventually valuable in the battle. See Dupuy, p.608.
203   Adan disagreed, pointing: Adan, op. cit., pp.206-13.
204   That evening Bar-Lev: Ibid., p.217.
204   As Adan left: Ibid., p.219.
204   "The decisiveness of: Shazly, *The Crossing of the Suez*, p.241.
204   "You know," Ismail: Heikal, *The Road to Ramadan*, p.220.
205   "The war should: Dayan, op. cit., p.519.
205   "And if we can't: Bartov, op. cit., p.406.
205   "We find ourselves: Ibid., pp.408-10.
206   "[The Syrians] would: Dayan, op. cit., p.516.
206   "If it is within: Bartov, op. cit., p.414.
206   Henry Kissinger heard: Kissinger, *Years of Upheaval*, pp.498-9, and 501, Kalb and Kalb, op. cit., p.469.
207   It was this news: Bartov, op. cit., p.414.
207   Kissinger also decided: Kissinger, op. cit., p.501.
207   Despite his busy: Kalb and Kalb, op. cit., pp.470-1.
207   Throughout the day: Kissinger, op. cit., p.503.

CHAPTER XXI: October 11-13—Attack in Syria

PAGE
208   For the first time: Bartov, *Dado*, p.425.
208   The expectation was: O'Ballance, *No Victor, No Vanquished*, p.195.
208   He was told: Ibid., p.195.
209   Israeli leaders were: Dayan, *Story of My Life*, p.521.

209   The Israeli attack: Dupuy, *Elusive Victory*, p.463.

209   The Israeli plan: Bartov, op. cit., p.421.

209   The capture of Damascus: Dayan, op. cit., p.520.

209   General Eytan's 7th: There is some confusion whether Colonel Hilawi was killed in this battle or was later executed for cowardice. Herzog, *The War of Atonement*, p.312, claims he was executed. O'Ballance, op. cit., p.191, who in general appears less reliable than other historians of the war, reports that the Syrians "emphatically denied" the Herzog version. Dupuy, op. cit., a far more sophisticated commentator, says, p.464, rather than being executed the Druze commander was killed in action and posthumously promoted. He notes that Syrian officials believed Herzog's story was fabricated in an effort to alienate Syria's Druze community, an altogether believable suspicion since Herzog's book is heavily propagandistic. Such are the subtle traps for the unwary researcher. Whatever the fate of Hilawi, one thing that seems certain is the 68th did break because even El-Edroos, no Israeli supporter, refers to it in his *The Hashemite Arab Army 1908-1979*, p.517.

210   But then the Israelis: Herzog, op. cit., p.134.

210   "I knew it: Heikal, *The Road to Ramadan*, p.222.

211   Next came word: Lacey, *The Kingdom*, p.404.

211   Reported Heikal: "The atmosphere: Heikal, op. cit., pp.221-3.

211   "What a strange: Shazly, *The Crossing of the Suez*, p.238. Shazly says this visit occurred Monday, 10/8, but the reader must assume he was indulging in a bit of dramatic license since the fort did not fall until Tuesday.

211   After inspecting Egypt's: Ibid., p.243.

212   At the Israeli: Adan, *On both Banks of the Suez*, p.227.

212   In the afternoon: Ibid., pp.226 7.

212   Henry Kissinger was: Facts on File 1973, Vol. XXXIII, p.835.

212   The public boast: Kissinger, *Years of Upheaval*, p.504.

212   Israel's demands for: There is no reason to doubt Kissinger's protestations or his version of events. At first, he and nearly everyone else believed, and were encouraged to believe by Israeli reports, that the war would not last long. Therefore, before a resupply operation could get underway the war would be over and the supplies unneeded. A prime reason that this view prevailed was the fact that the US had no independent surveillance of the battlefield at the time, as the hearings of the 1976 Pike report of the House Select Committee on Intelligence showed. Second, it was suspected by most members of the administration, including Kissinger for a time, that Israel was using the war as way to gouge more supplies out of America. This was not an unworthy thought, as various remarks by Israeli military men indicate that there was no real shortage of any military items. For instance, Bartov, p.423, reports one general exulting: "The end of war will see the IDF in better shape than it's ever been," adding that it will be "gorged with ammunition." Behind this suspicion also lurked the logical thought that Israel had got itself into its difficult position by its stubborn policies and it could get out by itself. It was not a US matter. As important as all these aspects was the warning by Saudi Arabia not to openly resupply and thereby exert pressure for an Arab oil boycott. Despite all these cogent reasons not to resupply, the fact is that the US did immediately release a number of valuable weapons for carriage on Israeli planes and, when it became obvious that they could not carry the load, it then tried to hire charter planes to do the work. Kissinger appears fully justified in writing, p.496, that the charge was a "canard." On a darker level, what it appears to have really been was a clever ruse to accomplish exactly what many in the administration suspected and what it eventually did: bounteous US supplies far beyond Israel's needs or losses or America's duty to provide.

213   Senator Henry Jackson: Ibid., p.504.

213   The aggressive Israeli: Kalb and Kalb, *Kissinger*, p.472.
213   Later that night: Kissinger, op.cit., p.506.
213   Though the Israelis: Dupuy. op. cit., p.485.
214   The best strategy: O'Ballance, op. cit., p.147.
214   Chief of Staff Shazly: Shazly, op. cit., p.246. A number of writers, Dupuy, O'Ballance
       and Herzog in particular, claimed that it was actually Shazly who was the one who
       recklessly wanted to take the attack beyond the missile screen. But their books were written
       before Shazly published his memoirs in 1980, in which he made a very vigorous, and
       convincing, denial. It is certainly true that he detested Ismail and probably thought him
       to be too cautious, which he probably was. But both men agreed that the Egyptian defense
       should be "the rocks upon which the Israeli waves would be shattered." That did not
       imply an Egyptian thrust forward, nor did it suggest a basic dispute over strategy. In
       addition it is inconceivable that a commander of Shazly's experience, however great his
       egoism, could have failed to see the complete vulnerability of Egypt's troops once they
       moved beyond their missile protection and exposed themselves to Israel's air force. That
       it was a political decision made by Sadat to accommodate the Syrians and probably also
       the Saudis—who had warned him not to stop fighting too soon—seems unavoidable.
214   To accomplish the: Ibid., p.247. Sadat does not mention the decision or the 10/14 attack
       in his memoirs.
214   During his tours: Dayan, op. cit., p.521.
215   Northern commander Hofi: O'Ballance, op. cit., p.192.
215   Ben-Gal moved: Herzog, op. cit., p.133.
215   Ben-Gal decided: Ibid., p.133. Israel finally did take the village 11/13 with an attack by
       a parachute brigade, which suffered almost no casualties.
215   While Ben-Gal was: Ibid., p.137.
216   They were from: O'Ballance, op. cit., pp.195 and 202.
216   Although major battles: Bartov, op. cit., p.466; Dupuy, op. cit., p.532.
216   The Israeli advance: O'Ballance, op. cit., p.218; Dupuy, op. cit., p.537.
217   In a meeting: Bartov, op. cit., p.436-7.
217   Egypt was obviously: Ibid, p.441; Herzog, op. cit., p.202.
217   Arik Sharon was: Dan, *Sharon's Bridgehead*, p.93.
218   "What's happened, he's: Yael Dayan later discussed with brutal candor in her memoir (*My
       Father, His Daughter*) her father's philandering and other character flaws.
218   Richard Nixon was: Kissinger, op. cit., p.509. This is at odds with Bartov's claim, p.444,
       that the Israeli cabinet only took this decision at the end of 10/12. The discrepancy is
       probably explainable by Golda Meir's habit of making decisions on her own and then
       getting cabinet approval.
218   "...Israel would prefer: Kissinger, op. cit., p.509.
218   At his first news: Ibid., p.508.
218   Afterwards, Kissinger had: Ibid., p.508.
219   Kissinger's response was: Ibid., p.510-1.
219   Dinitz's session with: Bartov, op. cit., p.399.
220   The Kalb brothers: Kalb and Kalb, op. cit., p.475.
220   Despite this implied: Kissinger, op. cit., p.515.
220   That same day: Washington Post, 10/11/73.
220   Amid all the frantic: Lacey, op. cit., p.408.
220   Kissinger met with: Kissinger, op.cit., p.514.
221   At a meeting: Kissinger, op. cit., p. 514. Aviation Week and Space Technology, 12/10/73,
       pp.16-9, reports approximately 11,000 tons of supplies were airlifted to Israel between
       10/14 and 10/25; in the same period 40 F-4s, 36 A-4s and 12 C-130s were flown there
       and turned over to Israel. By the time the airlift ended on 11/15, a total of 22,300 tons

NOTES

had been airlifted in 421 sorties by C-141s and 147 by C-5s.
221 No European nation: Insight Team, *The Yom Kippur War*, p.284.
221 As a symbol: *The Pike report on the hearings of the House Select Committee on Intelligence*, published 2/16/76 in the Village Voice. There has been much speculation that photographs from this flight revealed the "seam" between the Egyptian Second and Third armies, thus allowing Israel to plan its crossing of the canal at that point. Actually, the seam had been discovered by Sharon's troops on 10/9, and the decision to cross at that point was taken as early as 10/11, according to Adan, p.227. In addition, intelligence sources claim that at the time there was a long lag-time between taking the photos and processing them—as much as 24 hours—therefore making it unlikely the photos played any pivotal role in Israel's decision. In fact, as the Pike report claimed, US reconnaissance apparently was so poor during the war that it had little influence.
221 At 3:30 PM, Scowcroft: Kalb and Kalb, op. cit., p.478.
222 Yamani did not: Lacey, op. cit., pp.402-5.
222 "I haven't agreed: Sadat, *In Search of Identity*, p.257-8.
223 "To go home: Ben-Porat et al, *Kippur*, pp.96-7.
223 With the International: Herzog, op. cit., p.176-9.
223 Chief of Staff Elazar: Ibid., p.203-4.
224 Gonen, stricken by: Ben-Porat, op. cit., p.202.
224 Elazar immediately promoted: Bartov, op. cit., p.453.
224 When he returned: Ibid., p.457.
224 The Iraqi division: Herzog, op. cit., p.138.
225 Meanwhile, the latest: Bartov, op. cit., p.458.

CHAPTER XXII: October—Egypt Gambles
PAGE
226 Chief of Staff Elazar: Bartov, *Dado*, pp.459.
226 Despite the bloodying. Ibid., pp.459 and 466.
227 During the past two: Ibid., pp.465-6; Shazly, *The Crossing of the Suez*, pp.244-5.
227 Whatever the precise: Bartov, op. cit., p.466.
227 The Egyptian plan: Shazly, op. cit., p.248.
227 As the Egyptian: O'Ballance, *No Victor, No Vanquished*, pp.160-2.
228 The attack in the: Dupuy, *Elusive Victory*, p.486.
228 The two brigades: Adan, *On the Banks of the Suez*, pp.238-9.
228 "Anyone who visualized: Dan, *Sharon's Bridgehead*, p.129.
228 Bar-Lev told Elazar: Bartov, op. cit., p.467.
228 In the south Adan, op. cit., p.238.
228 By noon, the worse: Shazly, op. cit., p.248.
228 The most they: O'Ballance, op. cit., p.165.
228 At the height: Shazly, op. cit., p.249, says he suffered a "breakdown." Others, including Dupuy, p.487, say he had a heart attack. Whatever the ailment, it occurred in the first hours of the attack and no doubt contributed to the Egyptian debacle.
229 "As news had come: Shazly, op. cit., p.249.
229 At the end: Ibid., p.248.
229 Israel claimed it: Adan, op. cit., p.241.
229 Shazly's estimate of: Shazly, op. cit., p.248.
229 One reason explaining: Dupuy, op. cit., p.488.
229 That night Bar-Lev: Meir, *My Life*, p.432.
230 The Egyptians' position: Bartov, op. cit., p.471.

230 At the end: Ibid., p.471.
231 "The airlift was: Meir, op. cit., p.431.
231 When Kissinger went: Kissinger, *Years of Upheaval*, p.515.
231 "I assured him: Nixon, *The Memoirs of Richard Nixon*, p.927.
231 Kissinger, who now: Kissinger, op. cit., p.518 and 531.
231 Despite such strutting: Ibid., p.528.

CHAPTER XXIII: October 15-17—Battle for the Chinese Farm
PAGE
232 The Israeli plan: Dan, *Sharon's Bridgehead*, p.146.
233 Sharon's mission was: Adan, *On the Banks of the Suez*, p.255.
233 The time schedule: Bartov, *Dado*, p.477.
233 Then Sharon, with: Adan, op. cit., p.253.
233 Southern Command optimistically: Bartov, op. cit., p.477.
233 Tuesday would be: Adan, op. cit., p.254.
234 The attack got off: Dupuy, *Elusive Victory*, p.497.
234 There was no opposition: Dan, *Sharons Bridgehead*, p.154.
234 The combat became: Adan, op. cit., p.266.
234 An attempt by: Dupuy, op. cit., p.499.
234 Repeated attacks to open: Adan, op. cit., p.269.
234 But still, the Egyptians: Dan, op. cit., p.154.
235 "I'm the man: Herzog, *The War of Atonement*, p.218.
235 But there was another: Ibid., p.218.
235 Then the timing: Ibid., p.218.
235 It was the only: Ibid., p.218.
235 It took the brigade: Ibid., p.218.
235 By this time: Bartov, op. cit., p.481; Dupuy, op. cit., pp.498-9; Adan, op. cit., p.336.
236 "Acapulco!" Matt radioed: Adan, op. cit., p.267.
236 "Everything is all: Ben-Porat et al, *Kippur*, p.190.
236 Israel had two: Adan, op. cit., pp.245-7; Bartov, op. cit., p.476.
236 The self-propelled: Bartov, op. cit., p.482-3.
236 "The Egyptians didn't: Ibid., pp.484-5.
237 "...I suddenly saw: Adan, op. cit., p.276.
238 Israel's losses were: Bartov, op. cit., p.485.
238 Arik Sharon repeatedly: Dan, op. cit., p.166.
238 Instead of sending: Bartov, op. cit. p.487; Herzog, op. cit., p.224.
238 The order infuriated: Dupuy, op. cit., p.503.
238 "There was an absence: Dayan, *Story of My Life*, 529.
239 "I do not know: Ibid., p.524.
239 After being ordered: Dan, op. cit., p.167.
239 This was, as: Adan, op. cit., p.280.
240 Golda Meir made: Facts on File 1973, Vol. XXXIII, p.860.
240 Then, to the consternation: Bartov, op. cit., p.489.
240 Now any hope: Ibid., pp.492-3.
240 Shortly after Golda: Dayan, op. cit., p.526.
241 A precious advantage: Dan, op. cit., p.194. Adan, op. cit., p.296, writes, without mentioning Meir's speech, that by the morning of 10/17 the "Egyptians had in the meantime pinpointed the crossing site and were bombarding it fiercely." Bartov, p.497, also notes, without mentioning Meir, that the heavy Egyptian bombardment began shortly after 7

NOTES

AM on 10/17. It seems clear that Meir's boast was a costly one on the battlefield, a sacrifice she perhaps thought necessary to bolster Israeli morale.

241   "I am not prepared: Sadat, *In Search of Identity*, p.258.

241   The OPEC producers: Lacey, *The Kingdom*, p.406.

242   As he confessed: Adan, op. cit., p.286.

242   Fire was so heavy: Herzog, op. cit., p.225.

242   Adan finally had: Adan, op. cit., pp.292-4.

243   All told, about: Dupuy, op. cit., p.508.

243   "What you people: Herzog, op. cit., p.230.

243   "I am no novice: Dayan, op. cit., p.532.

243   Meanwhile, under the: Adan, op. cit., p.291.

243   This was the opening: Shazly, *The Crossing of the Suez*, pp.259-60.

243   In a sharp clash: Adan, op. cit., pp.296-7.

244   I don't accept: Bartov, op. cit., p.500.

244   He was furious: Dan, op. cit., p.202.

244   "What can I: Bartov, op. cit., p.500.

244   Sharon said sarcastically: Dan, op. cit., p.202.

244   "I have decided: Adan, op. cit., p.299.

244   At that point Adan: Shazly, op. cit., p.257.

245   By the time: Adan, op. cit., p.303.

245   "He's worth gold: Bartov, op. cit., p.502.

245   "It's good that: Ibid., p.503.

246   "The option you: Adan, op. cit., pp.305-6.

246   Adan was extremely: Ibid., pp.305-7.

246   As Elazar prepared: Bartov, op. cit., p.504.

247   A delegation of: Kissinger, *Years of Upheaval*, p.535.

247   "Some of you: Heikal, *The Road to Ramadan*, p.233.

247   Kissinger noted in his: Kissinger, op. cit., p.535.

247   In his memoirs: Ibid., pp.534 and 536.

247   "I complacently observed. Ibid., p.536.

CHAPTER XXIV: October 18—Israel in Africa

PAGE

248   "The great moment: Adan, *On the Banks of the Suez*, p.310.

249   "If we can capture: Bartov, *Dado*, p.507.

249   By 5:15, Thursday: Ibid., pp.312-3.

250   As a result: Dupuy, *Elusive Victory*, p.514.

250   In addition, by now: Shazly, *The Crossing of the Suez*, pp.260-2.

250   "Every time a: Adan, op. cit., p.325.

251   One SAM base: Ibid., p.320.

251   The raids against: Ibid., pp.318-20.

251   The Israeli general: Bartov., op. cit., pp.515 and 522.

252   Meanwhile, Sharon's forces: Herzog, *The War of Atonement*, p.240.

252   Other elements of Sharon's: Ibid., p.139.

252   Elazar estimated that: Bartov, op. cit., pp.510 and 515. Since most of the major battles had been fought by this time and Israel's ultimate losses were 2,838 killed and 8,528 wounded, it seems this is a case of delayed reporting or perhaps a deliberate effort to hide while the war continued the true dimensions of Israel's losses.

341

253 "I'm sorry to: Sadat, *In Search of Identity*, p.259. It was during this Thursday meeting that Heikal, *The Road to Ramadan*, reported, p.235, Kosygin was probably able to show Sadat satellite photographs to prove how substantial the Israeli bridgehead really was. This is a claim that a number of writers have repeated. However, since Adan had crossed only that morning it was highly unlikely that there would have been time to retrieve a satellite photograph and get it to Cairo on the same day, according to high U.S. intelligence officials. Moreover, Sadat went out of his way to deny this claim in his memoirs, p.260, not always a dependable source, but by this time it could hardly have escaped any Egyptian official that there was now a major Israeli force on the west bank since numerous Egyptian units had been involved in fierce combat with them all day long.

253 To that end: Shazly, op. cit., pp.263-4.

253 "If we vetoed: Kissinger, *Years of Upheaval*, p.541.

253 "If the United States: Ibid., p.538.

254 Despite the Soviet: Ibid., pp.538-41.

CHAPTER XXV: October 19-21—Oil Embargo

PAGE

255 Never had the Arab: Nyrop, Richard F. et al, *Area Handbook for Persian Gulf States*, Washington, DC: American University, 1977, pp.77-83.

256 Since time is: Kissinger, *Years of Upheaval*, p.542.

256 This Soviet gambit: Ibid., p.542.

256 Before he left: Ibid., pp.542-3.

257 That same Friday: Nixon, *The Memoirs of Richard Nixon*, p.931.

257 King Faisal was: Lacey, *The Kingdom*, p.412.

257 Muammar Qadhafi was: Facts on File 1973, Vol. XXXIII, p.880.

258 By dawn Friday: Adan, *On the Banks of the Suez*, pp.326-8.

258 This was the moment: Ibid., p.347.

258 "Sudden fear—what: Ibid., pp.348-50

259 By the end: Ibid., pp.350; Bartov, *Dado*, p.523.

259 Sharon's division ran: Herzog, *The War of Atonement*, pp.240-1.

259 Despite this hard: Bartov, op. cit., p.520.

259 "I have fought: Ben-Porat et al, *Kippur*, p.245; compare with the paraphrase in Bartov, p.521.

259 This was a sentiment: Adan, op. cit., p.258.

259 Elazar was moved: Bartov, op. cit., p.521.

259 He later remarked: Ibid., pp.523-4.

259 In addition, Defense: Dayan, *Story of My Life*, p.533.

260 "I won't have: Sadat, *In Search of Identity*, p.259.

260 Sadat had another: Ibid, pp.262-3; Shazly, *The Crossing of the Suez*, pp.266-7. Shazly claims, p.296, that he was not fired until December 12. Obviously, the two versions are radically different in recalling events of that night. Mohamed Heikal, the usual source of endless inside information, is silent on the issue of Shazly's firing.

260 At 9 PM local: Lacey, op. cit., p.413; State Department Middle East Task Force, Situation report -51, 10/21/73, secret; declassified 12/31/81.

261 "To put it: Heikal, *The Road to Ramadan*, p.239.

261 When Ambassador Vinogradov: Sadat, op. cit., pp.263-4.

261 "'Full authority': Kissinger, op. cit., p.547.

262 The Israelis and: Ibid., p.551.

NOTES

262 "U.S. political: Ibid., pp.550-1.
262 Kissinger called this: Ibid., p.550.
262 His response was: Nixon does not mention in his memoirs the message, Kissinger's insubordination or the lost opportunity.
262 The Egyptians were: Adan, op. cit., p.355.
263 This arc of Egyptian: Dan, *Sharon's Bridgehead*, p.203.
263 Adan's forces continued: Dupuy, *Elusive Victory*, p.523.
263 He also tried: Adan, op. cit., p.359.
263 Nonetheless, his forces: Ibid., p.360.
263 Sharon's troops on: Dupuy, op. cit., p.528.
264 The gains by Adan: Bartov, op. cit., p.531.
264 In the morning: Adan, op. cit., p.373.
264 When a short: Bartov, op. cit., p.537.
264 Sharon agreed to attack: Adan, op. cit., p.374.
265 Gonen ordered Sharon: Ibid., p.376.
265 During the day's: Bartov, op. cit., p.538.
265 Things had not gone. Adan, op. cit., p.377.
265 Kissinger found the: Kissinger, op. cit., p.554.
266 To make sure: Department of State, Flash Top Secret Moscow Telegram #13139 strictly Eyes Only Scali from Kissinger, 10/21/73.
266 He then drafted: Kissinger, op. cit., pp.554-5.
266 Washington had flashed: Bartov, op. cit., p.540.
266 The best Israel: Insight Team, *The Yom Kippur War*, p.380, claims that Meir made her demand directly to Nixon in a telephone call Sunday night in Washington. Neither Nixon nor Kissinger mentions such a call.
267 "Delicately, Golda had: Kissinger, op. cit., p.559.
267 If there remained: Heikal, op. cit., pp.248-9.

CHAPTER XXVI: October 22-23—Ceasefire

PAGE
268 After only two hours: Text of Resolution 338:

"The Security Council:

1. Calls upon all parties to the present fighting to cease all firing and terminate all military activity immediately, no later than 12 hours after the moment of adoption of this decision, in the positions they now occupy;
2. Calls upon the parties concerned to start immediately after the ceasefire the implementation of Security Council Resolution 242 in all of its parts;
3. Decides that, immediately and concurrently with the ceasefire, negotiations will start between the parties concerned under appropriate auspices aimed at establishing a just and durable peace in the Middle East.''
The resolution passed with a vote of 14-0; China abstained because the resolution did not condemn Israel. Although the actual passage time was 12:52, the council rounded it off to 12:50 as the time for implementation.
269 As the cabinet: Bartov, *Dado*, pp.544-5.
269 Almost immediately, coordination: Ibid., p.546.
270 Fighting was fierce: Asher, *The Duel for the Golan*, p.269.

343

CHAPTER XXVII: October 24-25—Nuclear Alert

NOTES

282 At a WSAG meeting: Department of State Operations Center, Situation Report, 0600 EDT, 10/26/73; secret/exdis, declassified 4/3/85; Kalb and Kalb, *Kissinger*, p.488.

282 "We were determined: Kissinger, op. cit., pp.579-80.

283 But before the: Ibid., pp.581-2. An indication of just how far removed from the crisis Nixon was by now comes in his memoirs, p.938, when he reports a Brezhnev charge of Israeli fighting on 10/24 and asserts that "we knew that this was not true; it had been a relatively quiet day on the battlefront." This was the day of Israel's greatest gains on the west bank.

284 There now followed: Facts on File 1973, Vol. XXXIII, p.878.

284 "Mr. President" and concluding: Kissinger, op. cit., pp.583-4. Dobrynin later claimed Kissinger had misunderstood "adhere" in the first sentence; it actually should have been "act here." Kissinger contends that the Dobrynin version does not change the meaning of the sentence. But it certainly does change its tone, since a command to "adhere" sounds more peremptory and therefore more threatening—and may have influenced Kissinger's sense of threat in the tense atmosphere. In fact, the other sentence quoted by Kissinger from the Brezhnev message did not sound threatening at all: "Let us together, the USSR and the United States, urgently dispatch to Egypt the Soviet and American military contingents, to insure the implementation of the decision of the Security Council of October 22 and 23 concerning the cessation of fire and of all military activities and also of our understanding with you on the guarantee of the implementation of the decisions of the Security Council."

284 Kissinger's reaction was: Ibid., p.585.

285 When the senior: Kalb and Kalb, *Kissinger*, p.491.

285 They expected that: Kissinger, op. cit., p.587.

285 Kissinger and his: Reports at the time of a Soviet ship carrying nuclear warheads to Egypt did not play any part in the declaration of the alert. These reports first emerged 10/25, after the alert was ordered. Neither Kissinger nor Nixon mentions the reports in his memoirs and the reports were likely false. A Rand Corporation study of the issue concluded that "there is no reliable evidence that nuclear weapons ever entered Egypt"; see letter from Shmuel Meir of the Tel Aviv Jaffee Center for Strategic Studies in The International Herald Tribune, 8/19/85.

285 They also took: Kissinger, op. cit., pp.587-8 and 591.

285 Dobrynin was once: Nixon, *The Memoirs of Richard Nixon*, p.938.

287 It was decided: Kissinger, op. cit., p.593.

287 At 5:40 AM: Nixon, op. cit., pp.939-40.

287 Kissinger awoke after: Kissinger, op. cit., p.591.

289 In addition, despite; Even the existence of Brezhnev's message and its contents, a very closely held secret, were known by Senator Henry M. Jackson. Although no direct evidence exists to this day, these leaks could have been made by Ambassador Dinitz, who had been kept closely apprised during the evening and early morning by Kissinger of the details of the crisis, including Brezhnev's letter. Kissinger repeatedly talked with Dinitz during this night and morning, even to the point of leaving a WSAG meeting so he could brief the Israeli envoy; see Kissinger's memoirs, volume two, 582-90. Dinitz was the only one of the insiders who was not completely absorbed with handling the crisis and had the time and opportunity—and the motive—to pass the word not only onto Israel, which was his duty, but to others as well. The leak could have come from Israel, but it seems unlikely since Kissinger indicates (p.591) the leak came as early as three hours after the alert, i.e., before 3 AM, which even for the Middle East would be an unusually swift time for the leak to spread from Israel back to Washington. Also, at 3 AM all the American participants were still working on the response to Brezhnev and would have barely have had time to talk with reporters. Thus circumstantial evidence makes Dinitz look like a fair suspect, if not a proven one. He knew Jackson well and Jackson was

known as Israel's best friend in the senate, where he invariably championed Israeli causes; his ties with Israel were extremely close. Only Israel would have profited by disclosure of the crisis, since the one thing it feared most was a superpower-imposed settlement. In this sense, any action it could take to worsen relations between Washington and Moscow were to its advantage, and leaking details of the crisis could certainly have achieved that end if the Kremlin had not maintained its restraint.

289 Good news began: Kissinger, op. cit., p.591.
289 In the afternoon: Ibid., p.598.
289 Resolution 440 was: Facts on File 1973, pp.878-9. Text of Resolution 440:

The Security Council,
Recalling its Resolutions 338 (1973) of 22 October, 1973, and 339 (1973) of 23 October, 1973,
Noting with regret the reported repeated violations of the ceasefire in noncompliance with Resolutions 338 (1973) and 339 (1973),
Noting with concern from the secretary General's report that the United Nations military observers have not yet been enabled to place themselves on both sides of the ceasefire line,
1. Demands that immediate and complete ceasefire be observed and that the parties return to the positions occupied by them at 16:50 GMT on 22 October, 1973;
2. Requests the Secretary General, as an immediate step, to increase the number of United Nations military observers on both sides;
3. Decides to set up immediately under its auspices a United Nations emergency force to be composed of personnel drawn from states members of the United Nations except permanent members of the Security Council, and requests the Secretary General to report within 24 hours on the steps taken to this effect;
4. Requests the Secretary General to report to the Council on an urgent and continuing basis on the state of implementation of this resolution as well as Resolutions 338 (1973) and 339 (1973);
5. Requests all member states to extend their full cooperation to the United Nations in the implementation of this resolution as well as Resolutions 338 (1973) and 339 (1973).
289 Quite suddenly, the: Kissinger, op. cit., p.597.

CHAPTER XXVIII: Shuttle Diplomacy—1974-75
PAGE
291 After three days: Dayan made these remarks in a lecture at Bar Ilan University in Ramat Gam, Israel, 12/19/74. He had begun them by saying: "The Americans said no more nor less than this...." Maariv printed a transcript of the lecture eight days later, but, as I learned while serving in Israel, an alteration was made in the text. A colleague, Leslie Hazelton, took the time to listen to the tape and discovered the actual quote. She discovered it was at the government's request, and with Dayan's concurrence, that Maariv changed the quote to make it read less threatening: "...then we, the United States, will dissociate from you." The issue was written about from an Israeli view by Theodore Draper in The United States and Israel: Tilt in the Middle East, Commentary 59, no. 4, April/1975; also see exchange of letters in Commentary 60, no. 3, Sept/1975.
291 That kind of unusually: Kissinger, Years of Upheaval, p.611.
291 "[It] was not: Facts on File 1973, Vol. XXXIII, p.897.
291 "Then we would: Kissinger, op. cit., p.1057.
292 Kissinger thought he had: Ibid., p.615. Kissinger repeatedly refers to this theme; see for

346

instance pp.608 and 1138-9 in *White House Years.*

292 "...from that time onward: Ibid., pp.646 and 648.
292 ". . .from that time onward: Ibid., pp.646 and 648.
292 In talks in Cairo: Veteran ambassador Hermann F. Eilts took up his post in Cairo within days, on Nov. 11, 1973; Ashraf Ghorbal was named Egypt's ambassador to Washington.
292 From Egypt, Kissinger: Ibid., pp.656 and 665.
293 Kissinger's hidden plan: Ibid., p.747; also Quandt, *Decade of Decisions*, p.213.
293 By using the forum: When Kissinger appeared at the press room during one of the crises of Sinai II in 1975 at the King David Hotel in Jerusalem and found only the foreign press there, he demanded: "Where is *my* press corps?" By that he meant the small group of reporters who regularly covered him at the state department and whom he assiduously cultivated. He was careful, for instance, to mention all the reporters by name in his memoirs. How friendly he became with the corps is indicated by his routine endorsement of their later books. See for instance his favorable treatment of books by the Kalb brothers, by Ted Koppel and Richard Valeriani, among others.
294 Kissinger's progress in convening: Quandt, op. cit., pp.221-3.
294 "I could tell Golda: Kissinger, op. cit., pp.768-9.
294 In Damascus, Hafez Assad: Ibid., p.779.
294 Assad, Kissinger found: Ibid., p.779.
295 "In the Syrian context: Ibid., p.781.
295 At their first: Ibid., pp.784-5.
295 Kissinger's visit to Israel: Ibid., p.775.
295 "All our sympathy: Ibid., p.790.
295 Even though President: Ibid., p.759. Quandt, op. cit., p.222, says there were two presidential letters to Meir, but he appears to be confusing a separate note that was addressed to Kissinger on the same subject and relayed indirectly to Meir.
295 In particular, they refused: Golan, *The Secret Conversations of Henry Kissinger*, p.127.
296 After the spotlight: Kissinger, op. cit., p.833.
296 "You must take: Ibid., p.836.
296 In the end, it was: Shechan, *The Arabs, Israelis, and Kissinger*, p.112; also see Quandt, op. cit., p.228.
296 "I am deeply conscious: Kissinger, op. cit., p. 844.
297 Though the withdrawal: For text of the pact, see Sheehan, op. cit., Appendix Six.
297 "In October we had: Golan, op. cit., p.122.
297 The rub, of course: Kissinger, op. cit., p.1133.
297 Despite Israel's seeming: Facts on File 1974, Vol. XXXIV, p.337.
298 It was, for instance: Kissinger, op. cit., p.953.
298 With Israel, Kissinger's: Quandt, op. cit., p.235,
298 This became clear: Ibid., p.237.
298 Kissinger leaned on both: Ibid., p.239.
298 (On June 30, he: Ibid., p.249.
299 Under Kissinger's constant badgering: For text, see Kissinger, op. cit., pp. 1257-8.
299 The agreement won: Ibid., 1111.
299 No similar praise: The Meir government had been reelected on December 31, 1973, but with a reduced mandate, going from 56 seats in parliament to 54, while Menachem Begin's nationalist Likud gained strength, up to 39 seats from 32.
299 But this, Kissinger: Kissinger, op. cit., pp.1139-40.
300 "In my view: Ibid., p.803.
300 "...a President facing impeachment: Ibid., p.1140.
300 "I played for time: Ibid., p.1141.
300 Egypt was becoming: Golan, op. cit., p.229. In the interveiw, Rabin admitted, among other

things, that Israel was aiming to split Egypt from Syria and would try to delay negotiations until the the 1976 U.S. elections.

300 Similarly, Moscow by now: Quandt, op. cit., pp.261 and 263.
301 "I am disappointed: Sheehan, op. cit., p.159.
301 On Kissinger's return: Ibid., p.165.
302 Many of the men: Ibid., p.165; also see Quandt, op. cit., p.269.
302 All this made: Quandt, op. cit., p.270.
302 Once again, Israel: Sheehan, op. cit., p.178.
302 In a secret memorandum: Text of the MOU and its secret addenda are in Sheehan, op. cit., Appendix Eight.
303 For all this: Ibid., p.190.
303 As Shimon Peres: Ibid. p.192. At the time, Peres refused to be identified in the article but he was the source of the quote since I was Time's Jerusalem bureau chief in 1975 and he made the remark to one of my reporters.
304 "I have come: Text is in Quandt. *Camp David*, Appendix C.

EPILOGUE
PAGE
305 The costs to Egypt: Dupuy, *Elusive Victory*, p.609.
305 But it was only: Adan, *On the Banks of the Suez*, p.405.
306 While Israel paraded: Kissinger, *Years of Upheaval*, p.801.
306 On the Golan: O'Ballance, *No Victor, No Vanquished*, p.215.
306 As Yitzhak Rabin later: Viorst, *Sands of Sorrow*, p.170.
307 I did not: Kissinger, *White House Years*, pp. 1138-9.

Chronology

1967   Israel attacks Egypt, Jordan and Syria.

In lightening air strikes, Israel on June 5 wiped out the combined air forces of Egypt, Jordan and Syria. In six days, Israel's land forces swept over the Sinai Peninsula, the West Bank of Jordan and Syria's Golan Heights, capturing land equal to three times its original size of 8,000 square miles. In the process, 323,000 Palestinians were turned into new refugees, 113,000 of them for the second time since 1948, and nearly 1.3 million Palestinians were left under Israeli military occupation. As in 1956, the war again brought the superpowers close to a direct confrontation. After Israel broke the ceasefire to invade the Golan Heights on June 9, the Soviet Union the next day broke diplomatic relations with Israel and warned Washington that Moscow was ready to take military action if Israel did not stop fighting. By then Israel had captured the Golan Heights and it abided by the ceasefire. Arab resentment at U.S. support for Israel resulted in the breaking of diplomatic relations by Algeria, Egypt, Iraq, Mauritius, Syria and Yemen.

1967   USS Liberty attacked by Israel.

During the war, on June 8, Israeli warplanes and torpedo boats repeatedly attacked the U.S. intelligence ship, *Liberty*, off the Sinai coast, killing 34 men and wounding 162. The attack involved the use of napalm, rockets, machine guns and torpedoes. It had been preceded by reconnaissance by Israeli planes for at least five and a half hours, during a time when the ship was flying a new flag that flew freely in a light breeze. The Johnson Administration accepted Israel's claim that the assault resulted from misidentification.

1967   Passage of U.N. Security Council Resolution 242.

With private U.S. assurances that the terms of Resolution 242 meant an Israeli withdrawal to the June 4, 1967 lines with only "minor modifications" of the frontier, Jordan and Egypt accepted the November 22 resolution calling for an exchange of land for peace. However, Israel later refused to withdraw without prior concessions by the Arabs and the United States made little effort to enforce the resolution.

1968   Growth of the Palestinian Guerrillas.

After the 1967 war the Palestinian guerrilla groups began growing for the first time in significant numbers. The various competing guerrilla groups in 1968 formed themselves within the Palestine Liberation Organization into eight separate factions; the PLO had been formed in 1964 largely as a way for Egypt to control the Palestinians. On February 3, 1969, Yasser Arafat, the leader of Fatah, which had begun operations in 1965, was also elected chairman of the PLO. The first Palestinian hijacking of a civilian airliner came in July 23, 1968, when the PFLP, the Popular Front for the Liberation of Palestine which had been formed after the 1967 war, captured an Israeli EI-AL jet. All of the passengers and crew were eventually released unharmed, but what would become a deadly technique of terrorism had been inaugurated.

1968   The Bar-Lev Line.

Late in 1968 Egypt began massive artillery shellings of Israeli troops who were still occupying the east bank of the Suez Canal in Egypt's Sinai Peninsula. In response, Israel launched a major construction effort to build a line of heavily fortified positions the length of the canal. The implications of the major effort to construct what became known as the Bar-Lev Line were extremely grave for Gamal Abdel Nasser. From his view, it was a dramatic demonstration that Israel had no intention of returning the territory it had captured a year and a half earlier.

1969-70   The War of Attrition.

The military strategy adopted by Gamal Abdel Nasser to win back Arab lands was designed to take advantage of the few options Egypt had along the Suez Canal. It capitalized on Egypt's greatest strength, artillery and manpower, while at the same time concentrating on the weakest part of Israel's strategy, which was now anchored on the fixed positions of the Bar-Lev

350

Line forts. The goal of his strategy was twofold: Either to force the super-powers to pressure Israel into returning captured territory or to inflict so many casualties on Israel, which had always been extremely sensitive to combat losses, that it would be forced away from the canal. Egypt began daily artillery attacks against the Bar-Lev Line on March 8, 1969, opening the seventeen-month war. By July 7, Secretary-General U Thant declared that ''the level of violence in the Middle East has never been higher [since the 1967 war] than it is at present.'' The war escalated on January 7, 1970, when Israel began employing its new U.S.-made Phantom war-planes in a campaign of raids deep inside Egypt, including targets on the outskirts of Cairo. The Soviet Union responded by making an unprecendented commitment to protect Egypt's skies. In all, it sent to Egypt two Soviet air force brigades and an air defense division. A ceasefire finally went into effect at 1 AM Cairo time, August 8, 1970. Israel admitted to more than 1,100 casualties, including over 400 deaths; Egypt lost as many as 5,000 killed during the war.

1970   Black September.

Growth of the Palestinian guerrillas in Jordan became so great after 1967 that the guerrillas openly began to challenge the authority of King Hussein. By 1970, repeated clashes were occurring between the Palestinians and royal troops. Finally, on September 17, open warfare broke out. Jordanian armor and troops entered Amman and fierce fighting raged in the capital and the northern strongholds of the guerrillas. On September 19, Syrian tanks entered northern Jordan on side of the guerrillas. The United States responded by urging Israel to go to the aid of Hussein, but before Israel could act royal troops gained the upperhand and the crisis was defused. However, the incident convinced the Nixon Administration that Israel was a strategic ally that could forward U.S. interests in the region.

1972   Egypt expels the Soviets.

Impatient with Russia's stalling on arms aid and resentful at what he took to be the Soviet leadership's cool treatment of him, Egyptian President Anwar Sadat expelled Russia's 15,000 military experts. Sadat announced the expulsion publicly on July 18, 1972 and it was confirmed the next day by Moscow. Although Sadat had calculated that the expulsion would attract interest in Washington, the Nixon Administration chose to continue to ignore Egypt's efforts to get back its territory from Israel. After this,

Sadat decided to go to war with Israel to regain Egyptian land.

1973 War

On October 6, the combined armies of Egypt and Syria attacked Israel; the fighting lasted until October 25.

Selected Bibliography

Abu Iyad with Eric Rouleau. *My Home, My Land: A narrative of the Palestinian struggle*. New York: Times Books, 1978.

Adan, Avraham. *On the Banks of the Suez*. London: Arms and Armour Press, 1980.

Ajami, Fouad. *The Arab Predicament: Arab political throught and practice since 1967*. London: Cambridge University Press, 1981.

Aronson, Shlomo. *Conflict & Bargaining in the Middle East: An Israeli perspective*. Baltimore: The Johns Hopkins University Press, 1978.

Asher, Jerry with Eric Hammel. *Duel for the Golan: The 100-hour battle that saved Israel*. New York: William Morrow and Company, Inc., 1987.

Badri, Hassan, Taha Magdoub and Mohammed Dia Din Zohdy. *The Ramadan War, 1973*. New York: Hippocrene Books, Inc., 1978.

Ball, George W. *Error and Betrayal in Lebanon*. Washington, DC: Foundation for Middle East Peace, 1984.

Bar-Siman-Tov, Yaacov. *The Israeli-Egyptian War of Attrition, 1969-1970: A case study of limited local war*. New York: Columbia University Press, 1980.

Bartov, Hanock. *Dado: 48 Years and 20 Days*. Israel: Maariv Book Guild, 1981.

Bar-Zohar, Michael. *Ben-Gurion: A biography*. New York: Delacorte Press, 1978.

Bell, J. Bowyer. *Terror Out of Zion*. New York: St. Martin's Press, 1977.

Ben-Porat, Yeshayahu et al (trans. Louis Williams). *Kippur*. Tel Aviv: Special Edition Publishers, 1973.

Benziman, Uzi. *Sharon: An Israeli Caesar*. New York: Adama Books, 1985.

Bethell, Nicholas. *The Palestine Triangle: The struggle for the Holy Land,*

1935-48. New York: G.P. Putnam's Sons, 1979.

Blair, John M. *The Control of Oil.* New York: Vintage Books, 1978.

Bober, Arie (ed.), *The Other Israel: The Radical Case Against Zionism,* New York: Anchor Books, 1972

Brecher, Michael. *Decisions in Israel's Foreign Policy.* London: Oxford University Press, 1974.

————- with Benjamin Geist. *Decisions in Crisis: Israel, 1967 and 1973.* Berkeley: University of California Press, 1980.

Cattan, Henry. *Palestine, The Arabs and Israel: The search for justice.* London: Longman, 1969.

Chomsky, Noam. *The Fateful Triangle.* Boston: South End Press, 1983.

Cobban, Helena. The Palestinian Liberation Organization: People, power and politics. New York: Cambridge University Press, 1984.

Cooley, John K. *Green March, Black September: The story of the Palestinian Arabs.* London: Frank Cass, 1973.

————- *Libyan Sandstorm.* New York: Holt, Rinehart and Winston, 1982.

Dan, Uri. *Sharon's Bridgehead.* Tel Aviv: E. L. Special Edition, 1975.

Davis, Uri & Norton Mezvinsky, *Documents from Israel 1967-73: Readings for a critique of Zionism,* London: Ithaca Press, 1975.

Dayan, Moshe. *Story of My Life.* New York: William Murrow amd Company, Inc., 1976.

————- *Breakthrough.* New York: Alfred A. Knopf, 1981.

Dupuy, Colonel Trevor N. *Elusive Victory: The Arab-Israeli wars, 1947-74.* New York: Harper & Row, 1978.

Eban, Abba. An Autobiography. Tel Aviv: Steimatzky's Agency Ltd., 1977.

Eisenhower, Dwight D. *Waging Peace: 1956-61.* Garden City, N.Y.: Doubleday & Company, Inc., 1965.

el-Edroos, Brigadier S.A. *The Hashemite Arab Army 1908-1979.* Amman, Jordan: The Publishing Committee, 1980.

Elon, Amos. *The Israelis: Founders and sons.* New York: Holt, Rinehart and Winston, 1971.

Ennes, James M. Jr. *Assault on the Liberty.* New York: Random House, 1979.

Epp, Frank H. *Whose Land is Palestine?* Grand Rapids, Michigan: William B. Eerdmans Publishing Company, second printing, July 1974.

Eveland, Wilbur Crane. *Ropes of Sand: America's failure in the Middle East.* New York: W.W. Norton & Co., 1980.

Fahmy, Ismail. *Negotiating for Peace in the Middle East.* Baltimore: The Johns Hopkins University Press, 1983.

Feuerlicht, Roberta Strauss. *The Fate of the Jews: A people torn between Israeli power and Jewish ethics.* New York: Times books: 1983.

Findley, Paul. *They Dare to Speak Out: People and institutions confront Israel's lobby.* Westport, CT: Lawrence Hill & Co., 1985.

Ghilan, Maxim, *How Israel Lost Its Soul,* Middlesex, England: Penguin Press, 1974

Glassman, Jon D. *Arms for the Arabs: The Soviet Union and war in the Middle East.* Baltimore: The Johns Hopkins University Press, 1975.

Golan, Matti. *The Secret Conversations of Henry Kissinger.* New York: Quadrangle/The New York Times Book Co., 1976.

Green, Stephen. *Living by the Sword.* Brattleboro, VT: Amana Books, 1988.

Grose, Peter. *Israel in the Mind of America.* New York: Alfred A. Knopf, 1983.

Halabi, Rafik. *The West Bank Story.* New York: Harcourt Brace Jovanovich, Publishers, 1981.

Halsell, Grace. *Journey to Jerusalem.* New York: Macmillan Publishing Co., Inc., 1981.

———, *Prophesy and Politics: Militant evangelists on the road to nuclear war.* Westport, CT: Lawrence Hill & Company, 1986.

Harris, William Wilson. *Taking Root: Israeli settlement in the West Bank, the Golan and Gaza-Sinai, 1967-1980.* New York: Research Studies Press, 1980.

Hart, Alan. *Arafat: Terrorist or peacemaker?* London: Sidgwick & Jackson, 1985.

Heikal, Mohamed. *Autumn of Fury: The assassination of Sadat.* New York: Random House, 1983.

——— *Nasser: The Cairo Documents.* London: New English Library, 1973.

——— *The Road to Ramadan: The inside story of how the Arabs prepared for and almost won the October war of 1973.* London: Collins, 1975.

——— *The Sphinx and the Commissar: The rise and fall of soviet influence in Middle East.* New York: Harper & Row, 1978.

Hersh, Seymour M. *The Price of Power: Kissinger in the Nixon White House.* New York: Summit Books, 1983.

Herzog, Chaim. *The War of Atonement.* Tel Aviv: Steimatzky's Agency Ltd., 1975.

Hirst, David. *The Gun and the Olive Branch: The roots of violence in the Middle East.* New York: Harcourt Brace Jovanovich, 1977.

——— and Irene Beeson. *Sadat.* London: faber & faber, 1981.

355

Hoopes, Townsend. *The Devil & John Foster Dulles.* London: Andre Deutsch, 1974.

Hurewitz, J.C. *The Middle East and North Africa in World Politics: a documentary record,* Vols. 1, 2 and 3. New Haven: Yale University Press, 1975 and 1979.

Insight Team of the London Times. *The Yom Kippur War.* New York: Doubleday & Company, 1974.

Isaacs, Stephen D. *Jews and American Politics.* Garden City, NY: Doubleday & Company, Inc., 1974.

International Commission of Jurists and Law in the Service of Man. *The West Bank and the Rule of Law.* International Commission of Jurists, 1980.

Jackson, Elmore. *Middle East Mission: The story of a major bid for peace in the time of Nasser and Ben-Gurion.* New York: W.W. Norton & Company, 1983.

Kalb, Marvin and Bernard. *Kissinger.* Boston: Little, Brown and Company, 1974.

Kahane, Rabbi Meir. *They Must Go.* New York: Grosset & Dunlap, 1981.

Kenen, I.L. *Israel's Defense Line: Her friends and foes in Washington.* Buffalo, NY: Prometheus Books, 1981.

Khouri, Fred J. *The Arab Israeli Dilemma* (3rd ed.) Syracuse, NY: Syracuse University Press, 1985.

Kissinger, Henry A. *White House Years.* New York: Boston: Little, Brown and Company, 1979.

——— *Years of Upheaval.* Boston: Little, Brown and Company, 1982.

Lacey, Robert. *The Kingdom.* London: Hutchinson & Co. (publishers) Ltd., 1981.

Langer, Felicia, *These are My Brothers: Israel and the occupied territories,* London: Ithaca Press, 1979.

Laqueur, Walter. *The Israel-Arab Reader.* New York: Bantam Book, 1971.

Lenczowski, George. *Soviet Advances in the Middle East.* Washington, DC: American Enterprise Institute for Public Policy Research, 1971.

Lilienthal, Alfred M. *The Zionist Connection: What price peace?* New York: Dodd, Mead & Company, 1978.

Love, Kennett. *Suez: The twice-fought war.* New York: McGraw-Hill Book Company, 1969.

Lucas, Noah. *The Modern History of Israel.* London: Weidenfeld and Nicolson, 1974.

Lustick, Ian, *Arabs in the Jewish State: Israel's control of a national minority,* Austin, Texas: University of Texas Press, 1980.

Luttwak, Edward and Dan Horowitz. *The Israeli Army*. London: Allen Lane, 1975.

Magnus, Ralph H., ed. *Documents on the Middle East*. Washington, DC: American Enterprise Institute, 1969.

Mayhew, Christopher and Michael Adams. *Publish it not...The Middle East cover-up*. London: Longman, 1975.

Medzini, Meron. *Israel's Foreign Relations: Selected Documents, 1947-1974*, Vols. 1 and 2. Jerusalem: Ministry of Foreign Affairs, 1976.

————, *Israel's Foreign Relations: Selected Documents, 1974-1977*, Vol. 3. Jerusalem: Ministry of Foreign Affairs, 1982.

————, *Israel's Foreign Relations: Selected Documents, 1977-1979*, Vols. 4 and 5. Jerusalem: Ministry of Foreign Affairs, 1981.

Meir, Golda. *My Life*. New York: G.P. Putnam's Sons, 1975.

Metzger, Jan, Martin Orth and Christian Sterzing (trans. Dan and Judy Bryant, Janet Goodwin and Stefan Schaaf). *This Land is Our Land: The West Bank under Israeli occupation*. London: Zed Press, 1983.

Miller, Merle. *Lyndon: An oral history*. New York: G. P. Putnam's Sons, 1980.

Morris, Roger. *Uncertain Greatness: Henry Kissinger and American foreign policy*. New York: Harper & Row, Publishers, 1977.

Moskin, J. Robert. *Among Lions: The Battle for Jerusalem June 5-7, 1967*. New York: Arbor House, 1982.

Mosley, Leonard. *Power Play. The tumultuous world of Middle East oil 1890-1973*. Great Britain: Weidenfeld and Nicolson, 1973.

Neff, Donald. *Warriors for Suez: Eisenhower takes America into the Middle East*. New York: Linden Press/Simon & Schuster, 1981.

———— *Warriors for Jerusalem: The Six Days that changed the Middle East*. New York: Linden Press/Simon & Schuster, 1984.

Nixon, Richard M. *The Memoirs of Richard Nixon*. New York. A Fllmways Company, 1978.

Nutting, Anthony. *Nasser*. London: Constable, 1972.

Nyrop, Richard F. and Beryl Lieff Benderly, William W. Cover, Darrel R. Eglin and Robert Kirchner. *Area Handbook for Egypt (3rd ed.)*. Washington, D.C.: U.S. Government Printing Office, 1976.

———— (ed.). *Syria a country study (3rd ed.)*. Washington, D.C.: U.S. Government Printing Office, 1979.

O'Ballance, Edgar. *No Victor, No Vanquished: The Yom Kippur War*. San Rafael, CA: Presidio Press, 1978.

———— *The Electronic War in the Middle East: 1968-70*. London: Faber and Faber Limited, 1974.

O'Brien, Lee. *American Jewish Organizations & Israel.* Washington, DC: Institute for Palestine Studies, 1986.

Petran, Tabitha. *Syria.* New York: Praeger Publishers, 1972.

Pollock, David. *The Politics of Pressure: Americans arms and Israeli policy since the six day war.* London: Greenwood Press, 1982.

Quandt, William B. *Decade of Decisions: American policy toward the Arab-Israeli conflict.* Berkeley: University of California Press, 1977.

————- *Camp David: Peacemaking and Politics.* Washington, DC: The Brookings Institution, 1986.

Rabin, Yitzhak. *The Rabin Memoirs.* Boston: Little, Brown and Company, 1979.

Rafael, Gideon. *Destination Peace: Three decades of Israeli foreign policy. A personal memoir.* London: Weidenfeld and Nicolson, 1981.

Riad, Mahmoud. *The Struggle for Peace in the Middle East.* New York: Quartet Books, 1981.

Rokach, Livia. *Israel's Sacred Terrorism: A study based on Moshe Sharett's Personal Diary and other documents.* Belmont, MA: Association of Arab-American University Graduates, Inc., 1980.

Rubenberg, Cheryl A. *Israel and the American National Interest: A critical examination.* Chicago: University of Illinois Press, 1986.

Rubinstein, Alvin Z. *Red Star on the Nile: The Soviet-Egyptian influence relationship since the June war.* Princeton: Princeton University Press, 1977.

Sachar, Howard M. *A History of Israel: From the rise of Zionism to our time.* Tel Aviv: Steimatzky's Agency Ltd., 1976.

Sadat, Anwar. *In Search of Identity.* New York: Harper & Row, 1978.

Sadat, Jehan. *A Woman of Egypt.* New York: Simon and Schuster, 1987.

Said, Edward W. *The Question of Palestine.* New York: Times Books, 1980.

Sampson, Anthony. *The Seven Sisters: The great oil companies & the world they shaped.* New York: The Viking Press, 1975.

Saunders, Harold. *The Other Walls: The Politics of the Arab-Israeli Peace Process.* Washington, DC: American Enterprise Institute for Public Policy Research, 1985.

Schweitzer, Avram. *Israel: The Changing National Agenda.* Dover, NH: Croom Helm, 1986.

Sella, Amnon. *Soviet Political and Military Conduct in the Middle East.* New York: St. Martin's Press, 1981.

Shazly, Saad. *The Crossing of the Suez.* San Francisco: American Mideast

Research, 1980.

Sheehan, Edward R. E. *The Arabs, Israelis, and Kissinger: A secret history of American diplomacy in the Middle East.* New York: Reader's Digest Press, 1976.

Shipler, David K. *Arab and Jew: Wounded Spirits in a promised land*, New York: Times Books, 1986

Silver, Eric. *Begin: The haunted prophet.* New York: Random House, 1984.

Snow, Peter. *Hussein.* London: Barrie & Jenkins, 1972.

Stevens, Stewart. *The Spymasters of Israel.* New York: Macmillan Publishing Co., Inc., 1980.

Tawil, Raymonda Hawa. *My Home, My Prison.* New York: Holt, Rinehart and Winston, 1979.

Tillman, Seth. *The United States in the Middle East: Interests and Obstacles.* Bloomington: Indiana University Press, 1982.

Tivnan, Edward. *The Lobby: Jewish political power and American foreign policy.* New York: Simon and Schuster, 1987.

Turki, Fawaz. *The Disinherited.* New York: Monthly Review Press, 1972.

Urofsky, Melvin. *We Are One! American Jewry and Israel.* New York: Anchor Press/Doubleday, 1978.

Viorst, Milton. *Sands of Sorrow.* New York: Harper & Row, Publishers, 1987.

Weissman, Steve and Herbert Krosney. *The Islamic Bomb: The nuclear Threat to Israel and the Middle East.* New York: Times Books, 1981.

Weizman, Ezer. *On Eagles' Wings: The personal story of the leading commander of the Israeli air force.* Tel Aviv: Steimatzky's Agency Ltd., 1976.

——— *The Battle for Peace.* New York: Bantam Books, 1981.

Whetten, Lawrence L. *The Canal War: Four-power conflict in the Middle East.* Cambridge, MA: The MIT Press, 1974.

Wilson, Evan M. *Decision on Palestine: How the U.S. came to recognize Israel.* Stanford, CA: Hoover Institution Press, 1979.

Wright, John. *Libya: A modern history.* Baltimore: The Johns Hopkins University Press, 1982.

Wright, Robin. *Sacred Rage: The crusade of modern Islam.* New York: Linden Press/Simon & Schuster, 1985.

Yale, William. *The Near East: A modern history.* Ann Arbor: The University of Michigan Press, 1958.

Yodfat, Aryeh Y. and Yuval Arnon-Ohanna. *PLO: Strategy and tactics.* London: Croom Helm, 1981.

Index

Azores, 220–221

Baathist Government, 19
Bab al Mandab, 296
Badri, Maj. Gen. Hassan, 118
Baghdad, 108, 123
Ball, George W., 302
Baluza (Israeli command post), 227
"Bambi", 149, 151
Barak Brigade, 148, 150, 157–158–161, 169, 209
Bahrein, 150, 260
Bar-Lev, Haim (Israeli former chief of staff), 78, 137, 168, 196, 204, 206, 228–229, 235–236, 244, 246, 263–264
Bar-Lev Line (Israeli canal defense), 79, 81–82, 102, 116, 119, 121, 124–125, 132–133, 137, 141–142, 145, 163–164, 174, 180, 211, 214, 223, 232, 261, 306
Bar-Lev Line forts, 141–143
Bartov, Hanoch, 167
Bathir, Hussain, 108
Begin, Menachem, 19, 51, 196
Beirut, 107–108, 195
Ben-Ari, Uri, 178–179
Ben-Gal, Avigdor, "Yanush" (Israeli brigade commander), 148, 163, 187, 193–194, 202, 209, 215
Bergus, Donald, 53, 63–66, 89
Bitar, Brig. General Gabriel (Syrian director of intelligence), 148
Black September (terrorist movement), 73, 94–97, 108
Bloom, Captain Harry, 149
Bnot Yakov (Jacob's Bridge), 187
Bouchiqui, Achmed, 108
Boudia, Mohammed, 108
Boumedienne, Houari (president of Algeria), 211
Brezhnev, Chairman Leonid (chairman of Soviet Union), 66, 70, 120, 281–287, 289; Nixon and, 120,171, 256, 261–262; role in ceasefire, 253, 256, 265–266, 276, 278; Sadat and, 49, 69, 82–86, 88, 92, 170, 176

Britain, 6, 266
Bruce, David, 302
Budapest (fort), 174, 191, 223
Bundy, McGeorge, 302

"C Alert", 131, 133
Cairo, 13, 16, 23, 32, 37, 41–2, 46–7, 53–4, 58, 60, 62–65, 68, 71, 76, 84–87, 103–106, 139, 169–172, 197, 204, 210–211–214, 222, 229, 240–241, 250–253, 260–264, 271, 279, 282, 289, 292
Canada, 149
Ceasefire of October War, 268–277, begins, 271, violation by Israel, 277
Center 10 (headquarters of Egyptian forces), 139–141, 152–153, 169, 260–261
Central Intelligence Agency (CIA), 27, 34, 53, 61–62, 64, 89, 130, 188, 199, 285
Chase Manhattan Bank, 66
China, 28, 66, 68, 71, 256
Chinese Farm, 232–247, 249, 257
Churchill, Winston, 35
Cohen, Baruch, 108
Colby, William, (CIA Director), 199, 285
Committee (Egyptian) for Preparing the Country for War, 50
Communism, 110
Congo, 102
Congress, 213, 302, 308
Cooperman, Lieut. Colo. Pinie, 159
Cox, Archibald, 261–262
Compagnie Universelle du Canal Maritime de Suez, 6
Customs House, 187
Cyprus, 108–9
Czechoslovakia, 49, 59

Dail, 103
Damascus, 97, 103, 146, 153, 192, 194, 201–202, 205–207, 208–213, 216–219, 225, 255, 294, 300, 306
Damascus Highway, 187, 193, 215
Damascus International Airport, 216

ACKNOWLEDGEMENTS

IT IS ONE OF THE SADDER FACTS of our national life to report that by 1988 the Reagan Administration had effectively smoothered the Freedom of Information Act, one of the most enligthened pieces of legislation in our time. The bureauracy has now wrapped FOIA requests in such tangles of red tape that the relationship has become an adversarial one, usually resolved only in the courts. Without legal mediation, FOIA requests now go unanswered for years, or documents are surrendered with information totally blacked out. While the act obviously has its pitfalls, such as its use by gangsters and foreign nations to unearth the identities of confidential sources, the fact is that its judicious use allowed the healthy light of reality to shine on our policics. It is a tragcdy that light has now been all but extinguished. Our democracy is the loser.

A far happier subject is the continued support of friends and those who gave so freely of their time to the creation of this volume and, at last after nearly a decade, the conclusion of the Warriors' trilogy. These include James Abourezk, Elyse Alterowitz, George Ball, Barbara Shahin Batlouni, William Brubeck, Hanja Cherniak-Mach, Robert Fleetwood, Murray Gart, Ben Gurtizen, Risque Harper, Donald Lund, Dennis Mullin, Richard Powell, Robbin Reynolds, Richard Viets, and, foremost, Abigail Trafford.

ABOUT THE AUTHOR

DONALD NEFF was Time's bureau chief in Jerusalem for four years and has traveled extensively in the region. His story on the Colombian cocaine trade was winner of the New York Press Club's best foreign story in a magazine in 1979, and the first book in his Warrior's trilogy , *Warriors at Suez*, was an alternate selection of the Book of the Month Club and the History Book Club as well as a finalist in the history category in 1981 of the American Book Awards. Mr. Neff now lives in Washington, D.C.

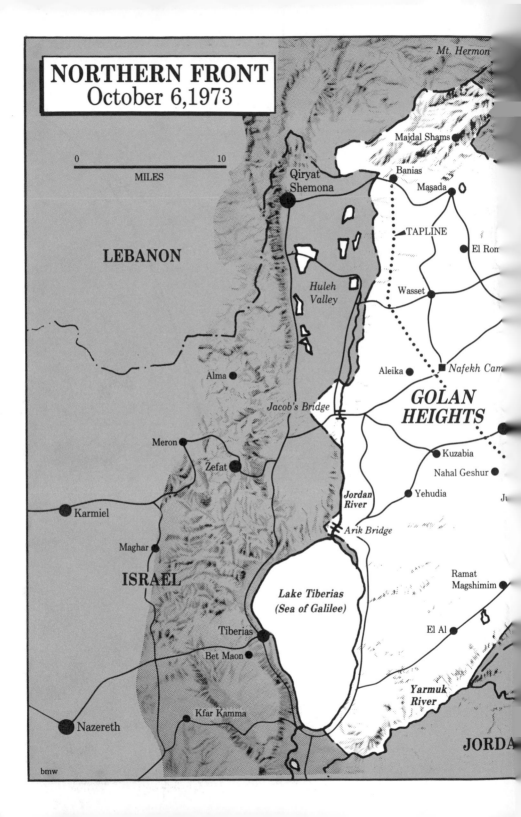

NORTHERN FRONT
October 6, 1973

0   10

MILES

Mt. Hermon

LEBANON

Majdal Shams

Banias

Qiryat
Shemona

Maşada

TAPLINE

El Rom

*Huleh
Valley*

Wasset

Alma

Aleika

Nafekh Cam

Jacob's Bridge

*GOLAN
HEIGHTS*

Meron

Kuzabia

Zefat

Nahal Geshur

Karmiel

*Jordan
River*

Yehudia

Arik Bridge

Maghar

Ramat
Magshimim

ISRAEL

*Lake Tiberias
(Sea of Galilee)*

El Al

Tiberias

Bet Maon

*Yarmuk
River*

Kfar Kamma

Nazareth

JORDA

bmw